The New Penguin Book of English Folk Songs

EDITED BY

STEVE ROUD

AND JULIA BISHOP

PENGUIN CLASSICS

an imprint of

PENGUIN BOOKS

Penguin Group (USA) Inc., 375 Hudson Street, New York, New York 10014, USA
Penguin Group (Canada), 90 Eglinton Avenue East, Suite 700, Toronto, Ontario,
Canada M4P 2Y3 (a division of Pearson Canada Inc.)
Penguin Ireland, 25 St Stephen's Green, Dublin 2, Ireland (a division of Penguin Books Ltd)
Penguin Group (Australia), 250 Camberwell Road, Camberwell, Victoria 3124,
Australia (a division of Pearson Australia Group Pty Ltd)
Penguin Books India Pvt Ltd, 11 Community Centre,
Panchsheel Park, New Delhi – 110 017, India
Penguin Group (NZ), 67 Apollo Drive, Rosedale, Auckland 0632, New Zealand
(a division of Pearson New Zealand Ltd)
Penguin Books (South Africa) (Pty) Ltd, 24 Sturdee Avenue,
Rosebank 2196, South Africa

Penguin Books Ltd, Registered Offices: 80 Strand, London WC2R 0RL, England

www.penguin.com

First published 2012
003

Selection, introductions and additional material copyright © Steve Roud and Julia Bishop, 2012
The moral right of the authors has been asserted

Set in Bembo Mt Std 12/14.75pt
Typeset by Penguin Books
Music set by Julian Elloway
Printed in Great Britain by Clays Ltd, St Ives plc

ISBN: 978-0-141-19461-5

www.greenpenguin.co.uk

Penguin Books is committed to a sustainable
future for our business, our readers and our planet.
This book is made from Forest Stewardship
Council™ certified paper.

MIX
Paper from
responsible sources
FSC® C018179

ALWAYS LEARNING   **PEARSON**

To Kate, Mark, Jacqueline and Stephanie
To Robin and the girls, who have held the fort so valiantly
during the preparation of this book

Contents

The Songs

General Introduction

This book presents the core tradition of English folk song, as reflected in the major and minor collections compiled from about 1870 to the 1970s and 1980s. It therefore includes many of the most popular traditional songs from the long-gone era when singing out loud was normal everyday behaviour and music was largely a participatory rather than a spectator activity.

The original edition of *The Penguin Book of English Folk Songs*, edited by Ralph Vaughan Williams and A. L. Lloyd, was a brilliant piece of work and has been a classic ever since it was published in 1959. Vaughan Williams was one of the last survivors of the great days of the Edwardian folk-song collectors and the grand old man of the English musical establishment, although he died just before the project was completed. By contrast, Lloyd was a journalist and freelance writer who was one of the most vocal of the new Folk Revival activists, criticizing, questioning, and politically committed to spreading the word of folk song to the people. The book came at just the right moment, when there was a groundswell of feeling among the Folk Revivalists in England that the national tradition was being neglected in the welter of American, Irish and Scottish material which had thus far fuelled the movement. In an uncanny parallel to the general perception in the Victorian and Edwardian eras that the English had no decent music, it was felt there was a danger the new generation of 'folk singers' would know about songs from every nation but their own. The word 'English' in the new title was therefore a significant element. The book quickly became a key text for the Folk Revival in this country, and not only supplied the repertoire for countless club singers (being conveniently pocket size), but also prompted enthusiasts to seek out other English sources.

Vaughan Williams and Lloyd took their material from a single, albeit long-running, source: the journals of the Folk-Song Society (1899–1932) and its successor, the English Folk Dance and Song Society (1932 onwards). Both societies had prided themselves upon presenting the material in their journals in a plain and unadulterated fashion, with the tunes printed exactly as collected from the original singers, without amendment or accompaniment, therefore making them the real thing. In the earlier volumes of the journals, however, the texts were not so delicately handled. They were often cut short, with only one verse or a representative sample given, and if they were printed in full were sometimes completed from broadsides. Vaughan Williams and Lloyd therefore had to complete many of their texts by taking elements from other versions.

As with most folk-song collections down the years, Vaughan Williams and Lloyd were not looking for the normal and typical, or to present a view of the tradition as a whole, but were concerned with choosing the 'best' of folk songs. They therefore often selected the special and unusual, based largely on aesthetic grounds. 'All Things are Quite Silent', for example, the first song in the book, was extremely rare in the tradition, having been collected only once. The present volume takes a different tack, and is the first to do so for some time. Conscious of the fact that we now have access to much more material than any of our predecessors, we have tried to ascertain which songs were collected most often, and to use this as a ranking, however crude, of popularity within the tradition at large.

If one follows the theory that it is selection by the community which ensures continuity (see below), it can be inferred that the songs which were widely sung must have had some quality that made them survive better than others. From the thousands of examples of songs in books, manuscripts, sound recordings and videos, we have looked specifically at those which were collected widely, and made our selection from them. This may well be a simplistic evolutionary argument, and we are aware that in other contexts, such as the modern world of pop music, it could be maintained that widespread popularity is a sign of the lowest common denominator rather than of quality. There is no objective standard here, all is necessarily subjective, but as stated already, what we have tried to do is reflect the core tradition of the

English folk-song repertoire, on the evidence of those collections and such ancillary historical information at our disposal.

This is not as simple as it sounds. The available collections were selective and patchy when compiled (see below), and some have not yet been indexed, but with these reservations a fairly clear picture emerges. We set the lower limit of a song's inclusion in this volume at about fifteen versions (from different singers across the country), but in this context it is not so much the absolute numbers which are significant, but the relative proportions. Some of the songs just scrape in at the lower level, while others romp home with dozens of versions and some with well over a hundred. In other words, in terms of popularity, some songs stand in a completely different class to the mass.

Using this method, we had an overall corpus of about 300 from which to make our selection. However, the book is not simply an exercise in ranking songs solely by popularity (*The Folk Song Index* can do that, see pp. xl–xli), and we decided not to take this scheme to its logical conclusion and merely present the most collected songs as a sort of 'top 151'. We also wanted to indicate the range of songs and tunes available, and to provide the next generation of enthusiasts with a corpus of material which we considered worth investigating in order to build an all-round knowledge of the field.

We have tried to present versions that use the tune and text from the same singer, and if possible to select texts which are sufficiently complete for us not to need to do too much patching from other versions, although a certain amount of that is always necessary in a book aimed at the general public. Our other selection criteria have been concerned with geographical coverage, gender balance, and roughly equal numbers from the different periods in our date range. About half the songs are taken from sound recordings of some sort, so those who wish to hear them sung in the old way can do so, while the others exist in written form and need more expert interpretation. In the latter case, it is often possible to find recorded examples of other versions (again, see *The Folk Song Index*) for those who wish to seek them out.

Inevitably, some imbalances have been introduced by our selection criteria. Selecting material on a national scale necessarily militates against songs which are popular only locally. The insistence on text and tune from one singer excludes important collections, such as the one made by Alfred Williams in the Upper Thames region, as he did not note down the tunes. We have also largely avoided versions printed in Vaughan Williams and Lloyd's Penguin volume and in current English Folk Dance and Song Society publications, notably from the Hammond and Gardiner manuscript collections. And we have left out some categories altogether – sea shanties and other work songs, songs related to calendar customs (for example, May garlands and wassailing), children's games and rhymes – and have included only a small selection of carols and religious items.

Folk-Song Characteristics

The definition of 'folk song' is fraught with difficulty, and many researchers even avoid the term altogether. Those who are interested in pursuing the subject will find some discussion on the matter later in this Introduction, but for now a simple description will suffice. Folk songs are learnt and performed by non-professionals in informal, non-commercial settings. They are 'traditional' in that they are passed on from person to person, and down the generations, in face-to-face performance. It is not the origin of a song which makes it a 'folk song', but the process by which ordinary people learn it, perform it and pass it on. It is therefore not really the song which is 'folk', but the process of learning and performance.

In 1907 Cecil Sharp proposed a three-part scheme – continuity, selection and variation – which goes some way to describing the characteristics of a folk song. Continuity refers to the song's surviving by being passed on from person to person, and down the generations; selection refers to the role played by the community in choosing which songs survive – if no one chooses to learn a song it will not survive; variation highlights the fact that because songs travel informally from singer to singer, changes will always occur, whether consciously or not, and even successive performances by the same singer will never be exactly the same.

While we tend to think of folk songs as special, they were in their time everyday music. The 'educated' classes may not have performed them, or even recognized them as culturally significant or valid, but the bulk of 'the people' did. Nevertheless, such singing traditions gradually, inexorably, went out of fashion and ceased to be viable.

In the period with which we are concerned, farmworkers sang these songs in fields, barns and at harvest homes, as did milkmaids in their cowsheds, factory workers at their machines, coal miners above and below ground, women doing the washing or sweeping up at home, families round the fireside, drinkers in the pub, nursemaids to their infant charges, scullery maids sweeping the area steps, delivery and messenger boys going down the street, carriers driving their horses and the people sitting in the cart behind them, children on their way to school, sailors at rest in the forecastle, fishermen hauling nets, ballad singers in city streets and at country fairs, and so on. They were sung solo and in unison, to large crowds or for the singer's own pleasure, raucously and tenderly, extremely well and rather badly. A handful of songs were centuries old, while others had recently filtered through from the pleasure gardens or music halls, that is, they were the pop music of the day, or rather the day before. But all had been around long enough to have been passed on from person to person and to have had their corners knocked off, and all were performed in the locally accepted and sanctioned style.

No subjects are barred to folk song, but the genre is hardly suited to heavy discussion of politics, religion or other weighty matters, and protest songs rarely lasted long. In fact, the songs are usually about the daily concerns of the time – drinking, poaching, hunting, seafaring, battles, highwaymen, farmwork and murder – and the vast majority are simply about love, sex and relationships. In folk songs, parents object to suitors (and sometimes murder them), ladies fancy ploughboys, squires pursue milkmaids, lovers go to war and return in disguise or are killed, girls dress as sailors to follow their lovers to sea, sweethearts get married or are abandoned, women become pregnant and sing ruefully of their condition, commit suicide, shrug philosophically or get their own back on their seducers.

It is not exactly real life that is reflected in the song repertoire, of course, but the stylized and romanticized view which one encounters in all forms of fiction. And as the times move on faster than the folk songs do, a song about the press gang can still be sung fifty years after the last man was forced to sea, and a ballad about Dick Turpin is not likely to be about the real man and his sordid career, but the one whom legend has refashioned as a hero. Songs about Van Diemen's Land were written by those who had never been there, and remnants of stage fashions for pseudo-classical pastoral shepherdesses and Gipsies rub shoulders with songs about the real thing. Songs can be funny, tragic, complete nonsense or deadly serious; some tell a detailed story while others are lyrical explorations of feelings. Some have rousing choruses, others are more introspective, but all have great tunes – or they would not have survived.

History of Folk-Song Collectors and Collecting

To understand the genre of folk song, and the selection process involved in writing books such as this one, it is necessary to investigate two very different types of history. One is the history of vernacular songs and singing – where the songs came from; who sang them; how, why, where they were sung, and so on – which will be tackled later. The other history, an account of how people (that is, educated, book-writing people) discovered folk song, defined it, collected it and published it, explains not only the corpus of material that is at our disposal, but also how we define and view the genre. It has to be remembered, of course, that the 'folk' did not need to discover folk song: they had it all along, although they did not call it that.

The folk-song 'movement' began to take real shape in the last quarter of the nineteenth century, but its intellectual roots go back more than one hundred years before that. These roots are usually traced to the publication, in 1765, of Thomas Percy's *Reliques of Ancient English Poetry*, which sent shock waves across the literary establishments of Europe. Percy had stumbled across an old manuscript, probably dating from about 1650, which contained a series of old ballads. Compared to the standard poetry of the time, they were a major blast of fresh air, and their publication started a fashion for heroic themes and direct language which lasted for decades.

Scottish editors were already moving in this direction, and following the publication of Sir Walter Scott's seminal *Minstrelsy of the Scottish Border* (1802), a group of Scottish collectors, including William Motherwell, James Maidment, George Kinloch and Robert Jamieson, published editions of ballads, many of which were noted down from 'the mouths of the people'. The collectors' motives were a combination of literary and nationalist, and one incidental effect of this early start was the notion, which still persists to this day, that the ballad tradition in the British Isles was primarily Scottish.

In England, there were also stirrings of interest in the 'songs of the people', although it was at this stage confined to isolated individuals. The working-class poet John Clare (1793–1864) deliberately noted down his parents' songs and used them in his poetry, while John Bell (1783–1864) demonstrated his interest in all things north-eastern by gathering local songs, published as *Rhymes of the Northern Bards* (1812). A strong interest in musical antiquarianism was also developing, which is reflected in Davies Gilbert's *Some Ancient Christmas Carols* (1822) and William Sandys's *Christmas Carols: Ancient and Modern* (1833). But the doyen of musical antiquarians was William Chappell, whose major work, *The Ballad Literature and Popular Music of the Olden Time* (1859), trawled through the history of music and assigned tunes to particular periods.

These writers used some material from 'traditional' sources, but this was not their primary concern, and they were more comfortable with older books and manuscripts than with real singers. This was about to change, albeit rather slowly.

In 1846 William J. Thoms wrote to the periodical the *Athenaeum* and proposed a new word, 'folk-lore', to describe the tales, beliefs, customs, songs and dances of the common people, which had previously been subsumed under the clumsy title 'popular antiquities'. He thus gave a name to a body of material, and the discipline which would soon develop to collect and study it. In the same year James Henry Dixon put together his *Ancient Poems* for the Percy Society, and in 1847 the Revd John Broadwood produced, as a private venture, the first collection gathered entirely from 'the people': *Old English Songs as now Sung by the Peasantry of the Weald of Surrey and*

Sussex (1847). More or less independent of this growing musical activity, a group of literary scholars with a specific interest in ballads were following in Percy's footsteps. This movement found its apogee in the publication of Francis J. Child's seminal *English and Scottish Popular Ballads* (1882–98). The 305 items included by Child rapidly became the accepted canon for ballad study, and we still refer to these as 'Child ballads'. He not only printed several early texts of each ballad, but also provided extensive comparative and historical notes on an international scale.

From the 1870s onwards, a number of individuals, including William Alexander Barrett, M. H. Mason, Sabine Baring-Gould, Lucy Broadwood (John Broadwood's niece) and Frank Kidson, all became interested in the history of vernacular music, but the key development was that in addition to finding songs in old manuscripts and books they began to collect them from living singers. Working in different parts of the country, these enthusiasts gradually came into contact with each other and began to formulate the theoretical framework which eventually turned their personal interests into a crusade, and the Folk-Song Society was formed in 1898. The society pledged to collect and publish folk songs, and after a few initial years without much sense of direction, it hit its stride in 1904. In the previous year, two of the leading lights of the next phase of the Folk-Song Revival, Cecil Sharp and Ralph Vaughan Williams, had collected their first songs and Sharp, in particular, with his flair for publicity and public controversy, rapidly brought folk music to the attention of the wider musical world and the general public.

So began the golden age of folk-song collecting: Janet Blunt, George Butterworth, Clive Carey, George Gardiner, Anne Gilchrist, Alice Gillington, Percy Grainger, Henry Hammond, Percy Merrick and others joined those already in the field, and between them amassed the major collections on which we still draw for our basic knowledge of the subject. Many of these are represented in this book.

What they found was a large repertoire of songs and styles of singing which were largely unknown to the 'educated' classes, and which had apparently existed in the mouths of the rural working people for generations. This 'folk' music had inherent qualities which, they thought, had been lost in both the more sophisticated art music and the raucous popular music of the time, and was therefore valuable enough to be rescued before it passed into oblivion. This notion of the solid old-world roots of the tradition led them to be highly selective in their collecting. They avidly sought out what they thought was old and genuine, and rejected anything which smacked of the modern and commercial world. Apparently unaware that the tradition had always been continuously reinforced and invigorated by infusions of 'new' material, they chose not to document the whole picture of vernacular song. They gathered an extremely rich harvest of material, for which we should be eternally grateful, but if only they had spread their net a little wider we would have a far better understanding of traditional song than the important but relatively narrow part which they chose to recognize.

One key characteristic of this new wave of enthusiasts was that they were primarily musicians, enamoured mainly with the tunes and less interested in the words of the songs. Nor were they interested in the social context in which the songs existed. They collected mainly from elderly people (because folk song was believed to be dying out), and in rural areas. For Sharp and Vaughan Williams, and several of the others, the real reason for collecting folk songs was nothing less than the revitalization of English music in general, and to this end, Sharp successfully lobbied the national education authorities to include 'folk' songs and dances in the curriculum of state schools.

For a time, Sharp and his colleagues were successful in getting folk music on the agenda in establishment musical circles, although whether or not they made any real difference to the musical tastes of the mass of the population is another question. It has to be said that there were some at the time who were not swept away with enthusiasm for the new folk-music movement and who thought it misguided and rather pointless, and there was a degree of public controversy in the musical press. Even more critical, however, was a more recent group of academics who began to argue, in the 1970s, that the main participants in the flurry of folk-song collecting before the First World War had systematically misrepresented the culture of the working people while pretending to champion it.

The folk-song collectors were drawn from such a narrow social background, it was argued, and their fieldwork so narrowly focused on a small section of working people's experience, that their work constituted a distortion of the vernacular culture of the time. Worse still, they invented the whole category of 'folk song' to serve their own class-based agenda and deliberately appropriated the workers' expressive culture for their own gain, in the same way as their parasitic class routinely expropriated the workers' labour and money.

As is usually the case with writing that has a strong political agenda, the initial premise (in this case of class conflict and conspiracy) was couched in such a way as to make the conclusion seem not only reasonable but inevitable, while the dogma was allowed to distort the evidence, to the point of misrepresentation. While an investigation into the motives and methods of the early collectors was long overdue, and could have been a useful corrective to the previous uncritical acceptance of their role, the polemic that was produced has seriously warped the debate ever since, and it is time that it be relegated to a brief historiographical footnote concerned with the follies of the era, and replaced by a more balanced, accurate and nuanced perspective.

A few collectors did operate outside the 'charmed circle' of Folk-Song Society members. Alfred Williams (1877–1930), for example, was from a different mould. He had been a railway factory worker in Swindon, but later tried to survive by writing poetry, and books and articles about the Upper Thames region (Berkshire, Wiltshire and Oxfordshire). His *Folk-Songs of the Upper Thames* (1923) was the result of intensive collecting around 1918, and although it includes a slightly different range of material than the others, on the whole it pretty much confirms their findings.

When enthusiasts got the collecting bug they faced the problem of how to find suitable people to collect from, which was a particular puzzle for many of them as they often had little meaningful contact with the 'working classes' in their daily lives. Some started with family members and neighbours, and their servants often proved an unexpectedly useful source. One regular scenario was middle-class collectors remembering songs taught to them by their nannies or maids many years before.

Once the movement got under way, lectures, articles and newspaper appeals spread the word and people from far afield started writing in with their finds, and although these contributions are numerically insignificant and of variable quality, they often offer evidence from the areas in which the main collectors were not active. One regular method of contacting a community at a distance was to write to the local clergyman, who was often surprised to find that he had singers in his parish, let alone good ones. A visit to the local pub frequently provided good contacts, and workhouses were also particularly fruitful places to find elderly singers. Some collectors, like Cecil Sharp, regularly visited people in their homes or even asked likely-looking passers-by in country lanes, while others, like Grainger and Broadwood, based themselves at a friend's house and invited singers to come there for collecting sessions. Each method had its advantages and drawbacks, and, however much we might wish they had done some things differently, was simply the best that could be done under the circumstances. Song collecting in that period was an arduous business and took a great deal of time, energy and expense.

Before the first decade of the twentieth century there was no option but to note down the songs with pencil and paper, and this was not as easy as it sounds. Not only were the tunes themselves unusual and difficult to the classically trained ear, but the performers were often elderly, out of practice and shy about singing to gentlefolk. It took an extraordinary level of musical skill to transcribe the songs well, and many of the enthusiasts, such as Sabine Baring-Gould and George B. Gardiner, felt they were not good enough and took along colleagues to take down the tunes. This had its advantages, as it was much more efficient for one person to note down the words while the other struggled to get the tune right, but it was sometimes difficult to find someone sufficiently skilled and sympathetic to undertake the work. Many trained musicians found unadulterated traditional singing very hard to take.

One of the advantages of being involved in a network is that expertise can be shared, and there was a great deal of correspondence between those in the field – often routed through Lucy Broadwood in her capacity as editor of the Folk-Song Society's journal – and the leading collectors, who commented on each other's work (not always completely amicably) and offered practical advice and assistance. Cecil Sharp, for example, edited the music for later editions of Baring-Gould's *Songs of the West* and sharpened up the musical side of Lady Gomme's publications of singing games. Ralph Vaughan Williams, too, made trips to note down the tunes of some of Ella M. Leather's Herefordshire singers and also helped to transcribe tunes from phonograph cylinders made by other collectors.

The phonograph could have revolutionized the collecting experience in England because in theory it gave people who lacked the skills to note down a tune in live performance the opportunity to capture a song and notate it at their leisure, or find someone else who could do so. Collectors in other countries, most notably Zoltán Kodály and Béla Bartok in Hungary, were already using it to document their folk traditions. It is not clear how far the English collectors were aware of developments abroad, but the new method met with only limited support over here. It has been argued that the main stumbling block was that the leading collectors were already set in their ways and rejected the phonograph as it threatened their hard-won position as gatekeepers in the folk-song world, but this is a parody of the truth. Certainly, many of them were sceptical about its use as the sole, or prime, collecting method, and valid objections were made on various grounds, including the perceived technical limitations of the media, the fear that it made the singers nervous and therefore falsified the record, and that its bulk and fragility made it difficult to transport and use, except in a highly controlled environment.

Nevertheless, the Folk-Song Society bought a machine in 1907 for use by members, and several of the leading collectors, including Ralph Vaughan Williams, George B. Gardiner, Cecil Sharp and Lucy Broadwood, experimented with the new technology, but with mixed results. The one collector who really took to the new machine, however, was Percy Grainger, and he became a strong advocate of its usefulness both in the field and in the study. He made numerous recordings in 1906 and 1908, mostly of his Lincolnshire singers, and maintained that the ability to play a performance over and over again, if necessary at a slower speed, gave him the opportunity to really get under the skin of the way a tune was sung; he produced detailed and complicated transcriptions, which baffled all but the most expert of his colleagues but which he claimed were more 'scientific' than those noted purely by ear. On the basis of this work he began to make claims about folk tunes that did not always agree with those of his more experienced colleagues.

It was this 'scientific' dissection of performances and his conclusions which caused other collectors to question his approach rather than the use of the phonograph per se. Cecil Sharp, for example, put forward a number of arguments in a detailed letter to Grainger, published by Michael Yates in 1982, in which he argues that the collector's job is not to document the minutiae of a performance but to get to the essence of the tune. Sharp goes on to make some very revealing remarks about his distinction between the tune itself and the singer's performance of it:

> No doubt it is much easier to note down the 'great or slight rhythmical irregularities ever present in traditional solo-singing' from a phonogram than from a singer. The question is, is this worth doing at all? The majority of these rhythmical minutiae have nothing to do with the song itself, but only with the artistic presentation of it. The difficulty, which is perpetually confronting the collector, is to decide which of these aberrations he should record and which he should omit, in other words to settle when a rhythmical irregularity belongs to the song itself and when it is merely a personal idiosyncrasy, or arises from some mechanical cause, the taking of breath, fatigue, clumsy vocalisation, hesitation due to the forgetfulness of the words, and so on.

Grainger's mercurial attention soon moved elsewhere and he did no more collecting in England after 1909, but many of his recordings, and a few made by others, have fortunately survived. Some can be heard on the British Library's Archival Sound Recording website, and they are rightly considered precious evidence of what traditional singers sounded like over one hundred years ago.

After the First World War, when the collecting boom was largely over, the phonograph was rapidly eclipsed in general use by the gramophone, which for all its advantages did not have the same portable recording applications. So there was little follow-up to these promising early experiments with sound recording, and apart from the visiting American collector James Madison Carpenter, no other collectors seem to have made fieldwork sound recordings in England till the 1940s. A few people were still noting songs up and down the country, such as E. J. Moeran, Francis Collinson and H. H. Albino, but their efforts were relatively small scale. The Folk-Song Society amalgamated with the English Folk Dance Society in 1932, to form the English Folk Dance and Song Society (EFDSS), and the prevailing opinion in the society was that there were no more folk songs to collect. But they were wrong. In the late 1930s there were signs of a renewed interest in folk-song collecting, and during the war there was an increased awareness (much of it government-sponsored) of 'the people' and their daily lives and concerns. The dramatic shift to the left in national politics, which resulted in the Labour Party's landslide victory in 1945, was another important indicator of a newly confident working-class sensibility. The seeds of a new interest in folk music were being sown, which blossomed into a full-blown Revival movement over the next two decades.

Beginnings of the Second Folk-Song Revival

For some years a small group of people, usually jazz fans, had been seeking out records of American blues and folk music, but the market for such material began to expand rapidly and in 1954 resulted in the skiffle boom, which swept like wildfire across the country. It seemed as if every male teenager in the land was singing Leadbelly songs and bashing out chords on a guitar or thumping a tea-chest bass. It did not last long, until around 1957, but it introduced the youth of the nation to the guitar, and many skifflers graduated to become folk fans.

As for traditional folk songs, the popular radio programme *Country Magazine* had started to feature them in 1942, usually sung by trained singers, although not all listeners appreciated the move: 'Can't you put a stop to those awful songs, doesn't the producer know that countrymen don't sing?' wrote one (Dillon (1949), p. 135). But in general the songs were widely appreciated, and largely as a result of the public interest aroused, the BBC launched its highly successful 'Folk Song and Dialect' collecting project, which ran from 1952 until 1957. Peter Kennedy, Seamus Ennis, Bob Copper and others went round the country toting newly invented portable tape-recorders and amassing a remarkable archive of field recordings of speech and song. The BBC also continued using folk songs in its programmes, and some, such as the *As I Roved Out* series, used field recordings to present folk songs sung by genuine traditional singers.

Meanwhile, left-wing activists such as Ewan MacColl and A. L. Lloyd had begun using folk song in their writing and their radio programmes, but it took an American, Alan Lomax, to suggest the deliberate founding of a Folk Revival in Britain, and the idea spread very quickly. Folk clubs sprang up all over the country, records and specialist magazines started to appear, and a group of semi-professional performers soon developed, who toured and were paid (very little) for their appearances. But there was a very strong do-it-yourself, nobody-gets-paid ethos in the Revival, and one of the worst things which could be said in some quarters was that so-and-so performer had 'sold out' or 'gone commercial'. For a while in the 1960s the commercial pop music industry did indeed take an interest in the folk boom, and some of the more accessible acts became household names and had hit records. This, too, did not last, but it had a significant impact, forcing the Revival further away from its roots in pre-war folk music.

Within the folk movement there were many different styles, tastes and fashions, and it is not our brief here to examine them all. One of the most important early divisions was between 'contemporary' and 'traditional', however, and the latter camp included those who eagerly sought out earlier books and recordings from which to draw their repertoire and inspiration. Many genuine traditional singers of the previous generation found themselves a new audience to sing to, and several made LPs for specialist folk labels. A significant new wave of collecting took place – seventy years after Sharp and his colleagues had pronounced folk song dead–and thousands more recordings were added to the national collection. The huge expansion of the higher education sector in the 1960s brought with it courses that included 'folk' topics, and for the first time real academic research in the subject was possible.

But it was the development of the Folk-Song Revival which ushered in the problems of definition that bedevil us today. For more than half a century, nobody had really questioned the received notions of folk music as laid down by the Sharp generation, although this was mainly because nobody seriously examined the question at all. But once the Revival took hold, the notion of 'folk' came under pressure from several directions and it soon collapsed under the strain.

First came the left-wing Revivalists, who argued that urban and industrial workers had just as much right to be considered 'folk' as their country cousins, and that their songs should be included in the genre—even those that were still being written. They also believed that folk song could be used by the workers in the fight against oppression, and they consequently accentuated the potential social protest aspect of folk music.

Other Revivalists soon realized that if the earlier definitions were valid then folk music must have died out with the fading of the unlettered peasantry and that they themselves could therefore never be 'folk'. But they were desperate for the status and security that roots can offer, so they started to turn the definition of folk music on its head, and to argue that rather than being a relatively conservative, backward-looking genre of long roots and slow adaptation, folk must be relevant to the times and should therefore change rapidly with them if necessary. The first result was to include singer-songwriters in the definition, and when the semi-commercial 'scene' developed, in which fashions came and went, the Revival took another step away from the old tradition. As young musicians moved on to other styles, as is in their nature, they still kept the media description of 'folk', at least for a while. The result was that the word 'folk' expanded to include people whose act once used to have some connection with the old folk songs, however tenuous, even if it did not any more. It is no exaggeration to say that performances which were in effect the opposite to what was previously described as 'folk' were now given that same label.

The post-war Revival was also primarily youth-based. It was young people who provided both the rank and file of the movement and the up-and-coming artists, and even those who had no overt political agenda often still appreciated the genre precisely because it was non-commercial, democratic and vaguely counter-cultural. The movement was also, at first, based heavily on American influences – most notably in the use of guitars and the incorporation into the folk fold of protest songs and singer-songwriters. When the commercial music industry got involved it started labelling anything vaguely acoustic as 'folk', the elastic word stretched further and further.

The breaking point was reached when the Marxist academics of the 1970s and 1980s, already mentioned as leading the attack against the collectors, pointedly destroyed earlier notions of a 'folk' or peasant class, and declared the whole notion of 'folk song' to be a fake anyway.

So we are left with a term that not only covers too many disparate forms of music to be of much use but is intellectually untenable. One strategy is to retreat into the anodyne and in response to the question, 'Is that a folk song?' to reply, 'Well, I never heard a horse sing it'; but that is hardly helpful. Another is to do what we are doing in this book and to assert that we are not concerned with the Revival or what came after it, or whether what happens now is 'folk' or not. We are only concerned with understanding and presenting what went on in former times, and that is plenty to keep us interested and busy.

Aspects of Tradition: Singers and Songs

We can now turn, with some relief, to an investigation of songs and singing in the period with which we are concerned. Our account will necessarily be impressionistic and somewhat superficial, but it is designed as an overview rather than an in-depth analysis, and we sincerely hope that it will stimulate further enquiry.

Although most of the pioneer collectors were not particularly interested in documenting all aspects of traditional song, we can go some considerable way to understanding the manner in which folk songs functioned within the community and how and when they were performed, at least during the nineteenth and twentieth centuries. Social and contextual evidence exists in a variety of sources but nobody yet seems to have gathered it together properly, although Roy Palmer's books go a long way in this direction (see the Bibliography).

Sabine Baring-Gould and Alfred Williams were two collectors who gave us pen portraits of their singers, plus some valuable information on how they learnt their songs and where they sang them. But the real gems are often to be found outside the folk-song literature. So, for example, there are many books on contemporary rural life which include valuable information about singing practices, although we do have to make allowances for the 'local colour' and notions of quaint rusticity with which they are often suffused. A great deal of information can be gleaned from memoirs and autobiographies, and works of popular social history such as Flora Thompson's incomparable *Lark Rise to Candleford* (1939–43). Some singers, such as Henry Burstow and Bob Copper, wrote their own accounts, and interviews with post-war singers have added a great deal of contextual information. Local newspaper reports of events, biographies of local characters, and so on, are well worth investigation, and even novels, plays and reports of court cases can be sifted for clues.

Similarly, there is no shortage of material on urban traditions, although never as much as we would like. Henry Mayhew's *London Labour* (1861) tells us a great deal about ballad singers and sellers, while *Tavern Singing in Early Victorian London*, edited by Lawrence Senelick (1997), includes the diary of Charles Rice, a semi-professional singer of comic songs. And in Charles Dickens's *Bleak House* (1853), for example, tangential details are given of the Harmonic Meetings at the local public house after the distressing occurrence of spontaneous human combustion. There are also numerous publications of the 'low life in London' type, which are the equivalent of the books on rural life already mentioned.

It is a bit misleading to speak of a 'local singing tradition', because there were semi-distinct groups within each community which had their own traditions. Thus, in a village, there might be differences between young and old people, men and women, those with different occupations, church and chapel, and so on, in addition to social class. But there would also be overlaps and occasions when they came together.

Songs could originate anywhere – from within the community or, more commonly, outside. For a 'pop' song to become 'folk', however, it needed to escape from the professional and commercial sphere and become amateur and vernacular, and it had to last long enough in the public 'voice' to be transmitted informally from person to person, and down the generations. But a folk song is not simply a pop song which has endured, because the song could have entered the folk tradition from another angle (for example, church music) or have been composed within the local folk tradition. What appears to have happened commonly is that young people picked up the latest songs, while (temporarily at least) rejecting those of the older generation as old-fashioned. There is evidence from Mayhew, for example, of youngsters deliberately buying and collecting the latest songsters from ballad sellers, and an elderly informant in the 1970s told me that in his youth he and his mates used to visit a local music hall to learn the new songs being performed there. Each of them learnt particular lines and they put the song together afterwards. In the nineteenth century, at least, in each successive generation, it seems that the young people's songs were sufficiently different from the norm for the older generation to be wary of them, but sufficiently similar to be incorporated into the 'local tradition' as the young singers got older. At the same time as introducing their 'new' songs (that is, new to the community), the younger people were being regularly exposed to the older repertoire and absorbing it, even if they did not realize it.

The point here is that 'new' and 'old' had to be capable of amalgamation, and the contexts for performance had to be shared between the generations so that cross-generational influences could take place. The polarization of 'youth' and 'adult' culture, in both content and performance venue, is one of the reasons for the death of the old folk-song style.

It stands to reason that a song with similar characteristics to songs already in the tradition has more chance of being adopted than one perceived to be too 'foreign'. So, for example, if it has a tune that is amenable to unaccompanied singing and words that are readily understandable, it is more likely to catch on and be accepted. A case in point here is the craze for 'blackface minstrelsy', which swept the country in the 1840s and remained popular for decades. The songs in these shows were catchy, singable and constructed on similar lines to traditional songs, and young people especially took to them enthusiastically. A number of minstrel songs stayed in the traditional repertoire for generations.

It is clear from the experience of the earlier collectors and later evidence that there was a marked difference between members of the same community when it came to songs and singing. Some people could not or did not sing, while the majority knew a handful of songs. But a small minority had dozens or even hundreds. In the case of the latter it was usually because they had taken a particular interest in the subject and gone out of their way to learn more – investing a certain amount of their personality in being known as a singer. Harry Cox (1885–1971) from Norfolk and Henry Burstow (1826–1916) from Sussex are examples of singers who went to considerable lengths to increase their repertoire. Others, such as Bob Copper (1915–2004) from Sussex, simply had prolonged exposure to a strong singing experience, whether through parents or other family members or in the workplace, and picked up songs almost by osmosis.

We know that some singers deliberately sought out songs that they fancied. Harry Cox, for example, stated that he would walk to another village and pay someone sixpence to sing a song that he was after, while others plied potential sources with drink to get them to sing. But many singers reported that they learnt their songs simply by hearing them over and over again – in the pub every Saturday, or in the home whenever family members thought fit to sing.

It is also clear that there is often a big difference between performers' active and passive repertoires. The former category contains the items which a singer regards as his or her own and which will be sung when the opportunity arises, but the passive repertoire will include songs known but not usually performed – either because they belong to another person, do not appeal sufficiently or are considered incomplete. In most cases the passive repertoire will also include a whole host of ditties, catches, fragments, rhymes, toasts and other flotsam and jetsam of a life of oral tradition.

But attitudes can change over time, and many collectors have come across people who, as they have grown older, have started to take more of an interest in the old songs, and have deliberately tried to recall those that their mother or father sang, or were popular in the barracks or factory at some point in their lives. The Folk-Song Revival also caused a fair amount of 're-remembering'. Collectors started visiting older singers – many of whom had not sung for years – and stimulated them with their interest and questions. Those who then became involved in the Revival, by singing in folk clubs and at festivals, had an incentive to resurrect half-forgotten songs or even to learn new ones.

We also know that it was common practice for people to 'own' particular songs. These were songs for which they were so well known that no one else in the community would dream of singing them in their presence, even though they knew them perfectly well.

People sang in all kinds of places and contexts, and there was probably no situation in which people did not sing at one time or another – even funerals – but certain milieux seem to have been particularly conducive to song. The local pub is the obvious place to look for social music, and there is strong evidence that this was one of the primary locations for singing in urban as well as rural areas. In many cases it would happen on a Friday or Saturday night, but singing could break out at any time or on special occasions, provided, of course, that the landlord or landlady was amenable to such goings-on.

Most communities had more than one pub, and particular locations often acquired a name in the locality for being good 'singing pubs', to which those who liked to perform or listen would naturally gravitate. In many cases there were local rules covering singing sessions, with a recognized chairman who called for 'order', and even rules about who would sing and when. On the whole this kind of pub singing was a male province, as in many communities there was strong disapproval of women visiting pubs on a regular basis. Nevertheless, Ginette Dunn's research into Suffolk traditions around the turn of the twentieth century has shown that while some women would go to the local pub only on special occasions, others went regularly but usually sat in a different room from the men. They too had a strong singing tradition, but it was quite separate from the men's, and is less well documented.

The home was probably the most important singing environment for most women, who sang to themselves while doing the daily chores, to amuse, quieten or instruct the children, and with the whole family in the evenings and at weekends. Many children absorbed the local repertoire and singing style from hearing it constantly around the house long before they met it in other social settings. In many households, hymn singing was a particularly important part of family life.

There were also a number of special occasions within the family and the community when singing was expected—weddings, Christmas parties, harvest-home gatherings, for example—and at any time locals might organize their own 'concert party' or talent show. Whenever people went on trips, whether in the carrier's cart or a motor 'charabanc', singing was a regular part of the fun of the day. Many people belonged to local social clubs, whose monthly or yearly meetings nearly always included singing sessions, while musical enthusiasts within the community might well form a glee club or a minstrel troupe.

People also sang regularly at the workplace, whether on the farm or in the factory. If people were together, and other factors did not prevent it (for example deafening machinery), singing was one way to pass the time. This was particularly likely if the tasks were skilled but sedentary, such as hand lace-making and straw-work, or if the workers lived in—on farms, ships or in army barracks. But others sang precisely because they were alone during much of the day—plough-boys and shepherds, for example.

Local fairs, revels, wakes, and so on—the name changes with the locality—were very important social events and often one of the few times in the year when young rural workers could mix with the opposite sex unsupervised by families or employers. A holiday atmosphere prevailed, and there was always plenty of eating and drinking, dancing and singing, as well as the chance to buy the latest broadside from a ballad seller.

No community was completely isolated from outside musical influence. Ballad singers and itinerant pedlars have already been mentioned, but a village could be visited by a German band or other itinerant group, and there were also professional travelling concert parties and theatre companies who would hire a barn or other space for a show. Many people would make trips to nearby towns to attend concerts or music halls, and outside influence would also operate through the singing in church or chapel, and as taught in the local school. These would all be based on different conventions and involve different repertoires. Children at school would not be taught to sing like their parents, or to perform the same songs their uncles sang every Saturday night after a few pints, and each individual chose which musical path to follow. But it is probably true to say that except in families with marked musical tastes, or strict religious principles, the local vernacular singing tradition formed the bedrock of most people's everyday musical experience.

It is easy to romanticize the world of folk song and to claim its deep psychological value as the glue which held communities together before society fractured into isolated pursuits like watching TV, but there is some truth in the idea that singing and playing gave people a communal experience which we nowadays appear to lack. It is not simply that in previous generations amusements had to be self-made and singing cost nothing, but that there was often a generalized reverence for things which had stood the test of time, and a comfort in knowing where you stood in the community and what to expect. Obviously, there would be some in the community who hated all this 'old' stuff, who craved novelty and found the weight of tradition stifling, or who simply wanted a better class of music, and these people opted out of the traditional activities and found other outlets. Religious people were often encouraged to eschew worldly songs and music, for example, but many people cheerfully straddled two or more spheres. You could sing in the church choir as well as in the pub, play the melodeon for local step-dancing as well as trumpet in a brass band, and ring the church bells on a Sunday.

Decline and Fall

The founders of the Folk-Song Society and the individuals who answered their call to get out into the field and 'collect' songs claimed that folk singing had been in decline for some time and that the songs would be lost if swift action were not taken. They were convinced that the elderly people of the time were the last generation from which genuine folk songs could be obtained, and many of them had trouble remembering songs which they said had gone out of fashion years before. The collectors were right about the decay of the tradition, of course, but they got the timescale wrong, and folk song turned out to be tougher than they had bargained for. Many of the singers recorded by post-Second World War fieldworkers were children, or not even born, when Sharp and his colleagues were active.

Modern enthusiasts often find it difficult to come to grips with folk song being declared dead, and, as discussed earlier, sometimes attempt to circumvent the diagnosis by redefining what is meant by the term 'folk song'; although those who define 'folk' in terms of performance and context within communities rather than simply by repertoire are more willing to accept the verdict, however harsh it may sound. But if 'folk song', in the old sense, is dead, who killed it? What was it that broke down? Was there one trigger or several? All the evidence points in one direction: 'folk song' flourished in a certain type of social context, and they declined and died together.

Not only is the term 'folk song' annoyingly ambiguous, but the other terms used in this discussion are similarly vague, including the word 'tradition', which we have already employed frequently as both adjective and noun and will do so again. In the present context, the phrase 'the tradition' is a useful shorthand term for the bundle of things which are pertinent to folk song within a community, and it is the identification of these things that will help us deconstruct the internal workings of what we are arguing is a particular form of vocal expression, different from other forms.

The key point has been made several times already; it is not simply the repertoire – the songs themselves – which matter, but also the place of singing within the community. 'The tradition' encompasses the singers themselves and their attitudes to singing; the audience's attitudes; the songs (words and tunes), what they say and where they come from; the performance styles; venues and social contexts; who attends and participates; local rules (for example, who sings when, song ownership, and so on), and the frequency of singing opportunities. There is also the question of the degree of openness – how often songs from outside are introduced and whether they are welcomed.

To oversimplify: in a 'healthy' tradition there is plenty of opportunity to perform and an incentive to do so. With much singing going on, there is opportunity to learn new songs and to further imbibe stylistic features which come with repeated hearing. Singing has (usually) a positive social function and good, or effective, singers gain credit for being able performers.

In a 'declining' tradition there are fewer opportunities to perform and to learn, and little incentive. Singers get out of the habit and out of practice. In practical terms, songs become lost or fragmented because people who know only part of a song cannot easily find someone else who knows it to help them out. A 'tipping point' is reached when folk songs become disliked and disowned by significant parts of the community and are actively discouraged. Even in Sharp's day many elderly singers were worried that the collectors were asking them to sing to make fun of their 'old-fashioned' songs.

The early collectors already regarded the urban population as too corrupted by modern influences to be worth considering, and they believed that rural areas were going the same way. They blamed the increased sophistication of the rural population on general social changes such as education, literacy, travel, the rise of commercial mass entertainment and the fact that it was penetrating to every corner of the land. When singers' views are recorded, which is not very often, they usually blame young people for not being interested in the 'old ways'.

The fact of decline is hardly to be disputed, but there is a problem with the timescales involved, and the whole process now looks a lot messier than it seemed in Edwardian times. Modern researchers looking back at social change and its effect on the 'old ways' often focus on the period just before and after the First World War as a time of major upheaval, and this period is seen as the end of a golden age of rural community, contentment and innocence. But if the early collectors' assessment of the health of the tradition was correct, it was already in terminal decline well before the turn of the twentieth century. The twentieth-century acceleration of urbanization, mass entertainment and universal education may have exacerbated the situation but can hardly have caused it.

Flora Thompson's perceptive description of pub-singing at the Wagon and Horses in her village on the Northamptonshire–Oxford-shire borders in the 1880s highlights the changes in the air at the time and is worth quoting in extenso, although those interested should read the whole piece:

> While the talking was going on, the few younger men, 'boy-chaps', as they were called until they were married, would not have taken a great part in it. Had they shown any inclination to do so they would have been checked, for the age of youthful dominance was still to come; and as the women used to say, 'The old cocks don't like it when the young cocks begin to crow'. But, when singing began they came into their own, for they represented the novel.
>
> They usually had first innings with such songs of the day as had per-colated so far, 'Over the Garden Wall', with its many parodies, 'Tommy Make Room for Your Uncle', 'Two Lovely Black Eyes', and other 'comic' or 'sentimental' songs of the day. The most popular of these would have arrived complete with tune from the outer world; others, culled from the penny song-book they most of them carried, would have a tune fitted to them by the singer. They had good lusty voices and bawled them out with spirit. There were no crooners in those days.
>
> The men of middle age inclined more to long and usually mournful stories in verses, of thwarted lovers, children buried in snowdrifts, dead maidens, and motherless homes. Sometimes they would vary these with songs of a high moral tone, such as 'Waste not, Want not' …
>
> But this dolorous singing was not allowed to continue long.
>
> 'Now, then, all together, boys,' someone would shout, and the com-pany would revert to old favourites. Of these, one was 'The Barleymow'… Another favourite for singing in chorus was 'King Arthur'… Then Lukey, the only bachelor of mature age in the hamlet, would oblige with 'My Feyther's a Hedger and Ditcher'…
>
> But, always, sooner or later, came the cry 'Let's give the old 'uns a turn. Here you, Master Price, how about "It was My Father's Custom" or "Lord Lovell" or summat of that sort as has stood the testing o' time?' and Master Price would rise from his corner of the settle, using the stick he called his 'third leg' to support his bent figure as he sang …

[Eventually] someone would say 'What's old Master Tuffrey up to, over in his corner there? Ain't heard him strike up tonight', and there would be calls for old David's 'Outlandish Knight', not because they particularly wanted to hear it – indeed they had heard it so often they all knew it by heart – but because, as they said, 'Poor old feller be eighty-three. Let 'un sing while he can.' So David would have his turn. He only knew the one ballad, and that, he said, he had heard his own grandfather sing it. Probably a long chain of grandfathers had sung it; but David was fated to be the last of them. It was out of date, even then, and only tolerated on account of his age ...

Songs and singers have all gone, and in their places the wireless blares out variety and swing music, or informs the company in cultured tones of what is happening in China or Spain...

Writing in 1943, Flora can be forgiven a touch of nostalgia, but her description rings true for the period and is confirmed by other sources. Of particular interest are the stratification by age, the different types of repertoire, the respect for the old alongside the introduction of the new, and even the printed songbooks, which had largely replaced the broadsides and supplied some of that new material. But also of note is the fact that young and old were still sharing the same performance space, taking their part in the same social event and doing the same thing: singing.

Neither collectors nor performers in the early twentieth century could have foreseen the other major change which would revolutionize the world of song and music: the development of sound recording and broadcast media. Slowly but surely as the century progressed, records and radio removed the face-to-face element of music-making, brought a much higher degree of homogeneity, and introduced a commercial imperative which emphasized professionalism and the constant need for novelty rather than the slow change of local tradition. It is worth remembering that before the invention of the phonograph, if you wanted to hear a song you had to be in the presence of the performer.

The new recording technology was not totally inimical to 'folk' singing. The new sound media also gave people access to songs which they may never have encountered otherwise, and therefore helped to spread them around. Albert Richardson's recordings of 'The Old Sow' and 'Buttercup Joe', for example, issued in 1928, were extremely influential and his versions turned up in singers' repertoires all over the country many years later. In Ireland, Scotland and, particularly, in America, records in vernacular styles were deliberately made and marketed, and certainly supplied local singers with new ways to use their skills. And in America, because radio was local and often drew on local talent, many traditional performers had an opportunity to turn at least semi-professional.

But again the decline was not as fast as many people predicted. Pub sessions roughly similar to those described by Flora Thompson were still found in the 1930s (see, for example, H. Harman's *Sketches of the Bucks Countryside* (1934)) and even after the Second World War, as the remarkable film of an evening at The Ship in Blaxhall, Suffolk, in 1952 (recently reissued on the British Film Institute's DVD set *Here's a Health to the Barley Mow*) amply demonstrates. And, as mentioned earlier, post-war collectors gathered a harvest of hundreds of old songs still being sung in the old style.

Whether or not the Folk Revival, or rather Revivals, continue a tradition or have started a new one is open to debate, and, as already stated, depends largely on your definition of 'folk'. In this sense, its very elasticity can be either a curse or a blessing.

Editors and Performers

Following the original definition of folk song, however flawed, the key feature the folk-song researcher will look for is whether the song in question was 'collected' from actual singers or culled from another book, from a commercial or professional source (that is, trained musicians or professional singers) or even simply made up. Without this information it is impossible to be sure how 'authentic' the information is.

The next litmus test is the quality of the evidence presented: whether the collector or previous editor/author has faithfully reported what he or she found. It is notoriously difficult to represent a sung performance in standard music notation, and it is even surprisingly hard to fully represent a vernacular text in normal writing, but at the least the editor should make the effort.

These problems are well understood and can be compensated for, but the real difficulty is when editors have 'improved' the music by correcting notes or intervals to conform with what they think it should be, or have altered the words to scan better or to change the meaning. In the past, folk songs published by both musicians and poets had routinely been subject to these cavalier editorial attitudes, and it is not always easy to tell how trustworthy a particular editor is, although whether the reader cared or not depended very much on what they wanted from the material.

Performers, of course, are under no such obligations as regards fidelity to source, although in the folk world there have often been strong notions of being grounded in 'tradition', which at least implies a degree of authenticity. Many performers were happy with previous editorial practices, because they usually enhanced the modern 'performability' of the songs, while researchers deplored them and consigned the perpetrators to that corner of hell reserved for untrustworthy editors.

This divergence of expectation between scholars and performers has resulted in a regular irritating misunderstanding on the question of accuracy and alteration in folk music. One argument runs that because folk songs change in transmission and performance it is therefore perfectly acceptable for collectors and editors to alter the songs they are presenting to their public. They are simply another link in the chain of transmission. By the same token, some performers assume that editors who are pernickety in preserving the exact details of their informants' texts and performances are being 'purist' (a favourite pejorative word in this debate) and are attempting to straitjacket future performance by dictating exact fidelity to the source.

The fact of the matter is that editors' and performers' needs may overlap, but are very different. It is the editor's task to present the data as accurately and honestly as possible, so that future users have the choice whether to change things or not—although if you are simply looking for a good song, it matters little how it has come to you, and questions of historical accuracy and authenticity will probably come a poor second to notions of singability. But if you wish to say, to yourself or others, 'This is how it was sung in Sussex in 1907,' then you need to be confident that the editor has not interpolated verses from Scotland, changed the notes to suit a personal notion of how songs should sound, or omitted verses because they offended some notion of propriety. The question is whether or not you can trust the editor, but the rest is up to you.

Broadsides and Street Literature

Something needs to be said about broadsides and other street literature, because they are intimately connected with the history of folk song and are mentioned frequently in the Notes in this book. 'Street literature' is the usual term for cheap printed material which poured from the back-street presses of jobbing printers from the sixteenth to the late nineteenth centuries, and was designed to entertain and inform the masses. The genre includes broadsides (single sheets printed on one side), chapbooks (made by printing a large sheet and folding it into a small booklet), prints (woodcuts and engravings) and other forms of cheap printed material.

Songs constituted an important part of street literature, but there was also a huge range of prose pieces which described local crimes and scandals, offered last dying speeches purportedly written by condemned criminals, told amazing stories of monstrous births, sea serpents and other wonders, or related traditional stories like 'Jack the Giant Killer', or the exploits of Robin Hood or Dick Turpin, while a great number were devoted to the interpretation of dreams, how to tell the future, and so on.

Street literature was available in various ways. Broadsides were sold in city streets and at rural markets and fairs by itinerant vendors who sang the songs to attract attention and teach the tunes, as well as by static 'stationers' who pinned them up on street walls or railings for their customers to peruse. They were also included in the packs of itinerant pedlars and were stocked by shops which specialized in toys and other cheap sundries, and sold retail and wholesale by the printers themselves; the better class of broadside was also sold in book shops. We know that sheets on popular subjects sold in their hundreds of thousands, and, judging by the number of printers who specialized in their production, there must have been a steady and lucrative market.

Cheap printed material came in many types, shapes and sizes, but for songs the standard forms were the broadside and the chapbook, or garland. The most common broadside pattern in the nineteenth century was a quarto (10 in. x 8 in.) sheet, printed on one side of flimsy paper. The words were printed in two columns; occasionally there would be one long song but more commonly two songs were printed side by side, and a sheet could be cut in half to make two separate 'slip songs'. The sheet would often be decorated with one or two woodcuts, which were used again and again and frequently had little connection with the song.

The quality of the printing varied enormously. Some were carefully and professionally typeset, but the majority were rough and ready, and many were very crude indeed, on poor-quality paper, with letters missing, inserted in the wrong place or upside down. Larger sheets were also available, with lots more songs, and there was a special annual trade in large, lavishly illustrated sheets of Christmas carols. Some of the song chapbooks were issued in series with a generic title (for example, *A Garland of New Songs*), presumably to encourage people to collect them. Even within street literature, there were fashions brought about by changes in taste and/or developments in paper-making and printing technologies. Eighteenth-century broadsides were usually larger than nineteenth-century sheets, and songs could therefore be much longer. Chapbooks of songs proliferated in the eighteenth and early nineteenth centuries but gradually gave way to more substantial 'songsters', which had more pages and were more professionally produced.

Many local printers produced a few broadsides from time to time as a sideline, but there were some who specialized in this type of material and the most prolific advertised that they held over 4,000 or more different ballads in stock, offering items at prices ranging from a halfpenny to sixpence. London was the most important place for broadside printing, but there were significant producers in Newcastle, Manchester, Liverpool and other regional centres, as well as in Scotland and Ireland.

The main broadside market seems to have faded away by the 1880s, but a few printers specialized in song sheets well into the twentieth century. These catered for customers who were nostalgic for old songs as well as those who wanted the latest music-hall or comic songs.

It is now clear that the vast majority of the songs which were collected as folk songs had previously appeared on broadsides and in chapbooks, and we know that many people learnt their new songs in this way. This does not negate the theory of an oral tradition, because the person who bought a broadside and learned a song may then have sung it to dozens of other people, who picked it up by ear. But it does make the idea of a purely oral tradition untenable, except perhaps in regard to the tunes. Although sheet music for many songs was available, this was an expensive format and required the ability to read music. Most people therefore learnt the tune aurally even if they got the words from a printed source.

Most modern researchers accept the role played by print in the folk-song tradition, although there is still debate about the relative proportions of print/oral influence, and what this means to our overall notion of folk song as an identifiable category of music. Even if we think that broadsides had a minimal effect on the song tradition, they are still essential for historical research. Street literature is rarely dated, but it often includes datable clues, such as printers' names and addresses, which enable us to get a handle on how old particular songs are. What also seems clear is that some, perhaps most, folk songs started life as songs written specifically for broadside production, and were probably written by poorly paid urban versifiers usually referred to as 'broadside hacks'.

The Folk Song Index *and* The Broadside Index

These have been mentioned several times in the Introduction and therefore need some explanation. *The Folk Song Index* is an online database which seeks to list all the English-language folk songs ever collected in the English-speaking world. A very tall order, of course, and it will always be a work-in-progress, but a good start has been made and it already contains 180,000 references. The most complete section is that devoted to material collected in England, and nearly all the major publications and unpublished collections have already been included. Each entry includes the song title, first line, performer's name, collector's name and date and place of collection, and whether the text or tune is available. As each element is fully searchable and sortable, it is relatively easy to isolate songs from a particular singer or geographical location, or all the versions of a particular song. A numbering system allows users to find versions of a song, even if they appear under different titles.

The Broadside Index simply gives details of songs which appeared on broadsides, chapbooks, songsters and in other cheap literature up to about 1920. It is very useful in its own right as a finding aid for popular songs, and for the history of street literature, but is particularly valuable for tracing the history of songs which appear in *The Folk Song Index*. Both indexes are freely available on the Vaughan Williams Memorial Library website: www.efdss.org.

The Folk Song Index underpins much of the commentary of the present book in two significant ways. Firstly, the 'Roud number' quoted when song titles are mentioned is not only a way of identifying the song and distinguishing it from others with the same name, but also offers the interested reader the key to other publications and collections. And secondly, the gathering of large quantities of data provides the present-day researcher with opportunities which were not previously available. The quantitive evidence supplied by the *Index* is the basis of many of the judgements and statements made in the present notes – such as 'This song was widely collected in England but not often in Scotland.' Nevertheless, as the *Index* is still growing, such statements must always be taken as at least partly provisional.

Steve Roud

Introduction to the Music

This section focuses on English folk-song tunes, their characteristics, methods of study and history. It tackles the question of why English folk song sounds the way that it does. As A. L. Lloyd wrote in the original *Penguin Book of English Folk Songs* (1959), 'None of this need frighten the reader who has no mind for musical technicalities.' Such technicalities are explained here as clearly and straightforwardly as possible with examples drawn from the present volume. Nevertheless, nothing can take the place of actually listening to traditional singing. Some recordings from the last 110 years are commercially available and can be located through the *Folk Song Index* mentioned in the General Introduction.

Despite the interest in folk-song melodies of the Edwardian collectors and others, there are in general fewer studies of the music of folk songs than of their words. Indeed, some of the earlier published folk-song collections, such as Thomas Percy's *Reliques of Ancient English Poetry* (1765) and John Bell's *Rhymes of the Northern Bards* (1812), contained only the words. Literary scholars like Francis J. Child (1825–96) were similarly concerned with ballads as poetic texts rather than songs and left the consideration of the tunes out of their accounts. Fortunately, from John Broadwood's *Old English Songs* (1847) onwards, folk-song collecting was frequently undertaken by musically trained individuals and their methods set the pattern. Few of the major collections published post-Broadwood omitted the tunes, with the exception of Alfred Williams's *Folk-Songs of the Upper Thames* (1923).

When collecting from a living tradition of folk singing became the vogue, the ability to document the tunes rested on the collector not only being musically literate but having the skill to take down tunes by what was effectively oral dictation. This was no mean feat when he or she was noting down the words as well, and some employed an assistant for that very reason. Others used the sound-recording technology of their time. At the dawn of the twentieth century, this was the phonograph, which recorded up to two minutes of sound on to wax cylinders. It was not commonly employed by collectors during this period, however, except Percy Grainger. By the time of the Second Revival after the Second World War, technology had improved in fidelity, portability and ease of operation, and the use of audio-recording equipment became the norm in folk-song collecting.

Prior to this, though, the favoured method was the notation of tunes by ear directly from the performances of singers. As a result, much of the tune evidence dating from Victorian and Edwardian times takes the form of a skeletal notation (excluding details of singing style such as ornamentation) of a single stanza of music. This may represent the first stanza of the song or a 'normal' form of the melody as it developed during the performance and was apprehended by the collector. Without sound recordings of these singers we have no independent check as to the accuracy of the transcription in relation to what was sung or how typical the normal form of the melody was in terms of both rhythm and pitches. Judgements as to the reliability of tune transcriptions have then to be made on the basis of what we know about the musical skills of the collector in question and their experience of, and attitude towards, folk song.

Even with the more widespread use of electronic sound recording, transcription was still not a straightforward matter. Its ability to allow repeated playback and the slowing down of renditions led to some highly detailed notations by Grainger, which others found very difficult to follow, and some, like Cecil Sharp, felt exaggerated aspects of the singer's performance style (see 'Bonny Bunch of Roses O' (No. 2), for an example, albeit simplified, of a Grainger transcription). As Charles Seeger has pointed out, it is important to consider the purpose of the transcription and to reflect that in the level of detail adopted. He distinguished between 'prescriptive music-writing', which acts as a blueprint for performance, and 'descriptive music-writing', which takes place after the performance and attempts to describe what happened in it. Since a major reason for the transcription of later sound recordings of folk song has been so that new audiences could learn and sing them, the notations have needed to function as prescriptive music and have thus remained single-stanza, skeletal transcriptions. Some do note variations in pitches and rhythm occurring from one stanza to another, though, as Sharp also tried to do.

Singing Style

Although music notations can give us pitches and rhythms, they cannot convey the way the singing sounded. What we know about performance style is almost entirely based on evidence from the late nineteenth century on, in literary accounts (such as Flora Thompson's *Lark Rise to Candleford* (1939–43), mentioned in the General Introduction), collectors' descriptions of singing as they witnessed it in the collecting situation, the home and the pub, and on sound recordings.

It is important to bear in mind that traditional singers had no formal musical training. This is not to say that they were not accomplished musicians or that there was no learning process or practice involved, but rather to emphasize that the techniques and conventions of art and popular music are not of relevance here. Many were not musically literate and, even if they were, this skill seems to have been little used in this context, where tunes were generally learnt from listening to others' song performances. Words and music would be taken in as a conjoined unit, therefore. Sharp went so far as to claim that singers could not remember the words of songs if they could not remember the tune. This may have been true for some singers but has not been universally found. What Sharp's observation does highlight, though, is the vital importance of the tune as the means by which the words are both expressed and recalled in an oral song tradition. Songs were rarely 'taught' as such, except perhaps to children, meaning that they were usually learnt from repeated listening to complete performances (not necessarily always by the same singer), or re-created from a single hearing by recall of the melody, the storyline and some of the specific lines of the song's text. The manner in which songs were performed was taken in as part of the same process of watching and listening and was not taught separately.

A key feature of traditional singing in England is that it has been widely found to be solo in style (except where the audience joins in with a chorus), and does not use any accompanying instruments. There are exceptions to this, the Copper family of Rottingdean in Sussex who sing in harmony being an important one, and it has been suggested that unaccompanied singing is a relatively recent phenomenon (Gammon (1981)). Two examples of part-singing have been included here: 'The White Cockade' (No. 20) and 'The Hungry Fox' (No. 110).

In the solo performance tradition, the manner in which singers perform a song can vary according to their identity, ability, the context and function of performance (including the amount of alcohol they have drunk) and the kind of song being sung. By and large, the overriding focus of singers is on putting across the words of the song clearly. Too many histrionics, changes in tempo, articulation and dynamics are felt to detract from this and so are avoided, although there is often more leeway in a comic song. Hence English traditional singing has often been described as 'plain' or matter-of-fact, even impassive, and this is reinforced by the predominantly syllabic setting of the words to the music (discussed below).

Sharp commented that the traditional singer 'is a past-master in the art of welding together words and tune, i.e., in enunciating his syllables with great clearness, while maintaining an unbroken stream of melody' (*English Folk-Song: Some Conclusions* (1907), p. 107). This highlights a subtle but crucial difference between the singing style of traditional and trained singers. Trained singers are basically taught to prolong the vowel sounds of words in order to sustain the notes. Traditional singers, on the other hand, tend to keep the length of vowels closer to speech and do a greater amount of singing on voiced and hummed consonants. This can sometimes lead to the creation of an extra syllable, the word 'plough', for example, becoming 'pl-ough'. When the consonant cannot be voiced, a momentary staccato-like effect is produced. This method of vocalization contributes to the buoyancy and lilt of much English traditional singing.

Musical Characteristics of Folk Song

Form, Rhythm and Metre

English folk songs, in common with those from elsewhere in northern and western Europe, are frequently made up of two- or four-line stanzas of text matched by a four-phrase melody. The melody and stanzaic form are repeated while the words that fill them are changed in order to recount a story or evoke a scene and its attendant mood. The repetition of the melody makes it familiar and predictable, even mesmerizing, to the listener as the rendition progresses. It also means that when someone else learns the song the melody is usually the first element to be picked up and in turn helps in remembering the words.

Sometimes stanzas are lengthened by the repetition of one or more lines in the manner of a chorus, or refrain (as in 'Bold Grenadier', No. 77, for example), or they may have new lines which recur at the end of each stanza (as in 'Bonny Light Horseman', No. 41, and 'The Cunning Cobbler', No. 78). Refrain lines are also found interpolated as lines 2 and 4 of the verse, in which case they are technically known as a burden (see 'The Cruel Mother', No. 116).

The words of each line commonly consist of four stresses with a varying number of unstressed syllables in between. Many songs are in 'ballad metre', which at first sight seems to be a four-stress line followed by a three-stress one, although in reality the melody to which they are sung contains a pause or held note at the end of the three-stress lines, implying a fourth stress. Ballad metre is often accompanied by a rhyme scheme of abcb, which may become abcbb when the final line is repeated (as in 'Barbara Allen', No. 40). When the song has a burden, however, lines 1 and 3 carry the rhyme abac (as in 'The Frog and the Mouse', No. 108). Another common verse pattern consists of four lines with four explicit stresses. It is often found in broadside verse but is not confined to it (see 'Golden Glove', No. 26, and 'Blackberry Fold', No. 131, for example). More complex verse forms are also found.

The musical stanzas have been moulded to fit the length of the

verse forms and the length of the lines within them. They thus typically consist of four phrases, each ending with a brief moment of
repose though this can vary depending on the singer's style of singing
and whether or not the line has a masculine (stressed syllable) or feminine (unstressed syllable) ending (see, for example, 'The Painful
Plough', No. 101, and 'Spanish Ladies', No. 19). There is generally a
more pronounced pause midway through the stanza (at the end of the
second line or phrase).

The form of folk tunes is commonly described in terms of their
phrase structure, with letters denoting each phrase and indicating any
recurrences of it. Common patterns range from ABCD in which no
two phrases are alike, to AAAB, ABCA, ABAC and ABBA. Sometimes
a phrase may be repeated in a slightly differing form, which is often
denoted by the use of a straight apostrophe, for example, the common
pattern ABB'A.

In terms of rhythm and metre there is also a close fit between the
melody and the words, with the textual stresses usually coinciding
with the musical metre. The number of unstressed syllables between
each stressed beat can vary and this leads to rhythmic variation by the
singer, who adds, repeats or omits notes accordingly. Most singers
seem able to do this with ease, and this is an important skill given that
in the English tradition the words are married up to the notes of
the tune in a highly syllabic manner, that is, with one or two notes
allotted to each syllable. At the opposite extreme is melismatic word-
setting in which multiple notes coincide with a single syllable of the
text, as found in Irish sean-nós singing, for example. A glimpse of
this is found in 'The Bold *Princess Royal*' (No. 1) as sung by Ned
Adams, but in general this kind of singing is rare in England.

The syllabic setting of the words to the music is highlighted by a
relatively regular feeling of pulse underlying many singers' renditions (sometimes described by tune commentators as *tempo giusto*
style, drawing on the Italian performance direction meaning 'in exact
(that is, strict) time'). This does not always result in bars of regular
length, singers often adding an extra beat to the bar at the end of the
phrase, for example, but it does allow rhythms to be reasonably well
represented by Western art-music notation. As anyone who has

attempted to transcribe a song from a sound recording will know, however, some singers perform in a stricter style than others, and for several songs in the present collection it has been necessary to make the notation more complex in order to convey this subtle elasticity. This results in what Percy Grainger described as 'a regrettably disturbing impression to the eye' (Grainger (1908), p. 152).

It is also notable that syncopation, in which a stress is diverted to a beat that the listener is expecting to be unstressed, is not commonly found in English folk-song melodies. Upbeats (pick-up notes), on the other hand, are almost invariably the rule for each phrase.

The four-stress textual line tends to result in musical phrases which are notated as four bars in length. The number of beats in these bars is usually two, three or four, in either simple or compound time (in which the beats can be subdivided into two or three quicker notes respectively). Melodies either wholly or partially in five time are also found. Indeed, this metre seems to be associated with certain song examples, including 'Bold Fisherman' (No. 21), 'Barbara Allen' (No. 40) and 'Basket of Eggs' (No. 59) in the present volume. Five time produces asymmetrical bars, which in these examples always follows a 2+3 pattern.

Tonality and Range

Although the majority of English folk-song melodies draw on the notes in the major scale, their tonality has been something of a preoccupation among those who have collected and published them. Writing in 1833, for example, William Sandys noted that some folksong tunes do not conform to either the major or the two forms of the minor scale found in Western art-music theory. Instead, the scales of such tunes have frequently been described in terms of the 'medieval' or 'church' modes. References to the names of modes, such as Ionian, Dorian, Aeolian and Mixolydian, are commonly found in folk-song publications, and can appear arcane and offputting to the non-music specialist. They are doubly confusing in that some commentators have chosen to treat the major scale as modal because another of the modes replicates the constituents of that scale under the name of the Ionian mode. Not surprisingly, some analysts have questioned the usefulness of the modes on various grounds. Nonetheless, they refer to a real aural characteristic of English folk song, and understanding modal terminology and the reasons for its use is important to the history of English folk-song collecting and publication.

What is a mode? It can be narrowly defined here as a type of scale, a scale being a sequence of notes abstracted from a piece or style of music and placed in ascending or descending order of pitch. In Western art music, scales consist of seven different notes, the eighth note being the same as the first note but at a higher or lower pitch. The difference between one pitch and another in a scale is described in terms of two basic intervals, the half step (semitone) and whole step (tone). Much popular and art music, though not world musics, that we hear today conforms to the major scale and/or the two forms (harmonic and melodic) of minor scale. These scales, and the tonal conception of music that they imply, became the norm in Western music in the seventeenth century and they have been with us ever since. The crucial difference between tunes cast in these scales and those cast in the modes was that the former implied certain harmonies or underlying chords as part of a simultaneous accompaniment, while the modes did not. This is because mode theory was developed to describe and account for plainsong, an unaccompanied chant used in church liturgy. The sixteenth-century theorist Glareanus presented a reformulation of the modes introducing what he maintained were two previously overlooked modes – the Aeolian and Ionian – and established the system of terminology, based on ancient Greek writings, that is used in discussions of folk song.

We can begin to appreciate the different sound of modal music compared to tonal harmonic music if we take a well-known tonal tune and 'translate' it into the various modes. Take, for example, the opening of the carol 'The First Nowell', which makes use of all the notes in the major scale:

'The First Nowell' (major)

The distribution of steps and half steps in the major scale, also sometimes referred to as the Ionian mode, is as follows:

Major-scale tones (T) and semitones (S) arrangement

If we alter the seventh note of the scale (C sharp) and make it a semitone lower (C natural), this modifies the tone-semitone pattern, turning it into the Mixolydian mode. When applied to 'The First Nowell', this produces an obvious difference in sound:

'The First Nowell' (Mixolydian)

If we then retain this modification and additionally lower the third degree of the scale (F sharp) by a half step (F natural) we arrive at the Dorian mode, again with obvious aural results:

'The First Nowell' (Dorian)

Finally, if we retain both of the above modifications and lower the sixth degree (making B into B flat), we create the Aeolian mode:

'The First Nowell' (Aeolian)

There are other modes, but these are the three, or four if the Ionian is counted, that are noted as prevalent in English folk-song tunes.

Although the example just given is highly artificial ('The First Nowell' was conceived as a tonal tune, implying a certain harmonic accompaniment, not as a non-harmonic, modal melody), we can at least gain some idea of the impression that the apparently modal folk tunes made on nineteenth-century musicians. At best they sounded 'quaint' and at worst 'wrong' or 'out of tune', and they presented obvious problems when folk songs were set to a piano accompaniment. Champions of folk song around the mid nineteenth century nevertheless began to make a virtue of them, the attribution of 'modal' lending the melodies greater validity at the same time as tending to lead to claims of their consequently being 'ancient'. Towards the end of the century, in the years leading up to the formation of the Folk-Song Society, the modality of English folk tunes was made increasingly explicit by collectors who again, under the influence of an evolutionary perspective on music, and a Tylorian theory of survivals, believed modality to be evidence of a tune's antiquity.

The aesthetic appeal of modal folk-song tunes came to the fore in the early twentieth century in the writings of collectors such as Lucy Broadwood, Ralph Vaughan Williams and Cecil Sharp. Sharp at first appears to have equated modality with the ancientness of a tune but he quickly changed tack, insisting that the modes were 'no test of age' in folk song. He countered the idea that modal folk tunes may have become part of country singers' repertoire from church music, implying as this did a process of cultural 'descent', and instead suggested that folk singers had probably always used the modes. He also began to stress the freshness of modal folk tunes and their potential for the modern composer.

That modes came to be so prized among Sharp and his contemporaries is very much due to the musical climate of their time. English composers in the late nineteenth century had been striving to overcome a 200-year-old tradition of musical impotence and were trying to develop a distinctively national musical style by which to counter the late Romantic idiom then dominant in most of Europe and emanating largely from Germany. It was partly through their contact with folk-song melodies that certain English composers, such as Vaughan Williams, were propelled towards the final realization that the modes could form a viable point of departure for the new musical idiom they sought to create. This idiom had connotations of 'Englishness' by virtue of being found in folk-song melodies collected in the English countryside, and had the musical potential to furnish an alternative to the lush chromaticism of much contemporary music from the Continent.

While Sharp insisted that each mode had its own individual character, which in turn affected the character of a folk song, Grainger, who had made a detailed study of songs he had collected using the phonograph, emphasized the tendency of singers to alter the third and seventh degrees of the scale, and occasionally the sixth, in their performances by up to a semitone. These are the very degrees which differentiate the different modes from each other and from the major scale. Thus, Grainger proposed that modal songs were cast in 'one single loosely-knit modal folk-song scale' that combined Mixolydian, Dorian and Aeolian characteristics (Grainger (1908), p. 158). This model was not received favourably by members of the Folk-Song Society and was not widely taken up, and modal terminology persisted throughout the twentieth century.

Modal terminology was most notably employed by Bertrand Bronson in his 'mode star', which was intended to demonstrate the points of overlap between the modes and also between pentatonic and hexatonic tunes (drawing on a five- and six-note scale respectively). Norman Cazden, another American folk-song scholar, was an outspoken critic of modal terminology in folk-tune analysis and attacked Bronson's mode star in particular.

It is almost impossible for us to escape the major and minor tonality to which we have been conditioned when we listen to the melodies of folk song. There is also little evidence as to how singers themselves 'heard' modal tunes and even if they were aware of them, how they might have articulated their qualities. Singers were likewise not isolated from standard major and minor tonality, which permeated church music and commercial forms and would have been reinforced by the tuning of certain musical instruments. Rather, it seems that the flexible tuning of certain notes may arise at least partly from their position in relation to other notes of a phrase and their association with certain formulaic melodic patterns that can be found in folk-song tunes.

We are on firmer ground when we consider the note range of tunes commonly used for folk songs. In England, this is usually no greater than the interval of an eleventh, that is, one and a half octaves. Tunes can be divided into two categories according to where the 'tonal centre' – often the final note of the tune – lies in relation to the other notes. In tunes with a so-called 'authentic' range, the tonal centre lies at the extremes of the range, with the rest of the notes used in the tune being located in between. By contrast, in tunes with a plagal range the tonal centre lies more or less halfway between the lowest notes of the tune and the highest ones.

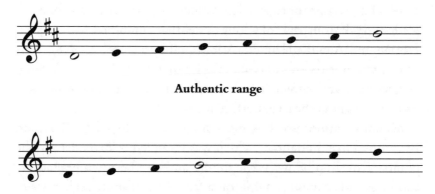

Authentic range

Plagal range

Stability and Change in Folk-Song Melodies

One consequence of the unwritten nature of English folk-song tradition was that the melodies associated with the songs were not fixed. There was usually no original version to which performers had access and could refer, and sheet music and latterly even commercial recordings, when used as sources, might be regarded as starting points rather than models that must be precisely imitated. Performers also varied as to how much they aspired to sing songs in the way that they heard them sung and how much they liked to innovate, consciously or unconsciously.

Changes could occur in one or more elements of the tune, such as pitches, tonality, rhythm, speed, metre and structure. Some of these could be introduced in the course of a song as the singer fitted the tune to the differing number of syllables of the words, for example, or if the number of textual stresses varied from the norm. Variation in one element could also lead to variation in another, a change in the order of the phrases, for example, sometimes necessitating adjustments to individual pitches. These changes have been regarded as the result of either creative or degenerative processes (individual artistry versus forgetting, for example) but there is a sense in which all change requires creativity, whatever the impetus for it in the first place.

Given the scope for altering a song's melody, then, it may come as something of a surprise to the uninitiated to learn that many of the tunes noted from English folk singers sound markedly similar to each other. This was constantly noted by folk-song collectors, not only in England but also in Scotland and Ireland, who commented not on how many tunes they encountered but, conversely, how few. The same basic tunes cropped up over and over again but in slightly differing forms, or 'variants' as they called them. The existence of these flexible and variable melodies raised many questions. What makes one tune variant sound 'the same' as another? Where is the dividing line between one tune, in all its variant forms, and another? Are all variants descended from one original tune? Why are some variants from geographically distant places very similar and others from the same location very different? Is close resemblance between variants evidence of their genetic connection?

Folk-song scholars have come up with the concepts of 'melodic contour' and of 'tune families' to help tackle these kinds of questions. The outline of the melody, or its contour, has been observed to be one of the most stable elements of a tune. At the most general level, many tunes in Anglo-American, Scandinavian and German folk-song traditions are essentially arc-shaped in that their first phrase is confined to the lower part of the melodic range and the phrases in between rise to one or two melodic peaks before descending to the same level as the initial phrase. At a more specific level, though, it has been hard to pinpoint the exact combinations of elements that make one melody strike the listener as 'the same' as another, and it is quite possible that shifting criteria come into play in different cases. This difficulty has hampered the classification and comparative study of folk-song tunes, which, despite digital technology and developments in music information retrieval, still relies principally on the human ear and a wide-ranging knowledge of traditional tunes.

The American scholar Samuel Bayard made an extensive study of Anglo-American folk-song tunes and their resemblances. He identified a number of what he called 'tune families'. These were groups of related variants that he presumed had descended from a single original melody and taken on multiple forms due to variation, imitation and assimilation. In total, Bayard identified more than forty tune families among the folk songs of England, Ireland and Lowland Scotland and their descendants in the New World. The crossings and overlap between these areas show that a pure English tradition of folk music is a myth and the assertion of a tune as, for example, 'English' or 'Irish' in origin or character belies the complex history of melodic relationships and interchange between England and other countries.

Bayard's tune families also highlight another feature of folk-song tunes. Despite the close relationship of music and words in oral tradition, singers were clearly able to separate the two when needed to fit the tune to a different set of words, such as those taken from a broadsheet. The recycling of melodies in this way was commonplace and explains why there are fewer tunes than songs. Intriguingly, when one studies the tunes associated with particular songs, as Bronson did with each of the Child ballads, for example, and as has been done with some of the songs in this volume, it seems that some songs have been strongly associated with just one tune, while others are associated with many distinct melodies. It is tempting to interpret the former situation as indicative of the vitality of a song in oral tradition through time and space, and the latter situation as being related to the influence of print in perpetuating or reviving a song that has lost vitality in oral tradition. Alas, it is difficult, if not impossible, to substantiate these speculations.

Tune History

While it is likely that the majority of folk-song melodies originated in a single composition by an individual composer, these compositions

have generally not been preserved. In addition, it was not only traditional singers who recycled melodies. Trained musicians and
professional composers have likewise drawn on folk-song melodies,
making arrangements of them and recasting them in their own works.
When it appears that we have found the origin of a song in such a
source, then, it can turn out that the composer was 'borrowing' from
oral tradition in this way. On the other hand, there are instances of
composed pieces from other performance traditions, such as the
eighteenth-century glee club, and music hall, parlour ballads and
blackface minstrelsy in the nineteenth and early twentieth centuries,
being adopted by traditional singers and becoming widespread
through oral transmission and, more recently, electronic media such as
radio and gramophone records.

Where these sources exist they provide some of the scant datable
evidence we have relating to melodies sung by traditional singers.
They also provide glimpses of the complex ways in which, during
specific eras, songs and tunes were appropriated and re-appropriated
by performers in different spheres of professionalized and non-pro-
fessionalized music-making and among performers and audiences of
different social classes.

Despite tonalities that resembled the modes of pre-harmonic
music, and the fact that Bronson and others have found melodic
resemblances between some examples of plainchant and folk songs
(see the headnote to 'Lady Isabel and the Elf-Knight', Child 4, in his
Traditional Tunes of the Child Ballads, I (1959), p. 39), few of the tunes
noted from oral tradition in the nineteenth and twentieth centuries
can be shown to have originated in or date back to medieval music.
The earliest evidence for many English folk-song tunes is the seventeenth and eighteenth centuries although, of course, they may be
older. Some occur in the sets of variations written on popular tunes
by Renaissance composers such as William Byrd (*My Ladye Nevell's
Book*, 1591) and the contributors to the *Fitzwilliam Virginal Book*. Others were published in Thomas Ravenscroft's collections *Pammelia*,
Deuteromelia (both of 1609) and *Melismata* (1611). In the second half of
the seventeenth century, folk-song tunes crop up in the enormously
popular and much reprinted publication by John Playford, *The*

English Dancing Master (1651–1728). In the eighteenth century, two major sources of evidence stand out. One is *Wit and Mirth; or, Pills to Purge Melancholy*, first published in 1699–1700 but, again, much reprinted in expanded editions and latterly edited by Thomas D'Urfey, himself a composer of stage songs set to ballad tunes. The other is *The Beggar's Opera* (1728), by John Gay, a highly successful work which spawned many imitations. The work was satirical in intention, with Gay substituting the arias that characterized contemporary operas with short songs set to well-known tunes of his day. Music performed in pleasure gardens also entered the repertoires of folk singers and was itself influenced by songs in oral tradition. By the second half of the nineteenth and the early twentieth centuries, songs from minstrel shows, parlour ballads, evangelical hymns and music-hall songs (often comic) were often adopted into folk singer's repertoires as well, as noted above.

Despite this, the historical record for a great many English folk-song tunes remains patchy and still more sources may yet come to light or become accessible through indexing and digitization. For this reason the definitive history of most folk tunes has yet to be written, although two major contributions are to be found in Bronson's *Traditional Tunes of the Child Ballads* (1959–72) and Simpson's *British Broadside Ballad and Its Music* (1966). Rather more haphazard are the notes that folk-song collectors provided on tunes in the *Journal of the Folk-Song Society*.

Julia Bishop

Note on Editing and Transcription

Text Editing and Transcription

Apart from the considerable difficulties of representing vital vernacular speech in cold print, one of the most problematic areas of any attempt to make the transition from ear to eye is punctuation. Many of the songs are not grammatical in the strictest sense, and if a text is punctuated according to the formal rules it becomes burdened with marks – particularly commas – which destroy the rhythm. We have therefore decided to strip the punctuation to the minimum, and have always favoured rhythm over grammar. For example, the line which could be given as 'So, fare ye well, my own true love, for ever, ever more' becomes 'So fare ye well my own true love, for ever ever more'. Punctuation at the end of each line has been particularly severely suppressed.

It is a well-known characteristic of folk songs that titles vary considerably from singer to singer, which presents editors and researchers with major problems. We have decided to give a generally known title as the main heading for each song, while the singer's or editor's title is given in the Notes.

Music Editing

The songs in this volume have been taken from a variety of sources, each of which presents the tune in a slightly different way. Some are notations made by ear directly from a singer's rendition, others are transcriptions from sound recordings. Some are highly detailed, while others are more skeletal or composite in their conception. Some include melodic and rhythmic variation to a greater or lesser extent, others do not.

There has, of necessity, then, been some degree of standardization in the presentation of the tunes here. Where necessary, they have been transposed so that they fit the stave without the need for notes using more than one ledger line and so that they are presented in keys of no more than two sharps, as follows:

- Major and Mixolydian tunes
  (plagal range) → tonal centre on G
- Major and Mixolydian tunes
  (authentic range) → tonal centre on D
- Minor, Dorian and Aeolian tunes
  (plagal range) → tonal centre on A
- Minor, Dorian and Aeolian tunes
  (authentic range) → tonal centre on E

Other editorial emendations, such as the addition of slurs or the sub-division of notes to accommodate the words of the first verse, and the correcting of obvious mistakes, have also been made. More major changes, such as editorial solutions to anomalies in the text, have been documented in the written notes for the relevant song.

Music Transcription

Some audio-recorded songs appear here in transcription for the first time. In addition, most previously notated songs for which it has been possible to obtain the source sound recording have been newly transcribed to increase the consistency of transcribed examples, such as in the presentation of melodic variation.

A fairly straightforward level of transcription has been adopted so that the transcribed tunes are easy to read and more closely resemble the other tune notations in appearance. Ornaments and grace notes have therefore, for the most part, been omitted unless they are very prominent, and rhythmic subtleties have mostly been notated in the nearest conventional note values and combinations. Sometimes these latter have been supplemented by impressionistic symbols, especially the pause sign, which obviates the need for too many changes of time signature and unexpected time values. In some songs, where the length of the bars alternates between two different time signatures, or sometimes even three, the additional time signatures have been noted in parentheses at the start of the transcription rather than at the point at which they occur in the notation. Music theory has not been strictly adhered to in the final bar of each tune, which reflects the length singers give it rather than being made up to one full bar with the addition of the upbeat (pick-up) note with which the tune starts. Rests have also been omitted for the most part, as have indications of where singers took breaths.

Since, by convention, it is usual to present the music and words of the first stanza in folk-song collections, it was decided to follow this practice in the transcribed examples here. This is despite the fact that, in performance, it is often the case that singers take a while to get into their stride with a tune and the first verse may be the least typical rendition of it.

For reasons of space and clarity, it has been necessary to be selective with regard to the notation of rhythmic and melodic variations introduced by singers in the course of singing a song. Since rhythmic changes are often made in response to the words, they have been omitted and only variations which introduce changes of pitch through omission, addition, substitution or reordering at a specific point have been included. Other notable features of individual performances are mentioned in the written notes to the song.

Notes on the tunes of the songs have been provided in many cases. Although not exhaustive, they attempt to bring together salient comments by others relating to the song and its tune and to highlight particular musical features of the melody and its performance. Resemblances with other tunes have also been noted, but adopting a rather more narrow definition of resemblance than that which characterizes Samuel Bayard's tune family research.

Mode names have been used in describing the tonality of some of the melodies, but only as a shorthand method by which to indicate the occurrence of inflected notes within a tune. We have also tended to distinguish between the major modes (the major scale or Ionian mode and the Mixolydian mode), on the one hand, and the minor modes (the Dorian and Aeolian modes, which, like minor scales, flatten the third degree), on the other.

The Songs

I

'Tis True My Love's Enlisted ...
Soldiers and Sailors

'Tis True My Love's Enlisted ...
Sailors and Soldiers

Britain has prided itself on its military and maritime prowess for centuries, and it is no surprise that these subjects feature widely in traditional song, either by providing the main backdrop to the story or simply by having soldiers and sailors as main characters.

It is interesting to note that whereas the songs on rural life and work are mostly positive and do not dwell on the poverty and the unpleasant realities of everyday life, many songs of the sea take a much more realistic view and do not shrink from the hardships involved. This is not to argue that there were no romanticized portrayals; there were also plenty of those, and writers like Charles Dibdin made a comfortable career out of them. However, one reality of naval life which impinged directly on the general population, from Tudor times to the early nineteenth century, was the system of forcible impressment. The press gang was a very real threat to working people, especially in coastal areas in times of war, and therefore features often in songs, as a means of removing unwanted suitors, for example. The army had no such powers of enforcement, but had to rely on roaming recruiting parties to persuade likely candidates to enlist, often getting them drunk first. The allure of an army life is sometimes treated positively in traditional song, but recruiting parties are usually portrayed as something to be mistrusted and resisted.

The 'female warrior' motif, of young women disguising themselves as soldiers or sailors, is a very common one, and over one hundred different songs with the theme have been identified, the earliest being 'Mary Ambree', from about 1600. Cross-dressing characters also became stock figures in popular culture and appeared regularly in plays and novels as well as songs. From the late seventeenth to the early nineteenth centuries, at least twenty verifiable cases of women joining the Royal Navy or Marines have been identified, and three became famous in their day – Hannah Snell (1723–92), Mary Lacy (b.1740) and Mary Ann Talbot (1778–1808), although the latter is now thought to be fictional. Wishful thinking on the part of servicemen starved of female company is sometimes cited as the basis of these songs, but this is unlikely. Most navy ships carried some women as a matter of course and while in port they were, according to the moralists of the day, quite overrun with them. Similarly most armies were attended by whole troops of wives, cooks, washerwomen and general camp followers.

Many songs which feature soldiers and sailors are not about the armed services at all, but simply use them as characters in daily life. Many songs are about 'Jack on shore', invariably portrayed as carefree, free-spending, drinking, singing and dancing, with a girl in every port, and whose only enemies are landladies who will not serve him when his money is gone, and whores who seek to cheat him at every turn. Jack usually gets the better of them and the songs are usually on his side, the only criticism of his behaviour being the muted one from the girls left holding the babies.

It is not just in song that blue jackets and red coats seemed irresistible to young women. In the mid nineteenth century, so taken were young women of what was termed the 'servant-girl class' with military uniform that the popular press referred to it as the 'scarlet fever', and even ladies of higher social standing were hardly immune.

Not all songs about the sea are about the navy or pirates, and there are many which deal with the fishing industry, of which 'The Greenland Whale Fishery' (No. 11) is probably the widest known example.

The Bold *Princess Royal*

On the fourteenth of February we sailed from the land
In the bold *Princess Royal*, bound for Newfoundland
We had forty brave seamen for the ship's company
And boldly from the eastward to the westward bore we.

We had not been a-sailing scarce days two or three
When a man from our mast-head strange sails did he see
He came bearing down on us for to see what we were
And under his mizzen, black colours he wore.

'O Lord,' cried our captain, 'what shall we do now?
Here comes a bold pirate for to rob us, I know.'
'Oh no,' cried the chief mate, 'that will not be so
We'll shake out our reef, my boys, and away from him we'll go.'

[At last this bold pirate he hove alongside
With a loud-speaking trumpet; 'Whence came you?' he cried
Our captain standing aft, my boys, he answered him so
'We've come from fair London town, we're bound for Cairo.']

['Come lay up your course-sails and heave your ship to
For I have some letters for to send home by you.'
'I will lay up my course-sails and I'll heave my ship to
But that's home in harbour, boys, not alongside of you.']

He chased us to the westward all that livelong day
And he chased us to the eastward but he couldn't get no way
He fir-ed shots after us but none did prevail
And the bold *Princess Royal* soon showed him her tail.

'O Lord,' cried the captain, 'the pirate he is gone
Go down to your grog, my boys, go down everyone
Go down to your grog, my boys, and be of good cheer
For while we have sea-room, brave lads never fear.'

2

Bonny Bunch of Roses O

By— the dan-gers of the o - cean, one mor-ning in the

month of June The— fea - thered war - bling

song - sters their charm-ing notes so sweet did tune

There I es-pied a fe - male, seem-ing - ly in grief and

woe Con - ver-sing with young Bon - a - parte, con -

cern - ing the bon - ny bunch of ro - ses O.

By the dangers of the ocean, one morning in the month of June
The feathered warbling songsters their charming notes so sweet did tune
There I espied a female, seemingly in grief and woe
Conversing with young Bonaparte, concerning the bonny bunch
    of roses O.

When first you saw great Bonaparte, you fell upon your bended knee
And asked your father's life of him, when he granted it most manfully
'Twas then he raised an army and o'er the frozen Alps did go
He said, 'I'll conquer Moscow, then go to the bonny bunch of roses O.'

But when he came near Moscow he was overpowered by driven snow
All Moscow was a-blazing, so he lost the bonny bunch of roses O.

'Then son, don't be so venturesome, for England is the heart of gold
There is England, Ireland and Scotland, their unity shall ne'er be broke
Then son, look at your father, on St Helena his body lies low
[And if] you will go to the war, sir, beware of the bonny bunch
    of roses O.'

It's mother adieu for ever, it's now I'm on my dying bed
But if I'd lived I should have been clever, but now I droop my youthful
    head
For the while our bones do moulder and weeping willows o'er us grow
The deeds of bold Napoleon still sting the bonny bunch of roses O.

3

Captain Ward and the *Rainbow*

Come all you sea-men bold,— with cour-age beat your drum

I'll sing you of— a rov - er who on the sea did roam

Whose name it was bold Cap-tain Ward as you shall quick-ly hear

(a)

O such a rov-er has not been known for ma-ny a long year.

(a)

Come all you seamen bold, with courage beat your drum
I'll sing you of a rover who on the sea did roam
Whose name it was bold Captain Ward as you shall quickly hear
O such a rover has not been known for many a long year.

It was on the first of July we sailed from the west
Loaded with silks and satins, a cargo of the best
Until we met bold saucy Ward all on the watery main
He robbed us of our wealthy stores and sent us back again.

Now he sent a letter to our Queen, he sent it with courage bold
To know if he might come, my lads, old England to behold
[And if your Queen will let me come till he his tale has told]
Now for this parting he would give five hundred tons of gold.

Now our Queen was building a fine ship, a ship of noted fame
She was called the *Rainbow*, you may have heard her name
She was called the *Rainbow* and on the seas went she
With four or five hundred seamen bold to bear her company.

Now she went on till she came where saucy Ward did lie
'Where is the admiral of your ship?' our Captain he did cry
'I'm here, I'm here,' cried saucy Ward, 'my name I'll never deny
If you be one of the Queen's fine ships you're welcome to pass by.'

'Oh no,' cried the Captain, 'that grieves our Queen full sore
To think that our rich merchant ships can't pass as they've done before.'
He says, 'Come on, bold saucy Ward, I value you not one pin
If you've got brass for outward show, I have got steel within.'

So at eight o'clock in the morning, this bloody fight begun
That lasted till eight in the evening, the setting of the sun
'Fight on, fight on,' cried saucy Ward, 'your style so well please me
For I will fight for a month or two and your master I will be.'

Now gallant *Rainbow* he fought but all in vain
Till sixty and five of his men all on his decks lie slain
'Go home, go home,' cried saucy Ward, 'and tell your Queen for me
If she reigns Queen of England, I will reign king at sea.'

4
The *Dolphin*

Our ship she laid in har - bour, in
Liv-er-pool Docks she lay A - wait - ing for fresh
or - ders and her an-chor for to weigh
Bound down to the coast of A - fri - ca, our
or - ders did__ run so We're go-ing to sink and destroy, my boys, no mat - ter where we go.

Our ship she laid in harbour, in Liverpool Docks she lay
Awaiting for fresh orders and her anchor for to weigh
Bound down to the coast of Africa, our orders did run so
We're going to sink and destroy, my boys, no matter where we go.

We had not been sailing scarce fifty leagues or more
For there we espied a lofty ship and down on us he bore
He hailed us in French colours, he asked us where and whence we came
'We just came down from Liverpool town and the *Dolphin* is our name.'

'Are you a man-of-war, sir? Pray tell me what you be.'
'I am no man-of-war, sir, but a pirate ship you see
Come heave up your fore and main yards and let your ship come to
For our tackles are overhauled and our boats are all lowered, or else we
    will sink you.'

Now our captain stood on the quarter deck, he was brave and fearless too
'It's three to one against us,' he cried unto his crew
'If it hadn't have been for my younger brother, this battle would never
    been tried
Let every man stand true to his gun and we'll give to them a broadside.'

Now broadside to broadside, which caused all hands to wonder
To see that lofty tall ship's mast come rattling down like thunder
We shot them from our quarterdeck till they could no longer stay
Our guns being smart and we played a fine part and we showed them
    Liverpool play.

Now this large tall ship was taken and in Liverpool Docks was moored
We fired shots with our sweethearts and with the fancy girls ashore
We lowered down the French colours, we hoisted the red, white and blue
We drink success to the *Dolphin* and all her jovial crew.

5

Faithful Sailor Boy

It was a stormy winter's night, the snow lay on the ground
The sailor boy stood on the quay, his ship was outward bound
His sweetheart standing by his side shed many a silent tear
And as he pressed her to his breast, he whispered in her ear.

Chorus
Farewell, farewell, my own true love, this parting brings me pain
I'll be your own true guiding star when I return again
My thoughts shall be of you, of you, when the storms are raging high
So fare ye well, remember me, your faithful sailor boy.

Without a gale the ship set sail, he kissed his love goodbye
She watched the craft till out of sight and a tear bedimmed her eye
She prayed for him in heaven above to guide him on his way
His last and loving words that night re-echoed o'er the bay.

But sad to say the ship returned without her sailor boy
He died whilst on the voyage back, the flag 'twas half-mast high
And when his comrades came on shore they told her he was dead
A letter he had sent to her, and the last line sadly read.

Last chorus
Farewell, farewell, my own true love, on earth we meet no more
I soon shall be from storm and sea on that eternal shore
I hope to meet you in that land, that land beyond the sky
Where you shall not be parted from your faithful sailor boy.

6

The Female Cabin Boy

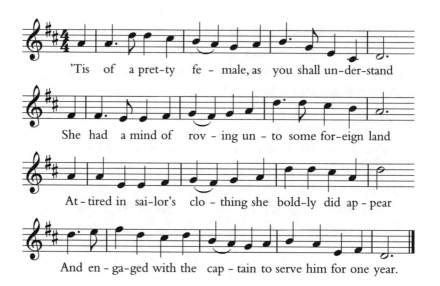

'Tis of a pret-ty fe - male, as you shall un-der-stand

She had a mind of rov - ing un - to some for-eign land

At - tired in sai-lor's clo - thing she bold-ly did ap - pear

And en - ga-ged with the cap - tain to serve him for one year.

'Tis of a pretty female, as you shall understand
She had a mind of roving unto some foreign land
Attired in sailor's clothing she boldly did appear
And engaged with the captain to serve him for one year.

She engaged with the captain as cabin boy to be
The wind it was in favour and so they put to sea
The captain's lady being on board she seemed for to enjoy
And glad the captain had engaged with a female cabin boy.

So nimble was this pretty girl, she did her duty well
Only mark what follows after, the song it soon will tell
By eating the captain's biscuits her colour did destroy
And the waist did swell of pretty Nell, the female cabin boy.

[It was through the Bay of Biscay our gallant ship did plough]
One night among the sailors there was a pretty row
They bundled from their hammocks, which did their rest destroy
They swore about the groaning of the female cabin boy.

'O doctor, O doctor,' the cabin boy did cry
The sailors swore by one and all the cabin boy will die
The doctor ran with all his might a-smiling at the fun
To think a sailor lad should have a daughter or a son.

O when the sailors heard the joke they all began to stare
The child belongs to none of them they solemnly declared
The lady to the captain said, 'My dear I wish you joy
'Twas either you or I betrayed the female cabin boy.'

7

The Female Drummer

When I was a young girl, the age of sixteen
I from my parents ran away and went to serve the queen
I enlisted in the army like another private man
And very soon they learnt me for to beat upon the drum
For to beat upon the drum, for to beat upon the drum
And very soon they learnt me for to beat upon the drum.

They sent me to my quarters, they sent me to my bed
And lying by a soldier's side I did not feel afraid
For in taking off my red coat I oftentimes did smile
To think myself a drummer but a maiden all the while
But a maiden all the while, etc.

They sent me up to London for there to mind the Tower
And there I might have been until this very day and hour
Till a young girl fell in love with me, I told her I was a maid
She went unto my officer, my secret betrayed
My secret she betrayed, etc.

My officer sent for me to see if it was true
I smiled, O I smiled, I told him it was true
He looked upon me kindly and these are the words he said
'It's a pity we should lose you, such a drummer as you made
Such a drummer as you made', etc.

O fare you well, dear officer, you have been kind to me
And fare you well, dear colonel, will you please remember me
If the war it should break out again and you are short of men
I'll put on my hat and feathers and I'll beat the drum again
And I'll beat the drum again, etc.

8

General Wolfe

Bold General Wolfe to his men did say
'Come come my lads, to follow me
See yonder cliffs, oh they look so high
Through smoke and fire, through smoke and fire
There lies the path to victory
All for the honour, all for an honour
All for a king and a country.'

You see brave men on the hill so high
While we poor lads in the valley lie
You see them fall like gnats in the sun
Through smoke and fire, through smoke and fire
They're falling to our frigate guns
All for the honour, all for the honour
All for a king and a country.

Now the first volley that they gave to us
They hit our Wolfe in his left breast
And he lay bleeding no more to stand
Saying, 'Fight on so boldly, fight you on so boldly
For while I live I shall give command.'
All for the honour, all for the honour
All for a king and a country.

'In my left pocket and in my chest
My money and jewels there lie at rest
Divide this money, this jewels and gold
Drink to me boldly, drink to me boldly
It is no good when the blood is cold.'
All for the honour, all for an honour
All for a king and a country.

'Now when to old England you do return
Go to the village where I was born
Say unto my old mother dear
"Weep not for me, weep you not for me
A soldier's death I had wished to share."'
All for the honour, all for the honour
For the second George and the country.

9

The *Golden Vanity*

It's I have got a ship in the north coun-try___
She goes by___ the name of the *Gol-den Va - ni - ty*___
I'm a-fraid she will be ta-ken by the Span-ish gal-leon___
As she sails___ on the Low-lands, Low-lands low
As she sails___ on the Low - lands___ low.___

It's I have got a ship in the north country
She goes by the name of the *Golden Vanity*
I'm afraid she will be taken by the Spanish galleon
As she sails on the Lowlands, Lowlands low
As she sails on the Lowlands low.

Then up stepped a little cabin boy
Saying, 'Master what will you give me if I will them destroy?'
'I'll give you gold and silver and you shall have my daughter
If you'll sink her in the Lowlands, Lowlands low
If you'll sink her in the Lowlands low.'

This boy he undaunted and soon jump-ed in
He leant upon his breast and so gallantly did swim
He swam till he came to the Spanish galleon
As she lies in the Lowlands, Lowlands low
As she lies in the Lowlands low.

This boy had an auger that bored two holes at once
While some was playing cards and the others playing dice
He let the water in and it dazzled in their eyes
And he sank her in the Lowlands, Lowlands low
And he sank her in the Lowlands low.

He leant upon his breast and he swam back again
'O master take me up, for I'm sure I will be slain
For I have offended the total of the crew
And I've sunk her in Lowlands, Lowlands low
And I've sunk her in Lowlands low.'

'I will not take you up,' the master he cried
'I will not take you up,' the captain replied
'I will shoot you, I will kill you, I will send you with the tide
And I'll sink you in the Lowlands, Lowlands low
And I'll sink you in the Lowlands low.'

He leant on his breast and swum round the larboard side
His strength began to fail him, most bitterly he cried
'O messes take me up, for I'm sure I shall be slain
For I've sunk her in the Lowlands, Lowlands low
For I've sunk her in the Lowlands low.'

His messes took him up and on the deck he died
And then they wrapped him up in an old cow's hide
They threw him overboard to go with the wind and tide
And they sank him in the Lowlands, Lowlands low
And they sank him in the Lowlands low.

10

The Green Bed

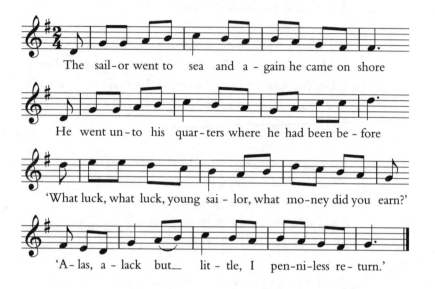

The sail-or went to sea and a-gain he came on shore

He went un-to his quar-ters where he had been be-fore

'What luck, what luck, young sai-lor, what mo-ney did you earn?'

'A-las, a-lack but— lit-tle, I pen-ni-less re-turn.'

The sailor went to sea and again he came on shore
He went unto his quarters where he had been before
'What luck, what luck, young sailor, what money did you earn?'
'Alas, alack but little, I penniless return.'

'Where is your daughter Molly? Come fetch her down to me
Her own true love she'll welcome, returning from the sea.'
'My daughter is too busy and cannot come to you
I cannot think to trust you above a pot or two.'

The sailor he was drowsy, and weary hung his head
He called for a candle to light him to his bed
'My beds are all engaged, they have been full a week
So if you need a lodging, some other tavern seek.'

'Come, for the ale I'll pay you, I'm making here too bold.'
He drew from out his pocket three handfuls all of gold
Upstairs the mother hasted, 'Come come my Molly dear
The sailor rolls in riches, make him the best of cheer.'

Downstairs came Molly quickly, and pleasantly she smiled
She patted Jack upon the back and called him her dear child
She pulled his hair, she plucked his cheek, and said, 'My duck, my dear
The green best bed is empty and you shall lie in there.'

'Nay rather than I'd lie in there, I'd lie out in the street
I'd rather eat a crust of bread than touch of your best meat
So fare thee well, false Molly, and fare thee well, old mother
My golden store and wealth galore I'll spend upon another.'

11

The Greenland Whale Fishery

We may no longer stay on shore
Since deep we are in debt
So off to Greenland let us steer
Some money, boys, to get, brave boys
So to Greenland we'll bear away.

In eighteen hundred and twenty-four
On March the twenty-third
We hoist our colours to th' mast-head

And for Greenland bore away, brave boys
And for Greenland we bore away.

John Paigent was our captain's name
Our ship the *Lion* bold
We weigh-ed anchor at the bow
To face the storm and cold, brave boys
And to Greenland we bore away.

We were twelve gallant men on board
And to the north did steer
Old England left we in our wake
We sailors knew not fear, brave boys
And to Greenland we bore away.

Our boatswain to the mast-head went
With a spyglass in his hand
He cries, 'A whale! A whalefish blow
She blows at every span', brave boys
And to Greenland we bore away.

Our captain on the quarterdeck
A violent man was he
He swore the Devil would take us all
If that fish were lost to we, brave boys
And to Greenland we bore away.

Our captain on the quarterdeck
A violent man was he
'Overhaul, overhaul,' he loudly cried
'And launch our boat to sea', brave boys
And to Greenland we bore away.

Our boat being launched, and all hands in
The whale was full in view
Resolved was every seaman bold

To steer where the whalefish blew, brave boys
And to Greenland we bore away.

The whale was struck, the line paid out
She gave a flash with her tail
The boat capsized, we lost five men
And never caught the whale, brave boys
And for Greenland we bore away.

Bad news we to the captain brought
We'd lost five 'prentice boys
Then down his colours he did haul
At hearing the sad news, brave boys
And from Greenland we bore away.

'The losing of the whale,' said he
'Doth grieve my heart full sore
But the losing of my five brave men
Doth grieve me ten times more,' brave boys
And from Greenland we bore away.

The winter star doth now appear
So boys the anchor weigh
'Tis time we leave this cold country
And for England bear away, brave boys
And for England bear away.

For Greenland is a barren place
A land where grows no green
But ice and snow where the whalefish blow
And daylight's seldom seen, brave boys
And for England bear away.

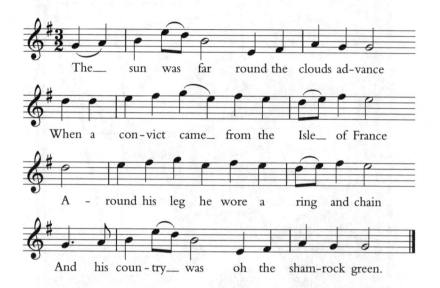

12

The Isle of France

The sun was far round the clouds advance
When a convict came from the Isle of France
Around his leg he wore a ring and chain
And his country was oh the shamrock green.

Then the coastguards waited all on the beach
Till the convict's boat was all in reach
The convict's chains did so shine and spark
Which opened the veins of the coastguard's heart.

Then the coastguard launched his little boat
And on the ocean he went afloat
The birds at night took their silent rest
But the convict here had a wounded breast.

Then the coastguard came to the Isle of France
Toward him the convict did advance
While tears from his eyes did fall like rain
'Young man I hear you are of the *Shamrock Green*.'

'I am a Shamrock,' the convict cried
'That has been tossed on the ocean wide
For being unruly I do declare
I was doomed to transport for seven years.'

'When six of them were past and gone
We were coming home for to make up [for] one
When the stormy winds did so blow and roar
Which cast me here on this foreign shore.'

Then the coastguard played a noble part
And with some brandy cheered the convict's heart
'Although the night be so far advanced
You shall find a friend in the Isle of France.'

Then a speedy letter went to the Queen
Of the dreadful shipwreck of the *Shamrock Green*
And his freedom came by a speedy post
To the absent convict they thought was lost.

'God bless the coastguard,' the convict cried
'He saved my life from the ocean wide
I'll drink his health in a flowing glass
So here's success to the Isle of France.'

13

The Mermaid

On Fri-day mor-ning as we set sail It was not far from land O— there we es-pied a— fair pret-ty maid With the comb and a glass in— hand, her hand, her hand With the comb and— glass— in— hand.

Chorus

O the storm-y winds they did blow And the ra-ging seas did roar While we— poor sai-lor boys go— up a-loft And the land-lub-bers lie—down be-low, be-low, be-low— And the land-lub-bers lie—down be-low.

On Friday morning as we set sail
It was not far from land
O there we espied a fair pretty maid
With the comb and a glass in hand, her hand, her hand
With the comb and glass in hand.

Chorus
O the stormy winds they did blow
And the raging seas they did roar
While we poor sailor boys go up aloft
And the landlubbers lie down below, below, below
And the landlubbers lie down below.

Then up spake a boy of our gallant ship
And a well-spoken boy was he
'I've a father and mother in fair Portsmouth town
This night they will weep for me.'

Then up spake a man of our gallant ship
And a well-spoken man was he
'I have married a wife in fair London town
This night she a widow will be.'

Then up spake the captain of our gallant ship
And a valiant man was he
'For want of a longboat we all shall be drowned
And sink to the bottom of the sea.'

The moon shone bright and the stars gave light
And my mother is looking for me
She may look, she may weep, O with watery eyes
That I lie at the bottom of the sea.

14

Nancy of Yarmouth

Come my pretty Nan-cy,— my love and de-light

Here is this kind let-ter to you I in-dite

It— is to— in-form you, wher-ev-er we go

On the salt stor-my o-cean, I'm faith-ful to you.

Come my pretty Nancy, my love and delight
Here is this kind letter to you I indite
It is to inform you, wherever we go
On the salt stormy ocean, I'm faithful to you.

When the seas they are roaring and tossing about
Five hundred bright sailors both valiant and stout
Stand shiv'ring and shaking 'twixt hope and despair
One moment they're in the deep, the next in the air.

It was early one morning before it broke day
Our hon'rable captain unto us did say
'Be all of good heart, boys, be all of good cheer
For whilst there is sea-room, brave boys we don't fear.'

It was early one evening, before it grew dark
Our hon'rable captain kind showed us a mark
It was something that threatened he knew by the sky
And this was the meaning, a tempest drew nigh.

O a ship that's distressed is the dismalest sight
Like an army of soldiers just routed in flight
But a soldier can fly, love, from beat of the drum
But a sailor must lie, love, in a watery tomb.

Soon as the storm was over, if God spares our lives
We'll return to our sweethearts, likewise to our wives
Here's a health to sweet Nancy as we sail on the main
And I hope to old England we shall come again.

15

The *Rainbow*

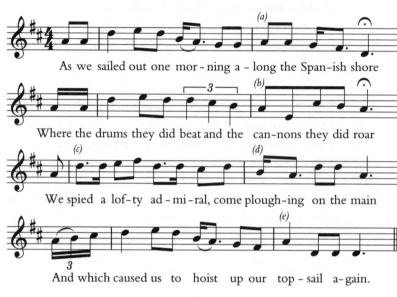

As we sailed out one mor-ning a-long the Span-ish shore

Where the drums they did beat and the can-nons they did roar

We spied a lof-ty ad-mi-ral, come plough-ing on the main

And which caused us to hoist up our top-sail a-gain.

As we sailed out one morning along the Spanish shore
Where the drums they did beat and the cannons they did roar
We spied a lofty admiral, come ploughing on the main
And which caused us to hoist up our topsail again.

Come come my lads get ready, come come my lads be true
To face this French admiral, that's all that we can do
If he should overtake us all on the ocean wide
We will nearly draw up to him and give him a broadside.

Now a broadside, a broadside, and at it we went
For killing one another that was their full intent
The very second broadside our admiral he got slain
And a young damsel stepp-ed up in his place to remain.

'For quarters, for quarters,' this damsel replied
'We'll give you the best of quarters that ever we can afford
And we'll offer you the finest quarters that ever we can afford
You must fight, sink or swim, my boys, or else jump overboard.'

Now we fought there four hours, four hours severe
We fought till there was not a man he could stand on board
We fought till not a man on board could fire off a gun
And the blood from our quarterdecks like water did run.

And now we are gained a victory we'll take a glass of wine
You drink luck to your true love and I'll drink luck to mine
But there's good luck to the damsel who's fought with us on the main
To our good ship the *Royal*, called *Rainbow* by name.

16

Rambling Sailor

I've sailed the seas, fought battles too
Long time I've ploughed the ocean
I've fought for my Queen and my country too
Won medals and promotion
But now I've bid shipmates adieu
I've left behind both ship and crew
To travel the country through and through
And be a rambling sailor.

And if you want to know my name
My name it is young Johnson
I have a mission from the Queen
To court all girls that are handsome
With my false heart and flattering tongue
I'll court them all but I'll marry, marry, none
I'll court them all both old and young
And still be a rambling sailor.

And when I came to Greenwich town
There I saw lasses in plenty
I boldly stepp-ed up to them
To court them for their money
With my false heart and flattering tongue
I'll court them all but I'll marry, marry, none
I'll court them all both old and young
And still be a rambling sailor.

17

The Saucy Sailor Boy

'Come my own love, come my true love
Come my darling unto me
Will you wed with a poor sailor that's
Just returned from sea?'

'But you are dirty, love, you are ragged, love
And you smell so strong of tar
So begone, you saucy sailor lad
So begone, you Jack Tar.'

'If I'm dirty, love, if I'm ragged, love
If I smell so strong of tar
I have silver in every pocket, love
And gold in great store.'

As soon as she had heard these words
On her bended knees she fell
Crying, 'I will wed with Henery
For I love the jolly sailor well.'

'If I'm dirty, love, if I'm ragged, love
If I smell so strong of tar
I have silver in every pocket, love
And gold in great store.'

'Far across the briny ocean
Where the meadows are so green
Since you've refused to be my bride
Some other girl shall wear the ring.'

'If I'm dirty, love, if I'm ragged, love
If I smell so strong of tar
I have silver in every pocket, love
And gold in great store.'

'But I am frolicsome, I am easy
Good-tempered and free
And I don't care a single pin, my boys
What the world says about me.'

'If I'm dirty, love, if I'm ragged, love
If I smell so strong of tar'
'So begone, you saucy sailor lad
So begone, you Jack Tar.'

18

The Silk Merchant's Daughter

As I was a-walking all up New York street

O I made it a matter my true love to meet

What ship-wreck-ed sai-lor can tell un-to me

Be-longs to the *Nan-cy*, for old Eng-land I be

What ship-wreck-ed sai-lor can tell un-to me

Be-longs to the *Nan-cy*, for old Eng-land I be.

As I was a-walking all up New York street
O I made it a matter my true love to meet
What shipwreck-ed sailor can tell unto me
Belongs to the *Nancy*, for old England I be.
What shipwreck-ed sailor can tell unto me
Belongs to the *Nancy*, for old England I be.

O we want a sailor, for we've lost a man
O we want a sailor to do what he can
Although I'm no sailor, if you want a man

For my passage over I'll do what I can.
Although I'm no sailor, if you want a man
For my passage over I'll do what I can.

All things were got ready for setting the sail
The wind it blew west and a sweet pleasant gale
As we were a-sailing to our heart's content
Our ship sprang a leak, to the bottom she went, etc.

Then twenty-four of us got into a boat
And on the wide ocean we went for to float
Provisions grew short and starvation drew nigh
Then we all did cast lots which of us should die, etc.

The lots were surely ready, all in a bag shift
And every man took in hand his own life
This poor innocent virgin the short lot she drew
And was doomed to be killed to feed the ship's crew, etc.

'You inhuman butchers,' the damsel she said
''Tis true that I am a poor innocent maid
A rich merchant's daughter of London I be
You may see what I've come to for loving of thee', etc.

O then the red colour flew into his face
With his eyes full of tears and his heart full of grace
With his eyes full of tears and his heart nigh to burst
'To save your sweet life, I'll surely die first', etc.

O the lots they were thrown in the shift for to see
Who then of this young man the butcher should be
'O pray and be quick, let the business be done.'
But before the blow fell, we heard sound of a gun, etc.

'O hold now your hand,' the captain did cry
'Some ship or some harbour I know we are nigh.'

As we were a-sailing in the sweet flowing tide
We came to a city the salt sea beside, etc.

When this couple got married then I have heard say
The bells they rang out and sweet music did play
The birds in the valleys did echoing ring
Where the old women dance and the young women sing, etc.

19

Spanish Ladies

Fare - well and a - dieu   to you fair Span-ish   la - dies

Fare - well and a - dieu   to you la - dies of   Spain

For we've re-ceived or - ders for to sail for old   Eng-land

But we hope in   a   short while to   see you a - gain.

Chorus

We'll rant and we'll roar   like   true Brit-ish   sai - lors

We'll rant and we'll roar   a - cross the wide   sea

Un - til we strike sound-ings in the chan-nel of old   Eng-land

From the Ush-ant   to the Scil-lies   is   thir - ty - five leagues.

Farewell and adieu to you fair Spanish ladies
Farewell and adieu to you ladies of Spain
For we've received orders for to sail for old England
But we hope in a short while to see you again.

Chorus
We'll rant and we'll roar like true British sailors
We'll rant and we'll roar across the wide sea
Until we strike soundings in the channel of old England
From the Ushant to the Scillies is thirty-five leagues.

Now we hove our ship to with the wind at sou'west, boys
We hove our ship to for to make soundings clear
We had forty-five fathom and a fine sandy bottom
So we filled the main topsail and up channel steered.

Now the first land we met it is known as the Dead Man
Next Ramhead off Plymouth, Start, Portland and Wight
For we sailed past Beachy passed Fairlee to Dungeness
Then we bore her away for the South Foreland light.

Now the signal was made for the grand fleet to anchor
All day in the Downs that night for to moor
Stand by your shank painter, let fly your cat stopper
Haul up your clew garnets, stick out tacks and sheets.

Now let every man swig off a full bumper
Now let every man swig off a full bowl
So drink and be merry, drive away melancholy
For we'll drink to each jovial good-hearted soul.

20

The White Cockade

As I one sum-mer's mor-ning, as I crossed o'er yon moss

I had no thoughts of 'list-ing till a sol-dier did me cross

He kind-ly in-vi-ted me to drink a flow-ing glass

He ad-van-ced, He ad-van-ced,

he ad-van-ced he ad-van-ced

Me my mon-ey, ten guin-eas and a crown.

As I one summer's morning, as I crossed o'er yon moss
I had no thoughts of 'listing till a soldier did me cross
He kindly invited me to drink a flowing glass
He advanc-ed, he advanc-ed
He advanc-ed, he advanc-ed
Me my money, ten guineas and a crown.

'Tis true my love's got 'listed and he wears a white cockade
He is a handsome young man, likewise a roving blade
He is a handsome young man, just right to serve the King
Oh my very, oh my very

Oh my very, oh my very
Heart is breaking all for the loss of him.

Oh may he never prosper, oh may he never thrive
Or anything he takes in hand so long as he's alive
The very ground he treads upon may the grass refuse to grow
Since he has been my, since he has been my
Since he has been my, since he has been my
Only cause of my sorrow, grief and woe.

She then pulled out her handkerchief to wipe those flowing eyes
Dry up, dry up those mournful tears, likewise those mournful sighs
And be thou of good courage till I return again
You and I, love, you and I, love
You and I, love, you and I, love
Will be married when I return again.

II

Down in Cupid's Garden ...
Happy Relationships

Down in Cupid's Garden ...
Happy Relationships

It is impossible to be numerically accurate, but it would not be far wrong to say that at least half of all traditional songs are concerned with love and relationships. As Frank Kidson and Mary Neal write in *English Folk-Song and Dance* (1915), p. 57:

> Love holds first place in all lyrics, and there is no exception to this rule in the folk-song. There is, however, this difference – whilst the art song is frequently couched in language abstract and sentimental, and enriched with metaphor and simile, the folk-song is almost always direct, and from its baldness of diction possessed of great force. The declaration of love in a folk-song is simple, and there is no mincing of words. It is unmistakably fervent and in earnest. The tragedy of a girl's forsakenness is biblical in its plainness.

The pleasure gardens, from which many of our love songs originate, specialized in pastoral idylls in which shepherds and shepherdesses (or milkmaids) met and fell in love among the groves and meadows of an idealized rural setting, in a perpetual spring or summer. A number of these songs survived in the tradition, and the genre is typified by 'Searching for Lambs' (No. 36) and 'The Spotted Cow' (No. 38), in both of which the lovers meet while the girl is searching for animals under her care. This may be seen as romanticism, pure and simple, but in the real world of long working hours, cramped living conditions and strict moral supervision of female staff, it was a fact that often the only place young people could meet relatively freely was out in the open.

Others make more of a story about the path of true love. 'Golden Glove' (No. 26), for example, is typical of the kind of love story popular with broadside printers, although it too emanated from the pleasure gardens. Among the Child ballads, not generally known for their happy endings, stories such as 'Lord Bateman' (No. 33) can be found, where the lovers survive and prosper.

Although it is usually a case of boy pursuing girl, a number of active females take the initiative too, as in 'Little Gipsy Girl' (No, 32) and 'The Knight and the Shepherd's Daughter' (No. 31), while in songs such as 'Madam, Will you Walk?' (No. 34) and even 'Dabbling in the Dew' (Part IV, No. 67), it is the girl's sassy answers that provide the main interest.

21

Bold Fisherman

As I walked out one__ May mor-ning

Down by the ri — ver - side

(a)
And__ there I saw a young fish - er - man__

Come a - row - ing down__ the tide

Come a - row - ing down__ the tide

And__ there I saw a young fish - er - man__

Come a - row - ing down__ the tide.

(a)

As I walked out one May morning
Down by the riverside
And there I saw a young fisherman
Come a-rowing down the tide
Come a-rowing down the tide
And there I saw a young fisherman
Come a-rowing down the tide.

'Good morning to you, young fisherman
How come you fishing here?'
'I'm fishing for some pretty fair maid
All on this river clear', etc.

He pulled his boat up to the side
And tied it to a stake
And he got out all on the shore
All for her hand to take, etc.

He pulled off his morning gown
And softly laid it down
And there she saw three chains of gold
All round his neck hung down, etc.

Down on her bended knees she fell
'O pardon, pardon me
For calling you young fisherman
Come a-rowing down the sea', etc.

['Arise, arise, my sweet pretty maid
Arise, arise,' said he
'For there is not one word that you have spoke
The least offended me', etc.]

'Rise up, rise up, my fair lady
And come along with me
And you shall have a fisherman
To row you down the sea', etc.

He took her to his father's house
And now both married be
And now she's got a captain
To row her down the sea, etc.

22

Cupid the Pretty Ploughboy

As I walked out one May mor-ning when may was all in bloom I went in-to the mead-ows to taste the sweet per-fume___ I went in-to the flower-y fields to turn my head a while___ Where I saw Kil - pit the pret-ty plough-ing boy, who did my heart be - guile.___

As I walked out one May morning when may was all in bloom
I went into the meadows to taste the sweet perfume
I went into the flowery fields to turn my head a while
Where I saw Kilpit the pretty ploughing boy, who did my heart beguile.

As this young man was ploughing his furrows deep and low
Breaking the clods to pieces, some barley for to sow
I wish that pretty ploughing boy my eyes had never seen
Was Kilpit the ploughing boy with his harrows sharp and keen.

A worthy rich gentleman a-courting to me came
Because I would not marry him my parents did me blame
Adieu young men for ever, farewell for ever adieu
It's Kilpit the pretty ploughing boy that have caused my heart to rue.

The ploughboy hearing the lady most sadly to complain
Crying, 'Oh my dearest jewel I will ease you of your pain
If you will wed a ploughing boy for ever I'll prove true
It's you my heart have wondered and I love no one but you.'

The lady then consented to be his lawful bride
And there they went up to the church and there the knot was tied
And now they live in pleasure for they have gold in store
The lady and the ploughing boy each other do adore.

Cupid's Garden

It was down in Cu-pid's gar - den for plea-sure I did go___ To view the fair-est flow - ers that in that gar-den grow The_ first it was a jess-a-mine, oh the li_ ly, pink and rose_____ These are the fair - est flow - ers that_ in__ this gar - den grow That in this gar - den grow.

It was down in Cupid's garden for pleasure I did go
To view the fairest flowers that in that garden grow
The first it was a jessamine, oh the lily, pink and rose
These are the fairest flowers that in this garden grow
That in this garden grow.

I had not walked the garden the space of half an hour
Before I saw two very pretty girls sitting under a shady bower
The one was lovely Nancy, most delicate and fair
The other she was a virgin, and she the laurels wear
And she the laurels wear.

I boldly stepp-ed up to them and this to them did say
'Are you engaged with any young man? Come tell to me, I pray.'
'I am not engaged with any young man I solemn will declare
For I mean to live a virgin and still the laurel wear
And still the laurel wear.'

Then hand in hand together this loving couple went
Resolv-ed was the sailor to know her true intent
For to know if she would slight him while he to the sea must go
'Oh no, my love, my own true love, for I like a sailor well
I like a sailor well.'

'Then farewell, lovely Nancy, since I to the sea must go
Through many a dark and dismal night while the stormy winds do blow
But if ever I do return again how happy we shall be
With you, my love, my own true love, sat smiling on my knee
Sat smiling on my knee.'

'So now my ship's returned again, I'm landed safe on shore
God bless me now and for ever if I go to the sea any more
So come, my lovely Nancy, how happy I can be
With you, my love, my own true love, sat smiling on my knee
Sat smiling on my knee.'

24

The Game of Cards

As I walked out on a midsummer's morning
To view the fields and the meadows so gay
There I saw a sweet pretty damsel
As I was walking on the highway.

Chorus
Right fol the diddle doe
Right fol the diddle doe
Right fol the diddle doe
Right fol the day.

And he said, 'My dear, how far are you going
How far are you going so early in the morn?'
'I'm going down to my next-door neighbour
Down in Crompton where I was born.'

Then he said, 'My dear, are you fond of gaming?
One game of yours I should like for to learn
That would be a game of All Fours
I will bet you three to your one.'

Then they picked the pack for each turn to deal O
He dealt no trump tricks off but a Jack
She had the Ace and very shortly beat him
To the best cards in the pack.

Then she played off her Ace and she stole Jack from me
 Made she high-low-Jack and the game
She said, 'Young man, as I fairly have beat you
We'll play that same game over again.'

Then he took up his hat and he bid her good morning
So she said she was high-low-Jack and the game
She said, 'Young man if you'll call again tomorrow
Play that same game over again.'

25

The Garden Gate

The day was gone, the moon shone bright
The village clock struck eight
Young Mary hastened with delight
Unto the garden gate
But what was there to make her sad?
The gate was there but not the lad
Which made poor Mary say and sigh
'Was ever poor girl so used as I?'

She waited here, she waited there
The village clock struck nine
Which made poor Mary to sigh and to swear
'You shan't, you shan't be mine
You promised to meet me here at eight
You have deceived me and made me wait
But I'll let all such sweethearts see
They never shall make a fool of me.'

She traced the garden here and there
The village clock struck ten
When William caught her in his arms
Oh ne'er to part again
For he had been for the ring that day
Which took him from home such a long, long way
Then how could Mary cruel prove
To banish the lad she dearly did love?

Up with the morning sun they rose
To church they went away
And all the village joyful were
Upon their wedding day
Now in a cot by a riverside
William and Mary both reside
And she blesses the night that she did wait
For her absent swain at the garden gate.

26

Golden Glove

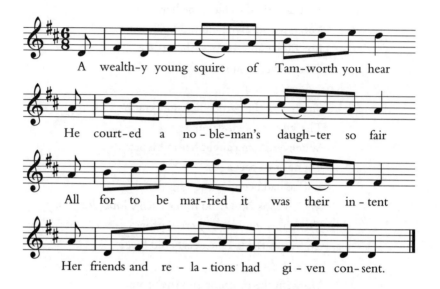

A wealth-y young squire of Tam-worth you hear

He court-ed a no-ble-man's daugh-ter so fair

All for to be mar-ried it was their in-tent

Her friends and re-la-tions had gi-ven con-sent.

A wealthy young squire of Tamworth you hear
He courted a nobleman's daughter so fair
All for to be married it was their intent
Her friends and relations had given consent.

The time was appointed for the wedding day
A farmer was chosen to give her away
As soon as this lady the farmer did spy
Love inflamed her heart, 'O my heart!' she did cry.

She turned from the squire, but nothing she said
Instead of being married she went to her bed
The thoughts of the farmer still run in her mind
A way for to gain him she soon then did find.

Coat, waistcoat and breeches this lady put on
And a-hunting she went with her dog and her gun
She hunted all round where the farmer did dwell
Because in her heart she lov-ed him so well.

She oftentimes fired, but nothing she killed
At length the young farmer came into the field
[And to discourse with him it was her intent
With her dog and her gun to meet him she went.]

'I thought you had been at the wedding,' she cried
'To wait on the squire and give him his bride.'
'Oh no,' said the farmer, 'if the truth I must tell
I'll not give her away, for I love her too well.'

The lady was pleased for to hear him so bold
She gave him a glove that was flowered with gold
And told him she'd found it as she came along
As she was a-hunting with her dog and her gun.

The lady went home with her heart full of love
And gave out a speech that she had lost her glove
The man that will find it and bring it to me
The man that will find it, his bride I will be.

The farmer was pleased for to hear of such news
With his heart full of love to the lady he goes
Saying, 'Dear honoured lady, I've picked up a glove
If you will be pleased for to grant me your love.'

'It's already granted,' the lady replied
'I love the sweet breath of a farmer,' she cried
'I'll be mistress of his dairy and the milking of his cow
While my jovial brisk young farmer goes a-whistling to plough.'

27

Green Mossy Banks of the Lea

When first in this coun-try__ a stran-ger Cur-i - os - i - ty
caused me__ to roam   O-ver Eur-ope re - solved for__ to
ram-ble When I   left Phil - a - del-phi-a my home   Un -
til   I____   came to old   Eng-land Where forms of great
(a)
beau - ty   do   shine   There I   be - held   a____   fair
dam - sel   And I wished in   my   heart she__ was   mine.

When first in this country a stranger
Curiosity caused me to roam
Over Europe resolved for to ramble
When I left Philadelphia my home
Until I came to old England
Where forms of great beauty do shine
There I beheld a fair damsel
And I wished in my heart she was mine.

One morning I careless did ramble
Where the pure wind soft breezes did blow
It was down by a clear crystal river
Where the sweet pearly waters did flow
It was there I espied this fair creature
Some goddess appearing to be
As she rose from the reeds by the water
On the green mossy banks of the Lea.

I stepped up to this fair creature
Her fair cheeks did blush like a rose
Says I, 'The green meadows are charming
Your guardian I'll be if you choose.'
She said, 'Sir, I do not want no guardian
Young man, you're a stranger to me
And yonder my father is coming
On the green mossy banks of the Lea.'

I waited till up came her father
I plucked up my spirits once more
Saying, 'Kind sir, if this be your daughter
She's the beautiful girl I adore
Five thousand a year is my portion
And your daughter a lady shall be
She shall ride in her chariot and horses
On the green mossy banks of the Lea.'

Then they welcomed me home to their cottage
Soon after in wedlock we joined
And there I erected a castle
With grandeur and splendour did shine
So now the American stranger
All pleasure and pastime doth see
With adorable gentle Matilda
On the green mossy banks of the Lea.

28

Hares on the Mountains

If maidens could sing like blackbirds and thrushes
If maidens could sing like blackbirds and thrushes
How many young men would hide in the bushes?
Sing fal-de-ral, tal-de-ral, fal-ral-lal-day.

If maidens could run like hares on the commons
If maidens could run like hares on the commons
How many young men would take horse and ride hunting?
Sing fal-de-ral, tal-de-ral, fal-de-ral-day.

If maidens could swim like fish in the water
If maidens could swim like fish in the water
How many young men would undress and dive after?
Sing fal-de-ral, tal-de-ral, fal-de-ral-day.

If maidens could dance like rushes a-growing
If maidens could dance like rushes a-growing
How many young men would get scythes and go mowing?
Sing fal-de-ral, tal-de-ral, fal-de-ral-day.

If maidens could sleep like sheep on the mountains
If maidens could sleep like sheep on the mountains
How many young men would lie down beside them?
Sing fal-de-ral, tal-de-ral, fal-de-ral-day.

29

The Indian Lass

Now as I was a-walk-ing down a far—dis-tant shore

I walked in-to an ale-house to spend half an hour

And whilst I sat a-smo-king and a-tak-ing my glass

By chance there step-ped in— a young In-di-an lass.

(c) Stanza 3

(d) Stanza 6

Now as I was a-walking down a far distant shore
I walked into an alehouse to spend half an hour
And whilst I sat a-smoking and a-taking my glass
By chance there step-ped in a young Indian lass.

She sat down by the side of me and she squeez-ed my hand
'You are a young sailor, not one of this land
I have got good lodgings if along with me you'll stay
While my fortune I will share it without no delay.'

So with a drop of good liquor, boys, she welcomed me in
And all that night long this was her tune
And all that night long, my boys, why this was her tune
'You are a young sailor so far from your home.'

Now we tossed and we tumbled into each other's arms
I embraced this charming damsel, I embraced her sweet charms
A night of enjoyment, till the time passed away
I did not go and leave her until nine that next day.

Now the day being appointed for our ship to set sail
This loving young Indian on the beach did revail [= bewail]
When I took my handkerchief and all wiped her eyes
'Oh do not go and leave me, young sailor,' she cried.

Now we whipped up our anchor, straight away we did steer
We'd a fair and a pleasant breeze which soon parted our view
And if ever I get over and sat taking my glass
I will drink a success to this young Indian lass.

30

Just as the Tide was a-Flowing

One— mor - ning in— the month of June down
by— a rol - ling ri - ver There a jol - ly sai - lor
chanced to stray where he— be - held some lov - er
Her cheeks were red, her eyes were brown, her hair in wrin-kles a-
hang - ing— down And her love - ly brow— with -
out a frown, just as— the tide was a - flow - ing.

One morning in the month of June down by a rolling river
There a jolly sailor chanced to stray where he beheld some lover
Her cheeks were red, her eyes were brown, her hair in wrinkles a-hanging
   down
And her lovely brow without a frown, just as the tide was a-flowing.

'My pretty maid,' to her he said, 'How come you here so early?
My heart by you it is betrayed and I might love you dearly
For I am a sailor come from sea, if you will accept of my company
For to walk and view the fishes play, just as the tide was a-flowing.'

No more did say but on her way they both did gang together
The small birds sang and the lambs did play, how pleasant was the weather
And they being weary both sat down beneath a tree with the branches
   around
And what was said shall never be known, just as the tide was a-flowing.

And upon the grass she then did roll and her colour it kept changing
And the pretty maid called out, 'Alas, don't let your mind be ranging.'
And she gave him twenty pound in store, saying, 'Meet me when you
   will, there's more
For a jolly sailor I adore', just as the tide was a-flowing.

So they kissed, shook hands and then did part, Jackie Tar drank rum and
   brandy
And to keep my shipmates in good cheer the lady's gold came handy
And with some other young girl you'll go to the public bar where the
   brandy flow
Give me the lad that will do so, just as the tide was a-flowing.

31

The Knight and the Shepherd's Daughter

It's of a shepherd's daughter keeping sheep on yonder hill
A roving blade came riding by and vowed he'd have his will
'Then if you have your will of me pray tell to me your name
That when my baby it is born I may put it the same.'

'Oh some do call me Jack, fair maid, and some do call me John
But when I'm in the King's fair court they call me sweet William.'
Then he mounted on his milk-white steed and away from her did ride
She picked her petticoats under her arm and she ran close by his side.

She ran till she came to the riverside and she fell on her breast and swam
She swam till she came to the other side and she picked up her clothes and ran
She ran till she came to the King's fair court and she loudly rang the ring
There was no one so ready as the King himself to loose this fair maid in.

'What do you want of me, fair maid, what do you want of me?'
'There is a man in your fair court and he has robb-ed me.'
'What has he robbed you of, fair maid, of your gold or of your fee?'
'He's robbed me of my maidenhead, the chief of my body.'

'Then if he be a married man, oh hang-ed he shall be
And if he be a single man, his body I'll give to thee.'
So the King he called his merry, merry men by one by two by three
Young William he came last of all when first he used to be.

He pull-ed out a handful of gold and wrapped it in a [glove]
'Take this, take this, my pretty fair maid and seek for another to love.'
'I neither want any of your gold or any of your fee
But I will have your body as the King has granted me.'

Then he mounted on his milk-white steed and she upon another
They rode along the King's highway like a sister and a brother
They rode till they came to the first fair town and he bought her a gay gold
   ring
They rode till they came to the next fair town and he gave her a gay wedding.

'Oh I wish I'd been drinking of [barrel] water while I've been drinking wine
That ever a shepherd's daughter should have been a bride of mine
I wish I'd been drinking of white wine, while I've been drinking red
That ever a shepherd's daughter should have brought me to my wedding bed.'

32

Little Gipsy Girl

My father is the King of the Gipsies, that is true
My mother she learn-ed me some camping for to do
They put the pack upon my back, they all did wish me well
So I set out for London town some fortunes for to tell.

As I was a-walking up fair London street
A handsome young squire I chanc-ed for to meet
He view-ed my brown cheeks and he lik-ed them so well
He said, 'My little Gipsy girl, can you my fortune tell?'

'Why yes, kind sir, give me hold of your hand
Why you have got houses, you've riches and you've lands
But all those pretty ladies you must put them to one side
For I'm the little Gipsy girl that is to be your bride.'

Now once I was a Gipsy girl but now a squire's bride
I've got servants for to wait on me and in my carriage ride
The bells they rung so merrily and the sweet music did play
And a jolly time we had upon the Gipsy's wedding day.

33

Lord Bateman

Lord Bate-man was a no-ble lord__ A no-ble
lord of high de-gree He shipped him-self a-board a
ves-sel__ And said some coun - tries he would see.

Lord Bateman was a noble lord
A noble lord of high degree
He shipped himself aboard a vessel
And said some countries he would see.

He sail-ed east, he sail-ed west
Until he came to proud Turkey
Where he was taken and put in prison
Until his sweet life was quite weary.

The Turk he had an only daughter
The fairest creature you e'er did see
She stole the keys of her father's prison
And said Lord Bateman she would see.

'Oh are you, are you Lord Bateman
And does Northumberland belong to thee
And what would you give to the fair young lady
Who out of prison would set you free?'

'Oh yes, oh yes, I am Lord Bateman
And half Northumberland belongs to me
And I'd give it all to the fair young lady
If out of prison would set me free.'

When seven long years were gone and past
And fourteen days well known to me
She packed up her gay gold and clothing
And said Lord Bateman she would see.

When she came to Lord Bateman's castle
So boldly there she rang the bell
'Who's there, who's there?' cried the young proud porter
'Who's there, who's there? Come unto me tell.'

'Oh is this Lord Bateman's castle
And is his Lordship here within?'
'Oh yes, oh yes,' cried the young proud porter
He's just now taken his young bride in.'

'Tell him to send me a slice of cake
And a bottle of the best of wine
And not to forget the fair young lady
Who did release him when close confined.'

Away, away went the young proud porter
Away, away, away went he
Until he came unto Lord Bateman
When down he fell on bended knee.

'What news, what news, my young porter
What news, what news hast thou for me?'
'Oh there's the finest of all young ladies
That ever my two eyes did see.'

'She has got rings on every finger
And on one of them she has got three
She has as much gay gold about her middle
As would buy all Northumberland of thee.'

'She tells thee to send her a piece of cake
And a bottle of the best of wine
And not to forget the fair young lady
Who did release thee when close confined.'

Lord Bateman in a passion flew
He broke his sword in splinters three
'I'll give all my father's lands and riches
Now if Sophia has crossed the sea.'

Then up spoke the young bride's mother
Who was never heard to speak so free
'Don't forget my only daughter
Although Sophia has crossed the sea.'

'I'll own I've made a bride of your daughter
She's none the better nor worse for me
She came to me on a horse and saddle
She shall go back in a coach and three.'

Then another marriage was prepared
With both their hearts so full of glee
'I'll roam no more to foreign countries
Since my Sophia has crossed the sea.'

34

Madam, Will You Walk?

'I should like to buy thee a fine lace cap
With five yards of ribbon to hang down thy back
If thou wilt walk with me.'

'I will not accept of the fine lace cap
With the five yards of ribbon to hang down my back
Nor I will not walk with thee.'

'I will buy thee a fine silken gown
With nine yards of ribbon to trail upon the ground
If thou wilt walk with me.'

'I will not accept of the fine silken gown
With nine yards of ribbon to trail upon the ground
Nor I won't walk with thee.'

'I'll buy thee a fine golden chair
To sit in the garden and to take the pleasant air
If thou wilt walk with me.'

'I will not accept of thy fine golden chair
To sit in the garden and to take the pleasant air
Nor I will not walk with thee.'

'It's I will give thee the keys of my chest
To take gold and silver when thou art distressed
If thou wilt walk with me.'

'I will not accept of the keys of your chest
To take gold and silver when I am distressed
Nor I will not walk with thee.'

'I'll give thee the key, O the key of my heart
And thy heart and my heart shall never depart
If thou wilt walk with me.'

'I will accept of the key of your heart
And thy heart and my heart shall never depart
And I will walk with thee.'

35

Queen of the May

Now the winter is gone and the summer is come
And the meadows look pleasant and gay
I met a young damsel so sweetly sang she
And her cheeks like the blossoms of May.

I says, 'Fair maid, how came you here
In the meadows this morning so soon?'
The maid she replied, 'For to gather some may
For the trees they are all in full bloom.'

I says, 'Fair maiden, shall I go with you
To the meadows to gather some may?'
O the maid she replied, 'O I must be excused
For I'm afeared you will lead me astray.'

Then I took this fair maid by her lily-white hand
On the green mossy banks we sat down
And I placed a kiss on her sweet rosy lips
And the small birds were singing all round.

When we arose from the green mossy banks
To the meadows we wandered away
I placed my love on a primrosy bank
And I plucked her a handful of may.

When I returned she gave me a smile
And thanked me for what I had done
I placed a sprig on her snowy-white breast
And believe me there's never a thorn.

Then early next morning I made her my bride
That the world should have nothing to say
The bells they did ring and the bridesmaids did sing
And I crowned her sweet Queen of May.

36

Searching for Lambs

As Johnny walked out one day it was a summer morn
Himself he laid beneath the shade to rest him of a thorn
He had not long been lying there when his true love passed by
And 'twas down in yonder valley, love, where the water glideth by.

'Oh have you seen my pretty ewe that hath a pair of lambs?
They've strayed from their pasture, they've strayed from their dams.'
'O pretty maid,' he answered, 'I saw them pass me by
And 'twas down in yonder valley, love, where the water glideth by.'

She traipsed the country over, no lambs nor ewe could find
And many times upbraided she young Johnny in her mind
[Then turned herself most curiously and smiled with a blush
For young Johnny followed after her and hid him in a bush.]

The flame of anger kindled love and changed its kind of show
So Johnny laughed out and said, 'I'll lead the way below
I'll lead you to the meadows green, where you the lambs may spy
They are down in yonder valley, love, where the water glideth by.'

He held her hand, he whispered love, he swore his heart was true
He kissed her lips, the lambkins skipp'd about them in the dew
About them in the morning dew beneath a sunny sky
All a-down in yonder valley where the water glideth by.

So married were this happy pair, and joined in wedlock bands
No more they go to seek their lambs together hand in hand
They go no more a-searching for her sheep with tearful eye
And all a-down in yonder valley where the water glideth by.

37

Seventeen Come Sunday

O as I rose up one May morning
One May morning so early
I overtook a pretty fair maid
Just as the sun was dawning.

Chorus
With my rue dum ray, fother diddle ay
Whack fol air diddle I-do.

Her stockings white and her boots were bright
And her buckling [buckles] shone like silver
She had a dark and a rolling eye
And her hair hung round her shoulder.

'Where are you going, my pretty fair maid
Where are you going, my honey?'
She answered me right cheerfully
'I'm an errand for my mummy.'

'How old are you, my pretty fair maid
How old are you, my honey?'
She answered me right cheerfully
'I am seventeen come Sunday.'

'Will you take a man, my pretty fair maid
Will you take a man, my honey?'
She answered me right cheerfully
'I dar'st not for my mummy.'

'Will you come down to my mummy's house
When the moon shines bright and clearly?
You'll come down, I'll let you in
And my mummy shall not hear me.'

I went down to her mummy's house
When the moon shone bright and clearly
She came down and let me in
And I lied in her arms till morning.

O it's now I'm with my soldier lad
His ways they are so winning
It's drum and fife is my delight
And a pint of rum in the morning.

38

The Spotted Cow

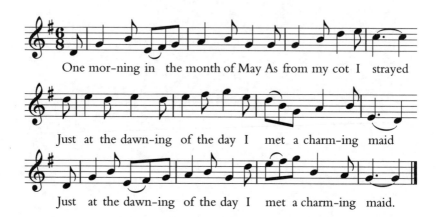

One mor-ning in the month of May As from my cot I strayed

Just at the dawn-ing of the day I met a charm-ing maid

Just at the dawn-ing of the day I met a charm-ing maid.

One morning in the month of May
As from my cot I strayed
Just at the dawning of the day
I met a charming maid.
Just at the dawning of the day
I met a charming maid.

'Good morning, fair maid whither,' said I
'So early, tell me now.'
The maid replied, 'Kind sir,' she said
'I've lost my spotted cow.'
The maid replied, 'Kind sir,' she said
I've lost my spotted cow.'

'No more complain, no longer mourn
Your cow's not lost, my dear
I saw her down in yonder bourne
Come love, and I'll show you where', etc.

'I must confess you're very kind
I thank you, sir,' said she
'You will be sure her there to find
Come sweetheart, go with me', etc.

Then to the grove we did repair
And crossed the flow'ry dale
We hugged and kissed each other there
And love was all our tale, etc.

And in the grove we spent the day
And thought it passed too soon
At night we homeward bent our way
When brightly shone the moon, etc.

If I should cross the flow'ry dale
Or go to view the plough
She comes and calls, 'Ye gentle swain
I've lost my spotted cow', etc.

III

Let No Man Steal Your Thyme ...
Unhappy Love

Let No Man Steal Your Thyme ...
Unhappy Love

There are many types of unhappy relationships in life, but it is really only the uncomplicated ones which get discussed in traditional songs – fickle sweethearts, unequal marriages, love triangles and the workings of cruel fate – with little attempt to explore the depths of psychology or offer couples counselling. Some of the songs in Part IV concerning obstacles and tricks could be included here, but the simple distinguishing feature is that those usually have a happy ending while the songs in this section do not. Similarly, many of the songs included in Part VIII, concerning death, hinge on love-life problems.

It is interesting to note that neither sex has a monopoly on laments for lost love, and there are many songs from the man's point of view as well as from the woman's. 'A Week Before Easter' (No. 56), for example, while usually sung by a man, can easily be recast to suit a female singer, although 'Susan, the Pride of Kildare' (No. 54) cannot. Songs in which fate carries off the husband, such as 'The Trees They Do Grow High' (No. 55), can be balanced by 'The Foggy Dew' (No. 44), where it is the wife who dies. The only area on which women can make sole claim is sweethearts killed by enemy action ('Bonny Light Horseman', No. 41, and 'Early, Early All in the Spring', No. 43).

How a jilted or forsaken lover handles the rejection also varies considerably. Barbara Allen's beau (No. 40), most famously, curls up and dies, while the young man in 'Green Bushes' (No. 45) takes a more pragmatic view of the situation. The girls in 'A Brisk Young Sailor (No. 42) and 'Rosemary Lane' (No. 51), being left pregnant, have little choice, while others simply complain of their lot, lyrically and often in the symbolism of the natural world ('If I Were a Blackbird', No. 47, 'The Seeds of Love', No. 52, and 'The Sprig of Thyme', No. 53).

As indicated in Part V, the section on lust and bad living, marital infidelity is usually treated as funny in traditional songs, but what we would now call 'love triangles' are far from comic. The inability of

'Lord Thomas' (No. 48) to stick to one woman, for example, has dire consequences for all, although 'Lord Bateman' (Part II, No. 33) gets away with it.

There are many song of unhappy marriages, not included here, in which one partner takes direct action or rejoices when the other dies; and it is usually the man who is hoping to get rid of a shrewish wife, the story often told in a humorous vein. Similarly, the theme of a young woman marrying an old man ('An Old Man Once Courted Me', No. 50) can be sung ruefully, or humorously, as the last verse indicates.

39
Banks of Sweet Primroses

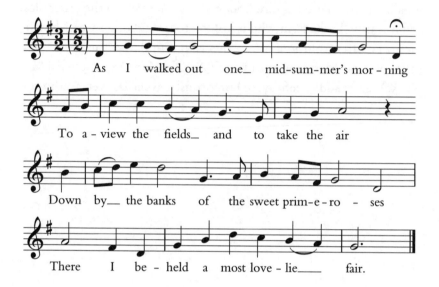

As I walked out one midsummer's morning
To a-view the fields and to take the air
Down by the banks of the sweet prim-e-roses
There I beheld a most lovelie fair.

Three long steps I stepped up to her
Not knowing her as she passed me by
I stepped up to her, thinking to view her
She appeared to me like some virtuous bride.

I said, 'Fair maid where are you going
Or what's the occasion of all your grief?
I'll make you as happy as any lady
If you will grant me some small relief.'

'Stand off, stand off, for you are deceitful
You've been a false and deceitful man
For it's you that have caused my poor heart to wander
And to give me comfort it's all in vain.'

I'll go down into some lonesome valley
Where no man on earth shall me never find
Where the pretty little small birds shall change their voices
And every moment blow blusterous and wild.

Now all young men that go a-courting
Come pay attention to what I say
For there's many a dark and a cloudy morning
Turns out to be a sunshiny day.

40

Barbara Allen

In Scotland I was born and bred
In London I was dwelling
I courted one a pretty maid
Her name was Barbara Allen, Allen
Her name was Barbara Allen.

I sent my servant to her town
To her town where she was dwelling
Saying, 'Come unto my master's house

If your name is Barbara Allen, Allen
If your name is Barbara Allen.'

How slowly I put on my things
And slowly I went to him
And when I came to his bedside
I said, 'Young man, you're a-dying, dying.'
I said, Young man, you're a-dying.'

'A dying man don't say I am
When one kiss from you will cure me.'
'One kiss from me you never shall have
While your false heart lie breaking, breaking
While your false heart lie a-breaking.'

'Last Saturday night you know very well
Sweet ale that you were a-drinking
You drank your health to all was there
But not to Barbara Allen, Allen
But not to Barbara Allen.'

'O mother, O mother, look at my bedside
There's my gold watch all hanging
There's my gold watch likewise my chain
Give it to Barbara Allen, Allen
Give it to Barbara Allen.'

'As I was going across the fields
I heard the bells all tolling
And every time the bell did toll
Hard-hearted Barbara Allen, Allen
Hard-hearted Barbara Allen.'

'O mother, O mother, go and make my bed
And make it long and narrow
For my true love he died today

And I will die tomorrow, morrow
And I will die tomorrow.'

'O father, O father, go and dig my grave
And dig it deep and narrow
For my true love was buried today
And I'll be buried tomorrow, morrow
And I'll be buried tomorrow.'

41

Bonny Light Horseman

Ye maids, wives and wi-dows, I__ pray give at - ten-tion

Un - to these few lines tho' dis-mal to__ men-tion

I'm a mai-den dis - tract-ed, in the des-ert I'll rove

To the gods I'll com-plain for the loss of my love.__

Chorus

Bro-ken-heart-ed I'll__ wan-der, bro-ken-heart-ed I'll wan-der

My bon-ny light horse-man that was slain in the wars.

Ye maids, wives and widows, I pray give attention
Unto these few lines tho' dismal to mention
I'm a maiden distracted, in the desert I'll rove
To the gods I'll complain for the loss of my love.

Chorus
Broken-hearted I'll wander, broken-hearted I'll wander
My bonny light horseman that was slain in the wars.

Had I wings of an eagle so quickly I'd fly
To the very spot where my true love did die
On his grave would I flutter my outstretched wings
And kiss his cold lips o'er and o'er again.

Two years and two months since he left England's shore
My bonny light horseman that I did adore
O why was I born this sad day to see
When the drum beat to arms and did force him from me?

Not a lord, duke or earl could my love exceed
Not a more finer youth for his king e'er did bleed
When mounted on a horse he so gay did appear
And by all his regiment respected he were.

Like the dove that does mourn when it loseth its mate
Will I for my love till I die for his sake
No man on this earth my affection shall gain
A maid live and die for my love that was slain.

42

A Brisk Young Sailor

A brave young sai - lor court - ed me

He stole a - way my li - ber - ty

He stole my heart with a free___ good will

Al - though he's false___ I love___ him still.

A brave young sailor courted me
He stole away my liberty
He stole my heart with a free goodwill
Although he's false I love him still.

It's once my apron did tie low
My love followed me through frost and snow
But now my apron is up to my chin
My love passes by and never looks in.

There is a seat on yonder hill
Where my false love is sitting still
He takes a strange girl on his knee
He kisses her and he frowns on me.

The reason is I'll tell you for why
Because she's got more gold than I
Her gold will wither, her beauty will blast
Poor girl she'll come like me at last.

It's down the green field I do go
Gathering flowers as they grow
I gather one of every kind
Until I gather my apron full.

I wish to God my baby was born
Sat smiling in his dada's arms
And me poor girl rolled in cold clay
And green grass growing all over my grave.

43

Early, Early All in the Spring

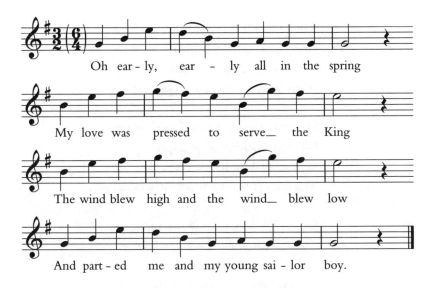

Oh ear-ly, ear - ly all in the spring

My love was pressed to serve__ the King

The wind blew high and the wind__ blew low

And part-ed me and my young sai - lor boy.

Oh early, early all in the spring
My love was pressed to serve the King
The wind blew high and the wind blew low
And parted me and my young sailor boy.

'O father, father, build me a boat
That on the ocean I may float
And every king's ship as I pass by
I will enquire for my sailor boy.'

She had not sailed far across the deep
Before five king's ships she chanced to meet
'Come, jolly sailors, come tell me true
Does my love sail in along with you?'

'What clothes does your true love wear?
What colour is your true love's hair?'
'A blue silk jacket, all bound with twine
His hair is not the colour of mine.'

'Oh no, fair lady, your love's not here
He has got drowned I greatly fear
For on yon ocean as we passed by
'Twas there we lost a young sailor boy.'

She wrung her hands and tore her hair
Like some lady in deep despair
Saying, 'Happy, happy is the girl,' she cried
'Has got a true love down by her side.'

She sat her down and wrote a song
She wrote it wide, she wrote it long
At every line she shed a tear
And at every verse she said, 'My dear.'

When her dear father came home that night
He call-ed for his heart's delight
He went upstairs, the door he broke
He found her hanging by a rope.

He took a knife and cut her down
Within her bosom a note was found
And in this letter these words were wrote
'Father, dear father, my heart is broke.'

'Father, dear father, dig me a grave
Dig it wide and dig it deep
And in the middle put a lily-white dove
That the world may know I died for love.'

44

The Foggy Dew

When I was young and in my prime I followed the weaving trade
And the only harm that ever I done I courted a fair young maid
I courted her in summertime and in the winter too
And many the times I rolled that girl all over the foggy dew.

One night she came to my bedside as I lay fast asleep
She laid her head upon my bed and bitterly she did weep
She raved, she swore, she tore her hair, she cried, 'What shall I do?
For tonight I'm resolved to sleep with you for fear of the foggy dew.'

Now all the first part of that night how we did sport and play
And all the second part of that night she in my arms did lay
And when broad daylight did appear, she cried, 'I am undone.'
I said, 'Hold your row, you foolish young girl, the foggy dew is gone.'

'Now suppose that you should have a child 'twould make you laugh
    and smile
Suppose that you should have another 'twould make you think awhile
Suppose that you should have another, another, another one too
'Twould make you give over your foolish young ways and think of the
    foggy dew.'

One night she woke with moans and groans, I said, 'What's up with you?'
She said, 'I should never have been this way if it hadn't have been for
    you.'
I pulled my boots and trousers on, I got my neighbour too
But do what we would we could do her no good and she died in the
    foggy dew.

Now I am a bachelor I live with my son and we work at the weaving
    trade
And when I look into his eyes I think of that fair young maid
I think of her in summertime and in the winter too
And of the times I held her in my arms for fear of the foggy dew.

45

Green Bushes

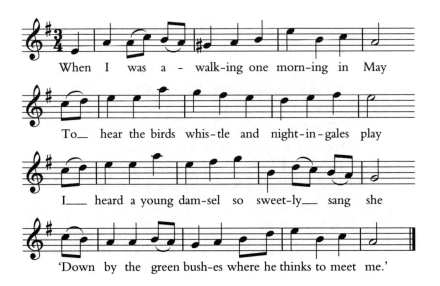

When I was a - walk-ing one morn-ing in May

To— hear the birds whis-tle and night-in-gales play

I— heard a young dam-sel so sweet-ly— sang she

'Down by the green bush-es where he thinks to meet me.'

When I was a-walking one morning in May
To hear the birds whistle and nightingales play
I heard a young damsel so sweetly sang she
'Down by the green bushes where he thinks to meet me.'

'I'll buy you fine beavers and fine silken gowns
I'll buy you fine petticoats flounced to the ground
If you prove loyal and constant to me
Forsake your own true love and marry with me.'

'I want none of your beavers nor fine silken hose
For I ne'er was so poor as to marry for clothes
But I will prove loyal and constant to thee
Forsake my own true love and married we'll be.'

'Come let us be going, kind sir, if you please
Come let us be going from under these trees
For yonder is coming my true love I see
Down by the green bushes, when he thinks to meet me.'

But when he got there and found she was gone
He stood like some lambkin was left quite forlorn
'She's gone with some other and forsaken me
So adieu the green bushes for ever adieu.'

'I'll be like some schoolboy, spend my time in play
For I never was so foolishly deluded away
There's no false-hearted woman shall serve me so more
So adieu the green bushes, it's time to give o'er.'

46

Green Grow the Laurels

I once had a sweet-heart but now I've got none

She's gone and she's left me a - lone, all a - lone

She's gone and she's left me, con - tent - ed I'll be

For she loves an - o - ther one bet - ter than me

Chorus

Green grow the lau - rel____ and so does the yew

And it's sor - ry I'll be at the part - ing of you

But at our next meet - ing I hope you'll prove true

And ex-change your green lau-rels for the red, white and blue.

I once had a sweetheart but now I've got none
She's gone and she's left me alone all alone
She's gone and she's left me, contented I'll be
For she loves another one better than me.

Chorus
Green grows the laurel and so does the yew
And it's sorry I'll be at the parting of you
But at our next meeting I hope you'll prove true
And exchange your green laurels for the red, white and blue.

I wrote my love a letter in red rosy leaves
She wrote me one back that was twisted and twined
Saying, 'Keep your love letters and I will keep mine
You can write to your true love and I'll write to mine.'

I passed my love's window both early and late
And the looks that she gave me my poor heart did ache
And the looks that she gave me ten thousand would kill
She's the heart of an innocent, she's the one I love still.

47

If I Were a Blackbird

I was once a poor maiden all lonely and sad
I once went a-courting a brave sailor lad
I courted him fondly by night and by day
And now like a sailor he's gone far away.

Chorus
If I were a blackbird I'd whistle and sing
I'd follow the vessel my true love sailed in
And in the top rigging I'd there build my nest
And pillow my head on his lily-white breast.

My love he was handsome in every degree
His parents despised him because he loved me
But they can despise him and say what they will
While I've breath in my body I'll love that lad still.

He promised to meet me at Bonnybrook Fair
With a bunch of blue ribbon to tie up my hair
With a bunch of blue ribbon he'd crown me with joy
While I'd kiss the lips of my own sailor boy.

48

Lord Thomas and Fair Eleanor

Lord Tho-mas he was a bold fo - rest - er
A - keep - ing of the king's deer
Fair E - li - nor she was the fair - est wo - man
Lord Tho - mas he lov - ed her dear.

Final stanza

Lord Thomas he was a bold forester
A-keeping of the king's deer
Fair Elinor she was the fairest woman
Lord Thomas he loved her dear.

'O riddle, O riddle, dear mother,' he said
'O riddle it both as one
Whether I shall marry fair Ellen or not
And leave the brown girl alone.'

'The brown girl she've a-got houses and lands
Fair Ellen she've a-got none
Therefore I charge thee to my blessing
The brown girl bring safe to home.'

Lord Thomas he rode to fair Elinor's gates
And loud he tirled at the pin
There was none so ready as fair Elinor
To let Lord Thomas in.

'What news, what news, Lord Thomas?' she said
'What news hast thou brought unto me?'
'I'm come to invite thee to my wedding
And that is bad news for thee.'

'O God forbid, Lord Thomas,' she said
'That any such thing should be done
I thought to have been the bride myself
And you to have been the bridegroom.'

'O mother, come riddle, come riddle to me
And riddle it all in one
Whether I be to go to Lord Thomas's wedding
Or whether to stay at home.'

'There's thousands are your friends, daughter
There's thousands are your foes
Betide your life, betide your death
To Lord Thomas's wedding don't go.'

'There's thousands are my friends, mother
There's thousands are my foes
Betide my life or betide my death
To Lord Thomas's wedding I go.'

She drest herself in her scarlet red
The merry maids drest in green
And every town that she rode through
They took her to be the queen.

She rode on to Lord Thomas's door
So loud did she pull at the ring
None so ready as Lord Thomas
To let fair Elinor in.

'Is this your bride?' fair Elinor said
'I think she looks wonderful brown
You may have had as fair a woman
As ever the sun shone on.'

'Despite her not,' Lord Thomas he said
'Despite her not unto me
For I love your little finger
Better than her whole body.'

The brown girl had got a little penknife
Which was both keen and sharp
Between the long ribs and the short
She pierced to fair Elinor's heart.

'Oh what is the matter?' Lord Thomas he said
'I think you look wondrous wan
You used to have as fair a colour
As ever the sun shone on.'

'Art thou blind, Lord Thomas?' she says
'Or canst thou not very well see?
Canst thou not see mine own heart's blood
Come trickling down my knee?'

Lord Thomas he had a long sword by his side
As he walked through the hall
Off he cut the brown girl's head
And dashed it against the wall.

Lord Thomas he had a long sword in his hall
He pointed it up to his heart
Was it ever so soon they met
Or ever so soon they did part?

'Pray those that dig my grave
Dig it both wide and deep
And bury fair Elinor at my right hand
And the brown girl at my feet
That if ever my mother she do pass by
She may sit down and weep.'

They grew and grew to a red rosebud
For thousands to admire
They grew up to the chancel wall
And the brown girl to a brier.

49

Mowing the Barley

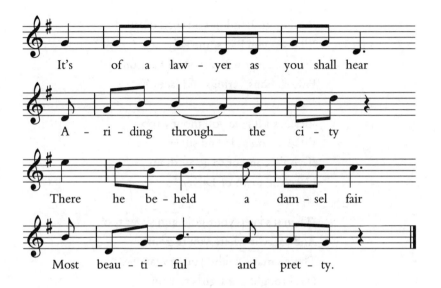

It's of a law - yer as you shall hear

A – ri – ding through__ the ci - ty

There he be - held a dam - sel fair

Most beau - ti – ful and pret - ty.

It's of a lawyer as you shall hear
A-riding through the city
There he beheld a damsel fair
Most beautiful and pretty.

'Where are you going, my fair pretty maid
Where are you going, my honey?'
'To yonder meadow,' she replied
'My father's there a-mowing.'

'Shall I go with you, my fair pretty maid
Shall I go with you, my honey?'
She answered me right cheerfully
'My father will be angry.'

Then quickly I tripped over the plain
And soon I overtook her
I whispered these kind words to her ears
'A lady I will make you.'

'And up to London you shall dwell
I'll dress you like some lady
Fine silken gowns you shall have on
Fine ribbons, strings and laces.'

'Besides I'll give you money too
I'll give you gold and silver
If you'll consent to go with me
Unto the town of Dover.'

'Then it's keep your gold and silver too
And carry it where you're going
There's many a false young man like you
Has brought poor girls to ruin.'

'I'd rather be a ploughman's wife
Sit at my wheel a-spinning
Than I'd be a lawyer's bride
Sit in some alehouse drinking.'

Come all young maids a warning take
In country, town or city
You never should listen to what a young man says
For a young man's got no pity.

50

An Old Man Once Courted Me

An old man once court-ed me   I ding doo-rum down

An old man once court-ed me   I doo-rum down

(a)

An old man once court-ed me   Fain would he mar-ry me

Maids, when you're young   Ne-ver wed an old man.

Chorus

For they've got no   fa-loo-ral   fa-lid-dle   fa-loo-ral

They've got no   fa-loo-ral   fa-lid-dle   all   day

They've got no   fa-loo-ral, they've lost their ding doo-rum

So   maids, when you're young   ne-ver wed an old man.

(a)

An old man once courted me
I ding doorum down
An old man once courted me
I doorum down
An old man once courted me
Fain would he marry me
Maids, when you're young
Never wed an old man.

Chorus
For they've got no falooral faliddle falooral
They've got no falooral faliddle all day
They've got no falooral, they've lost their ding doorum
So maids, when you're young never wed an old man.

Now when we went to church
Hay ding doorum down
When we went to church
Hay doorum down
When we went to church
He left me in the lurch
Maids, when you're young
Never wed an old man.

Now when we went to bed
Hay ding doorum down
When we went to bed
Hay doorum down
When we went to bed
He neither done nor said
Maids, when you're young
Never wed an old man.

Now when he went to sleep
Hay ding doorum down
When he went to sleep

Hay doorum down
When he went to sleep
Out of bed I did creep
Into the arms of a jolly young man.

Last chorus
And I found his falooral faliddle falooral
I found his falooral faliddle all day
I found his faloorum, and he got my ding doorum
So maids, when you're young never wed an old man.

51

Rosemary Lane

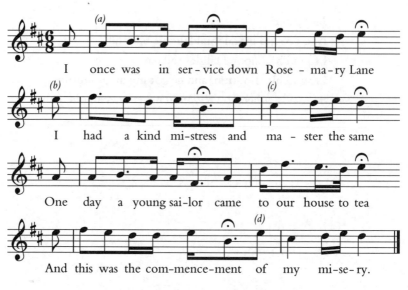

I once was in service down Rosemary Lane
I had a kind mistress and master the same
One day a young sailor came to our house to tea
And this was the commencement of my misery.

When supper was over he hung down his head
Then he asked for a candle to light him to bed
I gave him a candle as a maiden should do
But he vowed and declared that I should go too.

Early next morning when the young sailor rose
He threw in my apron two handful of gold
'Oh take it, oh take it, for the wrong I have done
I have left you a daughter or else a fine son.'

'If it be a daughter, she shall wait upon me
But if it's a sonny, he shall cross the deep sea
He shall wear a blue jacket and his cap lined with gold
He shall cross the blue ocean like his young father bold.'

Now all you young lasses take a warning from me
Never trust a young sailor whoe'er he may be
They give you, they court you, they swear they'll be true
But the very next moment they'll bid you adieu.

Like a flower in the garden when its beauty's all gone
So you see what I've come to through loving that one
No father, no mother, no friend in the world
So me and my baby to the workhouse must go.

52

The Seeds of Love

I sow-ed the seeds of love
For to last me all the spring
There was April, May and likewise June
When the small birds do sweetly sing.

My garden was well provided
With seeds of every kind
But I had not the liberty them for to choose
The flower that was on my mind.

My gardener was standing by
So I asked him to choose for me
He chose for me the violet, the lily and the pink
But I did refuse all three.

The reason I refused the lily
Was because it fades so soon
And the violet and the pink I over, overlooked
Then I vowed that I'd stop till June.

For in June there is the red rosebud
And that is the flower for me
But often have I snatched at the red rosebud
And have gained but a willow tree.

Oh the willow tree will twist
And the willow tree will twine
And I wish that I was in that young man's arms
That stole away this heart of mine.

As my gardener was standing by
He bade me then beware
For that underneath the blossom of the red red rose
Lies a thorn that would wound and tear.

Then of hyssop I will take a spray
And no other flower I'll touch
That all in the world may both see and say
That I've loved one flower too much.

So come all you pretty fair maids
That love for to chipper and to chase
The grass that is often trodden underfoot
In time will rise again.

53

The Sprig of Thyme

Come all you pretty fair maids
That are just in your prime
I would have you weed your garden clear
And let no one steal your thyme.

I once had a sprig of thyme
It prospered both night and day
By chance there came a false young man
And he stole my thyme away.

Thyme is the prettiest flower
That grows under the sun
It's time that brings all things to an end
So now my thyme runs on.

But now my old thyme's dead
I've got no room for any new
For in that place where my old thyme grew
Is changed to a running rue.

[But I'll put a stop to that running rue
And plant a fair oak tree
Stand you up you fair oak tree
And do not wither and die.]

It's very well drinking ale
And it's very well drinking wine
But it's far better sitting by a young man's side
That has won this heart of mine.

Susan, the Pride of Kildare

When first from sea I land-ed_ I_ had a ro-ving mind

Un - daunt-ed I ram-bled my true love to_ find

I_ met pret-ty Su - san with her cheeks like a_ rose

And her bo - som more fair - er_ than the li - ly that blows.

When first from sea I landed I had a roving mind
Undaunted I rambled my true love to find
I met pretty Susan with her cheeks like a rose
And her bosom more fairer than the lily that blows.

Her keen eye did glitter like the bright stars by night
The robe she was wearing was costly and white
Her bare neck was shaded with her long raven hair
And they called her pretty Susan, the pride of Kildare.

Long time her I courted till I wasted my store
My love turned to hatred because I were poor
She said, 'I love some other one whose fortune I'll share'
And I'll be gone from pretty Susan, the pride of Kildare.

As I roamed out one morning, being in the month of May
I met pretty Susan with her young lord so gay
And as I passed by them with my mind full of care
I sighed for pretty Susan, the pride of Kildare.

Then down to the seaside I resolv-ed to go
Bound down to East Indies, with my heart full of woe
There I spied fair ladies with their jewels so rare
But there's none like pretty Susan, the pride of Kildare.

Now sometimes I'm jovial and sometimes I'm sad
Since my love she's been courted by some other lad
Now since we're at a distance no more I'll despair
Here's a blessing on my Susan, she's the pride of Kildare.

55

The Trees They Do Grow High

The trees they do grow high and the leaves they do grow green

And ma-ny a cold win-ter's night my love and I__have seen

Of a cold win-ter's night, my love, you and I a-lone have been

Whilst my bon-ny boy is young, he's a-grow-ing   Grow-ing,

grow-ing Whilst my bon-ny boy is young, he's a-grow-ing.

(d) Stanza 6

The trees they do grow high and the leaves they do grow green
And many a cold winter's night my love and I have seen
Of a cold winter's night, my love, you and I alone have been
Whilst my bonny boy is young, he's a-growing
Growing, growing
Whilst my bonny boy is young, he's a-growing.

'Oh father, dearest father, you've done to me much harm
You've tied me to a boy when you know he is too young.'
'Oh daughter, dearest daughter, if you'll wait a little while
A lady you shall be whilst he's growing
Growing, growing
A lady you shall be whilst he's growing.'

'I'll send your love to college all for a year or two
And then in the meantime he will do for you
I'll buy him white ribbons, tie them round his bonny waist
To let the ladies know that he's married
Married, married
To let the ladies know that he's married.'

I went up to the college and I looked all over the wall
Saw four and twenty gentlemen playing at bat and ball
I call-ed for my own true love but they would not let him come
All because he was a young boy, and growing
Growing, growing
All because he was a young boy, and growing.

At the age of sixteen he was a married man
At the age of seventeen he was father to a son
At the age of eighteen the grass grew over him
Cruel death soon put an end to his growing
Growing, growing
Cruel death soon put an end to his growing.

And he shall have a shroud of the very best brown
And whilst in a-making the tears shall roll down
Saying, 'Once I had a sweetheart but now I've never a one.'
So fare you well my own true, for ever ever more
Saying, 'Once I had a sweetheart but now I've never a one.'
So fare you well my own true, for ever ever more.

And now my love is dead and in his grave doth lie
The green grass grows over him so very very high
I'll sit and I'll mourn his fate until the day I die
And I'll watch all over his child whilst he's growing
Growing, growing
And I'll watch all over his child whilst he's growing.

56

A Week Before Easter

'Twas a week before Easter, the days long and clear
So fine was the morning but keen blew the air
I went on the forest to gather wild flowers
But the forest didn't yield none but roses.

The roses are red and the leaves they were green
All the brambles and briars so plain to be seen
The small birds were singing and changing their note
Amongst the wild beasts on the forest.

The first time I saw my love was to the church go
Oh the bride and the bridegroom, they cut a fine show
And I followed after with my heart full of woe
To see how my false love was guarding.

The first time I saw my love was in the church stand
With the ring on her finger and the glove in her hand
Thinks I to myself, 'I might have been that man'
But I never once mentioned to have her.

The second time I saw my love we sat down to meat
Oh I sat down beside her but none could I eat
She thought her sweet company much better than mine
Although she was tied to some other.

The fourth time I saw my love she was all dressed up in white
Oh my eyes run half water quite dazzl-ed my sight
I picked up my hat and I wished her goodnight
There's adieu to false lovers for ever.

Go and dig me a grave both long, narrow and deep
And strow it all over with the roses so sweet
So that I can lay down and take a long sleep
And that's the right way to forget her.

IV

Since Love Can Enter an Iron Door ...
Lovers' Tricks, Disguises and
Obstacles Overcome

Since Love Can Enter an Iron Door ...
Lovers' Tricks, Disguises and Obstacles

When true love does not run smooth in folk song it is often because family members have placed obstacles in the way, and such opposition is invariably concerned with differences in social class and/or wealth, the song always being on the side of the lovers. It is not only parents who take against an unsuitable match – it can be uncles or guardians who interfere, and sometimes brothers ('The Constant Farmer's Son', No. 115), and their action is often the most directly violent.

What happens next varies considerably from song to song. Sometimes there is simply a threat – 'we will get him pressed to sea', or 'send her away' – but where real action is taken it can be against the recalcitrant family member, or against the sweetheart.

The rule for lovers seems to be 'get away quick', because any dalliance simply gives the forces of opposition time to make their move. It is most often the male who is deemed unsuitable and in extreme cases he is quietly murdered, but in others he is framed for theft or, in the case of a failed elopement, for kidnap. Getting pressed to sea is perhaps the least of his worries. Where the unsuitable sweetheart is female (almost always a servant), she is simply dismissed, sent away, or taken abroad and left there, but she can also be framed for theft. In an obtuse sort of way, these songs do reflect something of the reality of life in eighteenth- and nineteenth-century rural England, where young working people were indeed at the mercy of their social superiors and employers.

But the action may be against the family member rather than the suitor, and the girl who falls for a lower-class boy is often shut away and, in extreme cases ('The Daughter in the Dungeon', No. 69), beaten and starved into submission, although in these cases she is nearly always rescued.

One of the most common themes of lovers' tricks is the return of the man in disguise who tests the woman's love in some way

– usually by telling her that her sweetheart has died. Oddly enough, the girl on the receiving end of this treatment never gets indignant or gives him a clout round the ear, but always swoons into his arms. Another modern comment is, 'How come she did not recognize him?' But not only is the man often in disguise, it should also be pointed out that in the days before photographs ordinary people did not have any 'likeness' of their lover to pore over day by day. The 'broken token' theme, which occurs often in this context, is also a possible touch of reality, as people did (and still do) give each other such tokens on parting. It is not easy to break a gold ring in half, but it has been suggested that this refers to specially made lovers' rings which were designed to separate into two.

But women can also play tricks. When they don male attire it is nearly always to follow their lover into the army or navy (see Part I on soldiers' and sailors' songs), and only rarely is it just for the fun of it as in 'Polly Oliver's Rambles' (No. 72), or to test their lover's resolve (see 'The Female Highwayman', Part IX, No. 134).

Another regular theme in song are the clever tricks played by girls on putative suitors, either to preserve their virtue, as in 'Broom-field Hill' (No. 63), 'The Baffled Knight' (No. 57) and 'The Knight and the Shepherd's Daughter' (Part II, No. 31), or get their own back afterwards as in 'Basket of Eggs' (No. 59).

57

The Baffled Knight

There was a shep-herd and he Kept sheep u-pon a hill

And he would go each May mor-ning All for to drink his fill.

Chorus

So it's blow the win-dy mor-ning Blow the winds I - O

Clear a-way the mor-ning dew And sweet the wind shall blow.

There was a shepherd and he
Kept sheep upon a hill
And he would go each May morning
All for to drink his fill.

Chorus
So it's blow the windy morning
Blow the winds I-O
Clear away the morning dew
And sweet the wind shall blow.

He look-ed high and he look-ed low
And he gave a downward look
And there he spied a pretty maid
A-washing at the brook.

And then they rode along the road
Till they came unto the inn
And ready was the waiting maid
To let the lady in.

She jump-ed off her milk-white steed
And stepped within the inn
Crying, 'You're a beggar without
And I'm a maid within.'

'You may pull off your shoes and hose
And let your feet go bare
And if you meet a pretty girl
You touch her if you dare.'

'I won't pull off my shoes or hose
Or let my feet go bare
But if I meet with thee again
Be hanged if I despair.'

58

The Banks of the Sweet Dundee

It's of a farm-er's daugh-ter, so beau-ti-ful I'm told Her par-ents died and left___ her five hun-dred pounds in gold She liv-ed with her un-cle, the cause of all her woe And soon you shall hear this mai-den fair did prove his o-ver-throw.

It's of a farmer's daughter, so beautiful I'm told
Her parents died and left her five hundred pounds in gold
She liv-ed with her uncle, the cause of all her woe
And soon you shall hear this maiden fair did prove his overthrow.

Her uncle kept a ploughboy young Mary loved so well
And in her uncle's garden their tales of love did tell
There was a wealthy squire who oft her came to see
But still she loved her ploughboy on the banks of the sweet Dundee.

It was one summer's morning her uncle went straightway
He knocked at her bedroom door and unto her did say
'Come rise up, pretty maiden, a lady you may be
The squire is waiting for you on the banks of the sweet Dundee.'

'A fig for all your squires, your lords and dukes likewise
My William's hand appears to be worth diamonds in my eyes.'
'Begone, you unruly female, ne'er happy you shall be
I mean to banish William from the banks of the sweet Dundee.'

The uncle and the squire rode out one summer's morn
'Young William is in favour,' her uncle he did say
'Indeed 'tis my intention to tie him to a tree
Or else to bribe the press gang on the banks of the sweet Dundee.'

The press gang came to William when he was all alone
He boldly fought for liberty but they were six to one
The blood did flow in torrents; 'Pray kill me now,' said he
'For I'd rather die for Mary on the banks of the sweet Dundee.'

This maid one day was walking, lamenting for her love
She met the wealthy squire down in her uncle's grove
He put his arms around her; 'Stand off, base man,' cried she
'For you banished the only lad I love from the banks of the sweet Dundee.'

He clasped his arms around her and tried to throw her down
Two pistols and a sword she spied beneath his morning gown
Young Mary took the weapon, his sword he used so free
But she did fire and shot the squire on the banks of the sweet Dundee.

Her uncle overheard the noise and he hastened to the ground
Saying, 'Since you have killed the squire, I'll give you your death wound.'
'Stand off,' then cried young Mary, 'undaunted I will be.'
So the trigger she drew and her uncle slew on the banks of the sweet Dundee.

The doctor soon was sent for, a man of noted skill
Likewise there came his lawyer for him to make his will
He willed his gold to Mary, who fought so manfully
And now she lives quite happy on the banks of the sweet Dundee.

59

Basket of Eggs

There once two sailors were a-walking
Their pockets they were lined with gold
And as they were walking and kindly talking
A pretty fair damsel they did behold.

Now this pretty damsel carried a basket
She set it down to get some ease
One of those sailors said, 'May I take it?'
'Oh yes kind sir, if you please.'

Now these two sailors walked on quite briskly
At the halfway house they pass-ed by
Pretty Nancy stepp-ed and so much lighter
And on them she kept her eye.

Now these two sailors called at an alehouse
They called for a pot of the very best
Saying, 'Landlord, landlord, bring us some bacon
For in that basket there is some eggs.'

The landlord turned unto the basket
He turned away and with a smile
Said, 'Sailor, sailor, you are mistaken
For instead of eggs there is a child.'

One of those sailors let out to swearing
The other he said, 'It's not worth the while
Here's fifty guineas to any woman
Who'll take and nurse this lovely child.'

Pretty Nancy standing at the window
She heard what those two sailors said
Crying, 'Sir, I'll take it and kindly use it
If you will see the money down paid.'

'Are you that Nancy, that fairest Nancy
That I danced with last Easter day?'
'Oh yes kind sir, and pleased your fancy
And now the fiddler you must pay.'

'So let us go to yonder chapel
Where the knot it shall be tied
Where bells are ringing and sailors singing
And I'll make you my lawful bride.'

The Blind Beggar's Daughter
of Bethnal Green

It's of a blind beg-gar and he lost his sight

He had but one daugh-ter, most beau-ti-ful bright

'Shall I seek my for-tune, dear fa-ther?' said she

The fa-vour was grant-ed to pret-ty Bet-sey.

It's of a blind beggar and he lost his sight
He had but one daughter, most beautiful bright
'Shall I seek my fortune, dear father?' said she
The favour was granted to pretty Betsey.

She set out for London, as I have heard say
And arrived in Bloomford that very same day
And when she came there unto my lord's house
So handsomely admired was pretty Betsey.

She had not been there no length of time
Before a young lord a-courting her came
'Your clothes shall be lined with jewels,' said he
'If you will but love me, my pretty Betsey.'

'It's all for to do it I am willing,' said she
'You must first ask the father of pretty Betsey.'
'Then who is your father? Pray tell unto me
That I may go with you your father to see.'

'My father is every day to be seen
He is called the Blind Beggar of Bethlem Green
He is called the Blind Beggar, God knows,' says she
'He has been a good father to his daughter Betsey.'

'If you're a blind beggar's daughter you won't do for me
A blind beggar's daughter my lady shan't be
A blind beggar's daughter my lady shan't be'
So scornfully turned from his pretty Betsey.

Then up spake a young squire, with riches enough
'If she's a blind beggar's daughter she's never the worse
Your clothes shall be lined with jewels,' said he
'If you will but love me, my pretty Betsey.'

'Your daughter's not clothed so fine as she shall be
For it's I will drop guineas for you, my girl.'
He dropp-ed these guineas till they dropp'd on the ground
He dropp-ed till he dropp-ed ten thousand pound.

'Dear honoured father, I've dropped all my store
I've dropped all my riches and I can't drop no more
But grant me your daughter, and that's all I crave
That I might be married to pretty Betsey.'

'Oh take her and make her your lady so bright
There's many a rich lord will owe you great spite
And when you are married, I will lay her down
Ten thousand bright guineas to buy her a gown.'

It's Billy and Betsey to church they did go
It's Billy and Betsey they cut a fine show
The most beautiful creature that ever was seen
Was the Blind Beggar's daughter of Bethlem Green.

The Bonny Blue Handkerchief

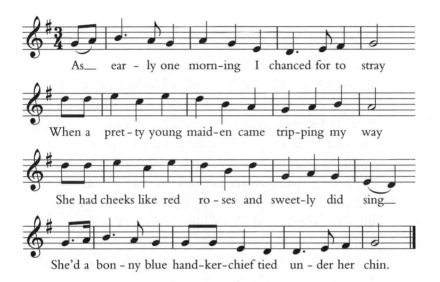

As___ ear - ly one morn-ing I chanced for to stray

When a pret - ty young maid-en came trip-ping my way

She had cheeks like red ro - ses and sweet-ly did sing___

She'd a bon - ny blue hand-ker-chief tied un - der her chin.

As early one morning I chanced for to stray
When a pretty young maiden came tripping my way
She had cheeks like red roses and sweetly did sing
She'd a bonny blue handkerchief tied under her chin.

'Where art thou going, pretty maid?' as I caught round her waist
'Oh sir, do not stop me for I am in great haste
I am going to yond' factory, there cotton to spin
With this bonny blue handkerchief tied under my chin.'

'Then why wear that handkerchief tied round thy head?'
'Because it's the fashion to, kind sir,' she said
'And the fashion you know, sir, we like to be in
With this bonny blue handkerchief tied under my chin.'

Then to kiss those fond lips he going to begin
'Oh stay, sir, oh stay, sir, whilst I tell you one thing
Who kiss these fond lips must show the gold ring
To the bonny blue handkerchief tied under my chin.'

'This bonny blue handkerchief my love gave to me
And told me to wear it whilst he was at sea
Unto him I've proved true as the colour therein
With this bonny blue handkerchief tied under my chin.'

When he heard her so [loyal], he could not forbear
But threw his arms around her and called her his dear
Saying, 'My dearest jewel, here is the gold ring
To the bonny blue handkerchief tied under your chin.'

When she heard him she knew him and went to his arms
And told of her love as he gazed on her charms
Forth to the church then they went and were married in speed
And this loving couple are happy indeed
When days are called over they sweetly do sing
Taken off the blue handkerchief tied under her chin.

62

Bonny Labouring Boy

It was early one May morning down in some shady grove
I heard a lovely maid complain so grieved as I've been told
'Oh cruel were my parents, they do me so annoy
For they would not let me marry my bonny labouring boy
Oh my bonny labouring boy, oh my bonny labouring boy
They would not let me marry my bonny labouring boy.'

It was early one May morning down in the shady grove
Pondering their hearts together some lovely band of love
Her father he came up to her, he took her by the hand
He swore he'd send young Johnny into some foreign lands
'He locked me in my bedroom my troubles to annoy
But he would not let me marry my bonny labouring boy
Oh my bonny labouring boy', etc.

'My mother came next morning and unto me did say
"Your father has appointed and fixed your wedding day."
But boldly I made answer and unto her did say
"Now single will I still remain for my bonny labouring boy
Oh my bonny labouring boy"', etc.

'So fill your glasses to the brim and drink so merrily round
Here's a health to every labouring boy that ploughs and sows the ground
And when his day's work's over it's oh my riddle and joy
So happy is the girl that weds my bonny labouring boy
Oh my bonny labouring boy', etc.

63

Broomfield Hill

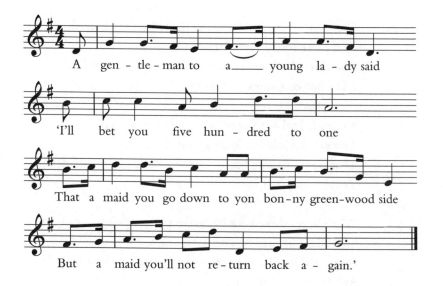

A gen - tle - man to a___ young la - dy said

'I'll bet you five hun - dred to one

That a maid you go down to yon bon - ny green-wood side

But a maid you'll not re - turn back a - gain.'

A gentleman to a young lady said
'I'll bet you five hundred to one
That a maid you go down to yon bonny greenwood side
But a maid you'll not return back again.'

'I'll bet you the same,' the young lady said
'And the money I'll freely lay down
That a maid I'll go down to yon bonny green woods
And a maid I'll return back again.'

Then she mixed him a glass of something so strong
He thought it had been some wine
And when he got down to yon bonny green woods
The sleep it came into his mind.

And when he got down to yon bonny green wood-side
Her lover he lie fast asleep
With his hare and his hounds in silk and satin gowns
And his ribbons hanging down to his feet.

Three times she walked round the crown of his head
And twice round the soles of his feet
And three times she kissed his cherry cherry cheeks
As he lied on the ground asleep.

She pulled off her finger her best diamond ring
And pressed it in her lover's right hand
That was to let him know when he awakened out of sleep
That his lady had been, but was gone.

When he awakened out of his sleep
So well a-wakened was he
He turned his face towards yon bonny bonny broom
And wept most bitterly.

'Oh where hast thou been to, my bonny greyhound?
And why did you stay so long?
And why did you not waken me out of sleep
Since the maiden has been but she's gone?'

'It's three times I tapped at your silk and satin robe
And twice I groaned so loudly
But I could not awaken you out of sleep
Since the lady had been, but she's gone.'

If I only had her fast in my arms
And I could but have my will
All the birds in the wood should drink of her blood
Until they had all had their fill.

64

Butter and Cheese and All

What a pi-ty it is to tease— me or try me for to sing When it does not lay in my pow-er to do a-ny such thing But since you have teased me so I'll try what I___ can do And when I come to the cho - rus, why you must bawl out too___ Why you must bawl out too.

What a pity it is to tease me or try me for to sing
When it does not lay in my power to do any such thing
But since you have teased me so I'll try what I can do
And when I come to the chorus, why you must bawl out too
Why you must bawl out too.

It's with a cook I fell in love and the truth I don't deny
For why a cook should have my choice I'll tell you the reason why
Because she has plenty of mince pies, plum puddings and roast beef
And when my belly was empty she gave to me a relief
She gave to me a relief.

She sent me an invitation some supper for to take
I kindly did accept it all for my belly's sake
And after supper was over of the cupboard I got the keys
One pocket I crammed with butter and the other I stuffed with cheese
The other I stuffed with cheese.

When supper being over about half an hour or more
When the master smelling of my cheese came tapping at the door
And I not knowing where to hide, up the chimney I did hide
And there I sat quite at my ease like a sweep exalted high
Like a sweep exalted high.

I hadn't been long there sitting, a-sitting at my ease
When the fire began to melt my butter, likewise to toast my cheese
And every drop that fell in the fire, it caused the fire to flare
The old man looked up the chimney and swore that Satan was there
And he swore that Satan was there.

Then up to the chimney top he got and down some water poured
And I came tumbling after, my butter and cheese and all
But I'm safe down from the chimney now with a smut and a greasy face
And out in the street I nimbly ran and down the street I was chased
And down the street I was chased.

The dogs did bark, the children screamed, up flew the windows all
And every soul cried out 'Well done' as loud as they could bawl
So to make an end to my ditty, boys, I hope I ain't kept you long
So we'll wish success to the chorus and sing another good song
And sing another good song.

65

Caroline and Her Young Sailor Bold

It's of a rich no - ble-man's daugh - ter

so come - ly and hand-some, we're told

Her par - ents pos-sessed a large for - tune,

of thir - ty - five thou-sands in gold

This no - ble - man had but one daugh - ter,

Ca - ro - line was her name we are told

One day from her draw - ing - room win - dow,

she ad - mir - ed the young sai - lor bold.

It's of a rich nobleman's daughter, so comely and handsome,
we're told
Her parents possessed a large fortune, of thirty-five
thousands in gold
This nobleman had but one daughter, Caroline was her
name we are told
One day from her drawing-room window, she admir-ed the
young sailor bold.

His cheeks, they appeared like two roses, his hair was as
black as the jet
Young Caroline watched his departure, when around with
young William she met
She says, 'I'm a rich nobleman's daughter, possessed of ten
thousand in gold
I'll forsake both my father and mother, to wed with the
young sailor bold.'

He said, 'My dear young lady, remember, your parents
you're bound for to obey
And in sailors there is no depending, when their true loves
are left far behind
I advise you to stay at home with your parents, and do by
them as you are told
And never let anyone tempt you, to wed with the young
sailor bold.'

She says, 'I'll be persuaded by no one one moment to alter
my mind
I'll ship and proceed with my true love, and he never shall
leave me behind.'
So she dressed like a gallant young sailor, in her trousers and
jacket we're told
Four years and a half on the salt seas, she ploughed with her
young sailor bold.

For three times with him she was shipwrecked, but she
    always proved like a man
And her duty she done like a sailor, when aloft in her jacket
    so blue
Her parents long wept and lamented, tears from their eyes
    in torrents did flow
Till at last they arrived in old England, Caroline and her
    young sailor bold.

Young Caroline went straight to her father, with her jacket
    and trousers so blue
Her father one moment lie fainting, when at first she
    appeared in his view
She said, 'My dear father, forgive me, deprive me for ever of
    gold
Grant me your request, I'm contented, to wed with my
    young sailor bold.'

Her father admir-ed young William, and vowed that in
    sweet unity
That if life should be spared until morning, they bound
    together should be
They were married and Caroline's portion was thirty-five
    thousands in gold
And now they live happy and cheerful, Caroline and her
    young sailor bold.

66

Claudy Banks

['Twas on one sum-mer's eve - ning all in the month of May Down by a flow'- ry] gar - den so care-less-ly I strayed I__ o-ver-heard a dam - sel in sor-row to__com-plain All for her ab-sent lov-(i)-er who'd gone to plough the main.

['Twas on one summer's evening all in the month of May
Down by a flowery] garden so carelessly I strayed
I overheard a damsel in sorrow to complain
All for her absent lov-i-er who'd gone to plough the main.

I boldly stepped up to her, which put she in surprise
She really did not know me, I being in disguise
[I said, 'My charming creature,] my joy and heart's delight
How far have you to wander this dark and dreary night?'

'It's all the way to Cloddy Banks, if you will please to show
Pity a maid distracted, not knowing where to go
I am in search of my true love and Johnny is his name
All on the Banks of Cloddy, I am told he do remain.'

'Oh it's six long weeks or better since your Johnny's left this shore
He's crossing the wide ocean where thundering billows roar
He's crossing the wide ocean for honour [and for gain]
Till I were told the ship got wrecked all on the coast of Spain.'

Oh hearing of this dreadful news, it put she in despair
Wringing her hands and crying and tearing of her hair
'Now Johnny's gone and left me, no other will I take
Once more to woods and valleys, I'll wander for his sake.'

Oh hearing of this pretty maid, he could no longer stand
For he fell into her arms, crying, 'Betsy, I'm that man
I am your false young man, which you thought was slain
But since we met on Cloddy Banks, we'll never part again'
Crying, 'Betsy I'm your false young man, which you thought was slain
But since we've met on Cloddy Banks we'll never part again.'
[spoken] Cloddy Banks.

67

Dabbling in the Dew

'O__ where are you go - ing, my sweet and pret-ty fair
maid   With your   red   ro - sy   cheeks   and your
cur - ly black hair?' 'O I'm go - ing a - milk - ing, kind
sir,' she ans-wered   me__   For it's   rol - ling in   the
dew__   makes   the   milk - maids   so   fair.

(a)   (b) Stanza 2

'O where are you going, my sweet and pretty fair maid
With your red rosy cheeks and your curly black hair?'
'Oh I'm going a-milking, kind sir,' she answered me
For it's rolling in the dew makes the milkmaids so fair.

'Shall I go along with you, my sweet and pretty fair maid
With your red rosy cheeks and your curly black hair?'
'Just as you please, kind sir,' she answered me
For it's rolling in the dew makes the milkmaids so fair.

'Supposing I should lay you down, my sweet and pretty fair maid
With your red rosy cheeks and your curly black hair?'
'Then you would have to pick me up again, kind sir,' she answered me
For it's rolling in the dew makes the milkmaids so fair.

'Supposing you should be with child, my sweet and pretty fair maid
With your red rosy cheeks and your curly black hair?'
'Then you would be the father of it, kind sir,' she answered me
For it's rolling in the dew makes the milkmaids so fair.

'What would you do for linen, my sweet and pretty fair maid
With your red rosy cheeks and your curly black hair?'
'My father he's a linen-draper, kind sir,' she answered me
For it's rolling in the dew makes the milkmaids so fair.

'What would you do for a cradle, my sweet and pretty fair maid
With your red rosy cheeks and your curly black hair?'
'My brother he's a basket-maker, kind sir,' she answered me
For it's rolling in the dew makes the milkmaids so fair.

'Supposing I should go to sea, my sweet and pretty fair maid
With your red rosy cheeks and your curly black hair?'
'Then I might follow after you, kind sir,' she answered me
For it's rolling in the dew makes the milkmaids so fair.

'Supposing I should jump overboard, my sweet and pretty fair maid
With your red rosy cheeks and your curly black hair?'
'Then the Devil would jump after you, kind sir,' she answered me
For it's rolling in the dew makes the milkmaids so fair.

68

Dark-Eyed Sailor

It___ was a come - ly young maid-en fair Who was
walk-ing out for to take the air She_ met a sai - lor all
on her way So I paid at - ten - tion I
paid at-ten - tion to hear what they_ did_ say.

It was a comely young maiden fair
Who was walking out for to take the air
She met a sailor all on her way
So I paid attention
I paid attention to hear what they did say.

Said William, 'Lady, why do you roam?
The night is coming and the day's near gone.'
She said, while tears from her eyes did fall
'It's my dark-eyed sailor
It's my dark-eyed sailor that's proved my downfall.'

'It's two long years since he left this land
He took a gold ring from off my hand
He broke it in two, one part's with me
And the other rolling
And the other rolling in the bottom of the sea.'

Said William, 'Drive him from your mind
Some other sailor as good you'll find
Love turns aside and soon doth grow
Like a winter's morning
Like a winter's morning when the land is covered with snow.'

Says Ada dear, 'I'll ne'er disdain
A tarr-ed sailor I'll treat the same
So drink his health, here's a piece of coin
But it's a dark-eyed sailor
It's a dark-eyed sailor still claims this heart of mine'

'For his coal-black eyes and his curly hair
His pleasing tongue doth my heart ensnare
Genteel he was, not a rake like you
To advise a maiden
To advise a maiden to slight the jacket blue.'

Said, 'Ada dear, this fond heart's in flame.'
She said, 'On me you shall play no game.'
She drew a dagger and then did cry
'For my dark-eyed sailor
For my dark-eyed sailor a maid I'll live and die.'

Then half the ring did young William show
She was distracted, mixt joy and woe
'O welcome William, I've land and gold
For my dark-eyed sailor
For my dark-eyed sailor so manly and bold.'

Then in a village down by the sea
They joined in wedlock and well do agree
So all maids be true when your love's away
For a cloudy morning
For a cloudy morning brings forth a pleasant day.

69

The Daughter in the Dungeon

It's— of a dam - sel so fair and hand-some

These lines been true so— I've been told

On the banks of Sha - ron a lof - ty man-sion

Her— par - ents claim - ed great stores of gold

Now her hair's been black as a— ra-ven's fea - ther

Her— form and fea - tures des - cribe who can

But— still 'twas fol - ly be - longs to na - ture

She— fell in love— with her ser - ving man.

It's of a damsel so fair and handsome
These lines been true so I've been told
On the banks of Sharon a lofty mansion
Her parents claimed great store of gold
Now her hair's been black as a raven's feather
Her form and features describe who can
But still 'twas folly belongs to nature
She fell in love with her serving man.

When these two true lovers was fondly talking
O the wicked father in anger flies
He swore two lovers he would have them parted
Her wicked father as he drew nigh
To build a dungeon was his intention
To part true lovers he continued a plan
He swore an oath, it was too vile to mention
He would part the fair one from her serving man.

To build a dungeon of bricks and mortar
A flight of steps it was underground
The food he gave her was bread and water
That was the only cheer for her was found
Young Edwin found out her habitation
'Twas well secured by an iron door
He swore in spite of all the nation
He would give her freedom and rest no more.

Then at his leisure he talked with pleasure
To gain releasement for Mary Anne
He found his object and winned his pleasure
She cried, 'My faithful young serving man.'
Now a suit of clothes he brought his Polly
'Twas a man's apparel for to disguise
'For your sweet sake I'll face your father
To see you here will him surprise.'

When the cruel father brought bread and water
Thus to her father she then began
'If I've disgraced my own dear father
I'll lay and die for my serving man.'
Three times a day he'd cruelly beat her
And thus to her father she then began
Young William entered, 'I've found your daughter
For the willing fault is your serving man.'

Soon he found his daughter vanished
Like a lion he did roar
He swored from Ireland he should be banished
'With my broadsword I'll spill your gore.'
'Agreed,' said Edwin, 'then at your leisure
Since I have freed her do all you can
Forgive your daughter, I'll die with pleasure
For the willing fault is your serving man.'

[When her father found him so tender-hearted
Then down he fell on the dungeon door
Saying that love should never be parted
Since love can enter an iron door]
Now they're joined and part no more
To roll in riches this couple can
Young Edwin and Mary they lives together
She'll have ever blessed her serving man.

70

Erin's Lovely Home

When I was young and in my prime, my age was twenty-
one   Then I be-came a   ser - vant un - to some gen-tle-
man   I___ served him true and   hon - est, and
that is___ ve-ry well known   But_ cru - el - ly he
ba - nished me from   E - rin's love - ly home.

When I was young and in my prime, my age was twenty-one
Then I became a servant unto some gentleman
I served him true and honest, and that is very well known
But cruelly he banished me from Erin's lovely home.

'Twas down in her uncle's garden all in the month of June
A-viewing of those pretty flowers all in their youthful bloom
She said, 'My dearest Johnny, if with me you will roam
We'll bid adieu to all our friends in Erin's lovely home.'

Now the very night I gived consent, along with her to go
From her father's dwelling place, which proved my overthrow
The night being bright by the moonlight, we both set off to roam
Thinking we had got safe away from Erin's lovely home.

But when we got to Belfast, 'twas by the break of day
My true love she got ready a passage for to pay
Five hundred pounds she did pay down, saying, 'That shall be your own
And never mourn the friends we've left in Erin's lovely home.'

But of our great misfortune I mean to let you hear
'Twas in a few hours or afterwards her father did appear
He marched me back to Omagh jail in the county of Tyrone
And then I was transported from Erin's lovely home.

But when I heard my sentence, it grieved my heart full sore
And parting from my sweetheart, it grieved me ten times more
I had seven lengths all on my chain and every link a year
Before I was returned again to the girl I loved so dear.

But when the rout came to the jail to take us all away
My true love she came on to me and thus to me did say
'Bear up your heart, don't be dismayed, for it's you I'll never disown
Until you do return again to Erin's lovely home.'

71

Fair Maid Walking in Her Garden

A fair maid walked all in the gar - den

A brisk young sai - lor she chanced to spy

He stepped up to her, think - ing to view__ her

He said, 'Fair maid__ can you fan - cy me?'

A fair maid walked all in the garden
A brisk young sailor she chanced to spy
He stepped up to her, thinking to view her
He said, 'Fair maid can you fancy me?'

'You seem to appear like some man of honour
A man of honour you seem to be
How can you impose on a poor young woman
Who is not fitted your servant to be?'

'I don't impose on a poor young woman
A great regard, love, I have for you
I mean to marry you, make you my lady
Servants I have to wait on you.'

'I have a sweetheart all of my own, sir
And seven long years he has been gone from me
And seven more I will wait for him
If he is alive he'll return to me.'

'If it's seven years since he has left you
Perhaps he is now dead or drowned?'
'And seven more I will wait for him
But if he is dead he is in glory crowned.'

He took his hands out of his bosom
His fingers being both long and small
Saying, 'I am your young, poor and single sailor
I am returned to marry you.'

'If you are my young, poor and single sailor
Show me the token of what you gave
Saying, "Here's the ring that was broke between us."'
Soon as she saw it then down she fell.

He took her up into his arms, love
He gave her kisses by one, two and three
Saying, 'I am your young, poor and single sailor
I am returned for to marry thee.'

So now this couple they are got married
In wedlock's bands they now both are joined
I hope they'll live and enjoy each other
And that's the end of my sailor song.

72

Polly Oliver's Rambles

One morn as Pol-ly O-li-ver lay dream-ing in bed

The thoughts of her true love came in - to her head

Nei-ther fa-ther nor mo-ther shall make me false prove

For I'll 'list for a sol-dier and fol-low my true love.

One morn as Polly Oliver lay dreaming in bed
The thoughts of her true love came into her head
Neither father nor mother shall make me false prove
For I'll 'list for a soldier and follow my true love.

Next morning Polly Oliver very early arose
And dressed herself up in a man's suit of clothes
With a waistcoat and jacket and a sword by her side
On her father's green dragon away she did ride.

On she rode till she came to the sign of the Crown
And called for a pint of strong ale that was brown
And the first that came in was a man from abroad
And the next that came in was Polly Oliver's true love.

'Oh good morning, kind captain, good morning,' said she
['Here's a letter from your true love Polly Oliver,' said she
He opened the letter and a guinea was found
'For you and your companion to drink your health all round.']

When supper was over she hung down her head
And called for a candle to light her to bed
The captain made this reply, 'There's a bed at my feet
And you may lie in it, countryman, if you please.'

['To lie with a captain is a dangerous thing]
I'm a new 'listed soldier to fight for my Queen
To fight for my Queen, my boys, on land or by sea
[Since you are my captain I'll be at your command.']

Next morning very early Polly Oliver arose
And dressed herself up in her own suit of clothes
[And downstairs she came from her chamber above
Saying, 'Here is Polly Oliver, your own true love.'

He at first was surprised, then laugh'd at the fun
And then they were married and all things were done]
If I lay with you the first time the fault was not mine
And I hope to use you better the very next time.

73

The Pretty Ploughboy

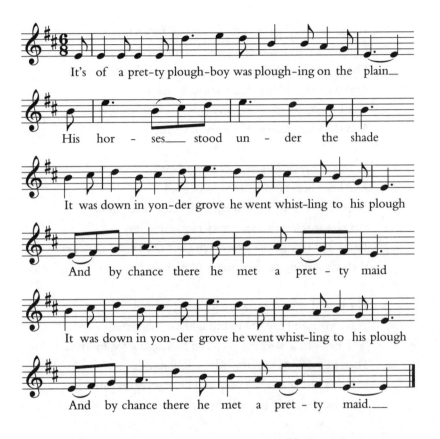

It's of a pret-ty plough-boy was plough-ing on the plain

His hor - ses stood un - der the shade

It was down in yon-der grove he went whist-ling to his plough

And by chance there he met a pret - ty maid

It was down in yon-der grove he went whist-ling to his plough

And by chance there he met a pret - ty maid.

It's of a pretty ploughboy was ploughing on the plain
His horses stood under the shade
It was down in yonder grove he went whistling to his plough
And by chance there he met a pretty maid
It was down in yonder grove he went whistling to his plough
And by chance there he met a pretty maid.

And this was his song as he walk-ed along
'I'm afraid, young maid, you're of some high degree

If I should fall in love and your parents they should know
The next thing they would send me off to sea
If I should fall in love and your parents they should know
The next thing they would send me off to sea.'

When her aged parents they came all for to know
This ploughboy was ploughing on the plain
The press gang they sent and they pressed her love away
And they sent him in the wars to be slain
The press gang they sent and they pressed her love away
And they sent him in the wars to be slain.

Then she dressed herself all in her best
And her pockets were lined with gold
To see her trudge the streets with the tears all in her eyes
She was seeking for her pretty ploughing boy
To see her trudge the streets with the tears all in her eyes
She was seeking for her pretty ploughing boy.

The first that she met was a jolly sailor bold
'Have you seen my pretty ploughboy?' she cried
'Yes, he's just across the deep and he's sailing for his fleet'
Then he said, 'My pretty lady, will you ride?
Yes, he's just across the deep and he's sailing for his fleet'
Then he said, 'My pretty lady, will you ride?'

She rode till she came to the ship her love was in
And unto the captain she complained
She said, 'I'm come to seek for my pretty ploughing boy
That was sent all in the wars to be slain'
She said, 'I'm come to seek for my pretty ploughing boy
That was sent all in the wars to be slain.'

Then five hundred bright guineas she fairly did pull out
And so gently she told them all over
And when she got her ploughboy all in her arms

She hugged him till she got him safe on shore
And when she got her ploughboy all in her arms
She hugged him till she got him safe on shore.

And when she got her ploughboy all in her arms
Where many a time he had been before
She set the bells to ring and so merrily she did sing
For she'd met with the lad whom she adored
She set the bells to ring and so merrily she did sing
For she'd met with the lad whom she adored.

Now it's God bless the day when these true lovers met
And their sorrows shall never be no more
For the last cruel war called so many lads away
And their true lovers they never saw them more
For the last cruel war called so many lads away
And their true lovers they never saw them more.

74

William and Mary

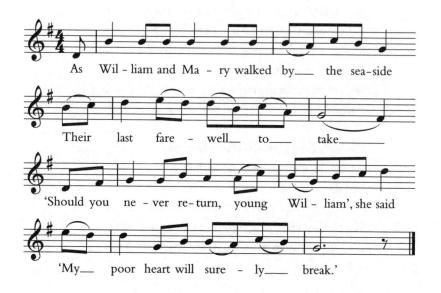

As Wil-liam and Ma-ry walked by__ the sea-side
Their last fare-well__ to__ take_____
'Should you ne-ver re-turn, young Wil-liam', she said
'My__ poor heart will sure-ly__ break.'

As William and Mary walked by the seaside
Their last farewell to take
'Should you never return, young William,' she said
'My poor heart will surely break.'

'Be not thus dismay'd,' young William he said
As he pressed the dear maid to his side
'Nor my absence don't mourn, for when I return
I will make little Mary my bride.'

Three years passed by without any news
When at last as she sat at her door
An old beggar came by, with a patch on his eye
Quite lame, and did pity implore.

Mary started and trembled; 'Oh tell me,' she cried
'All the money I've got I will give
Oh this I do ask you, if you will tell me true
Only say, does my dear William live?'

'Oh I love him so dear, so true and sincere
That no other I swear beside
If in riches he rolled and was clothed in gold
Should make little Mary his bride.'

'Forgive me, dear maid,' then William he said
'Your love it was only I tried
To church let's away, for ere the sun sets
I'll make little Mary my bride.'

75

William Taylor

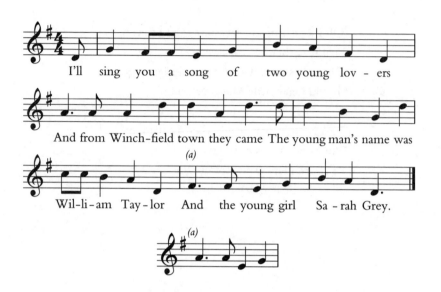

I'll sing you a song of two young lovers
And from Winchfield town they came
The young man's name was William Taylor
And the young girl Sarah Grey.

William 'listed for a soldier
To the army he did go
William 'listed for a soldier
Much to Sally's grief and woe.

Sally dressed in man's apparel
To the army she did go
Sally dressed in man's apparel
For to be with her Willie dear.

One day as they were exercising
She appeared among the rest
A silver locket flowed from her jacket
And it showed her milk-white breast.

The Captain he stepped up towards her
Asking her what brought her here
'Sir, I'm come for my own true lover
Who is fighting in this war.'

'If you want your own true lover
I pray to me then tell his name.'
'Sir, his name is William Taylor
And from Winchfield Town he came.'

'If you rise early tomorrow morning
Early at the break of day
There you'll see poor William Taylor
Walking out his lady gay.'

Sally rose early in the morning
Early at the break of day
There she saw her own true lover
Walking out his lady gay.

Sally called for a brace of pistols
Which was given at her command
There she shot poor William Taylor
With his bride at his right hand.

A few years after Sally got married
She became the Captain's wife
A few years after Sally got married
Now she lives a happy life.

V

My Parents Reared Me Tenderly ...
Lust, Infidelity and Bad Living

My Parents Reared Me Tenderly ...
Lust, Infidelity and Bad Living

In general in English folk song, marital infidelity is treated humorously: the drunken husband in 'Our Goodman' (No. 85) finds cumulative evidence of his wife's misdemeanours; in 'Marrowbones' (No. 82) the wife wants to get rid of her husband; the 'Cunning Cobbler' (No. 78) is found under the bed, the 'Molecatcher' (No. 83) traps the farmer, and so on. The cuckolded husband, 'wearing the horns', is a stock comic character in many forms of popular culture. But there are exceptions, especially in Child ballads like 'The Gipsy Laddie' (No. 81) and 'Little Musgrave' (Child 81, Roud 52), where the wife's adultery sets in train the tragic sequence of events related in the story.

Apart from this, the treatment of love and sex in the traditional repertoire varies so widely that it is foolish to attempt to portray folk song as primarily morally 'pure' or 'impure'. The tradition encompasses a broad spectrum from the risqué and mildly bawdy to the downright crude, and each individual will draw their own personal line in a different place, although it must be said that in a largely patriarchal society the songs are bound to reflect a male perspective on the whole. It must also be said that in this area context is all, and what is acceptable from one singer in a particular situation may not be in another. Taste and propriety are slippery concepts, and change over time.

We have come a long way from our Victorian and Edwardian predecessors who shied away from songs which nowadays do not register as bawdy at all, and a number of such cases are highlighted in the song notes. 'The Ball of Yarn' (No. 76), 'Bold Grenadier' (No. 77), 'The Nutting Girl' (No. 84) and 'Three Maidens to Milking Did Go' (No. 87), for example, all involve consensual sexual encounters of some sort, and each one made the earlier collectors uncomfortable, as did 'Young Sailor Cut Down' (No. 90), which in many versions makes clear that the main character is dying of venereal disease. But before we congratulate ourselves on our modern open-minded maturity, we should remember that we are just as uncomfortable publishing songs which include, for example, racist material, as our Edwardian ancestors were about the sexual.

There is a huge corpus of song which is concerned primarily and explicitly with sex, and it has been argued that one of the only areas in which true 'folk song' still exists is in the rugby clubs, barracks and other primarily male milieux. But we decided not to include any material which is explicit by today's standards, partly because this is a book for the general reader but also because much of that type of song is unacceptably misogynist and mostly puerile.

Many of the 'Jack on shore' type of song (see p. 5) feature a young buck who cares nothing for propriety and feels free to break hearts and steal maidenheads with impunity, and 'Young Ramble Away' (No. 89) here stands as an example of dozens of songs which feature young men whose attitudes and actions encapsulate what countless mothers have warned their daughters about since time immemorial.

76

The Ball of Yarn

Now it was on a sum-mer's day in the mer-ry month of May

(a) *(b)*

I was stroll-ing round my grand-fa - ther's farm

(c)

When a coun-try maid I spied and un-to her I cried

'May I wind up your lit - tle ball of yarn?'

(a) *(b)*

(b) *(b)*

(c)

Now it was on a summer's day in the merry month of May
I was strolling round my grandfather's farm
When a country maid I spied and unto her I cried
'May I wind up your little ball of yarn?'

'Oh no, kind sir,' said she, 'you're a stranger unto me
And you may love another, so be true.'
I said, 'My little miss you're the only one I want to kiss
And to wind up your little ball of yarn.'

So I took the country maid and I laid her in the shade
Not intending to do her any harm
And 'twas much to her surprise when I lay between her thighs
And wound up her little ball of yarn.

Now when the maid arose, after pulling up her clothes
She went to tell the people at the farm
So I slipped across the green, not intending to be seen
After winding up her little ball of yarn.

Now it was twelve months to the day, I was strolling down that way
Met a maid with a babe under her arm
I said, 'My little miss, sure I never thought of this
When I wound up your little ball of yarn.'

So all you country maids take warning from these days
And never go a-strolling round the farm
'Cause the blackbird and the thrush they still whistle in the bush
When he's winding up your little ball of yarn.

77

Bold Grenadier

As I was out walk-ing one fine sum-mer's day

I met a young cou-ple u-pon the high-way

One was a fe-male and a beau-ty was she

And the o-ther was a sol-dier in the Ar-til-ler-y

There was one was a fe-male and a beau-ty was she

And the o-ther was a sol-dier in the Ar-til-ler-y.

As I was out walking one fine summer's day
I met a young couple upon the highway
One was a female and a beauty was she
And the other was a soldier in the Artillery
There was one was a female and a beauty was she
And the other was a soldier in the Artillery.

Now the soldier and the female they strolled on together
They strolled side by side till they came to the river
And they sat themselves down by the side of the stream
For she loved to hear the water rattle and the nightingales sing
And they sat themselves down by the side of the stream
For she loved to hear the water rattle and the nightingales sing.

Then the soldier took the female with his arms round her middle
He out with his string and he up with his fiddle
And he played her a tune to the length of his string
For she loved to hear the water rattle and the nightingales sing
And he played her a tune to the length of his string
For she loved to hear the water rattle and the nightingales sing.

Said the soldier to the female, 'It's time to give o'er.'
Said the female to the soldier, 'Just play me one more
Just play one more tune to the length of your string
For I love to hear the water rattle and the nightingales sing
Just play one more tune to the length of your string
For I love to hear the water rattle and the nightingales sing.'

78

The Cunning Cobbler

A story, a story to you I will tell
Concerning of a butcher who in London did dwell
Now this butcher was possess-ed of a beautiful wife
And a cobbler he loved her dear as his life.

Chorus
Fol de-riddle-i-do, fol de-riddle-ay.

Now this butcher went to market to purchase an ox
And then the little cobbler as sly as any fox
Put on his Sunday clothing and a-courting he did go
To the jolly butcher's wife because he loved her so.

And as the little cobbler stepped in the butcher's shop
The butcher's wife knew what he meant and bid him to stop
He says, 'My little darling, have you got a job for me?'
She, smiling, said, 'I'll go upstairs and see.'

She went up to the bedroom and gave the snob a call
Saying, 'I've got a tidy job for you if you have brought your awl
And if you do it workmanlike some cash to you I'll pay.'
'I thank you,' said the cobbler and began to stitch away.

He hadn't been long at work before a knock came at the door
The cobbler crawled beneath the bed and lay upon the floor
'Lay still,' said the butcher's wife, 'what will my husband say?'
And then she let the policeman in along with her to play.

The butcher came from market and put them in a fright
The policeman scrambled down the stairs and soon was out of sight
The butcher's wife so nimbly did lock the bedroom door
And in her fright she quite forgot the cobbler on the floor.

And at night when the butcher lay down upon the bed
'There's something here is very hard,' unto his wife he said
His wife said, 'It's my rolling pin', the butcher could but laugh
Saying, 'How come you to roll your dough with a policeman's staff?'

And then he threw the truncheon underneath the bed
And broke the you-know-what to bits and cracked the cobbler's head
The cobbled called out, 'Murder!' Said the butcher, 'Who are you?'
'I am the little cobbler that mends the ladies' shoes.'

'If you are the little cobbler then come along with me
I'll pay you out for mending shoes before I've done with thee.'
So he locked him in the bullock's pen, the bull began to roar
And the butcher laughed to see the bull toss him o'er and o'er.

And early the next morning when the people were about
The butcher rubbed his face with blood and turned the cobbler out
He pinned a paper to his back and on it was the news
'The cobbler to the bedroom goes to mend the ladies' shoes.'

The people were all frightened, as home the cobbler ran
His coat and breeches being torn he looked an awful sight
His wife was amazed to see him so she shouted, 'O Lor!'
He says, 'My dear, I'll never go out stitching any more.'

79

The Devil and the Farmer's Wife

A man was walking the road one day
Right for lol for laddy fol ay
A man was walking the road one day
When he heard the Devil upon the highway.

Chorus
Singing right for the lol, tiddy fol ol
Right for lol, for laddy fol ay.

Said the Devil, 'My man, I have come for your wife.'
Right for lol for laddy fol ay
Said the Devil, 'My man, I have come for your wife
For I hear she's the plague and torment of your life.'

So the Devil he hoisted her up on his back
Right for lol for laddy fol ay
The Devil he hoisted her up on his back
And way off to hell with her straight did he pack.

There were three little devils a-playing at ball
Right for lol for laddy fol ay
There were three little devils a-playing at ball
She ups with her broom and she scatters them all.

There were three little devils all tied up in chains
Right for lol for laddy fol ay
There were three little devils all tied up in chains
She ups with a stick and she knocks out their brains.

So the Devil he hoisted her up on his back
Right for lol for laddy fol ay
So the Devil he hoisted her up on his back
And off to her old man so straight did he pack.

Said the Devil, 'My man, here's your wife back again.'
Right for lol for laddy fol ay
Said the Devil, 'My man, here's your wife back again
She wouldn't be kept, not even in hell.'

80

Flash Company

Once I loved a young girl as I loved my life

And to keep her in flash com-pa-ny has ru-ined my life

(a) Flash com-pa - ny, my boys, like a great ma-ny more If it

had-n't been for flash com-pa-ny I should ne-ver have been so poor.

Chorus
So it's take the yel-low hand-ker-chief in re-mem-brance of

me And tie it round your neck, love, in flash com-pa - ny

Flash com-pa - ny, my boys, like a great ma-ny more If it

had-n't been for flash com-pa-ny I should ne-ver have been so poor.

Once I loved a young girl as I loved my life
And to keep her in flash company has ruined my life
Flash company, my boys, like a great many more
If it hadn't been for flash company I should never have been so poor.

Chorus
So it's take the yellow handkerchief in remembrance of me
And tie it round your neck, love, in flash company
Flash company, my boys, like a great many more
If it hadn't been for flash company I should never have been so poor.

Once I had a colour as red as a rose
But now it's as pale as the lily that grows
Like a flower in the garden with all my colour gone
For you see what I'm coming to through loving that one.

Oh it's fiddling and dancing was all my delight
And to keep her in flash company has ruined my life
Flash company, my boys, like a great many more
If it hadn't been for flash company I should never have been so poor.

81

The Gipsy Laddie

O se - ven Gip - sies all in a gang

They were brisk and bon-ny O They went till they came to the

Earl Cas-tle's hall And there they sang so

sweet-ly O Sweet-ly O, sweet-ly O

They went till they came to the Earl Cas-tle's hall

And there they sang so sweet - ly O.

O seven Gipsies all in a gang
They were brisk and bonny O
They went till they came to the Earl Castle's hall
And there they sang so sweetly O
Sweetly O, sweetly O
They went till they came to the Earl Castle's hall
And there they sang so sweetly O.

They sang so sweet and so complete
Until downstairs came a lady O
And as soon as they saw her pretty, pretty face
They cast their gazes over her
Over her, etc.

She gave to them a bottle of wine
She gave to them some money O
She gave to them some far finer things
'Twas the gold rings off her fingers O
Fingers O, etc.

She pulled off her high-heeled boots
Put on her Highland plaidie O
'Last night I slept with my own wedded lord
And tonight with the Gipsies laddie O
Laddie O', etc.

When her dear lord came home that night
Enquiring for his lady O
The waiting maid made her reply
'She is gone with the black-hearted Gipsies O
Gipsies O', etc.

'So come saddle to me my best black horse
Come saddle it quite swiftly O
So I may search for my own wedded wife
Who is gone with the black-hearted Gipsies O
Gipsies O', etc.

He rode high and he rode low
He rode brisk and bonny O
He rode till he came to a far water-side
And there he found his lady O
Lady O, etc.

'What made you leave your house and land
What made you leave your money O
What made you leave your own wedded lord
To follow the black-hearted Gipsies O?
Gipsies O', etc.

'I know I've left my house and land
I know I've left my money O
But here I am and here I remain
So fare you well, my honey O
Honey O', etc.

Seven Gipsies all in a gang
They were brisk and bonny O
Tonight they are all condemned to die
For stealing Earl Castle's lady O
Lady O, etc.

82

Marrowbones

There was an old wo-man in York - shire In York-shire she did dwell___ She loved her old hus-band dear - ly And the lodg - er twice as well.

Chorus
Tid-dl-y whack fol did-dle um day Too-ral oo-ral day.___

There was an old woman in Yorkshire
In Yorkshire she did dwell
She loved her old husband dearly
And the lodger twice as well.

Chorus
Tiddly whack fol diddle um day
Tooral ooral day.

She sent for the doctor
And asked him oh so kind
Which was the narrowest way
To send her old husband blind.

He told her get some marrowbone
And scrape it fine and small
Rub it in the old man's eyes
Till he can't see at all.

The old man said, 'I'll go and drown myself
For I can't see one mite.'
The old woman said, 'Then I'll go with you
'Fraid you shouldn't go right.'

So arm in arm they went on
Till they came to the brim
The old man put his foot to one side
Popped the old woman in.

How the old woman did scream
And how the old woman did bawl
The old man said, 'I can't help you
For I can't see at all.'

She swam around and swam around
Until she came to the brim
The old man got the linen prop
And pushed her further in.

So now my song is ended
And I can't sing no more
My old woman is drownded
And I am safe on shore.

83

The Molecatcher

At Man-ches-ter ci-ty at the sign of the Plough

There lives an old mole-catch-er, I can't tell you how

He goes a-mole-catch-ing from mor-ning till night

While the jol-ly young farm-er goes playing with his wife.

Chorus

Sing-ing law-til-i-day, law-til-i-lit-tle-i, law-til-i-day.

At Manchester city at the sign of the Plough
There lives an old molecatcher, I can't tell you how
He goes a-molecatching from morning till night
While the jolly young farmer goes playing with his wife.

Chorus
Singing law-til-i-day, law-til-i-little-i, law-til-i-day.

The molecatcher jealous of the very same thing
So he hides in the bakehouse and saw him come in
And when that young farmer got over the stile
It caused the molecatcher to laugh and to smile.

He knocked at the door and thus he did say
'Pray where is your husband, good woman, I say?'
'He's gone a-molecatching, you need not fear.'
But little did she think the molecatcher was near.

She went upstairs, he followed the sign
And the molecatcher followed them closely behind
And when that young farmer was in the midst of his sport
The molecatcher caught him quite fast by his coat.

He clapped his hands and laughed at the sight
Saying, 'This is the finest mole I've catched in my life
I'll make you pay well for ploughing my ground
And the money it shall be no less than ten pound.'

'Very well,' said the farmer, 'the money I don't mind
For it only costs me about twopence a time.'
So come, all you young farmer chaps, mind what you're at
And never get caught in a molecatcher's trap.

84

The Nutting Girl

'Twas of a brisk young damsel, she liv-ed down in Kent
She arose one summer's morning and she a-nutting went.

Chorus
So a-nutting we will go, my boys
And a-nutting we will go

With a blue cockade all in our hats
We'll cut a gallant show.

'Twas of a brisk young farmer was ploughing of his land
He called to his horses and he bid them for to stand.

He sat himself down on his plough, a song for to begin
His voice was so melodious that it made the valleys ring.

Now John he sung so sweet-i-ly he charmed her as she stood
She had no longer power in that lonely wood to stay
But what few nuts she had, poor girl, she threw them all away.

She went unto her Johnny as he sat on the plough
She says, 'Young man I feels myself, for I feels I can't tell how.'

He says, 'My pretty damsel, come sit you down and hear
I'll keep you out of danger and I'll keep you out of fear.'

Now Johnny left his horses, and likewise left his plough
He took her in some shady dell his courage for to show.

He put his arms all round her and gently laid her down
'O John,' said she, 'I think I see the world go round and round.'

Now John returned to his horses all for to finish his song
He says, 'My pretty fair maid, your mother will think you long.'

But as they tripped along the plain, upon his breast did lean
'Oh John,' said she, 'I long to see the world go round again.'

Come all you pretty damsels, a warning take by me
If you should go a-nutting, I pray be home in time
For if you stay a little too long, to hear the ploughman sing
O you will have a little baby to nurse all in the spring.

85

Our Goodman

As— I came home so late last night And ve-ry late was I

I went in-to the sta-ble An-o-ther man's horse there lie

'Whose horse is this, whose horse is this Whose horse is this, my dear?'

'It's not a horse, but a milk-ing cow.' My gol-ly, did-n't that seem

queer I've—— tra-velled, I've——

(a)

tra-velled Ten thou-sand miles or more

But a milk-ing cow with a sad-dle on I ne-ver saw be-fore.

(a)

As I came home so late last night
And very late was I
I went into the stable
Another man's horse there lie
'Whose horse is this, whose horse is this
Whose horse is this, my dear?'
'It's not a horse, but a milking cow.'
My golly, didn't that seem queer
I've travelled, I've travelled
Ten thousand miles or more
But a milking cow with a saddle on
I never saw before.

As I came home so late last night
And very late was I
And on the table there
Another man's hat there lie
'Whose hat is this, whose hat is this
Whose hat is this, my dear?'
'It's not a hat, but a butter tub.'
My golly, didn't that seem queer
I've travelled, I've travelled
Ten thousand miles or more
But a butter tub with a brim all round
I never saw before.

As I came home so late last night
And very late was I
And underneath the table
Another man's boots there lie
'Whose boots are these, whose boots are these
Whose boots are these, my dear?'
'They are not boots, but flowerpots.'
My golly, didn't that seem queer
I've travelled, I've travelled
Ten thousand miles or more

But flowerpots with elastic sides
I never saw before.

As I came home so late last night
And very late was I
I went upstairs to get in bed
And another man there lie
'What man is this, what man is this
What man is this, my dear?'
'It's not a man, but a newborn babe.'
My golly, didn't that seem queer
I've travelled, I've travelled
Ten thousand miles or more
But a newborn babe with whiskers on
I never saw before.

86

Spencer the Rover

These words were com - pos-ed by Spen-cer the Ro-ver

Who trav -'led__ most parts of Great Bri - tain and Wales

He be-ing re - du-ced, which caused great con - fu-sion

And that is__ the__ rea-son a - ro-ving he went.

These words were compos-ed by Spencer the Rover
Who travell-ed most parts of Great Britain and Wales
He being reduc-ed, which caused great confusion
And that is the reason a-roving he went.

Through Yorkshire's broad valleys oh he travel'd for some years
Till being weary of rambling he sat down to rest
At the foot of yon mountain there runs a clear fountain
Of bread and cold water himself did refresh.

It tasted more sweeter than the gold he had wasted
Or the friends which for ever he'd left far away
But the thoughts of his children ever yearning for their father
Brought tears in his eyes and caused him to lament.

His children came round him with their sweet prattling stories
With their sweet prattling stories which drive care away
They were united together, like the birds all of a feather
Like bees in a hive, contented they would be.

So now I am arrived at me homestead so splendid
With roses and woodbines that hang round my door
I'm as happy as those that's got thousands
Contented I'll be and go rambling no more.

87

Three Maidens to Milking Did Go

Three mai - dens   to milk - ing did   go

Three   mai - dens   to milk - ing   did   go

And the wind it did blow high and the wind it did blow low—

And   it   tossed their milk - ing pails   to   and   fro.

Three maidens to milking did go
Three maidens to milking did go
And the wind it did blow high and the wind it did blow low
And it tossed their milking pails to and fro.

I met with a man I knew well
And I kindly asked of him if he had got any skills
For to catch me a small bird or two.

Oh yes I've got some excellent good skills
Now come along with me down by yonder shady tree
I'll catch thee a small bird or two.

He tapp-ed at the bush and the little birds flew out
Right into her lily-white breast.

Here's luck to the blackbird and thrush
Here's luck to the blackbird and thrush
It's a bird of one feather and we'll all flock together
Let the people say little or much.

Here's luck to the jolly dragoon
Here's luck to the jolly dragoon
We'll ramble all the day and at night we'll spend our play
And go home by the light of the moon.

88

The Wild Rover

I've been a wild ro-ver for ma-ny long year

I've spent all my mo-ney on wine, ale and beer

Now to give up all ro-ving, put my mo-ney in store

And ne'er will I play the wild ro-ver no more.

Chorus

Nay, no ne - ver, ne -ver no more

Ne'er will I play the wild ro-ver no more.

I've been a wild rover for many long year
I've spent all my money on wine, ale and beer
Now to give up all roving, put my money in store
And ne'er will I play the wild rover no more.

Chorus
Nay, no never, never no more
Ne'er will I play the wild rover no more.

I went into an alehouse where I used to frequent
And told the landlady my money was all spent
I called for a pint but she says to me, 'Nay
Such customer as you I can meet every day.'

I put my hand in my pocket, drew handfuls of gold
And on the round table it glittered and rolled
'Now here's my best brandies, my whiskey and all.'
'Begone, landlady, I'll have none at all.'

Now I'll go home to my parents, tell them what I've done
And ask to give pardon to a prodigal son
And if they forgive me, which they've done times before
Then ne'er will I play the wild rover no more.

89

Young Ramble Away

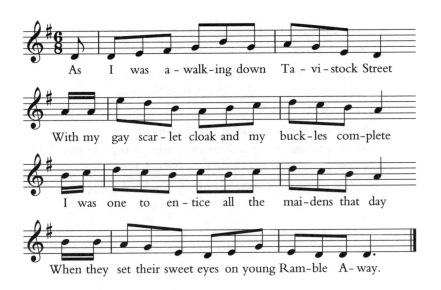

As I was a-walk-ing down Ta-vi-stock Street

With my gay scar-let cloak and my buck-les com-plete

I was one to en-tice all the mai-dens that day

When they set their sweet eyes on young Ram-ble A-way.

As I was a-walking down Tavistock Street
With my gay scarlet cloak and my buckles complete
I was one to entice all the maidens that day
When they set their sweet eyes on young Ramble Away.

As I was walking through Tavistock Fair
I saw my bright Nancy a-combing her hair
With my cap and my ribbons so bright and so gay
She could not but look at young Ramble Away.

As I was a-walking that night in the dark
I stood at her door and I shone as her spark
I whistled, she looked from her window to say
'Are you the young lad they call Ramble Away?'

When twenty-four weeks they were over and past
This fair pretty maiden did sicken at last
Her gown would not meet nor her apron strings stay
And 'twas all through the love of young Ramble Away.

'My dad and my mammy from home they are gone
But when they return I will sing them a song
I'll sing them a song and I'll have them to say
"Alas! you've been playing with Ramble Away."'

So come pretty maidens, wherever you be
With courting young fellows don't make yourselves free
For if you should be so you'll rue the sad day
When you met with the like of my Ramble Away.

90

Young Sailor Cut Down

One day as I strolled down by the Royal Al-bi-on

Dark was the mor-ning and cold was the day____

But who should I spy__ but one of my ship-mates

He was draped in a blan-ket far cold-er than clay.

One day as I strolled down by the Royal Albion
Dark was the morning and cold was the day
But who should I spy but one of my shipmates
He was draped in a blanket far colder than clay.

He called for a candle to light him to bed
Likewise a pillow to wrap round his head
For his poor head was aching, his poor heart was breaking
For he was a sailor cut down in his prime.

We'll beat the drums o'er him, we'll play the pipes merrily
We'll play the dead march as we carry him along
Take him to the churchyard and fire three volleys o'er him
For he was a sailor cut down in his prime.

His poor aged father, his dear old mother
Oftimes have told him about his fast life
Along with those flash girls his money he squandered
Along with those flash girls he took his delight.

But now he is dead and laid in his coffin
Six jolly sailor boys walk by his side
And each of them carrying a bunch of white roses
That no one might smell him as we pass them by.

At the top of the street you will see two girls standing
One to the other doth whisper and say
'Here comes the young sailor whose money we've squandered
Here comes the young sailor cut down in his prime.'

On top of the tombstone you will see these words written
'All you young fellows take a warning by me
And never go courting the girls of the city
For the girls of the city was the ruining of me.'

So we'll beat the drums o'er him, we'll play the pipes merrily
We'll play the dead march as we carry him along
Take him to the churchyard and fire three volleys o'er him
For he was a sailor cut down in his prime.

VI

I Can Guide a Plough …
Rural Life and Occupations

I Can Guide a Plough …
Rural Life and Occupations

The pastoral song is fairly frequent, especially in the southern counties of England. Its chief theme is the joys of country life. Such are the songs in which the ploughman is the chief personage, and one who glories in his calling … Then there are the sheep-shearing songs … Harvest home songs too are not lacking.

Frank Kidson and Mary Neal,
English Folk–Song and Dance (1915), pp. 60–61

It is not surprising that country life and rural affairs feature so strongly in the folk-song repertoire. Not only did many of the songs originate in a time when the majority of the population lived in the countryside (i.e. before 1850), but the Victorian and Edwardian enthusiasts worked mainly in rural areas, and indeed they often used 'country song' as a synonym for 'folk song'. But many of the songs actually originated in towns, written either for the predominately urban broadside trade or as pastoral ditties for pleasure gardens and other commercial entertainment venues, and the view of country life portrayed in folk song is not, on the whole, a realistic one.

Sociologists dubbed the twentieth-century farm employee 'the deferential worker', and earlier generations (notwithstanding occasional outbursts such as the 'Captain Swing' riots in the 1830s) appear to have been similarly unprotesting. There are exceptions, but the most well-known folk songs about farmwork ('All Jolly Fellows Who Follow the Plough', No. 91, and 'The Farmer's Boy', No. 94) are not critical or complaining. In England, there is little evidence of the 'bothy ballad' type of song which occurs frequently in Scottish tradition – songs that feature scathing comments on working conditions in general and even on specific farms and farmers. Pride in skilled work and contentment with one's lot is the more usual tone in England. It is perhaps curious that even parodies of the rural worker like 'Buttercup Joe' (No. 93) were adopted so enthusiastically by country folk, but they certainly were.

Harvest homes and other rural gatherings tied to the rhythms of the agricultural year were also noted as places where singing was expected and encouraged, and a high proportion of the songs performed in these contexts championed and celebrated rural life.

There is nothing particularly rural about drinking songs, of which there are many, although they may have had a particular resonance if sung in places where the barley or the hops were actually grown.

91

All Jolly Fellows Who Follow the Plough

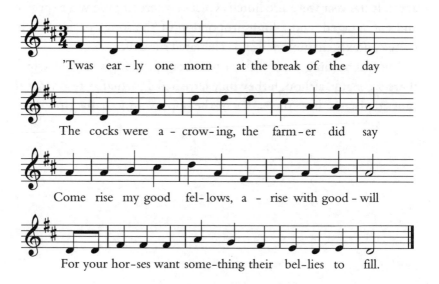

'Twas ear-ly one morn at the break of the day

The cocks were a - crow-ing, the farm-er did say

Come rise my good fel-lows, a - rise with good-will

For your hor-ses want some-thing their bel-lies to fill.

'Twas early one morn at the break of the day
The cocks were a-crowing, the farmer did say
Come rise my good fellows, arise with goodwill
For your horses want something their bellies to fill.

When four o'clock comes then up we do rise
And into the stable, boys, merrily flies
With a-rubbing and a-scrubbing our horses I'll vow
We're all jolly fellows who follow the plough.

When five o'clock comes at breakfast we meet
With beef, pork and bread, boys, so merrily eat
With a piece in our pockets I'll swear and I'll vow
We're all jolly fellows who follow the plough.

When six o'clock comes then out we do go
To see which of us a straight furrow could hold
In all kinds of weather I'll swear and I'll vow
We're all jolly fellows who follow the plough.

Our master came to us and this he did say
'What have you been doing, boys, all this long day?
You haven't ploughed an acre, I'll swear and I'll vow
You're all idle fellows who follow the plough.'

I turned myself round and made this reply
'Yes we have ploughed an acre, you're telling a lie
We have ploughed an acre, I'll swear and I'll vow
We're all jolly fellows who follow the plough.'

Our master turned round and laughed at the joke
'It's half past two o'clock, boys, it's time to unyoke
Unharness your horses and scrub them down well
And I'll give you a jug of the very best ale.'

So come all ye plough lads, where'er you may be
Never fear your master, take this advice from me
No, never fear your master, I'll swear and I'll vow
We're all jolly fellows who follow the plough.

92

The Barley Mow

Now   jol-ly good luck to the pint   pot   Luck to the bar-ley

mow   Jol-ly good luck to the pint pot Good luck to the bar-ley

mow___   Oh   the   pint pot, half pint, quar-ter pot,

gill pot, half gill, quar-ter gill   Fetch in   a   lit-tle drop

more Here's good luck, good   luck to the bar-ley mow.

Repeat these two bars, adapting rhythm as necessary, to accomodate text in subsequent verses.

Now jolly good luck to the pint pot
Luck to the barley mow
Jolly good luck to the pint pot
Good luck to the barley mow
Oh the pint pot, half pint, gill pot, half gill, quarter gill
Fetch in a little drop more
Here's good luck, good luck to the barley mow.

Now jolly good luck to the quart pot
Luck to the barley mow
Jolly good luck to the quart pot

Good luck to the barley mow
Oh the quart pot, pint pot, half pint, gill pot, half gill, quarter gill
Fetch in a little drop more
Here's good luck, good luck, to the barley mow.

Now jolly good luck to the half a gallon
Luck to the barley mow
Jolly good luck to the half a gallon
Good luck to the barley mow
Oh the half a gallon, quart pot, pint pot, half pint, gill pot, half
   gill, quarter gill
Fetch in a little drop more
Here's good luck, good luck, to the barley mow.

... the gallon

... the half a bushel

... the bushel

... the half a barrel

... the barrel

... the barmaid

... the landlady

... the landlord

... the brewery

... all this company

93
Buttercup Joe

Now I be a true-bred coun-try chap, me

fa-ther comes from Fare-ham_ Me mo-ther got some

more like I an' her well knows how to rare 'em

Some peo-ple calls I ba-con-fat and o-thers tur-nip 'ead

But I can prove I bain't no calf al-though I'm coun-try bred.

Chorus
For I can guide a plough and milk a cow And

I can rip or mow I'm as fresh as a dai-sy that

grows in the fields An' 'em calls I But-ter-cup Joe.

(a) Stanza 2

Now I be a true-bred country chap, me father comes from Fareham
Me mother got some more like I an' her well knows how to rare [rear] 'em
Some people calls I bacon-fat and others turnip 'ead
But I can prove I bain't no calf although I'm country bred.

Chorus
For I can guide a plough and milk a cow
And I can rip or mow
I'm as fresh as a daisy that grows in the fields
An' 'em calls I Buttercup Joe.

Now have you seen my young 'ooman, 'em calls her our Mary
Her works as busy as a bumblebee down in Sir Johns's dairy
And don't her make some dumplings nice, by joves I means to try 'em
An' ax her how her'd like to wed a country chap like I am.

Some folk they do like haymaking, there's others they likes mowin'
But of all the jobs that I loves best, then give I turnip hoein'
And don't I hopes when I gets wed to my old Mary Ann
I'll work for her and try me best, to please her all I can.

94

The Farmer's Boy

The sun went down beyond yon hill, across yon dreary moor
Weary and lame a boy there came up to the farmer's door
'Can you tell me if any there be that will give me employ
For to plough and sow, for to reap and mow, and be a farmer's boy
And be a farmer's boy?'

'My father's dead and my mother's left with her five children small
And what is worse for my mother still, I'm the oldest of them all
Though little I am I fear no work, if you'll give me employ

For to plough and sow, for to reap and mow, and be a farmer's boy
And be a farmer's boy.'

'And if that you won't me employ, one favour I've to ask
Will you shelter me till the break of day from this cold winter's blast?
At the break of day I'll trudge away, elsewhere to seek employ
For to plough and sow, for to reap and mow, and be a farmer's boy
And be a farmer's boy.'

The farmer said, 'I'll try the lad, no further let him seek.'
'Oh yes, dear father,' the daughter said, while tears ran down her cheek
'For them that will work it's hard to want and wander for employ
For to plough and sow, for to reap and mow, and be a farmer's boy
And be a farmer's boy.'

At length the boy became a man, the good old farmer died
He left the lad the farm he had and his daughter to be his bride
And now that lad a farmer is, and he smiles and thinks with joy
Of the lucky, lucky day he came that way, to be a farmer's boy
To be a farmer's boy.

95

Fathom the Bowl

Come all you old min-strels wher - ev - er you be

With com-rades u - ni - ted in sweet har-mo - ny

While the clear crys-tal foun-tain through Eng-land shall roll

Give me the punch la - dle, I'll fa-thom the bowl

O give me the punch la - dle, I'll fa-thom the bowl.

Come all you old minstrels wherever you be
With comrades united in sweet harmony
While the clear crystal fountain through England shall roll
Give me the punch ladle, I'll fathom the bowl
O give me the punch ladle, I'll fathom the bowl.

Let nothing but harmony reign in our breast
Let comrade with comrade be ever at rest
[Let's lift up our glasses, good cheer is our goal]
Give me the punch ladle, I'll fathom the bowl
O give me the punch ladle, I'll fathom the bowl.

From France cometh brandy, Jamaica gives rum
Sweet oranges, lemons from Portugal come
Of beer and good cider we'll also take toll
Give me the punch ladle, I'll fathom the bowl
O give me the punch ladle, I'll fathom the bowl.

Our brothers lie drowned in the depths of the sea
Cold stones for their pillows, what matters to we?
We'll drink to their healths and repose to each soul
Give me the punch ladle, I'll fathom the bowl
O give me the punch ladle, I'll fathom the bowl.

Our wives they may bluster as much as they please
Let 'em scold, let 'em grumble, we'll sit at our ease
[They may scold and grumble till they're black as the coal]
Give me the punch ladle, I'll fathom the bowl
O give me the punch ladle, I'll fathom the bowl.

Green Brooms

'Twas of a broom-dash-er who lived in the west

And his trade it was cut-ting of brooms, green brooms

'Twas of a broom-dash-er who lived in the west

And his trade it was cut-ting of brooms

He had a son Jack, an i-dle boy too

And he would lay in bed till 'twas noon, quite noon____

And he would lay in bed till 'twas noon.____

'Twas of a broomdasher who lived in the west
And his trade it was cutting of brooms, green brooms
'Twas of a broomdasher who lived in the west
And his trade it was cutting of brooms
He had a son Jack, an idle boy too
And he would lay in bed till 'twas noon, quite noon
And he would lay in bed till 'twas noon.

So the old man he rose and downstairs he goes
And he swore he would fire Jack's room, room room
The old man he rose and downstairs he goes
And he swore he would fire Jack's room
If he didn't arise and sharp up his knives
And go to the wood and cut brooms, green brooms
And go to the wood and cut brooms.

So Jack he arose and he put on his clothes
And he went to the wood to cut brooms, green brooms
So Jack he arose and put on his clothes
And he went to the wood to cut brooms
He vowed and he swore he'd do it no more
That he'd go to the wood to cut brooms, green brooms
He'd go to the wood and cut brooms.

So Jack trudg-ed on to where he's not known
Till he came to a castle of fame, fame fame
So Jack trudg-ed on to where he's not known
Till he came to a castle of fame
And there he did bawl as loud as could call
'Kind lady, do you want any brooms, green brooms?
Kind lady, do you want any brooms?'

The lady was there, and hearing Jack bawl
Said, 'Call the young man with his brooms, brooms brooms.'
The lady was there, and hearing Jack bawl
Said, 'Call the young man with his brooms.'

So Jack trudg-ed on to where he's not known
Till he came to the lady's fair room, room room
Till he came to the lady's fair room.

She said, 'You young blade, why not leave off your trade
And marry a lady in bloom, full bloom.'
She said, 'You young blade, why not leave off your trade
And marry a lady in bloom.'
So Jack gave his consent and to the church went
And he married the lady in bloom, full bloom
And he's married that lady in full bloom.

97

John Barleycorn

There were three men came from the west Their for-tunes for to try And these three men made a sol-emn vow John Bar - ley - corn should die.

There were three men came from the west
Their fortunes for to try
And these three men made a solemn vow
John Barleycorn should die.

So they ploughed and sowed and harrowed him in
Throwed clats upon his head
And these three men made a solemn vow
John Barleycorn was dead.

Then they let him lay for a long time
Till rain from heaven did fall
And little Sir John sprang up his head
And he amazed them all.

Then they let him stand for a long time
And he grew both pale and wan
And little Sir John grew with a long beard
And so he became a man.

They hired men with scythes so sharp
To cut him off at the knee
And the loader he served him worse than that
For he served him most barbarously.

Then they dragged him round and round the field
Till they came unto a barn
And there they made a solemn mow
Of poor John Barleycorn.

They hired men with crab-tree sticks
They cut him skin from bone
And the miller he served him worse than that
For he ground him between two stones.

Now here's little Sir John in a nut-brown bowl
And brandy in a glass
And here's little Sir John in a nut-brown bowl
He'll slay the strongest man at last.

For the huntsman he can't hunt the fox
Nor loudly blow his horn
Nor the tinker he can't mend kettles or pots
Without little Lord Barleycorn.

98

The Jolly Waggoner

When first I went a-wag-gon-ing, a-wag-gon-ing did go I broke my par-ents' hearts with sor-row, grief and woe For ma-ny were the hard-ships that we had to un-der-go— Sing-ing whoa, my lads, drive on, my lads, drive on, my lads, drive on For there's

Slows - - - - - - - - - - - - - - - -

none can drive a wag-gon when the hor-ses will not go.

When first I went a-waggoning, a-waggoning did go
I broke my parents' hearts with sorrow, grief and woe
For many were the hardships that we had to undergo
Singing whoa, my lads, drive on, my lads, drive on, my lads, drive on
For there's none can drive a waggon when the horses will not go.

On a cold and frosty morning I was wet through to my skin
And there we had to wander till we reached to yonder inn
There we sat a-talking to the landlord and his wife
Singing whoa, my lads, drive on, my lads, drive on, my lads, drive on
For there's none can drive a waggon when the horses will not go.

O the summertime is coming, what pleasures shall I see
The blackbird and the throstle sing in every greenwood tree
And every lass shall have a lad and sit her on his knee
Singing whoa, my lads, drive on, my lads, drive on, my lads, drive on
For there's none can drive a waggon when the horses will not go.

99

The Lark in the Morning

The lark in the morning she rises from her nest
She mounts into the air with the dew on her breast
'Twas down in yonder meadow I carelessly did stray
Oh there's no one like the ploughboy in the merry month of May.

When his day's work is over and then what will he do
He'll fly into the country, his wake to go
And with his pretty sweetheart he'll whistle and he'll sing
And at night he'll return to his own home again.

And when he returns from his wake unto the town
The meadows they are mowed and the grass it is cut down
The nightingale she whistles upon the hawthorn spray
And the moon is a-shining upon the new-mown hay.

So here's luck to the ploughboys wherever they may be
They'll take a winsome lass to sit on their knee
And with a jug of beer, boys, they'll whistle and they'll sing
For the ploughboy is as happy as a prince or a king.

100

The Miller's Three Sons

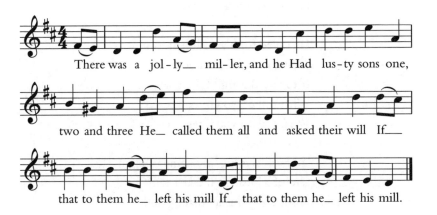

There was a jol-ly— mil-ler, and he Had lus-ty sons one,
two and three He— called them all and asked their will If—
that to them he— left his mill If— that to them he— left his mill.

There was a jolly miller and he
Had lusty sons one, two and three
He called them all and asked their will
If that to them he left his mill
If that to them he left his mill.

He called first to his eldest son
Saying, 'My life is almost run
If I to you this mill do make
What toll do you intend to take
What toll do you intend to take?'

'Father,' said he, 'my name is Jack
Out of a bushel I'll have a peck
From every bushel that I grind
That I may a good living find
That I may a good living find.'

'Thou art a fool!' the old man said
'Thou has not well learned thy trade
This mill to thee I ne'er will give
For by such toll no man can live
For by such toll no man can live.'

He called for his middlemost son
Saying, 'My life is almost run
If to you this mill I do make
What toll do you intend to take
What toll do you intend to take?'

'Father,' says he, 'my name is Ralph
Out of a bushel I'll take a half
From every bushel that I grind
That I may a good living find
That I may a good living find.'

'Thou art a fool,' the old man said
'Thou has not well learned thy trade
The mill to you I ne'er will give
For by such toll no man can live
For by such toll no man can live.'

He called for his youngest son
Saying, 'My life is almost run
If I to you this mill do make
What toll do you intend to take
What toll do you intend to take?'

'Father,' said he, 'I'm your only boy
For taking toll is all my joy
Before I will a good living lack
I'll take it all and forswear the sack
I'll take it all and forswear the sack.'

'Thou art the boy,' the old man said
'For thou hast right well learned thy trade
This mill to thee I give,' he cried
And then turned up his toes and died
And then turned up his toes and died.

101

The Painful Plough

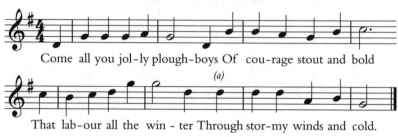

Come all you jol-ly plough-boys Of cou-rage stout and bold

(a)

That lab-our all the win - ter Through stor-my winds and cold.

(a)

Come all you jolly ploughboys
Of courage stout and bold
That labour all the winter
Through stormy winds and cold.

'Hold, ploughman,' says the gardener
'Count not your trade with ours
But walk you through the garden
And view the various flowers.'

'Likewise those curious borders
And pleasant walks renew
There's no such piece of pleasure
Performed by the plough.'

'Hold, gardener,' says the ploughman
'No calling I despise
For each man for a living
Upon his trade relies.'

'For Adam was a ploughman
When ploughing did begin
The next that did succeed him
Was Cain his eldest son.'

'Some of the generations
The calling to pursue
That bread might not be wanted
For needing of the plough.'

'For Samson was a strong man
And Solomon was wise
Alexander for the conquering
Was all that he did prize.'

'King David he was valiant
And many a man he slew
But none of these bold heroes
Can live without the plough.'

'Now all these wealthy merchants
Will plough the raging seas
That bring home foreign treasures
For those that live at ease.'

'And fine silks from the Indies
With flour and spices too
They all are brought to England
By virtue of the plough.'

I hope none are offended
At me for singing this
It never was intended
For to be taken amiss.

If it were not for the ploughboys
Both rich and poor might rue
For we are all depending
Upon the painful plough.

102

Twankydillo

Here's a health to the jol-ly black-smith, the best of all fel-lows

The man at his an-vil while the boy blows the bel-lows

For it makes our bright ham-mer to rise and to— fall

There's the old Cole and the young Cole and the old Cole of— all

Chorus

Twan - ky - dil - lo, Twan - ky - dil - lo, dil - lo,

dil - lo, dil - lo, dil - lo, dil - lo—— And a roar - ing pair of

bag - pipes made of a green wil - low.—

Here's a health to the jolly blacksmith, the best of all fellows
The man at his anvil while the boy blows the bellows
For it makes our bright hammer to rise and to fall
There's the old Cole and the young Cole and the old Cole of all
Twankydillo, Twankydillo, dillo, dillo, dillo, dillo, dillo
And a roaring pair of bagpipes made of a green willow.

Here's a health to that pretty girl, the one I love best
For she carries the fire within her own breast
For it makes my bright hammer to rise and to fall
There's the old Cole and the young Cole and the old Cole of all
Twankydillo, etc.

If a gentleman calls, his horse for to shoe
We make no deliance in one pot or two
For it makes our bright hammers to rise and to fall
There's the old Cole and the young Cole and the old Cole of all
Twankydillo, etc.

Here's a health to our queen, likewise all her men
And all the Royal Family that ever was seen
For it makes our bright hammers to rise and to fall
There's the old Cole and the young Cole and the old Cole of all
Twankydillo, etc.

VII

The Sons of Harmony …
Animals and Nonsense

The Sons of Harmony ...
Animals and Nonsense

Some of our best-known and oldest folk songs are apparently non-sensical or rely on the effect of a cumulative text for their impact, and much of their wide distribution stems from the fact that they have featured strongly in the 'nursery tradition' and have been taught to, and enthusiastically sung by, countless generations of English children. Nevertheless, their lively tunes and evocative words have also contributed to their staying power within the adult folk repertoire, and in some cases this is made possible by the availability of different sets of words for different audiences (for example, 'Old King Cole', No. 112) .

As noted in the individual song notes, nonsense, cumulative and hyperbolic songs such as 'The Derby Ram' (No. 106), 'The Herring's Head' (No. 109) and 'The Cutty Wren' (Roud 236) have often attracted fanciful explanations of origins in the religious rituals of our pagan past, but there is not the slightest evidence that this is the case, although no simple origin theory can be produced in its place. The first fallacy lies in expecting one single explanation to cover all such songs, and we should be ready to accept a more piecemeal explanation. 'The Herring's Head', for example, may have been originally a question-and-answer drinking game, while cumulative songs such as 'The Twelve Days of Christmas' (Roud 68) were certainly party games which tested the participants' memories, and 'The Wonderful Crocodile' (Roud 886) is simply an extended joke. Regardless of origin, it is the love of nonsense and hyperbole for its own sake, and the satisfaction of rhythm and rhyme, which are a sufficient explanation for the popularity of this type of song.

Songs about animals are not always nonsensical, of course, and 'Creeping Jane' (No. 105) and 'The Keeper' (No. 111) are here as brief examples of songs about sport, although the latter simply uses the chase as a metaphor for sex. There are also many traditional songs about hunting, which have been squeezed out from lack of space. The most widely known of these tend to be generic 'joys of the chase' songs, but there were (and still are) vigorous song traditions in some areas which remember particular local events or characters.

There are also plenty of songs about foolish people. In many cases these coalesce into pieces which rely on ethnic or regional stereotypes which are endemic to British society, and which play their small part in bolstering and legitimating traditional discrimination and persecution. But 'Bryan O'Lynn' (No. 103) and 'The Foolish Boy' (No. 107) are examples of a more generic silly person who has been a stock character in popular literature for centuries.

103
Bryan O'Lynn

O Brian O'Flynn had no trousers to wear
So he bought him a sheepskin and made him a pair
With the skinny side out and the furry side in
'Why, sure it'll do,' says Brian O'Flynn.

Chorus
'It'll do, do, do, do'
Says Brian O'Flynn, 'It'll do.'

O Brian O'Flynn had no shirt to his back
So he went to his neighbours to borrow a sack
He puckered the meal bags under his chin
'They'll take it for ruffles,' says Brian O'Flynn.

O Brian O'Flynn had no coat to put on
So he borrowed a goat skin to make him a one
He planted the horns right under his chin
'They'll answer for pistols,' says Brian O'Flynn.

O Brian O'Flynn had no watch for to wear
So he bought him a turnip and scooped it out fair
And he put him a cricket right under the skin
'They'll think it's a-ticking,' says Brian O'Flynn.

O Brian O'Flynn and his wife and wife's mother
They all went to sleep in the same bed together
The bed it was small and the clothes they were thin
'Lie close to the wall,' says Brian O'Flynn.

Brian O'Flynn and his wife and wife's mother
Were all going over the bridge together
The bridge it broke down and they all tumbled in
'We'll find ground at the bottom,' says Brian O'Flynn.

104

The Crabfish

'Oh fish-er-man, fish-er-man, one two three

Have you got a she-crab you can sell to me?'

(a)

'Oh yes sir, yes sir, one two three

I've got a she-crab I can sell to thee.'

(a)

'Oh fisherman, fisherman, one two three
Have you got a she-crab you can sell to me?'
'Oh yes sir, yes sir, one two three
I've got a she-crab I can sell to thee.'

I catched the little fellow up by the backbone
I put 'un in a bag and marched away home
Singing jimmy dingy ingy ding, jimmy ingy ingy ding
And the wind blew fair in the merry morning.

When I got home my wife was asleep
And I put 'un in the chamber alive to keep
Singing jimmy dingy ingy ding, jimmy ingy ingy ding
And the wind blew fair in the merry morning.

My wife got out to do what she want
And the crab jumped up and caught her by the
Jimmy dingy ingy ding, jimmy ingy ingy ding
And the wind blew fair in the merry morning.

'Oh John, oh John, there's something wrong
The Devil's in the chamber poking up his horns.'
Singing jimmy dingy ingy ding, jimmy ingy ingy ding
And the wind blew fair in the merry morning.

'Oh wife, oh wife, you must be mad
If you can't tell the Devil from a little she-crab.'
Singing jimmy dingy ingy ding, jimmy ingy ingy ding
And the wind blew fair in the merry morning.

So I took the chamber and missus took the broom
And we marched that little fellow right out of the room
Singing jimmy dingy ingy ding, jimmy ingy ingy ding
And the wind blew fair in the merry morning.

105

Creeping Jane

I will sing you a song and a ve - ry pret - ty one

Con - cern - ing Creep - ing Jane _____ O

Why she ne - ver saw a mare or a geld - ing in her life

That she va - lued to the worth of half a pin.

Chorus

Lol - the - day, dee - ay, the did - dle ol - the - die doh

Why she ne - ver saw a mare or a geld - ing in her life

That she va - lued to the worth of half a pin. Lol - the - day.

(d) Final stanza

I will sing you a song and a very pretty one
Concerning Creeping Jane O
Why she never saw a mare or a gelding in her life
That she valued to the worth of half a pin.

Chorus
Lol-the-day, dee-ay, the diddle ol-the-die doh
[Repeat last two lines of verse]
Lol-the-day.

When Creeping Jane on the racecourse came
The gentlemen view-ed her all around O
And all they had to say concerning little Jane
'She's not able for to gallop o'er the ground.'

Now when that they came to the second mile-post
Creeping Jane, she was far behind O
Then the rider flung his whip around her bonny little neck
And he said, 'My little lassie, never mind.'

Now when that they came to the third mile-post
Creeping Jane, she looked blithe and smart O
And then she lifted up her little lily-white foot
And she flew past them all like a dart.

Now Creeping Jane, she this race has won
And scarcely sweats one drop O
Why she's able for to gallop the ground o'er again
While the others is not able for to trot.

Now Creeping Jane, she is dead and gone
And her body lies on the cold ground O
I'll go down to her master one favour for to beg
That's to keep her little body from the hounds.

106

The Derby Ram

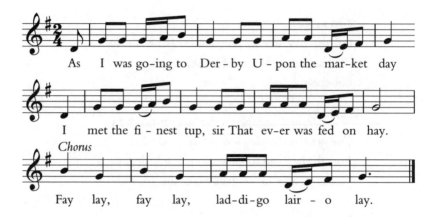

As I was go-ing to Der - by U - pon the mar-ket day
I met the fi - nest tup, sir That ev-er was fed on hay.

Chorus

Fay lay, fay lay, lad-di-go lair - o lay.

As I was going to Derby
Upon the market day
I met the finest tup, sir
That ever was fed on hay.

Chorus
Fay lay, fay lay, laddigo lairo lay.

This tup was fat behind, sir
This tup was fat before
This tup stood nine foot high, sir
If he didn't stand no more.

The wool that grew on his belly, sir
Was trailing all around
Every foot the tup set down, sir
He covered an acre of ground.

The wool that grew on his back, sir
It grew so mighty high
Eagles came and built their nests, sir
You could hear the young ones cry.

The horns that grew on his head, sir
They grew so mighty wide
That a coach and six could go betwixt
With a footman by the side.

The butcher that stuck the tup, sir
Was in danger of his life
He was up to his knees in blood, sir
Crying out for a longer knife.

The blood that ran from this tup, sir
It run down Derby moor
Turned the biggest waterwheel
That's ever been turned before.

And all the boys in Derby
Came begging for his eyes
To kick about in Derby streets
For they were football size.

And all the blacksmiths in Derby
Came begging for his ears
To make their leather aprons of
Cos they would last for years.

And all the women of Derby
Came begging for his bones
To get the marrow out of them
To nourish their old bones.

And now my singing's ended
We cannot sing no more
So p'raps you'll give us a trifle
Or else a glass of beer.

107

The Foolish Boy

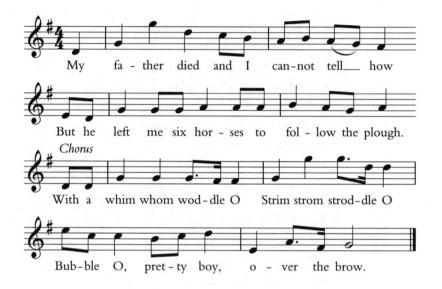

My fa - ther died and I can-not tell___ how
But he left me six hor - ses to fol - low the plough.
Chorus
With a whim whom wod - dle O Strim strom strod - dle O
Bub - ble O, pret - ty boy, o - ver the brow.

My father died and I cannot tell how
But he left me six horses to follow the plough.

Chorus
With a whim whom woddle O
Strim strom stroddle O
Bubble O, pretty boy, over the brow.

I sold my six horses to buy a new cow
Wasn't that a funny thing to follow the plough?

I sold my cow to buy me a calf
I never made a bargain but I lost the better half.

I sold my calf to buy me a cat
To sit down by the fire, warm her little back.

I sold my cat to buy me a mouse
She set fire to her tail and burnt up all my house.

108

The Frog and the Mouse

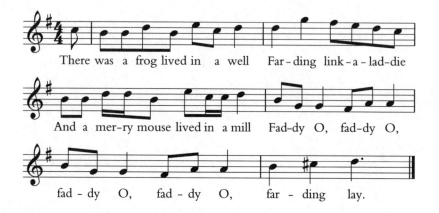

There was a frog lived in a well Far-ding link-a-lad-die
And a mer-ry mouse lived in a mill Fad-dy O, fad-dy O,
fad-dy O, fad-dy O, far-ding lay.

There was a frog lived in a well
   Farding link-a-laddie
And a merry mouse lived in a mill
   Faddy O faddy O faddy O faddy O farding lay.

The frog he would a-wooing ride
   Farding link-a-laddie
Sword and buckler by his side
   Faddy O faddy O faddy O faddy O farding lay.

He rode till he came to the mouse's hall
And there did knock and there did call.

'O Mistress Mouse, are you within?
Yes, kind sir, I sit and spin.'

'O Mistress Mouse, will you marriage make
With the frog that is so black?'

'Uncle Rat is not at home
I can't consent till his return.'

When Uncle Rat came home at night
'Has anyone been here since I went out?'

'Yes, there's been a gentleman
Who says he'll marry me if he can.'

'We'll have the marriage in the mill
The drums shall beat and the bells shall ring.'

The drums did beat and the bells did ring
When in came the cat and her kitling.

The cat she seized the rat by the crown
The kittling knocked the mousey down.

The frog he jumped into a brook
Where he was gobbled up by a duck.

109

The Herring's Head

Oh what-'ll I do with my her-ring's head
Oh what-'ll I do with my her-ring's head?
We'll make them in - to loaves of bread Her-ring's head,
loaves of bread And all man-ner of things.___
Chorus
Of all the fish that live in the sea The her-ring is the
one for me How are ye the day, how
are ye the day How are ye the day, me hin-ny O?

Repeat these two bars as necessary in subsequent verses.

Oh what'll I do with my herring's head
Oh what'll I do with my herring's head?
We'll make them into loaves of bread
Herring's head, loaves of bread
And all manner of things.

Chorus
Of all the fish that live in the sea
The herring is the one for me
How are ye the day, how are ye the day
How are ye the day, me hinny O?

What'll I do with my herring's eyes
Oh what'll I do with my herring's eyes?
We'll make them into puddings and pies
Herring's eyes, puddings and pies
Herring's head, loaves of bread
And all manner of things.

… herring's fins … needles and pins

… herring's guts … a pair of boots

… herring's belly … a lass called Nelly

… herring's tail … a barrel of ale

… herring's scales … a ship that sails

110

The Hungry Fox

A hungry fox jumped up in a fright
And he begged for the moon to give him light
For he had many miles to trot that night
Before he got back to his den O, den O, den O
For he had many miles to trot that night
Before he got back to his den O.

So he cocked up his head and out went his tail
And off he went on the long, long trail
Which he'd done many times in calm and gale
But he always got back to his den O, etc.

And soon he came to the old farmyard
Where the ducks and the geese to him were barred
But he always got one by working hard
To take back to his den O, etc.

He grabbed the grey goose by the neck
And he slung him right across his back
And the old grey goose went quack, quack, quack
But the fox was off to his den O, etc.

Old Mother Slipper Slopper jumped out of bed
And out of the window she poked her head
'Oh John, John, the grey goose is gone
And the fox is off to his den O', etc.

John went up to the top of the hill
And he blew a trumpet loud and shrill
Said the fox, 'That's very pretty music, still
I'd rather be in my den O', etc.

At last he got back to his den
To his dear little foxes eight, nine, ten
And they've had many fat geese since then
And sometimes a good fat hen O, etc.

The Keeper

The keep-er he a - shoot-ing goes   All   a-mongst his

bucks   and   does   All   for   to shoot   at   the

bar-ren doe She's a-mongst the leaves of the green   O.

Chorus
VOICE 1   2   1   2   1   2

Jack-y boy Ma-ster   Sing well Ve-ry well High down Ho down

Der-ry der-ry down A-mongst the leaves of the green   O To my

high down down To my ho down down   High down Ho down

Der-ry der-ry down   A-mongst the leaves of the green   O.

The keeper he a-shooting goes
All amongst his bucks and does
All for to shoot at the barren doe
She's amongst the leaves of the green O.

Chorus
Jacky boy – Master
Sing well – Very well
High down – Ho down
Derry derry down
Amongst the leaves so green O
To my high down down – To my ho down down
High down – Ho down
Derry derry down
Amongst the leaves so green O.

The first doe he shot at he missed
The second doe he trimmed he kissed
The third doe's away where nobody whist
She's amongst the leaves of green O.

The fourth doe she did cross the plain
The keeper fetched her back again
Where she is now she may remain
She's amongst the leaves of green O.

The fifth doe she did cross the brook
The keeper fetched her back with his hook
Where she is now you must go and look
She's amongst the leaves of green O.

Old King Cole

Now old King Cole was a mer-ry old soul

And a good old soul was he, was he

He called for his bot-tle and he called for his glass

And he called for his fid-d(e)-lers three, three

Now one of these fid-dlers had a ve-ry fine fid-dle

And a ve-ry fine fid-dle had he, he

(a) ★

Fid-dle did-dle dee, went the fid-d(e)-ler Fid-dle did-dle dee.

There's none so rare as can com-pare With the sons of har-mo-ny.

There's none so rare as can com-pare With the sons of har-mo-ny.

★ *Repeat this bar as necessary in subsequent verses.*

Now old King Cole was a merry old soul
And a good old soul was he, was he
He called for his bottle and he called for his glass
And he called for his fiddlers three, three
Now one of those fiddlers had a very fine fiddle
And a very fine fiddle had he, he
Fiddle diddle dee, went the fiddler
Fiddle diddle dee.
There's none so rare as can compare
With the sons of harmony.

Now old King Cole was a merry old soul
And a good old soul was he, was he
He called for his bottle and he called for his glass
And he called for his fifers three, three
Now one of those fifers had a very fine fife
And a very fine fife had he, he
Fi-fye fi-fye fi-fye, went the fifer
And fiddle diddle dee, went the fiddler
Fiddle diddle dee.
There's none so rare as can compare
With the sons of harmony.

Now old King Cole was a merry old soul
And a good old soul was he, was he
He called for his bottle and he called for his glass
And he called for his drummers three, three
Now one of those drummers had a very fine drum
And a very fine drum had he, he
Lie diddle de um dum dum, went the drummer, etc.

Now old King Cole was a merry old soul
And a good old soul was he, was he
He called for his bottle and he called for his glass
And he called for his harpers three, three
Now one of those harpers had a very fine harp
And a very fine harp had he, he
Clang clang clang, went the harper, etc.

Now old King Cole was a merry old soul
And a good old soul was he, was he
He called for his bottle and he called for his glass
And he called for his trumpeters three, three
Now one of those trumpeters had a very fine trumpet
And a very fine trumpet had he, he
Wum-pum pum pum pum, went the trumpeter, etc.

Now old King Cole was a merry old soul
And a good old soul was he, was he
He called for his bottle and he called for his glass
And he called for his tailors three, three
Now one of those tailors had a very fine needle
And a very fine needle had he, he
'Put it through his coat,' said the tailor, etc.

Now old King Cole was a merry old soul
And a good old soul was he, was he
He called for his bottle and he called for his glass
And he called for his cobblers three, three
Now one of those cobblers had a very fine cobble
And a very fine cobble had he, he
'Put it through his cut,' said the cobbler, etc.

Now old King Cole was a merry old soul
And a good old soul was he, was he
He called for his bottle and he called for his glass
And he called for his painters three, three

Now one of those painters had a very fine brush
And a very fine brush had he, he
'Dab it up against the wall,' said the painter, etc.

Now old King Cole was a merry old soul
And a good old soul was he, was he
He called for his bottle and he called for his glass
And he called for his parsons three, three
Now one of those parsons had a very fine book
And a very fine book had he, he
'Lord have mercy on his soul,' said the parson, etc.

Now old King Cole was a merry old soul
And a good old soul was he, was he
He called for his bottle and he called for his glass
And he called for his coachmen three, three
Now one of those coachmen had a very fine horse
And a very fine horse had he, he
[*spoken*] *Now, ladies and gentlemen as I was in the street walking along*
   one day a carriage and pair came and stopped outside a chemist shop.
   The horses took fright at something and dashed into the window
'Damn and blast his eyes,' said the coachman
'Hit him over the head,' said the bobbie
'Lord have mercy on his soul,' said the parson
'Dab it up against the wall,' said the painter
'Put it through his cut,' said the cobbler
'Put it through his coat,' said the tailor
Wum-pum pum pum pum, went the trumpeter
Clang clang clang, went the harper
Lie diddle de um dum dum, went the drummer
Fi-fye fi-fye fi-fye, went the fifer
And fiddle diddle dee, went the fiddler
Fiddle diddle diddle diddle dee.
There's none so rare as can compare
With the sons of harmony.

Three Sons of Rogues

Version 1

In good King Arthur's days
He was a merry king
He turned three servants out of doors
Because they wouldn't sing
Because they wouldn't sing
Because they wouldn't sing

He turned three servants out of doors
Because they wouldn't sing.

The first he was a miller
The second he was a weaver
The third he was a little tailor
Three thieving rogues together, etc.

The miller he stole corn
The weaver he stole yarn
The little tailor he stole broadcloth
To keep those three rogues warm, etc.

The miller was drowned in his dam
The weaver was hanged in his yarn
The devil ran off with the little tailor
With his broadcloth under his arm, etc.

Version 2

When good King Arthur ruled this land
He was a goodly king
He stole three pecks of barley-meal
To make a bag-pudding.

A bag-pudding the king did make
And stuffed it well with plums
And in it put great lumps of fat
As big as my two thumbs.

The king and queen did eat thereof
And noblemen beside
And what they could not eat that night
The queen next morning fried.

114

The Tree in the Wood

O in yon wood there was a tree
As nice a tree as e'er you saw
And the tree was in the wood
And the wood lies down in the valley O
And the wood lies down in the valley O.

And on that tree there was a limb
As nice a limb as e'er you saw
And the limb was on the tree
And the tree was in the wood
And the wood lies down in the valley O
And the wood lies down in the valley O.

And on that limb there was a branch, etc.

And on that branch there was a spray, etc.

And on that spray there was a nest, etc.

And in that nest there was an egg, etc.

And in that egg there was a bird, etc.

And on that bird there was a feather, etc.

VIII

Cruel Death Has Put an End ...
Songs of Death and Destruction

Cruel Death Has Put an End ...
Songs of Death and Destruction

After nineteen years' experience of the patter and paper line in the streets,
I find that a foolish nonsensical thing will sell twice as fast as a good moral
sentimental one; and, while it lasts, a good murder will cut out the whole
of them. It's the best selling thing of any. I used at one time to patter
religious tracts in the street, but I found no encouragement.

So said a broadside seller to Henry Mayhew in the late 1840s (Mayhew,
London Labour and the London Poor (1861) I, p. 235).

People of all ages have probably always loved a 'good murder', but
from the mid eighteenth to the late nineteenth centuries a veritable
'murder industry' developed which was fuelled by social changes
such as the expansion of transport networks and the availability of
cheap printed materials. Not only did thousands flock to see the regular public hangings (abolished in 1868), which were enjoyed as great
family outings, but they also visited crime scenes and other associated
places where there was always an owner or a neighbour willing to
show the very room, and point out the bloodstains. For a really well-
known crime, such as the murder of Maria Marten at the Red Barn,
you could even buy souvenir ceramic models of the building and the
key players to display on your mantlepiece.

Everyone followed the course of particular cases in newspapers and
on broadsides, which reported each crime in minute detail, but both
the legitimate press and street hacks were quite happy to include
spurious details based on rumour and prejudice, and it is often difficult for modern researchers to sort out fact from fiction. Melodramas,
puppet shows, peep shows, waxworks, print-sellers and countless
other manifestations of popular culture quickly followed and cashed
in on the latest sensation, keeping it in the public eye for a considerable time after the real perpetrator met his or her fate. The broadsides

and the stage shows often included songs written for the occasion.

But despite wide dissemination, few of the songs written about real murders seem to have lasted in singers' repertoires ('Maria Marten', No. 123, is an exception), and traditional singers seem to have preferred the generic fictional cases, of which the 'murdered sweetheart' songs are an important subcategory. 'The Cruel Ship's Carpenter' (No. 117), 'Mary in the Silvery Tide' (No. 125) and 'The Oxford Girl' (No. 129) are examples included here, but there were many others.

Child ballads also include more than their fair share of violence, and 'The Cruel Mother' (No. 116), 'Hugh of Lincoln' (No. 119) and 'The Outlandish Knight' (No. 127) each focuses on a different variety of human mortality, but for pure Gothic horror in song, nothing beats 'Lambkin' (No. 121).

Not all deaths in folk song were murders, of course. Many songs focused on shipwrecks and other disasters, executions or personal accidents ('The Lakes of Cold Finn', No. 120, and 'The Mistletoe Bough', No. 126), or used unexplained deaths as an element in a tragic love story ('The Trees They Do Grow High, Part III, No. 55; 'Lord Lovel', No. 122; and 'The Unquiet Grave', No. 130).

115

The Constant Farmer's Son

It's of a mer-chant's daugh-ter dear and in Lon-don she did dwell She was mod - est, neat and hand-some and her par-ents loved her well She was ad-mired by lords and squires but all their hopes were vain___ For she loved one and on - ly one For she loved one and on - ly___ one Her con-stant farm - er's son.

It's of a merchant's daughter dear and in London she did dwell
She was modest, neat and handsome and her parents loved her well
She was admired by lords and squires but all their hopes were in vain
For she loved one and only one
For she loved one and only one
Her constant farmer's son.

Her parents they consented, but her brothers they said nay
So they asked young William's company with them to spend the day

But mark, returning home again, how soon his race was run
For with a stake the life did take
For with a stake the life did take
Of her constant farmer's son.

As Mary on her pillow lay she had a dreadful dream
She dreamt she saw his body laid down by some crystal stream
Then she arose, put on her clothes, to seek her love did go
It's dead and cold she did behold
It's dead and cold she did behold
Her constant farmer's son.

With those cold tears all on his cheeks and mingled with his gore
She strived in pain to ease her pain, she kissed him ten times o'er
She gathered the green leaves from the trees to keep him from the sun
A night and day she passed away
A night and day she passed away
With her constant farmer's son.

Now hunger came creeping o'er the poor girl and homeward she did go
[To try to find his murderers she straightway home did go]
Saying, 'Parents dear, you soon shall hear, what a dreadful deed was done
In yonder vale lies dead and pale
In yonder vale lies dead and pale
My constant farmer's son.'

Up spoke the younger brother and he said, 'It was not I.'
The same replied the elder one, and he swore most bitterly
Young Mary said, 'Don't turn red, nor try the law to shun
You have done the deed and you shall bleed
You have done the deed and you shall bleed
For my constant farmer's son.'

116

The Cruel Mother

There was a lady that lived in York
  All alone and a loney O
She proved with child by her own father's clerk
  Down by a greenwood sidey O.

As she was walking down her father's lawn, etc.
She thought three times that her back would be broke, etc.

As she was walking down her father's lawn, etc.
She says, 'Honourable Mary, pity me', etc.

As she was walking down her father's lawn, etc.
Where her fine sons they were born, etc.

She pulled out her long penknife, etc.
And there she took away their three lives, etc.

Years went by and one summer's morn, etc.
She saw three boys they were playing bat and ball, etc.

'O my fine boys, if you were mine', etc.
'Sure I'd dress you up in silk so fine', etc.

'O mother dear, when we were yours', etc.
'You did not dress us in silk so fine', etc.

'You pulled out your long penknife', etc.
'And there you took away our three lives', etc.

'O my fine boys, what will become of me?', etc.
'You'll be seven long years a bird in a tree', etc.

'You'll be seven long years a tongue in a bell', etc.
And you'll be seven long years a porter in hell', etc.

117

The Cruel Ship's Carpenter

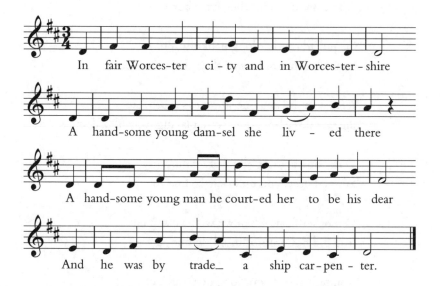

In fair Worces-ter ci-ty and in Worces-ter-shire
A hand-some young dam-sel she liv - ed there
A hand-some young man he court-ed her to be his dear
And he was by trade_ a ship car-pen - ter.

In fair Worcester city and in Worcestershire
A handsome young damsel she liv-ed there
A handsome young man he courted her to be his dear
And he was by trade a ship carpenter.

Now the King wanted seamen to go on the sea
That caused this poor damsel to sigh and to say
'O William, O William, don't you go to sea
Remember the vows that you made to me.'

It was early next morning before it was day
He went to his Polly, these words he did say
'O Polly, O Polly, you must go with me
Before we are married my friends for to see.'

He led her through groves and valleys so deep
And caused this young damsel to sigh and to weep
'O William, O William, you have led me astray
On purpose my innocent life to betray.'

'It's true, it's true,' these words he did say
'For all the long night I've been digging your grave'
The grave being open, the spade standing by
Which caused this young damsel to sigh and to cry.

'O William, O William, O pardon my life
I never will covet to be your wife
I will travel the world over to set you quite free
O pardon, O pardon, my baby and me.'

'No pardon I'll give, there's no time for to stand'
So with that he had a knife in his hand
He stabbed her heart till the blood it did flow
Then into the grave her fair body did throw.

He covered her up so safe and secure
Thinking no one would find her he was sure
Then he went on board to sail the world round
Before that the murder could ever be found.

It was early one morning before it was day
The captain came up, these words he did say
'There's a murderer on board, and he it lately has done
Our ship is in mourning and cannot sail on.'

Then up stepped one, 'Indeed it's not me.'
Then up stepped another the same he did say
Then up starts young William to stamp and to swear
'Indeed it's not me, sir, I vow and declare.'

As he was turning from the captain with speed
He met his Polly, which made his heart bleed
She stript him, she tore him, she tore him in three
Because he had murdered her baby and she.

118

Edwin in the Lowlands Low

Come all you feeling lovers, give ear unto my song
Concerning gold as we are told that leads so many wrong.

Young Emma was a servant maid; her love a sailor bold
He ploughed the main much gold to gain for his love as we are told.

Young Emma she would daily mourn since Edmund first did roam
And seven years have passed away since Edmund left his home.

He went up to young Emma's house his gold all for to show
What he had gained all on the main and down in the lowlands low.

'Oh my father keeps a public inn that stands down by the sea
And go you there, young Edmund, and there this night shall be.'

'I will meet you in the morning, love, don't let my parents know
That your name it is young Edmund who ploughs the lowlands low.'

As young Edmund he sat drinking until time to go to bed
But little was he thinking what sorrows crowned his head.

As soon as he had got to bed and scarcely got to sleep
When Emma's cruel father into his bedroom creep.

He robb-ed him, he stabb-ed him, until the blood did flow
And he sent his body a-rolling down in the lowlands low.

As young Emma she lay sleeping, she dreamt a dreadful dream
She dreamt she saw her own true love and the blood appeared in streams.

Young Emma got up at daybreak, down to her home did go
Because she loved him dearly, who ploughed the lowlands low.

'Oh father, dearest father, now tell me, I entreat
Oh where is that young man who came last night to sleep?'

'Oh Emma, dearest Emma, his gold will make a show
And I've sent his body a-rolling down in the lowlands low.'

'Oh father, cruel father, you shall die a public show
For murdering of my own true love, who ploughed the lowlands low.'

'Now the shells all in the ocean shall make my true love's bed
And the fish that swim all in the sea shall swim around his head.'

Faint, sick and broken-hearted to bed the maid did go
And her shrieks were of young Edmund who ploughed the lowlands low
[*spoken*] *Lowlands low.*

119

Hugh of Lincoln

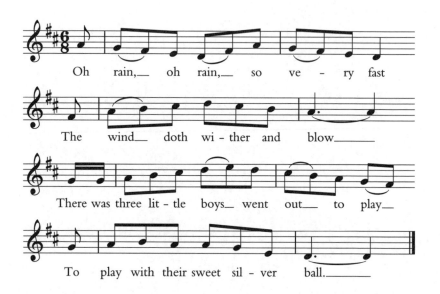

Oh rain, oh rain, so very fast
The wind doth wither and blow
There was three little boys went out to play
To play with their sweet silver ball.

They tossed him high, they tossed him low
They tossed him over into the Jew's garden
The very first of them that did come out
The Jewess, was dressed in green.

'Come in, come in, you little Sir Hugh
Come in and fetch your ball.'
'I can't come in, nor I won't come in
Without my playmates all.'

At first she showed me an apple so red
And next was a diamond ring
Next was the cherry so red as blood
And so she got me in.

She set me into a silver chair
And fed me with sugar so sweet
She laid me on the dressing board
And stuck me like a sheep.

She throwed me into a new-dug well
It was forty cubits deep
She wropped me up in a red mantle
Instead of a milk-white sheet.

'Twas up and down the garden there
This little boy's mammie did run
She had a little rod all under her apron
To beat her little son home.

'Oh here I am, dear mother,' he cried
'My grave is dug so deep
The pen-knife sticks so close to my heart
So 'long with you I can't sleep.'

120

The Lakes of Cold Finn

Early one morning young William arose
And straight to his comrade's bedchamber he goes
Saying, 'Comrade, oh comrade, let nobody know
For it is a fine morning and a-bathing we'll go.'

Young William tripped off till he came to Long Lane
The first that he met was a keeper of game
He advised him for sorrow to turn back again
For the lakes of cold water is the lakes of Cold Finn.

Young William stripped off and he swum the lake round
He swum round the island but not to right ground
Saying, 'Comrade, oh comrade, don't you venture in
For the depths of cold water are the lakes of Cold Finn.'

Early that morning his sister arose
And straight to her mother's bedchamber she goes
Saying, 'Mother, oh mother, I had a sad dream
That young William was floating on the watery stream.'

Early that morning his mother went there
She'd rings on her fingers and was tearing her hair
Saying, 'Where was he drownded, or did he fall in?
For the depths of cold water is the lakes of Cold Finn.'

The day of his funeral there shall be a grand sight
Four and twenty young men all dressed up in white
They shall carry him along and lay him on clay
Saying, 'Adieu to young William', they'll all march away.

121

Lambkin

Says the lord un-to the la-dy 'I'm a - going a-way from home

Be - ware of false Lamb-kin Un - til I re - turn.'

Says the lord unto the lady
'I'm a-going away from home
Beware of false Lambkin
Until I return.'

'What cares I for Lambkin
Or any of his kin?
While the doors they are fastened
And darkened within.'

As soon as my lordy
He was got out of sight
Then ready was that cruel Lambkin
To visit her that night.

He rapp-ed at the door
Says, 'Nurse, let me in
I'll make you a lady
And visit you in.'

He pinched that poor baby
For to make that for to cry
While Nurse sat a-singing
'Hush! hush-a by bye.'

So they pinched that poor baby
For to make that for to cry
While Nurse sat a-singing
Hush! hush-a by bye.

'I cannot keep it good, ma'am
With milk or with pap
So I pray you, kind lady
Come and nurse it in your lap.'

'How can I come down, nurse
At this time of the night
When there's no fire a-burning
Nor candle give light?'

'Put on your golden mantle
That will give you light
And I pray you, kind lady
Come and nurse it your lap tonight.'

She put on her golden mantle
Not thinking any harm
And Lambkin was ready
To catch her in his arms.

'Brother Lambkin, Brother Lambkin
Spare my life till ten o'clock
I'll give you as many guineas
As you can carry in your sack.'

'I want none of your guineas, love
I want none of your gold
For I want to see your heart's blood
Come trinkling quite cold.'

'Brother Lambkin, Brother Lambkin
Spare my life till ten o'clock
You shall have my daughter Betsy
As is up in the top.'

'You may fetch your daughter Betsy
She may do you some good
She may hold the silver basin
For to catch your heart's blood.'

There's blood in the kitchen
And there's blood in the hall
And there's blood in the parlour
Where the lady did fall.

As Betsy was a-looking
Out of the tower so high
She saw her worried father
A-coming riding by.

'Worried father! Worried father
Don't lay the blame on me
It was that cruel Lambkin
That murdered lady and baby.'

And Lambkin is a-hanging
On the high gallows tree
And the nurse is a-burning
In the fire close by.

Oh the death bell is a-knelling
For lady and baby
And the green grass is a-growing
All over they
And the green grass is a-growing
All over they.

122

Lord Lovel

Lord Lovel he stood at his own castle gate
All on a milk-white steed
And out came Lady Nancy Bell
And she wished him, Lord Lovel, God speed, God speed
And she wished him, Lord Lovel, God speed.

'Oh where are you going, Lord Lovel?' she cried
'Oh where are you going?' cried she
'I'm going, sweet Lady Nancy Bell
Strange countries for to see, to see
Strange countries for to see.'

'When will you come back, Lord Lovel?' she cried
'When will you come back?' cried she
'In a year or two, or three at the most

And I'll return to my Lady Nancy, Nancy
I'll return to my Lady Nancy.'

He hadn't been gone but a year and one day
Strange countries for to see
When all at once came into his mind
I'll return to my Lady Nancy, Nancy
I'll return to my Lady Nancy.

He mounted on his milk-white steed
And rode to London town
And there he saw a funeral
And the people were weeping around, around
And the people were weeping around.

123

Maria Marten

My name is Wil-li-am Cor-der, to you I do de-clare

I__ court-ed Ma-ri-a Mar-ten so__ beau-ti-ful__ and fair

I__ pro-mised her I'd mar-ry her all on a cer-tain day

In-stead of that I was con-tent to__ take her life a-way.

My name is William Corder, to you I do declare
I courted Maria Marten so beautiful and fair
I promised her I'd marry her all on a certain day
Instead of that I was content to take her life away.

I went unto her father's house on the eighteenth day of May
He said, 'I've come, my dearest Maria, we'll fix the wedding day
If you'll meet me at the Red Barn floor as sure as you're alive
I'll take you down to Ipswich Town and make you my dear bride.'

He straight went home and fetched his gun, his pickaxe and his spade
He went unto the Red Barn floor and he dug poor Maria's grave
This poor girl she thought no harm but to meet him she did go
She went into the Red Barn floor and he laid her body low.

Her mother dreamt three dreams one night, she ne'er could get no rest
She dreamed she saw her daughter dear lay bleeding at the breast
Her father went into the barn and up the boards he took
There he saw his daughter dear lay mingled in the dust.

Now all young men do you beware, take a pity look on me
For the time is past to die at last all on the gallus tree.

124

Mary Across the Wild Moor

It was one win - ter's night when the wind

It blew bit - ter a - cross the bleak moor___

When poor Ma - ry she came with her child

Wan - d'ring home to her own fa - ther's door.___

It was one winter's night when the wind
It blew bitter across the bleak moor
When poor Mary she came with her child
Wand'ring home to her own father's door.

She cried, 'Father, O pray let me in
Do come down and open your own door
Or the child at my bosom will die
With the wind that blows on the wild moor.'

'Why ever did I leave this cot
Where once I was happy and free
Doomed to roam without friend or home
O father, have pity on me.'

But her father was deaf to her cry
Not a voice nor a sound reached the door
But the watch dog's bark and the wind
That blew bitter across the wild moor.

Now think what her father he felt
When he came to the door in the morn
And found Mary dead, and her child
Fondly clasped in its dead mother's arms.

Wild and frantic he tore his grey hairs
As on Mary he gazed at the door
Who on the cold night there had died
By the wind that blew on the wild moor.

Now her father in grief pined away
The poor child to its mother went soon
And no one lived there to this day
And the cottage to ruin has gone.

The villagers point to the spot
Where the willow droops over the door
They cry out there poor Mary died
With the wind that blew o'er the wild moor.

125

Mary in the Silvery Tide

'Twas of— a love-ly crea-ture who dwelled by the sea - side

Her lov-e-ly form and fea - ture she was the vil-lage pride

There was a young sea cap-tain who Ma-ry's heart would gain

But she was true to Hen - ry, was on— the ra-ging main.

'Twas of a lovely creature who dwelled by the seaside
Her lovely form and feature she was the village pride
There was a young sea captain who Mary's heart would gain
But she was true to Henry, was on the raging main.

'Twas in young Henry's absence this nobleman he came
A-courting pretty Mary, but she refused the same
She said, 'I pray you begone, young man, your vows are all in vain
Therefore begone, I love but one, he's on the raging main.'

With mad desperation this nobleman he said
'To prove the separation I'll take her life away
I'll watch her late and early and then alone,' he cried
'I'll send her body a-floating in the rippling silvery tide.'

This nobleman was walking out to take the air
Down by the rolling ocean he met the lady fair
He said, 'My pretty fair maid, you consent to be my bride
Or you shall swim far, far from here in the rolling silvery tide.'

With trembling limbs cried Mary, 'My vows I never can break
For Henry I dearly love and I'll die for his sweet sake.'
With his handkerchief he bound her hands and plunged her in the main
And shrinking her body went floating in the rolling silvery tide.

It happened Mary's true love soon after came from sea
Expecting to be happy and fixed the wedding day
'We fear your true love's murdered,' her aged parents cried
'Or she caused her own destruction in the rolling silvery tide.'

As Henry on his pillow lay he could not take no rest
For the thoughts of pretty Mary disturbed his wounded breast
He dreamed that he was walking down by a riverside
He saw his true love weeping in the rolling silvery tide.

Young Henry rose at midnight, at midnight gloom went he
To search the sandbanks over down by the raging sea
At daybreak in the morning poor Mary's corpse he spied
As to and fro she was floating in the rolling silvery tide.

He knew it was his Mary by the ring on her hand
He untied the silk handkerchief which put him to a stand
For the name of her cruel murderer was full thereon he spied
Which proved who ended Mary's days in the rolling silvery tide.

This nobleman was taken, the gallus was his doom
For ending pretty Mary's days, she had scarce attained her bloom
Young Henry broken-hearted he wandered till he died
His last words was for Mary in the rolling silvery tide.

126

The Mistletoe Bough

The mis‑tle‑toe hung in the cas‑tle hall The

hol‑ly branch hung on the old oak wall The

Ba‑ron's re‑tain‑ers were blithe and gay Keep‑ing their Christ‑mas

hol‑i‑day The Ba‑ron be‑held with a fa‑ther's pride His

beau‑ti‑ful child, young Lov‑el's bride While she with her bright eyes

seemed to be The star of that good‑ly com‑pa‑ny.

Chorus

Oh_ the mis‑tle‑toe bough! Oh_ the mis‑tle‑toe bough.

The mistletoe hung in the castle hall
The holly branch hung on the old oak wall
The Baron's retainers were blithe and gay
Keeping their Christmas holiday
The Baron beheld with a father's pride
His beautiful child, young Lovel's bride
While she with her bright eyes seemed to be
The star of that goodly company.

Chorus
Oh the mistletoe bough!
Oh the mistletoe bough.

'I'm weary of dancing now,' she cried
'Here tarry a moment, I'll hide, I'll hide
And Lovel be sure thou'rt the first to trace
The clue to my secret hiding place.'
Away she ran and her friends began
Each tower to search and each nook to scan
And young Lovel cried, 'Oh where dost thou hide?
I'm lonesome without thee, my own dear bride.'

They sought her that night, they sought her next day
They sought her in vain till a week passed away
In the highest and the lowest and the loneliest spot
Young Lovel sought wildly but found her not
And years flew by and their grief at last
Was told as a sorrowful tale long past
When Lovel appeared the children cried
'See the old man weeps for his fairy bride.'

At length an old chest that had long lain hid
Was found in the castle, they raised the lid
A skeleton form lay mouldering there
In the bridal wreath of a lady fair
Oh sad was her fate in sporting jest

She hid from her lord in the old oak chest
It closed with a spring and her bridal bloom
Lay withering there in the living tomb.

127

The Outlandish Knight

An out-land-ish knight came from the north-west

He came__ a - woo - ing me__

He said he would take me un - to the north-west__

And there he would mar - ry me.

An outlandish knight came from the north-west
He came a-wooing me
He said he would take me unto the north-west
And there he would marry me.

'Go fetch me some of your father's gold
And some of your mother's fee
And two of the best nags out of the stable
Where there stand thirty and three.'

She fetched him some of her father's gold
And some of her mother's fee
And two of the very best nags out of the stable
Where there stood thirty and three.

She mounted on her lily-white steed
He on the dapple grey
They rode until they came to the seaside
Three hours before it was day.

'Mount off, mount off, thy lily-white steed
And deliver it unto me
For six pretty maidens I have drowned here
And the seventh thou shalt be.'

'Take off, take off thy silken dress
And deliver it unto me
For I think it looks too rich by far
To rot all in the salt sea.'

'If I must take off my silken dress
Pray turn your back to me
For it is not fitting that such a ruffian
A naked woman should see.'

He turned his back towards her
And viewed the lakes so green
She caught him round the middle so small
And bundled him into the sea.

He growped high and he growped low
Until he came to the side
'Take hold o' my hand, my pretty lady
And I will make you my bride.'

'Lie there, lie there, you false-hearted man
Lie there instead of me
For if six pretty maids thou hast drowned here
The seventh hath drowned thee.'

She mounted on her lily-white steed
And led the dapple grey
She rode till she came to her own father's door
Three hours before it was day.

The parrot being up in the window so high
And seeing the lady did say
'I fear that some ruffian hath led you astray
That you've tarried so long away.'

'Don't prittle nor prattle, my pretty Polly
Nor tell no tales of me
Your cage shall be made of some glittering gold
Although it is made of a tree.'

The King being up in his chamber so high
And hearing the parrot did say
'What ails you, what ails you, my pretty Polly
That you prattle so long before day?'

'It's no laughing matter,' the parrot replied
'That so loudly I called unto thee
For the cats have got into the window so high
And I'm afraid they will have me.'

'Well turned, well turned, my pretty Polly
Well turned, well turned, for me
Thy cage shall be made of some glittering gold
And the door of the best ivory.'

128

Oxford City

It was of a girl in Oxford city
The truth I now will tell to you
All by a young man this maid was courting
And he loved her as his life he gave.

She loved him too, but 'twas at a distance
She did not seem to be so fond
He said, 'My dear one, why can't we marry?
And then at once it would end all strife.'

'Oh no, I am too young to marry
Too young to incline on a marriage bed
For when we are married then we are bound for ever
And then at once all our joys are fled.'

As she was dancing with some other
This jealousy came to his mind
All for to destroy his own true loved one
This wicked young man he was inclined.

Some poison strong which he had conceal-ed
He mixed it in a glass of wine
Then he gave it unto his own true loved one
And she drank it up most cheerfully.

But in a very few minutes after
'Oh take me home, my dear,' said she
'For the glass of liquor you lately gave me
It makes me feel very ill indeed.'

'Oh I've been drinking the same before you
And I've been taken as ill as you
So in each other's arms we will die together'
Young men be aware of such jealousy.

129

The Oxford Girl

As I was fast - bound 'pren - tice boy, I was bound un-to__ a mill_____ And I served my ma - ster tru - ly for se - ven years and more_____ Till I took up a - court - ing with the girl with the rol - ling eye And I pro-mised that girl__ I'd mar - ry her__ if she would be__ my bride.__

As I was fast-bound 'prentice boy, I was bound unto a mill
And I served my master truly for seven years and more
Till I took up a-courting with the girl with the rolling eye
And I promised that girl I'd marry her if she would be my bride.

So I went up to her parents' house about the hour of eight
But little did her parents think that it should be her fate
I asked her if she'd take a walk through the fields and meadows gay
And there we told the tales of love and fixed the wedding day.

As we were walking and talking of the different things around
I drew a large stick from the hedge and knocked that fair maid down
Down on her bending knees she fell and so loud for mercy cried
'Oh come spare the life of an innocent girl for I am not fit to die.'

Then I took her by the curly locks and I dragged her on the ground
Until I came to the riverside that flowed through Ekefield town
It ran both long and narrow, it ran both deep and wide
And there I plunged this pretty fair maid that should have been my bride.

So when I went home to my parents' house about ten o'clock that night
My mother she jumped out of bed all for to light the light
She asked me and she questioned me, 'Oh what stains your hands and
    clothes?'
And the answer I gave back to her, 'I've been bleeding at the nose.'

So no rest, no rest, all that long night, no rest, no rest could I find
The fire and the brimstone around my head did shine
 It was about two days after this fair young maid was found
A-floating by the riverside that flowed through Ekefield town.

Now the judges and the jurymen on me they did agree
For murdering of this pretty fair maid so hang-ed I shall be
Oh hang-ed, oh hang-ed, oh hang-ed I shall be
For murdering of this pretty fair maid, so hang-ed I shall be.

130

The Unquiet Grave

Cold blows the winter wind, true love
With heavy cold showers of rain
The first true love that ever I had
In greenwood she was slain.

I'll do as much for my true love
As any young man may
I'll sit and mourn all on her grave
A twelvemonth and a day.

A twelvemonth and a day being gone
The ghost began to speak
'Why sit you here all on my grave
And never let me sleep?'

'What dost thou want of me, true love?
What dost thou want of me?'
'A kiss from off thy clay-cold lips
That's all I request of thee.'

'My lily-white lips are clayey cold
My breath smells earthy strong.'
'And if I kiss all off your lips
Your time will not be long.'

'My time be long, my time be short
Tomorrow or today
Sweet Christ in heaven will have my soul
And take my life away.'

'Don't grieve, don't grieve for me, true love
No mourning do I crave
I must leave you and all the world
And sink down in my grave.'

IX

Me and Five More ...
Poachers, Highwaymen and
Other Criminals

Me and Five More ...
Poachers, Highwaymen and Other Criminals

Many folk songs feature crime in one form or another, either as central to the plot or as a relatively incidental detail, but the moral stance varies considerably. In songs about murder, sympathy is invariably with the victims, but with lesser crimes it appears to lie as often with the perpetrators, and is rarely on the side of the authorities. Poachers and smugglers, in particular, are almost always treated sympathetically, and it is clear that the writers and singers did not count these activities as crimes at all, the perpetrators sometimes even taking on a heroic stance (*see* 'The Gallant Poacher', No. 135, and 'The Lincolnshire Poacher', No. 138). As James Hawker (1836–1921) writes in his journal, *A Victorian Poacher* (1961), p. 109:

> If I had been born an idiot and unfit to carry a gun – though with plenty of cash – they would have called me a grand sportsman. Being born poor, I am called a poacher.

Not for nothing has the struggle over the game laws been termed the 'poaching wars'.

But just because the game laws were draconian and unfair does not mean that all poachers were innocent labourers struggling to feed their starving families. Many did it precisely because it was reckless, and ruthless armed poaching gangs did not hesitate to intimidate locals as well as defying the gamekeepers, police and magistrates. Areas close to urban centres were often plagued with organized poaching gangs looking for easy money.

Songs about smuggling are a lot less common than ones on poaching, but as mentioned above they also exhibit sympathy for the smuggler – in 'The Poor Smuggler's Boy' (No. 140), for example, there is no sense that the father is responsible for the lad's plight by breaking the law, and the poor boy gets as much sympathy as any other orphan in the folk-song corpus.

Highwaymen get a mixed reception in English folk songs. Many of the most widespread songs are about specific real-life characters, and these are treated in a romantic light, which stems mainly from popular novels and other legend-creating publications. Dick Turpin is the most popular, but others (for example, 'Brennan on the Moor', No. 132) are also described in ways that bear little relationship to their real criminal careers, and they have nearly always taken on the Robin Hood characteristics of only robbing from the rich.

But generalized highwaymen in folk song are not usually heroic. They are often tricked by their victims ('Highwayman Outwitted', No. 137) and they can even be impersonated by a woman ('The Female Highwayman', No. 134). In songs like 'Wild and Wicked Youth' (No. 146), the focus is on the consequences of a young life gone wrong. Other forms of 'highway robbery' occur in songs like 'Three Butchers' (No. 143) and 'The Undaunted Female' (No. 144), and the perpetrators are here portrayed as unprincipled ruffians rather than 'gentlemen of the road'.

As is to be expected, other crimes make occasional appearances in folk-song narratives – kidnap in 'The Lost Lady Found' (No. 139), for example, and attempted rape in 'Blackberry Fold' (No. 131) – and sometimes the matter is a little more complicated, as in 'The Sheffield Apprentice' (No. 141), who is framed by his employer because he refused her advances.

131

Blackberry Fold

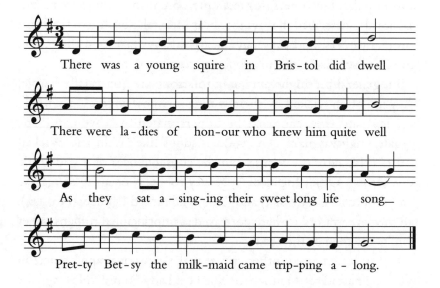

There was a young squire in Bris-tol did dwell

There were la-dies of hon-our who knew him quite well

As they sat a-sing-ing their sweet long life song—

Pret-ty Bet-sy the milk-maid came trip-ping a-long.

There was a young squire in Bristol did dwell
There were ladies of honour who knew him quite well
As they sat a-singing their sweet long life song
Pretty Betsy the milkmaid came tripping along.

'Do you want any milk?' pretty Betsy did say
'Oh yes, if you please, step in pretty maid
Step in pretty maid, 'tis you I adore
If ever a loved one was so honoured before.'

'Now hold your tongue squire, and let me go free
And do not make game of my poverty
There are ladies of honour more fitting for you
Than I a poor milkmaid brought up by my cow.'

A ring from his finger he instantly drew
And right in the middle he broke it in two
One half he gave to her so I have been told
And away they went walking down Blackberry Fold.

As they were a-walking in an open field
'And now,' said the squire, 'I must have my will
And if you deny me in this open field
With my glittering sword I will cause you to yield.'

With huggling and struggling pretty Betsy got free
And with his own weapon she pierced his body
And with his own weapon she pierced him right through
And home to her uncle like lightning she flew.

'Oh what is the matter?' her uncle did say
'I've wounded the squire, the squire,' she said
'With all his fair body he grew very bold
And I've left him a-bleeding down Blackberry Fold.'

The coach was got ready, the squire brought home
And likewise the doctor to heal up his wounds
To heal up his wound as he lay a-bed
'Go and fetch me my Betsy, my charming milkmaid.'

[Now Betsy was sent for, and shivering went on
'I'm sorry,' said Betsy, 'for what I have done.'
'The wound that you gave me was all my own fault
So don't let such things still remain in your thought.'

Now a parson was sent for this couple to wed
So happy they joined in their sweet marriage bed
So come maids, prove a virgin be you ever so poor
For 'twill make you a lady ten thousand times o'er.]

132

Brennan on the Moor

It's of a fearless highwayman a story I will tell
His name is Billy Brennan, in Ireland he did dwell
And on the Linwood Mountain he commenced his wild career
Where many a wealthy gentleman before him shook with fear.

Chorus
Crying Brennan's on the moor, Brennan's on the moor
So bold and undaunted stood Bill Brennan on the moor.

A brace of loaded pistols he carried night and day
He never robbed a poor man upon the King's highway
But what he'd taken from the rich like Turpin and Black Bess
He always would divide it with the widow in distress.

One day he met a packman, his name was Hillier Brown
They travelled on together till day began to dawn
The pedlar seeing his money gone, likewise his watch and chain
He at once encountered Brennan and robbed him back again.

Now Brennan seeing the pedlar was so good a man as he
Engaged him on the highway his companion for to be
The pedlar threw away his pack without any more delay
And proved a faithful comrade until his dying day.

One day as Billy he sat down upon the King's highway
He met the squire of Cashnel a mile outside the town
The squire he knew his features, 'I think, young man,' said he
'Your name is Billy Brennan, you must come along with me.'

Now it happened Billy's wife had gone to town provisions for to buy
And when she met her Billy, she began to sob and cry
He said, 'Give me the tenpence,' and as quick as Billy spoke
She handed him a blunderbuss from underneath her clothes.

Now by this loaded blunderbuss the truth I will unfold
He made the squire to tremble and robbed him of his gold
One hundred pound was offered for his apprehension there
And with his horse and saddle to the mountain did repair.

Brennan and his comrade, knowing that they was betrayed
With the mounted cavalry a noble battle made
He lost his foremost finger, which was shot off by a ball
So Bill Brennan and his comrade was taken after all.

Now they was taken prisoner and in irons bound
Conveyed to Clonmel gaol, strong walls did them surround
They was tried and then found guilty and the judge made this reply
For robbing on the King's highway you're both condemned to die.

Farewell unto my wife and to my children three
And to my aged father, who may shed tears for me
And to my loving mother, who tore her grey locks and cried
'O I wish, young Billy Brennan, in your cradle you had died.'

133

Dick Turpin

As Dicky rode across yon moor
He spied a lawyer ride before
He rode up to him and he thus did say
'Have you seen Dicky Turpin ride this way?'

Chorus
Singing hey ho, Turpin hero
I'm the valiant Turpin O.

'No, I've not seen him a many long day
No more do I want to see 'im ride this way
For if I did I would have no doubt
He would turn my pockets inside out.'

'Oh aye, lad,' Dick says, 'I'll be cute
I'll hide my money in my high top boot.'
The lawyer says, 'He shan't have mine
For I'll hide it in my great coat cape behind.'

They rode together till they came to a hill
Where he bid the bold lawyer to stand still
'Thy great coat cape it must come off
For my Black Bess wants a new saddle cloth.'

'So now I've robbed thee of all thy store
Thou now mayst go and work for more
And the very next town that thou rides in
Thou can tell 'em thou's been robbed by Dick Turpin.'

But wasn't Dicky hard and fast
For killing an old game cock at last
'But here's fifty pound before I die
To give Jack Catch for a lad like I.'

134

The Female Highwayman

Ce - ci - li - a on one cer - tain day

She dressed her-self in___ man's ar-ray

With a brace of pis - tols all by her side___

To meet her true__ love,___ to meet her true__ love

To meet her true love a - way did ride.

Cecilia on one certain day
She dressed herself in man's array
With a brace of pistols all by her side
To meet her true love, to meet her true love
To meet her true love away did ride.

She met him boldly on the plain
'Stand and deliver,' she said, 'young man
Stand and deliver, young man,' she say
'Or else this moment, or else this moment
Or this very moment your life I'll lay.'

She robbed him of his watch and gold
Gave him the empty purse to hold
Saying, 'There's one thing more on your finger now
Deliver it to me, deliver it to me
Deliver it to me, your life to spare.'

'That diamond ring a token was
Before I'd lose it my life I'd lose.'
She being tender-hearted more like a dove
She rode away, she rode away
She rode away from her own true love.

Early next morning plain to be seen
That couple walked on the garden green
When he saw his watch hanging by her clothes
Which made him blush, which made him blush
Which made him blush like the damask rose.

'How can you blush at such a thing
More if I'd had your diamond ring
For it's I that robbed you upon the plain
Now take your gold, love, now take your gold, love
Now take your gold, love, and your watch again.'

'Why did you enter such a foolish plot
Suppose your pistols you would have shot?
And if you had killed me out on that plain
For ever after, for ever after
For ever after you'd be brought to shame.'

'I did intend and 'twas to know
Whether your love was true or no
And now I have a contented mind
My love and all, my love and all
My love and all, my dear, are thine.'

Now this couple married were
And they do live a most happy pair
For the bells did ring and the music play
And they have pleasure, and they have pleasure
And they have pleasure both night and day.

135

The Gallant Poachers

Come all you lads of high renown That
love to drink strong ale that's brown And bring those lof - ty
phea-sants down With pow - der, shot and gun. He is a
gal - lant youth, he will tell you the truth He has
crossed all life's temp - ta - tion's ways No mor - tal man his
life could save He now is sleep - ing
in__ his grave His deeds on earth be done.

Come all you lads of high renown
That love to drink strong ale that's brown
And bring those lofty pheasants down
With powder, shot and gun
He is a gallant youth, he will tell you the truth
He has crossed all life's temptation's ways

No mortal man his life could save
He now is sleeping in his grave
His deeds on earth be done.

Me and five more a-poaching went
To kill some game 'twas our intent
Our money being gone and spent
We had nothing else to try
For the moon shone bright, not a cloud in sight
The keeper heard us fire a gun
And to the spot he quick-aly run
And swore before the rising sun
That one of us should die.

Now the bravest youth among the lot
'Twas his misfortune to be shot
His deeds shall never be forgot
By all his friends below
For help he cried, but was denied
His memory ever shall be blest
He rose again to stand the test
While down upon his gallant breast
The crimson blood did flow.

Now the youth he fell upon the ground
And in his breast a mortal wound
While through the woods the gun did sound
That took his life away
In the midst of life he fell, in suffering full well
Deep was the wound the keeper gave
No mortal man his life could save
He now lies sleeping in his grave
Until the Judgement Day.

It makes our hearts to mourn
Our comrades were to prison sent

It being our enemy's intent
That there they should remain
But fortune changed her mind, unto us proved kind
No more locked up in midnight cells
I hear the turnkey ring the bells
And bid those ponderous doors adieu
And the rattling of their chains.

Now the murderous man who did him kill
All on the ground his blood did spill
Must wander far against his will
And find no resting place
Destructive things his conscience stings
He must wander through the world forlorn
And ever feel the smarting thorn
And pointed at with finger scorn
And die in sad disgrace.

136

Geordie

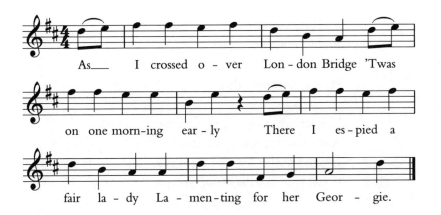

As — I crossed o - ver Lon - don Bridge 'Twas
on one morn-ing ear - ly There I es - pied a
fair la - dy La - men-ting for her Geor - gie.

As I crossed over London Bridge
'Twas on one morning early
There I espied a fair lady
Lamenting for her Georgie.

'Come fetch to me some little boy
That can go on an errand quickly
That can run ten miles in an hour
With a letter for a lady.'

'Come saddle me my milk-white steed
And bridle it most rarely
That I may go to Newcastle gaol
And beg for the life of Georgie.'

When she got to Newcastle gaol
She bowed her head so lowly
Three times on her bended knees did fall
Saying, 'Spare me the life of Georgie.'

'It is no murder George have done
Nor have he kill-ed any
But he stole sixteen of the King's fat deer
And sold them in the army.'

The judge looked over his right shoulder
And seeming very sorry
He says, 'My dear you are now too late
He is condemned already.'

'Oh six babies I have got with me
And I love them most dearly
I would freely part with them every one
If you spare me the life of Georgie.'

The judge looked over his left shoulder
And seeming very hard-hearted
He says, 'My dear you are too late
There is no pardon granted.'

'Oh George shall be hang in a chain of gold
Which a few there are not many
Because he became by a noble bride
And beloved by a vict'rous lady'. [= virtuous?]

137

Highwayman Outwitted

Good people draw near and a song you shall hear
'Tis of an old farmer in Oxfordshire
A shrewd Yorkshire boy he kept for his man
And [for] his business, whose name it was Jan.

Chorus
Ri fol de rital, fol de ral redo
Ri fol de redo, ri fol de rol dee.

In the morning quite early he called for his man
And his business, he called and said, 'Little Jan
Go take you my cow and away to the fair
She's in very good order and her I can spare.'

The boy took the cow and went off in a van
And came to the fair as we understand
And in a short time he met with three men
And sold them the cow for just six pound ten.

They went to an alehouse and there sat to drink
Where the purchaser paid to the boy all the chink
And then to the landlord the lad he did say
'With my money O what shall I do, I do pray?'

'I will sew it all in your coat lining,' said he
'Not upon the high road a-robbed should be.'
Now there sat there a highwayman drinking his wine
Said he to himself, 'Faith that money is mine.'

The boy took his leave and away he did go
The highwayman followed soon after also
'You're well overtaken, my boy,' he did say
'You're well overtaken upon the highway.'

'Will you get up behind me, my good boy?' he said
'How far are you going?' then answered the lad
'Four miles and yet further for aught that I know.'
So the boy jumped a horseback and away they did go.

They rode on their way till they reached a dark lane
When the highwayman says, 'I must tell you all plain
Deliver your money without any strife
Or instantly I will take off your sweet life.'

The boy saw no time and no chance to dispute
So he slipped from behind without any doubt
And then his coat lining he tore and pulled out
And among the green grass he strewed it about.

The highwayman instantly sprang from his horse
And little he counted the prospect of loss
But while he was seeking the highway beside
The boy jumped a horseback and away he did ride.

The highwayman shouted and bid him to stay
The boy made no answer but rode on his way
And to his old master in order did bring
Horse, bridle and saddle – a very fine thing.

His master he came to the door rather cross
'What the deuce, is my cow turned into a horse?'
'O no, my good master, the cow I have sold
She was ta'en on the way by a highwayman bold.'

They search-ed the bags and there speedily found
In silver and gold there was five hundred pound
And two brace of pistols, the boy said, 'I vow
I think, my good master, I've well sold the cow.'

Then the boy for his wit and his valour so rare
Three parts of the money was given as his share
And since that bold highwayman lost all his store
I reckon he's riding and robbing to get more.

The old master he laughed till his sides he did hold
Says he, 'Jan my boy, thou hast been very bold
And as to the villain, it serves him quite right
You have put on a robber a clean Yorkshire bite.'

138

The Lincolnshire Poacher

I was born a lab-our-er in fam-ous Glouces-ter - shire—

I served my ma-ster faith - ful for more than se-ven years—

Un - til I took to poach-ing, as quick-ly you shall hear—

For it's my de-light on a shi-ny night in the sea-son of the year.—

I was born a labourer in famous Gloucestershire
I served my master faithful for more than seven years
Until I took to poaching as quickly you shall hear
For it's my delight on a shiny night in the season of the year
For it's my delight on a shiny night in the season of the year.

As me and my companions were setting of a snare
'Twas then we spied the gamekeeper, for him we did not care
For we can wrestle and fight, my boys, [jump over anywhere]
For it's my delight on a shiny night in the season of the year, etc.

As me and my companions were setting four or five
[And taking of them up again] we caught a hare alive
We caught a hare alive, my boys, and through the woods did steer
For it's my delight on a shiny night in the season of the year, etc.

The gamekeeper came up to us and said, 'What does you here?
I'll send you both to prison for setting of a snare.'
With that we knocked the keeper down, the blow it warmed his ear
For it's my delight on a shiny night in the season of the year, etc.

Good luck to every gentleman that lives in Gloucestershire
Good luck to every poacher that goes to set a snare
Bad luck to every gamekeeper who will not sell his deer
For it's my delight on a shiny night in the season of the year, etc.

139

The Lost Lady Found

'Twas down in a val-ley a fair maid did_ dwell

She lived with her un-cle, as all knew full_ well

'Twas down in the val-ley where vi-o-lets were gay

Three Gip-sies be-trayed her and stole her_ a - way.

'Twas down in a valley a fair maid did dwell
She lived with her uncle, as all knew full well
'Twas down in the valley where violets were gay
Three Gipsies betrayed her and stole her away.

Long time she'd been missing and could not be found
Her uncle he search-ed the country around
Till he came to her trustee, between hope and fear
The trustee made answer, 'She has not been here.'

The trustee spake up with a courage so bold
'I fear she's been lost for the sake of her gold
So we'll have life for life, sir,' the trustee did say
'We shall send you to prison, and there you shall stay.'

There was a young squire that lov-ed her so
Oft times to the schoolhouse together they did go
'I'm afraid she is murdered, so great is my fear
If I'd wings like a dove I would fly to my dear.'

He travelled through England, through France and through Spain
Till he ventured his life on the watery main
And he came to a house where he lodged for a night
And in that same house was his own heart's delight.

When she saw him she knew him, and flew to his arms
She told him her grief as he gazed on her charms
'How came you to Dublin, my dearest, I pray?'
'Three Gipsies betrayed me and stole me away.'

'Your uncle's in England, in prison doth lie
And for your sweet sake is condemned for to die.'
'Carry me to old England, my dearest,' she cried
One thousand I'll give you, and will be your bride.'

When she came to old England, her uncle to see
The cart it was under the high gallows tree
'Oh pardon, oh pardon, oh pardon I crave
Don't you see I'm alive, your dear life to save.'

Then straight from the gallows they led him away
The bells they did ring and the music did play
Every house in the valley with mirth did resound
As soon as they heard the lost lady was found.

The Poor Smuggler's Boy

Oh my fa-ther and mo - ther was hap-py to dwell

In a neat lit - tle__ cot-tage, they reared me up well

Till fa-ther he ven-tured all on the__ salt__ sea

For a keg of good bran - dy, to the land of the free.

Oh my father and mother was happy to dwell
In a neat little cottage, they reared me up well
Till father he ventured all on the salt sea
For a keg of good brandy, to the land of the free.

It's for Holland we steer while the thunder do roar
And the lightning flash very far from our shore
Our topmast and rigging were blown to the waves
Leaving poor father with a watery grave.

Oh I jumped overboard, Oh I jumped in the main
To save my poor father but 'twas all in vain
Oh I clasped his cold clay and quite lifeless was he
And forced for to leave him sunk deep in the sea.

Which I clung to a plank, which I made for the shore
Bad news now for mother for father's no more
Mother, poor soul, broken-hearted she died
I was left for to wander, a poor smuggler's boy.

Now a lady of fortune she heard his complaint
She sheltered him in from the wind and the rain
She says, 'I've employment, no parents have I
I'll think of an orphan till the day I do die.'

Now he has done his duty and bears a good name
The mistress she died and the master he became
She leaved him five thousand pounds and some land
If you are poor you may live to be grand.

141

The Sheffield Apprentice

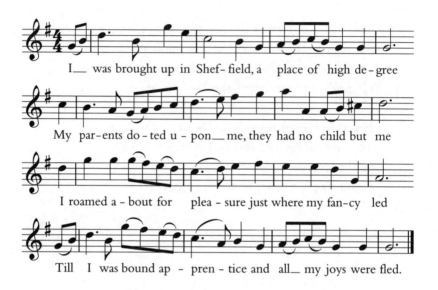

I_ was brought up in Shef-field, a place of high de-gree
My par-ents do-ted u-pon_ me, they had no child but me
I roamed a-bout for plea-sure just where my fan-cy led
Till I was bound ap - pren - tice and all_ my joys were fled.

I was brought up in Sheffield, a place of high degree
My parents doted upon me, they had no child but me
I roamed about for pleasure just where my fancy led
Till I was bound apprentice and all my joys were fled.

I did not like my master, he did not use me well
I made a resolution not along with him to dwell
I made a resolution not along with him to stay
Steering my course for London and cursed be the day.

I had not been in London scarce one month, two or three
Before my honoured mistress grew very fond of me
She said, 'I've gold, I've silver, I've houses and I've land
If you will marry me they shall be at your command.'

'Oh no dear honoured mistress, I cannot wed you now
For I have lately promised likewise a solemn vow
To wed with dearest Polly, your handsome chambermaid
So come my honoured mistress, she has my heart betrayed.'

She flew into a passion and turned away from me
Saying by he who made her she'll be revenged on me
Her gold ring on her finger, as she was passing by
She slipped it in my pocket and by it I must die.

For that before the justice, the justice I was brought
And there before the justice to answer for my fault
Long time I pleaded innocent but that was all in vain
She swore so false against me that I was sent to gaol.

Upon the day of execution and on that fateful day
I pray'd the people round me, 'Oh pray come pity me
Don't laugh at my downfall for I bid the world adieu
Farewell my dearest Polly, I died for the love of you.'

142

Thorneymoor Woods

In Thorn-ey-moor woods in Not-ting-ham-shire

Ri fal le - ro whack fal lad-die In Thorn-ey-moor woods in

Not-ting-ham-shire Fal the ral le - ro day____

The keep-ers' hou - ses stood three square A - bout a mile from

each they were Their or – der was to look

af - ter the deer Right fal the ral le - ro i day.____

In Thorneymoor woods in Nottinghamshire
Ri fal lero whack fal laddie
In Thorneymoor woods in Nottinghamshire
Fal the ral lero day
The keepers' houses stood three square

About a mile from each other they were
Their order was to look after the deer
Right fal the ral lero i day.

The moon was up and the stars gave light, etc.
O'er hedges, ditches, gate and rails
With my two dogs close at my heels
To catch a fat buck in Thorneymoor fields, etc.

The very next night we had bad luck, etc.
One of my very best dogs got stuck
He came to me both bloody and lame
And sorry was I to see the same
He was not able to follow the game, etc.

I searched his wounds and found them slight, etc.
Some keeper done it out of spite
I'll take my pike staff in my hand
I'll [range] the woods till I find that man
I'll tan his hide right well if I can, etc.

I searched the woods all that night, etc.
I searched the woods till it proved daylight
The very first thing that there I found
Was a good fat buck lie dead on the ground
I knew my dog had gave him the death wound, etc.

I out with my knife and I cut the buck's throat, etc.
I out with my knife and I cut the buck's throat
O how you would laugh to see limping Jack
Come trudging along with a buck on his back
He carried him off like a Yorkshire man's pack, etc.

We hired a butcher to skin the game, etc.
Likewise another to sell the same

The very first piece we offered for sale
Was to an old woman who sold bad ale
Who sent all us poor lads to gaol, etc.

The Nottingham 'sizes are drawing near, etc.
We poor lads shall have to appear
The magistrates they are all fully sworn
That such an old woman ought never been born
And into pieces she ought to be torn, etc.

The 'sizes are over and we are free, etc.
The 'sizes are over and we are free
Of all the games that here I see
A buck or a doe or a hare for me
In Thorneymoor woods this night I shall see, etc.

143

Three Butchers

It's of two jolly butchers, as I have heard them say
Were riding out of London all on one certain day.

As they were riding along the road as fast as they could ride
'Oh stop your horse,' said Johnson, 'I heard a woman cry.'

'I will not stop,' said Wilson, 'I will not stop,' said he
'I will not stop,' said Wilson, 'for robb-ed we shall be.'

Then Johnson he got off his horse and searched the woods around
And found a naked woman with her hair pinned to the ground.

'How came you here?' said Johnson, 'How came you here fast bound?
How came you here stark naked, with your hair pinned to the ground?'

'They whipped me, they stripped me, my legs and arms they bound
They left me here stark naked with my hair pinned to the ground.'

Then Johnson being a valiant man, a man of courage bold
He took the coat from off his back to keep her from the cold.

Then Johnson being a valiant man, a man of valiant mind
He wrapped his coat around her and took her up behind.

As they were riding along the road so fast as they could ride
She put her fingers to her lips and gave three dreadful cries.

Then up rode three young swaggering blades with staves all in their hands
A-riding up to Johnson and bidding him to stand.

'I'll stand, I'll stand,' said Johnson, 'I'll stand, I'll stand,' said he
'I never was in all my life afraid of any three.'

Then one of them he quickly slew, the woman he did not mind
She drew a knife and ripped him up behind.

'I must fall, I must fall,' said Johnson, 'I must fall upon the ground
It was this wicked woman who has give me my death wound.'

And she shall hang in iron chains for what she has just done
She's slain the fairest young butcher that e'er the sun shone on.

144

The Undaunted Female

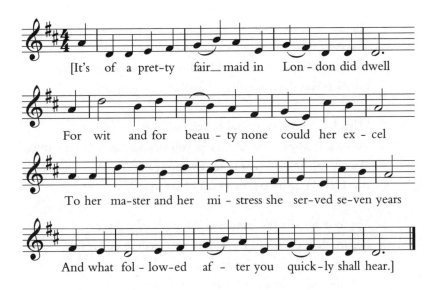

[It's of a pret-ty fair— maid in Lon - don did dwell

For wit and for beau - ty none could her ex - cel

To her ma-ster and her mi - stress she ser-ved se-ven years

And what fol - low-ed af - ter you quick-ly shall hear.]

[It's of a pretty fair maid in London did dwell
For wit and for beauty none could her excel
To her master and her mistress she serv-ed seven years
And what followed after you quickly shall hear.]

She put her box upon her head and gang-ed along
The first that she met was a surly-looking man
He said, 'My pretty fair maid, where are you going this way?
I will show you a nearer way across the counterie.'

He took her by the hand and he led her to a lane
And said, 'My pretty fair maid, I mean to tell you plain
Deliver up your money without a fear of strife
Or else this very moment I'll take away your life.'

The tears from her eyes like a fountain did flow
'Oh where shall I wander, or wither shall I go?'
And while this young fellow was feeling for his knife
This beautiful damsel she took away his life.

She put her box upon her head and gang-ed along
The next that she met was a noble-looking man
He said, 'My pretty fair maid, where are you going so late?
Or what was the noise that I heard at yonder gate?'

'That box upon your head to yourself it don't belong
To your mistress or your master you've done something wrong.'
'To my mistress or my master I've done nothing ill
But I feel in my heart it's a man I have killed.'

She took him by the hand and led him to the place
Where that surly-looking fellow lay bleeding on his face
He had some loaded pistols, some powder and some shots
A knife and a whistle, a robbery to call.

She put the whistle to her mouth and blew it loud and shrill
And four tall young fellows came trampling down the hill
And this gentleman shot one of them, whose name was Peter Lee
And the beautiful young damsel she shot the other three.

He said, 'My pretty fair maid, for what you have done
I will make you my bride for firing off your gun.'

145

Van Diemen's Land

Come all you gal-lant poach - ers that ram-ble free from care That walk out of— a moon-light night with your dog, your gun and snare Where the lof - ty hare and phea - sant you— have at your com - mand Not think-ing that your last ca-reer is on Van Die-men's Land.

Come all you gallant poachers that ramble free from care
That walk out of a moonlight night with your dog, your gun and snare
Where the lofty hare and pheasant you have at your command
Not thinking that your last career is on Van Diemen's Land.

There was poor Tom Brown from Nottingham, Jack Williams and poor Joe
Were three as daring poachers as the country well does know
At night they were trepann-ed by the keeper's hideous hand
And for fourteen years transported were unto Van Diemen's Land.

Oh when we sailed from England, we landed at the bay
We had rotten straw for bedding, we dared not to say nay
Our cots were fenced with fire, we slumber when we can
To drive away the wolves and tigers upon Van Diemen's Land.

Oh when that we were landed upon that fatal shore
The planters they came flocking round full twenty score or more
They ranked us up like horses and sold us out of hand
They yoked us to the plough, my boys, to plough Van Diemen's Land.

There was one girl from England, Susan Summers was her name
For fourteen years transported was, we all well knew the same
Our planter bought her freedom and he married her out of hand
Good usage then she gave to us upon Van Diemen's Land.

Often when I am slumbering I have a pleasant dream
With my sweet girl I am sitting, down by some purling stream
Through England I am roaming, with her at my command
Then waken, broken-hearted, upon Van Diemen's Land.

God bless our wives and families, likewise that happy shore
That isle of sweet contentment which we shall see no more
As for our wretched females, see them we seldom can
There are twenty to one woman upon Van Diemen's Land.

Come all you gallant poachers, give ear unto my song
It is a bit of good advice, although it is not long
Lay by your dog and snare, to you I do speak plain
If you knew the hardship we endure you ne'er would poach again.

146

Wild and Wicked Youth

I went to London both blithe and gay
My time I wasted in bowls and play
Until that my cash it did get low
And then on the highway I was forced to go.

O next I took to me a pretty wife
I loved her as dear and I loved my life
But for to maintain her both fine and gay
Resolved I was that the world should pay.

I robbed Lord Edgecombe I do declare
And my Lady Taunton of Melbourne Square
I bid then goodnight, sat in my chair
With laughter and song went to my dear.

I robbed them of five hundred pounds so bright
But all of it squandered one jovial night
Till taken by such as I never knew
But I was informed they were Fielding's crew.

The judge his mercy he did extend
He pardoned my crime, bade me amend
But still I pursued a thieving trade
I always was reckoned a roving blade.

O now I am judged and doomed to die
And many a maid for me will cry
For all their sighs and for all salt tears
Where I shall go the Lord knows where.

My father he sighs and he makes his moan
My mother she weeps for her darling son
But sighs and tears will never save
Nor keep me from an untimely grave.

X

What Is the Life of a Man ...
Traditional Religious Songs

What Is the Life of a Man ...
Traditional Religious Songs

There are numerous songs with religious themes, but it is not always easy to ascertain how many were sung by ordinary people of their own volition outside the confines of the church and school. Many certainly were, and a few examples are gathered here, but the folk-song collectors rarely took any notice of manifestations of 'official' culture in their fieldwork, so we often lack solid evidence.

It is misleading to think of 'folk-song' repertoire and style being totally isolated from commercial and 'art' music emanating from outside the community, and religious singing is a particular case in point. Week after week, year after year, throughout their lives, nearly everyone in rural England would have heard and participated in some form of religious music, although the exact nature of it would vary with the particular sect to which the individual belonged and the musical fashions of the time within that sect.

One example from many is 'Vital Spark of Heavenly Flame', originally a poem written by Alexander Pope about 1795 but so commonly sung as a funeral hymn that Vic Gammon writes, 'I venture to say that there was hardly a person in nineteenth-century England that was not familiar with it in the way that people today are familiar with "The National Anthem" or "Silent Night" (Gammon, 1988).

Carols were another special case and were immensely well known. In *English Folk-Song and Dance* (1915), pp. 74–5, Frank Kidson and Mary Neal write:

> That a large number of carols existed in a purely traditional form was somewhat of a revelation, even to the folk-song collector. When Miss Lucy Broadwood, Mr Cecil Sharp, and Dr Vaughan Williams published their 'finds' in the *Folk Song Journal*. Some of the folk-carols that have lately been recovered embody curious legends, the origin of which is difficult to trace.

Every year, broadside printers produced special carol sheets at Christmas (and sometimes Easter as well) which were larger, better printed and much more profusely illustrated than the average broadside and included the words to six or more songs. There was also a very strong tradition of village musicians and singers perambulating the parish to sing carols in the run-up to Christmas.

Most of the time, religious leaders took little notice of folk and popular song, apart from condemning it in general, although some evangelistic sects tried to stop their followers singing secular songs, and mostly the song tradition went on without direct interference or censure. Nearly all the Victorian and Edwardian collectors commented that the local clergyman was often totally oblivious to what his flock was singing in their leisure time and astonished to learn that there were expert ballad singers in his parish.

One organized attempt to directly influence popular taste was the *Cheap Repository Tracts* (1795–98), which were issued by a group of social conservatives led by Hannah More. These were ballads and stories, written in direct imitation of popular style and printed on broadsides and chapbooks for distribution among the working people. More's agenda was as much political as religious, and was prompted by fears that the ideas of the French Revolution would infect British society. Other would-be reformers followed suit, and such tracts were printed in their tens of thousands. But we are aware of no single case where any of these songs entered the tradition and lasted down the generations like true folk songs.

147

The Cherry-Tree Carol

Jo-seph was an old man And an old man was he
And Jo-seph mar-ried Ma-ry The Queen of— Ga-li - lee—
And Jo-seph mar-ried Ma-ry The Queen of— Ga-li - lee.

Joseph was an old man
And an old man was he
And Joseph married Mary
The Queen of Galilee.

Mary and Joseph
Together did go
And there they saw a cherry tree
Both red, white and green.

Then up speaks Mary
So meek and so mild
'O gather me cherries, Joseph
For I am with child.'

Then up speaks Joseph
With his words so unkind
'Let them gather thee cherries
That brought thee with child.'

Then up speaks the little child
In his own mother's womb
'Bow down, you sweet cherry tree
And give my mother some.'

Then the top spray of the cherry tree
Bowed down to her knee
'And now you see, Joseph
There are cherries for me.'

148

The Joys of Mary

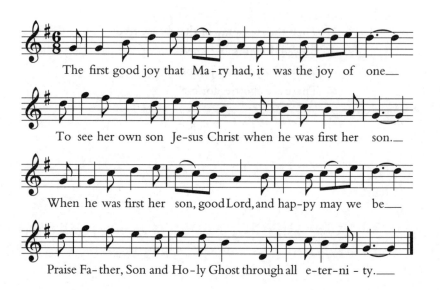

The first good joy that Ma-ry had, it was the joy of one___

To see her own son Je-sus Christ when he was first her son.___

When he was first her son, good Lord, and hap-py may we be___

Praise Fa-ther, Son and Ho-ly Ghost through all e-ter-ni-ty.___

The first good joy that Mary had, it was the joy of one
To see her own son Jesus Christ when he was first her son
When he was first her son, good Lord, and happy may we be
Praise Father, Son and Holy Ghost through all eternity.

The second good joy that Mary had, it was the joy of two
To see her own son Jesus Christ to make the lame to go, etc.

The third good joy that Mary had, it was the joy of three
To see her own son Jesus Christ to make the blind to see, etc.

The fourth good joy that Mary had, it was the joy of four
To see her own son Jesus Christ to read the Bible o'er, etc.

The fifth good joy that Mary had, it was the joy of five
To see her own son Jesus Christ to make the dead alive, etc.

The sixth good joy that Mary had, it was the joy of six
To see her own son Jesus Christ to carry the crucifix, etc.

The seventh good joy that Mary had, it was the joy of seven
To see her own son Jesus Christ to show the way to heaven, etc.

The eighth good joy that Mary had, it was the joy of eight
To see her own son Jesus Christ to make the crooked straight, etc.

The ninth good joy that Mary had, it was the joy of nine
To see her own son Jesus Christ to turn the water wine, etc.

149

The Life of a Man

As I was a-walk-ing one mor-ning at ease

View-ing the leaves as they fell from the trees

They were all in full mo-tion, ap - pear - ing to be

And— those that were wi-thered, they fell from the tree.

Chorus

What's the life of a man, a-ny more than a leaf?

A man has his sea-sons, then why should he grieve?

Al-though in this wide world he ap-pears fine and gay

Like a leaf he shall wi-ther— and soon fade a-way.

As I was a-walking one morning at ease
Viewing the leaves as they fell from the trees
They were all in full motion, appearing to be
And those that were withered, they fell from the tree.

Chorus
What's the life of a man, any more than a leaf?
A man has his seasons, then why should he grieve?
Although in this wide world he appears fine and gay
Like a leaf he shall wither and soon fade away.

You should have seen the leaves but a short time ago
They were all in full motion, appearing to grow
Till the frost came and bit them and withered them all
And the storm came upon them and down they did fall.

Down in yonder churchyard many names you will see
That are fallen from the world as the leaves from the tree
Old age and affliction upon them did fall
And death and disease came and blighted them all.

150

The Moon Shines Bright

The__ moon shines bright and the stars__ give a light

A____ lit - tle be - fore it was day

Our__ Lord our God he__ called on__ us

And__ bids us a - wake and__ pray.

The moon shines bright and the stars give a light
A little before it was day
Our Lord our God he called on us
And bids us awake and pray.

Awake, awake, good people all
Awake and you shall hear
Our Lord our God he died on the Cross
For those whom he lov-ed so dear.

And for the saving of our souls
Christ died upon the Cross
We ne'er shall do for Jesus Christ
What he has done for us.

The life of man is but a span
'Tis cut down like a flower
We are here today and we're gone tomorrow
We are all dead in an hour.

To teach your children well, dear man
The while that you are here
'Twill be better for your souls, dear man
When your corpse lies on the bier.

My carol's done and I must be gone
I can stay no longer here
So God bless you all, both great and small
And send you a happy New Year.

151

A Virgin Unspotted

A— vir-gin un - spot-ted the_ pro-phets fore - told

Should bring forth a__ Sav-iour which now we be - hold

To_ be our re - deem-er from death, hell and sin

Which A-dam's trans-gress-ion hath wrap-ped us in.

Chorus

And there-fore be mer - ry, set sor - row a - side

Christ Je - sus our Sav-iour was born on this tide.

A virgin unspotted the prophets foretold
Should bring forth a Saviour which now we behold
To be our redeemer from death, hell and sin
Which Adam's transgression hath wrapp-ed us in.

Chorus
And therefore be merry, set sorrow aside
Christ Jesus our Saviour was born on this tide.

Through Bethlehem's city in Judah it was
That Joseph and Mary together did pass
All for to be tax-ed with many one more
Since Caesar Augustus commanded the same.

Now Mary's full time being come as we find
She brought forth her firstborn to save all mankind
The inn being too full for this heavenly guest
No place could be found for to lay him to rest.

Then presently after the shepherds did spy
Vast numbers of angels for to stand in the sky
How happy they conversed, so sweet they did sing
All glory and praise to our heavenly King.

Notes to the Songs

The Roud numbers refer to the system adopted in Steve Roud's *Folk Song Index*, an online database available on the website of the Vaughan Williams Memorial Library, London (English Folk Dance and Song Society: http://library.efdss.org); the Child numbers refer to the system used in Francis J. Child's *English and Scottish Popular Ballads* (1882–98); and the Laws numbers to that in Malcolm G. Laws's *American Balladry from British Broadsides: A Guide for Students and Collectors of Traditional Song* (1957).

The number of 'entries' given for each song refers to the number of unique entries in *The Folk Song Index* for versions collected in England. See the General Introduction for further discussion of this aspect of song research.

List of Abbreviations

FMJ: *Folk Music Journal*
JEFDSS: *Journal of the English Folk Dance and Song Society*
JFSS: *Journal of the Folk-Song Society*
JIFSS: *Journal of the Irish Folk Song Society*

I
'Tis True My Love's Enlisted ...
Soldiers and Sailors

1 *The Bold* Princess Royal

Sung by Ned Adams, Hastings, Sussex (13 November 1954); recorded by
Bob Copper (BBC 22742).
Roud 528, Laws K29; 56 entries.

One of the best-known of our sea songs, collected all over the country. Some singers, at least, believed that it was a true story, but the *Princess Royal* was a very common name for a ship from the eighteenth to the twentieth centuries. The song is often set to fine stirring tunes, and it was also regularly printed on broadsides from the 1820s onwards.

The text presents us with an editorial quandary. The BBC recording has five verses, but Bob Copper's transcription of the text in his *Songs and Southern Breezes* (1973) gives two more. These additional verses are quite normally found in the song and it is possible that Bob heard Ned sing the song on another occasion, but given his reluctance to sing, as detailed in the book, this is unlikely. Bob was very familiar with the song, as it was included in his own family's repertoire, but the wording of the two verses in the book is not exactly the same as that sung by the Coppers. On balance, we have decided to leave them in (as verses 4 and 5) but have indicated their ambiguous status with square brackets.

The majority of tunes collected with this song are in triple time and bear a strong resemblance to the jaunty tunes associated with the song 'Flash Company' (No. 80), which, in turn, contain clear echoes of the very widespread tune known as 'Villikins and his Dinah' (see 'All Jolly Fellows Who Follow the Plough', No. 91). Ned Adams's melody is not of this group, being a very florid realization of a tune which has been noted elsewhere with this song in southern and eastern England. Adams's style of singing, with its melismas (in which one syllable of text is sung to several notes) and rhythmic freedom is not commonly found in English tradition, but it certainly lends his rendition a highly dignified and commanding feel. The transcription aims to strike a balance between incorporating some of these complexities (for example, through the use of 'pause' marks) while keeping the notation readable.

2 Bonny Bunch of Roses O

Sung by George Wray, Brigg, Lincolnshire (28 July 1906); collected by Percy Grainger (Grainger MSS, hectograph copy at VWML, song 189, CDA 6).
Roud 664, Laws J5; 54 entries.

'Bonny Bunch of Roses O', or 'Young Napoleon', was extremely widely known in England, and was also collected often in Ireland and Scotland. Some people have got into a tangle over the song, assuming that it features Napoleon Bonaparte speaking to his mother, and trying to fit its content into his historical life, but it is clearly a fictional account of a conversation between Napoleon's son, François Charles Joseph, and his mother. Some commentators have also made rather heavy weather of the meaning and social context of the song. Starting from the argument that many in Britain, and particularly in Ireland, saw Napoleon as a potential liberator rather than a tyrant, and assuming that 'Bonny Bunch of Roses O' was a pro-Napoleon song, it became common to maintain that the song was originally Irish. There is no evidence for this, and an Irish protest song would hardly include such a line as 'There is England, Ireland

and Scotland, their unity shall ne'er be broke', but there is a strong Irish connection.

In fact, the song was written by George Brown, who, from what little we know of him, was a prolific songwriter for the London broadside trade. Not only did Brown direct the song to be sung to the Irish tune 'The Bunch of Rushes' but he lifted wholesale some lines from an Irish broadside song, 'The New Bunch of Loughero' ('loughero' means 'rushes'). It is even possible that he got the idea for the telling phrase 'bonny bunch of roses' from 'bonny bunch of rushes'.

Given this information, we can use this song as a case study in what further can be teased out by a little detective work into broadside printings.

The song appeared numerous times on broadsides in the nineteenth century, but the earliest are by James Catnach, John Pitts and William Taylor of Waterloo Road, Lambeth. It is well known that the broadside printers simply stole each other's songs, and this is one of the reasons they claimed they could not pay their songwriters much for their work, because they could not protect their 'investment'. When different printers were in operation at the same time, it is usually impossible to know which issued a particular song first. But in the very few cases where the name of the writer appears on only one printer's sheet it is more than likely to be the original, simply because those who were copying an 'anonymous' song would not know who had written it and could not introduce the information from nowhere.

If we presume this song was written after the young Napoleon's death, in 1832, all three printers are still contenders: Catnach ceased in 1838 and Pitts in 1844, while Taylor was printing at Waterloo Road from 1831/2 to 1836/7. But it is the Taylor sheet which reveals Brown as the writer, so it is likely that the song was first published by Taylor between 1832 and 1837, and we can further hazard that the song was probably written soon after the young Napoleon's death, when he was in the news.

There is one factor that might throw some doubt on this identification of Taylor as the original printer. It is also claimed that songwriters would sell a song to one printer and then quickly sell it to another, on the assumption that the first printer would simply presume the second had copied his sheet as usual. There may, therefore, be two 'original' printers, but even if this were the case, Taylor would be one of them.

George Brown's name appears at the foot of at least eleven songs – ten of which were printed by William Taylor or his successors. It is also interesting to note that two other songs signed by Brown are Napoleonic songs – 'Bonaparte Again from St Helena' and 'The Grand Conversation on Napoleon' – and the latter also includes the 'bunch of roses' phrase.

George Wray sings a variant of the most widespread tune for this song as collected in England, which Frank Kidson considered 'a really fine air' (*JFSS*, 2 (1906), 277). The eponymous words 'the bonny bunch of roses O' occur at the end of each stanza and are almost invariably sung to the same distinctive melodic figure (bar 8 in the transcription), which falls from the seventh degree (often flattened) and concludes with the descending jump of a fifth.

As indicated, the tune is also associated with the song 'The Bunch of Rushes' in England and Ireland, and this tune name is cited for 'The Bonny Bunch of Roses O' on the Taylor printing of George Brown's song. According to D. J. O'Sullivan, this melody derives from an Irish love song, 'An Beinnsín Luachra' ('The Bundle of Rushes') (*JIFSS*, 6:27 (1967), 41–2). There is certainly a strong resemblance between the two in mode, range and phrase structure as well as melodic contour, although the Irish song is sometimes found in triple time. Its final A phrase also concludes with the hallmark melodic pattern, though finishing with a leap of a third or second rather than a fifth.

George Wray's singing is rhythmically very free and this is reflected in the complexity of Grainger's transcription of the cylinder recording. His notation is reproduced here in a simplified (and slightly re-barred) form. The tune for stanza 1 lacks the second line so this has been adapted from the corresponding phrase in stanza 2. The question marks in the variations are Grainger's. The tune's phrase structure varies from stanza to stanza, as follows:

stanza 1: A[A]BC
stanza 2: AABC
stanza 3: BCBC
stanza 4: BCBCBC
stanza 5: AABCBC

3 *Captain Ward and the* Rainbow

'Saucy Ward', sung by 'Skinny' Crow, Filby, Norfolk (March 1913);
collected by George Butterworth (Butterworth MSS, GB/5/28 &
GB/7d/39). One line was missing from verse 3, which has been supplied
from a version collected by Sabine Baring-Gould.
Roud 224, Child 287; 18 entries.

Collected a fair number of times, but nowhere near as often as other seafaring ballads such as 'The *Golden Vanity*' (No. 9) and 'The Bold *Princess Royal*' (No. 1). It was also noted occasionally in Scotland and Ireland and a few times in North America. Francis J. Child includes it in his *English and Scottish Popular Ballads*, but prints only one text, from a black-letter broadside in the Bagford collection, while Bertrand Bronson musters eleven tunes. Other black-letter sheets survive in the Pepys, Roxburghe and Euing collections, and were published in the mid to late seventeenth century – perhaps as early as the 1620s; the ballad remained in print on numerous broadsides and garlands throughout the eighteenth and nineteenth centuries.

The song does include some facts. Information given in Roy Palmer's *Oxford Book of Sea Songs* (1986) and Christopher Lloyd's *English Corsairs on the Barbary Coast* (1981) shows that John Ward (d. 1622) was indeed a Royal Navy man turned pirate, who, from his base in Tunisia, terrorized the shipping of the major maritime nations of the time. He was famous enough to inspire other ballads and a play, and he also appears to have tried to negotiate a pardon with James I, but was refused. But no fight with the *Rainbow*, or any other navy ship, is recorded.

Bronson finds the tune tradition for this ballad 'scattered and thin', often recalling the tunes of other songs (*The Traditional Tunes of the Child Ballads*, IV (1972), p. 363). 'Skinny' Crow's tune is no exception, for it is a version of the tune often associated with 'The Banks of the Sweet Dundee' (No. 58). With its ABBA structure, flattened seventh and the lack of the second degree of the scale, it is also particularly close to the tune found in this volume with 'The Knight and the Shepherd's Daughter' (No. 31). George B. Gardiner collected tunes for 'Captain Ward' in Hampshire (from Isaac Hobbs and Richard Haynes) whose first two lines comprise the B phrase of Crow's tune repeated.

Butterworth's manuscript lacks a time signature so one has been added to the notation here.

4 *The* Dolphin

Sung by Sam Larner, Winterton, Norfolk (7 March 1958); recorded by
Philip Donnellan (BBC 26075).
Roud 690; 21 entries.

A somewhat formulaic seafaring song, but very effective in the mouths of singers like Sam Larner and Bob and Ron Copper. Collected a fair number of times across the country, under various titles such as 'Warlike Seamen', 'London Man-o-War', 'Liverpool Play' and the very un-pirate-like 'The Sea-Lark'. Only a handful of broadside versions have survived, with the earliest, entitled 'The Bold Wasp', dating from about 1800.

It is the many versions which name the ship as the *Nottingham* which give a clue to the song's origins and reveal that it reports a real incident. In the laconic words of Captain Sainsbury's very useful *Royal Navy Day by Day* (1992), p. 288,

> 11th October 1746: *Nottingham* captured the French *Mars*, 70 miles to the southwestward of Cape Clear, after a gallant defence by an ailing crew.

What might be the original song (although the provenance is not given) appears in John Laffin's *Jack Tar* (1969), pp. 184–5.

The song is often associated with a four-time melody, such as that sung by Bob and Ron Copper, or a more lilting, compound-time tune of which Sam Larner's is an example. His rendition includes several vocal slides and grace notes, which add to the tune's swing.

5 Faithful Sailor Boy

Sung by George Spicer, Selsfield, Sussex (1974); recorded by Mike Yates;
issued on *Blackberry Fold*, Topic 12T235 (1974).
Roud 376, Laws K13; 25 entries.

'Faithful Sailor Boy' was immensely popular with twentieth-century singers and has
been widely recorded, but it does not appear in the manuscripts of the major Victorian and Edwardian collectors in England. Presumably, it was too modern to attract
them, although the less fastidious Gavin Greig noted no fewer than eight versions in
Scotland around 1908, which shows that it was already popular at that time. The
texts and tune are remarkably stable across all the known versions.

The song appeared on one or two late nineteenth-century broadsides, and was
probably written about 1880. Several sources claim that it was composed by the
well-known songwriters Thomas Payne Westendorf (1848–1923) and G. W. Persley
(1837–94), but we have not been able to confirm this, nor have we found any original
sheet music.

6 The Female Cabin Boy

Sung by Mrs Susan Williams, Haselbury Plucknett, Somerset (26 December
1905); collected by Cecil Sharp (Sharp MSS, FW 782–3/FT 698). In the
Sharp manuscript, the first line of verse 4 is missing, so we have supplied it
from a Hampshire version in the George B. Gardiner MSS (GG/1/18/1148).
The words in the last line have been amended from
'Twas you or either I betrayed ...'
Roud 239, Laws N13; 17 entries.

A reasonably widespread song in England, although it only just sneaks into our
category of 'most popular' songs, and was also found, but less frequently, in Scotland
and North America.

Although the cross-dressing motif usually gets this 'Cabin Boy' lumped in with
the category of 'female warrior' songs, there is nothing warlike about our heroine,
and really the song is simply an extended joke. Nevertheless, one can see, if one
chooses, a deeper significance, as in the comment on the song by Dianne Dugaw
in *Warrior Women and Popular Balladry* (1989), p. 84: 'Amidst its laughter, it warns of
the deep confusions and implicit dangers in such gender masquerading.' In other
versions the heroine is referred to as 'The Handsome Cabin Boy', which enhances
the gender ambiguity.

It was very widely printed on broadsides from at least the 1820s.

The same jaunty tune is nearly always used for this song, though in various forms.
It is also associated with 'The Female Drummer' (Frank Purslow, *Marrow Bones*

(2007), p. 141), although not in the case of No. 7 here, and 'The Little Gipsy Girl' (No. 32).

7 The Female Drummer

Sung by Mrs Elizabeth Smith, Copthorne, Surrey (1966); collected by
Ken Stubbs; printed in his *The Life of a Man* (1970), pp. 34–5. Stubbs added
the line 'He looked upon me kindly and these are the words he said' from
another local version.
Roud 226; 21 entries.

One of the few cross-dressing songs where the girl becomes a soldier, not to follow her lover, but just because she wants to. The song was collected quite widely in England and Scotland, but rarely in North America. It was also a favourite with broadside printers, and it must have been available for almost all of the nineteenth century.

The early broadside texts include the detail that our heroine fought at the Siege of Valenciennes, which took place in 1793. This has led some commentators to suggest that the song refers to Mary Ann Talbot (1778–1808), whose autobiography states that she was at that battle in the guise of a drummer boy. Talbot's claims were published, in ever-increasing detail, in the years 1799 and 1804, and finally in book form in 1809, after her death, but Suzanne Stark, in her book *Female Tars* (1996), claims that the whole story was spurious, and mostly concocted by a ghost writer. Nevertheless, the earliest broadside that we know of was published about 1802, so it is still possible that the song was inspired by her story, although beyond the name of the battle the narratives do not tally in any other detail. The subject was obviously popular at the time, as a different song telling a similar story and also called 'The Female Drummer' was in print in garlands and on broadsides in the same period.

The tunes associated with the song are appropriately march-like in their feel (see also the note to No. 6 above).

8 General Wolfe

'Bold General Wolfe', sung by Alec Bloomfield, Framlingham, Suffolk (27
August 1952); recorded by Peter Kennedy; and by Keith Summers, Newark,
Nottinghamshire (1975), issued on *A Story to Tell*, Musical Traditions
MTCD339 (2007). The text we have used incorporates both recordings,
which are slightly different.
Roud 624; 32 entries.

Writers of broadsides and folk songs certainly liked their military heroes to die in action, preferably after beating the French. Nelson and Wolfe managed it perfectly, whereas Wellington lived on too long to be truly heroic. James Wolfe (1727–59) died in command of the successful action to take Quebec from the French. Despite his youth, he had already seen action in several campaigns and he was a keen military theorist as well as a practical soldier. He introduced a number of basic improvements to the way our troops went into battle, which were acknowledged as important contributions to the effectiveness of the British army for several generations.

Numerous songs were written about him, but this was the one which took the popular fancy and lasted long enough to be collected 200 years after his death. It was widely known in England, but not apparently elsewhere, apart from some versions collected in Canada. The Americans and Canadians had their own traditional song, variously called 'Brave Wolfe' or 'Bold Wolfe' (Roud 961, Laws A1), which includes a delightful vignette of Wolfe and Montcalm (leader of the French) strolling together and chatting just before the battle.

Our Wolfe song also appeared widely on nineteenth-century broadsides, but no eighteenth-century examples of it have been found, although they probably did exist. It was certainly in existence in 1818, when it was included in the relatively upmarket *Vocal Library*, a hardback book of over 1,800 songs, which sold for 10s 6d, bound in red leather. Many of the songs in this book were assigned to named authors, but 'General Wolfe's Request' was anonymous.

Malcolm Douglas and Steve Gardham, the editors of Frank Purslow's *Marrow Bones* (2007), observe that the tunes for the song are all clearly related, although they show extensive variation (p. 125) and Alec Bloomfield's tune is no exception. His rendition is freer in rhythm than can be captured easily in music notation.

9 *The* Golden Vanity

Sung by Henry Hills, Lodsworth, Sussex (Jan 1900); collected by W. Percy Merrick; published in *JFSS*, 1 (1901), 104–5. 'Messes' in the last two verses means 'messmates'.
Roud 122, Child 286; 34 entries.

Widely collected across Britain and North America but not common, apparently, in Ireland, 'The *Golden Vanity*' is still well known because it was taught in school singing lessons after Baring-Gould and Sharp included it in their *English Folk Songs for Schools* (1906). Francis J. Child printed three early versions, but Bertrand Bronson found 110 tunes. The name of the ship varies considerably, especially in American versions, but in England *Golden Vanity* is by far the most common, although the song is sometimes called 'The Lowlands Low' after the repeated burden lines.

The earliest surviving text, which is probably the original, is found on a blackletter broadside in the Percy and Euing collections, entitled 'Sir Walter Raleigh Sailing in the Lowlands' and printed about 1682–5. It provides some details which were lost in later versions: Raleigh has built a ship called the *Sweet Trinity*, which has been captured by the enemy, and he asks for help getting it back. In this version, the

enemy is unspecified. The ending is inconclusive, as the captain agrees to the promised 'gold and fee', but refuses to hand over his daughter. The boy says goodbye,
'Seeing as you are not so good as your word'.

The core story remains the same in most later versions, although they name the
enemy variously as Turkish, Spanish, Dutch or French, and the ending often differs.
In most, as in Henry Hills's given here, the captain proves completely perfidious and
refuses to even take the boy back on board. The boy says that if it were not for his
crewmates on board he would serve the captain's ship as he had the enemy. Sometimes the crew take him on board anyway. But one way or another, the boy almost
always dies, and is often tossed back over the side quite unceremoniously.

The song was widely available on broadsides in the nineteenth century, and most
of the versions collected in England follow the printed texts quite closely, as does
the published school-book version.

Frank Kidson comments that 'though there is a great degree of similarity of
structure in the various versions of this widely distributed ballad, each one has a
distinct and separate tune' (*JFSS*, 1 (1901), 105).

10 The Green Bed

Sung by John Masters, Bradstone, Devon (*c.*1889); collected by Sabine
Baring-Gould (Baring-Gould MSS, SBG/1/1/426).
Roud 276; 26 entries.

The song was widely sung in England, Scotland and Ireland, and noted dozens of
times in North America; the theme of the land dwellers being out to cheat the poor
sailor is clearly universal. In general in folk songs, sailors can be as free and easy with
their affections as they wish, but women on shore must not, and there are apparently
no songs from the landlady's point of view complaining about feckless customers
who try to get things on credit and never pay their tab.

The song was also widespread on nineteenth-century broadsides, but it was
already in print well before that time. A chapbook in the British Library, for example, entitled *Philander's Garland* (*c.*1780), includes a song called 'A Comical Dialogue
Between an Honest Sailor and his Deluding Landlady; Shewing the Diverting
Compliments between him and her Daughter'. Another, *Four Excellent New Songs*
(National Library of Scotland), printed in Falkirk by Patrick Mair and dating from
the 1760s, includes the song as 'Green Bed's Empty'. It is interesting to note that
although patently the same song, these two eighteenth-century texts differ markedly and were clearly not simply copied one from the other or from a common
printed source. This might be taken as evidence that the song was already circulat-
ing orally before this time. In the *Philander's Garland* version Jack does not mince his
words at the end: 'O the pox may light on such a parcel of whores.'

John Masters's tune is a little reminiscent of 'Three Maidens to Milking Did Go'

(No. 87). The dotted minim in bar 8 has been changed to a dotted crotchet to fit the bar.

11 The Greenland Whale Fishery

Sung by Richard Gregory, Two Bridges, Devon (January 1890); collected by
Sabine Baring Gould (Baring-Gould MSS, SBG/1/2/196).
Roud 347, Laws K21; 21 entries.

This song was popular across England, and also collected often in Scotland and North America. Of several songs about whaling, this was easily the most widely known, and the one which lasted in traditional singers' repertoires. It was also widely printed on broadsides, with the earliest surviving examples dating from about 1820. We have evidence that it appealed to at least two real whalers, as copies are found in the journals of the ships *Bengal* from Salem, in 1833, and *Euphrasia* from New Bedford, in 1849 (Gale Huntington, *Songs the Whalemen Sang* (1964), pp. 9–13). By the time this song appeared, the Greenland whale fishery was already in decline and the ships were moving elsewhere.

Catching whales from small boats, as described in the song, was an arduous and dangerous business. *An Authentick Narration of all the Occurrences in a Voyage to Greenland in the Year 1772* contains the following description:

> The manner of killing a whale is as follows. As soon as a whale is perceived, the word
> is immediately given and every man hastens from the ship into the boat to which he
> properly belongs: for every ship has seven or eight boats, to each of which six men
> are appointed. As soon as the boats come sufficiently near the whale, the harpooner
> strikes him with his harpoon, or barb'd dart, and the fish, feeling himself wounded,
> shoots, with the swiftness of an arrow, down to the bottom of the sea. Great precau-
> tion is therefore necessary that the line, one end of which is fastened to the harpoon,
> runs freely out, for should it by any accident be stopped there will be a necessity of
> cutting it immediately to keep the boat from sinking ... After the whale has continued
> some time near the bottom of the sea, which is here some hundred fathoms deep, he
> is forced to come up to the surface of the water for air ... While he continues on the
> surface, a second harpoon is fixed in him, on which he again plunges into the deep, but
> cannot continue so long under water as the first time. On his coming up they pierce
> him with spears ...

The 'Greenland Whale Fishery' melodies vary considerably in their contour but often show a marked resemblance to each other in their final two phrases. Here, the penultimate note of the music notation has been changed from a quaver to a minim. The melodic variation is indicated in the manuscript source by the words 'or else' and appears to apply from the end of bar 4 to bar 8; it is set out beneath these bars.

12 The Isle of France

Sung by Captain Lewis, Minehead, Somerset (15 January 1906); collected by
Cecil Sharp (Sharp MSS, FW 835–7/FT 779).
Roud 1575; 30 entries.

This song was collected a respectable number of times in England, but was rare in
Scotland and apparently not collected at all in Ireland or North America, although
it appeared on broadsides there. It was also very common on English broadsides, but
only from perhaps the 1840s. The collected texts follow the broadsides quite closely,
although there is some confusion in the story. When the coastguard asks the convict
if he is of the Shamrock Green, this is often taken as meaning 'Are you Irish?', but it
is clear from the rest of the song that the *Shamrock Green* is the name of the ship which
has just been wrecked. In at least one collected version, the convict replies, 'I am not
of the shamrock.' But some versions start with a verse about a grieving female, which
confuses things further as 'my shamrock green' appears to be the convict's nickname:

> *The constant girl was heard to cry*
> *And drop't the tear from her tender eye*
> *Saying the cruel laws of our gracious Queen*
> *They have transported my Shamrock green.*

Even for a song written for the broadside trade, which it almost certainly was, the
song is rather sentimental and does not ring true. It is not clear, for example, why
the convict was still so heavily chained if he was on his way home, presumably under
some form of parole or licence, apart from the stereotype that convicts have to be in
irons. It is also not clear whether latter-day singers knew where the 'Isle of France'
was, or even whether they cared. It is sometimes suggested that it refers to the Channel Islands, but this is simply guesswork. 'Isle of France' was an early name for
Mauritius, which was taken from France by Britain after the fall of Napoleon, and
this is presumably the original location for the song. At least we can rule out the
other Isle of France, the French administrative region, which includes Paris and is
inland, so not known for its shipwrecks.

The tune to which 'The Isle of France' is often sung, as here, is also associated
with 'Early, Early All in the Spring' (No. 43).

13 The Mermaid

Sung by Robert Hard, Thrushelton, Devon, and others; collected by Sabine
Baring-Gould (Baring-Gould MSS, SBG/1/2/657).
Roud 124, Child 289; 28 entries.

Not one of the 'big five' Child ballads in terms of popularity, but still collected a respectable number of times in Britain and even more often in North America. Francis J. Child printed six versions, and Bertrand Bronson amassed forty-two tunes. The song goes under various titles, including 'The Stormy Winds Do Blow' and 'Three Times Round Went Our Gallant Ship', but the simple 'The Mermaid' is by far the most common, and highlights the key element of the plot, the significance of which modern readers or listeners might easily miss, but which our predecessors would have taken for granted.

Most seafaring cultures in the world seem to have some sort of lore about semi-human marine creatures, and these take many different forms, including, in Britain, the belief in the existence of seal-folk and mermaids. In Britain, mermaids were accepted as real by many until quite recently, and the idea that the sight of them presages disaster to sailors was also widespread. As Richard of Gloucester says, in Shakespeare's *Henry VI, Part 3* (III.2), 'I'll drown more sailors than the mermaid shall.' But there is another possible superstition lurking in our text and many other versions: that it is unlucky to start any new project, especially a journey, on a Friday. This was ultimately based on Christian teaching, as Friday was a general day of penance and abstinence in commemoration of it being the day of the Crucifixion. The idea of unlucky Friday is well documented in England at least since Chaucer's time, although the notion that Friday 13th is particularly bad only dates from late Victorian times.

Although 'The Mermaid' is often assumed to be ancient, largely because of its subject matter, Child found no earlier version than the one called 'The Seamen's Distress' in a chapbook, *The Glasgow Lasses Garland*, in the British Library, which is tentatively dated to about 1765 but could be at least two decades later. This is definitely our song, but takes fourteen verses to tell the story rather than the usual five or six of the collected versions. But this eighteenth-century song is in turn clearly based on a much earlier twenty-two-verse black-letter broadside 'The Praise of Saylors here set forth', which has the explanatory subtitle, 'With the hard fortunes which do befall them on the seas, when landsmen sleep in their beds', dating from about the 1670s and found in the Douce and Rawlinson collections (both available on the Bodleian Library Broadside Ballads website). This has the mermaid and the shipwreck, but they are part of a much longer account of the dangers and discomforts of a seafaring life.

The only evidence as to the song's melody on the black-letter broadsides is the instruction 'To a pleasant new tune'. This makes William Chappell's printing of 'The Stormy Winds Do Blow', 'a fragment of an old sea song, contributed by Mr Charles Sloman in 1840, and the tune noted down from his singing', the earliest tune record for this ballad (Bronson, *The Traditional Tunes of the Child Ballads*, II (1962), p. 742). Robert Hard's tune is very similar to this in terms of its pitches, rhythm and form. This last consists of a five-line stanza, the final line of which forms a refrain and is set to an embellished repeat of the previous musical phrase and linked to it by means of a 'bridge' of four notes (bar 8). This is followed by a burden, or chorus, set to the same music as the verse but with some notable alterations (see Bronson, *The Traditional Tunes of the Child Ballads*, IV (1972), p. 370). In common with most of the tunes for this song, which are of the same basic type, Hard's melody is major in tonality and authentic in range, with the first-phrase cadence on the first degree and a mid-stanza cadence on the fifth.

The first note of the source transcription has here been raised by a semitone, a dot added to the first minim of bar 12 and the final note of bar 14 changed from a quaver to a crotchet to fit the bar.

14 Nancy of Yarmouth

'Nancy', sung by James Parsons, Lewdown, Devon (1888?); collected by
Sabine Baring-Gould (Baring-Gould MSS, SBG/3/1/253 & SBG/1/246).
Baring-Gould also collected a very similar version from William Friend,
Lydford, Devon (January 1889) (SBG/1/1/245 & SBG/3/1/252). Neither text
was quite complete, and verses 2 and 6 in the above are
from Friend's version.
Roud 407; 30 entries.

Widely known in England, and with a number of versions reported from Canada, this song does not seem to have been popular elsewhere in Britain or in the USA. Several of the Edwardian collectors commented how common it was in their time, including H. E. D. Hammond in Dorset and Cecil Sharp in Somerset, and it was still being regularly collected in East Anglia in the post-war period. The wording varies little from version to version, although Nancy often comes from London, Plymouth, Weymouth, and so on, and the title is sometimes 'The Sea Storm'.

The song was printed on many nineteenth-century broadsides, but the earliest known examples are in undated eighteenth-century chapbooks, such as *Lord Anson's Garland* and *The Lover's Jubilee*, which were probably printed between 1760 and 1780.

The tune given here is from James Parsons, that of William Friend being a quite different melody. Parson's tune, as notated in the manuscript, is pretty clearly in C major, the F sharp in the key signature probably being a mistake (it has been transposed into G major here so the sharp is correct).

15 The Rainbow

'A Broadside', sung by Bob Scarce, Blaxhall, Suffolk (c. 1971); recorded by
Keith Summers; issued on *A Story to Tell*, Musical Traditions MTCD339-0
(2007), also on the British Library Sound Archive's Traditional Music
in England website.
Roud 492, Laws N4; 26 entries.

A rousing sea song full of blood and valour, which was popular with singers across the country. It goes by many titles, such as 'As We Were a-Sailing', 'Down by the

Spanish Shore' and 'A Broadside'. Likewise the ship's name is not fixed, including *Rainbow*, *Resolution*, *Lion*, *Britannia* and, in the older versions, the *Union*.

It is probably the concentration by successive singers on the naval action at the core of the song which has contributed to a slight problem in the storyline – where on earth does the damsel come from in verse 3? The answer is simple. Earlier versions start with a verse that describes a girl dressing as a sailor to follow her lover to sea; as in this example from another Suffolk singer, Bob Hart from Snape:

> Oh a story, a story I'm just about to tell
> It's a fair damsel who in London she did dwell
> And before I conclude, well you will quickly hear
> How she ventured her life for the one she loved so dear.

They usually also have verses at the end explaining how she brought the ship back to port and was given a pension for her valour. These earlier versions were called 'The Female Captain' or 'The Bold Damosel', which indicates that this was probably the central motif of the song.

No one has yet been able to date the song, but it is certainly at least eighteenth century and some authorities suggest a seventeenth-century origin, although they are probably confusing it with other *Rainbow* songs.

There is no one widespread tune for 'The *Rainbow*'. Several, including this one, are sung to a tune whose first and last phrases strongly echo those of 'The Female Cabin Boy' (No. 6), another song in which a girl dresses up as a sailor. Bob Scarce sings the rhythm very freely, so the transcribed rhythm is an approximation only. Variation (e) is sung in two different places and the change to the minor third (F natural) seems deliberate.

16 Rambling Sailor

Sung by William Bartle, Bedfordshire (1962); recorded by Fred Hamer;
published in Hamer's *Garners Gay* (1967), p. 12.
Roud 518; 23 entries.

The free-and-easy nature of sailors is proverbial and well represented in folk song; 'Rambling Sailor' was found widely in England, fairly regularly in Scotland, but not so often elsewhere. Although most of the early collectors noted it, often in several versions, they chose not to publish unedited texts in full because they found some of it objectionable. Their manuscripts, and the broadside texts, show that the verse they found difficult was on the lines of the following (collected by H. E. D. Hammond from F. Stockley in Wareham, Dorset, in 1906):

> Oh I got up early in the morning
> I left my love a-sleeping

I left her there for an hour or two
While I did go court some other
But if she stays there till I return
She may stay there till the doom
For I travel like a rambling sailor.

There was also a very similar 'Rambling Soldier' song, popular on broadsides but not so often collected from singers. Sabine Baring-Gould, Cecil Sharp and others assumed that 'Rambling Soldier' came first, but this does not seem be correct. Early broadsides of 'Rambling Soldier' were designed to be sung to the tune of 'Rambling Sailor', and there is evidence that it was written by broadside writer John Morgan, in the 1820s or 1830s, whereas the earliest 'Rambling Sailor' texts date from before 1800. There were also other songs on the same model – 'Rambling Female Sailor', 'Rambling Comber', 'Rambling Miner', and so on.

Many broadside copies of 'Rambling Sailor' have survived, and the traditional versions are usually very close to the printed texts.

Sharp notes that the song's tune is 'always in the hornpipe measure and usually in the mixolydian mode' (*Folk Songs from Somerset*, IV (1908), p. 73), and William Bartle's is no exception.

17 The Saucy Sailor Boy

'Jack Tar', sung by Emily Bishop, Bromsberrow Heath, Herefordshire (13 October 1952); recorded by Peter Kennedy.
Roud 531, Laws K38; 42 entries.

'The Saucy Sailor Boy' was collected widely in England, though more rarely elsewhere, but few of the collectors took much notice of it. William Alexander Barrett noted in his *English Folk-Songs* (1891), p. 55, 'The song is a great favourite with factory girls in the East of London', and J. Horsfall Turner wrote in *The Yorkshire Anthology* that it was 'formerly much sung at Whitby and Hull and in other parts of Yorkshire'.

The song was printed by many of the mid nineteenth-century broadside houses, with the earliest extant sheet by John Pitts of London, which could be from the first decades of the century. But Barrett noted that it was in print 'as far back as 1781', so he must have seen some earlier manifestation. This is quite possible, as the song has the feel of an eighteenth-century duet stage song.

Sailors in the days of sail really did 'smell so strong of tar', and the nickname 'Jack Tar' was an accurate one. Not only was tar used liberally on the wood, metal, cloth and ropes of the ship in an attempt to preserve them and keep them waterproof, but the men also used it on their clothes and hats to keep out the weather.

The same nineteenth-century printers also issued a song called 'The Saucy Plough Boy', which includes some of the lines of 'The Saucy Sailor Boy', and although the two songs are otherwise very different it is likely that the latter was written as a parody of the former.

The tunes found with this song are mostly very similar and a subgroup of these also have the distinctive dotted rhythm patterns like those sung by Emily Bishop. Frank Kidson found that 'in all copies of the air there appears to be too much of the "Swiss" waltz character to suggest English folk-melody' and Lucy Broadwood was of the opinion that it was 'a German-Swiss tune imported at the beginning of the last century together with ... similar foreign airs beloved by our guitar-playing great aunts'. Cecil Sharp, on the other hand, suggested that the tune was a variant of 'Chevy Chase' and 'The Two Children in the Wood' (*JFSS*, 4 (1913), 343–44).

18 *The Silk Merchant's Daughter*

'New York Street', sung by J. Masters, Devon (30 May 1891); collected by
Sabine Baring-Gould (Baring-Gould MSS, SBG/1/2/465).
Roud 552, Laws N10; 18 entries.

Collected fairly often in England and quite frequently in North America, but not much elsewhere, the song was common on broadsides from at least the 1820s onwards.

The theme of cannibalism at sea (or at least the threat of it) as a dramatic device is not uncommon in folk songs, and some broadsides claimed to report actual occurrences of the practice. On this topic, see Paul Cowdell's article 'Cannibal Ballads' in *FMJ* (2010). But what has survived in the collected versions is not the whole original story. These start some way in, leaving the listener to catch up as the song progresses. The original starts with the familiar tale of an old miser taking against his daughter's boyfriend and getting him 'pressed to sea'. She then dresses as a sailor and follows him to America. After some adventures of her own, she finally finds herself shipping on board the same ship as her still unaware lover.

The nineteenth-century broadsides, from which all the collected texts seem to derive, present the shortened version, either starting with an explanatory verse, 'There was a silk merchant's daughter' or going straight in with 'As I was walking down New York street', which is why many versions were simply called 'New York Street'. The longer version was printed in garlands in the late eighteenth century, usually under the title of 'The Silk Mercer's Daughter'.

J. Masters's tune, in its triple time and distinctive mid-point cadence on the lower fifth, is typical of those associated with this song. His tune is noted twice in the Baring-Gould manuscripts, both times without the F sharp in the key signature. The melodic movement in bars 15 and 23 definitely suggest that F sharp is correct, however, and a major tune is the norm in other collected versions, so it has been added here.

19 Spanish Ladies

Sung by Tommy Morrissey, Padstow, Cornwall (*c.*1992); recorded by John
Howson; issued on *Romany Roots*, Veteran VT153CD (2006).
Roud 687; 30 entries.

A widely collected song, usually set to a rousing tune, which was sung equally by
seafarers (including Tommy Morrissey, a retired fisherman) and land dwellers. At
sea, according to Stan Hugill in his *Shanties from the Seven Seas* (1961), who learnt it
from his father, it could also be used as a shanty: 'It was a homeward-bound song,
sung at the capstan' (pp. 384–7). The catalogue of place names along the English
Channel is interesting, and varies little from version to version. Sabine Baring-Gould,
on the authority of his sea-going cousin Alexander Baring, comments that they are
the sequence of *lights* sighted, not land (*English Minstrelsie*, III (1895), p. iii).

Many people in the nineteenth century knew the song because it appeared in the
novel *Poor Jack*, published in 1840 and written by Captain Frederick Marryat (1798–
1848), who first went to sea in September 1806. He clearly thought of it as an old song:

> 'Give us Spanish Ladies, Dick?' said my father. As this song was very popular at that
> time among the seamen, and is now almost forgotten, I shall, by inserting it here, for
> a short time rescue it from oblivion.

Marryatt gives a text which is remarkably similar to Tommy Morrissey's, recorded
over 150 years later. The song also appeared on broadsides, some of which were
probably printed in the 1820s or 1830s, but it may have been in circulation sometime
before that. James Anthony Gardner, who entered the navy in 1782, quoted a verse
in his *Recollections* (Naval Record Society, 1894) under the heading of '1794', and this
is sometimes quoted as evidence of its existence at that date. But he compiled his
memoirs in the 1830s and was clearly simply quoting an 'old song' which seemed
appropriate to the subject in hand.

The 'Spanish Ladies' tune is found in both major (as here) and minor tonalities.
Cecil Sharp regarded the former as a 'modernized' and 'far less beautiful' form of
the tune (*Folk Songs from Somerset*, V (1909), p. 90).

20 The White Cockade

'The Summer Morning', sung by 'Mr Alderson and men', Redmire,
Wensleydale, Yorkshire; collected by Mary and Nigel Hudleston; published
on their *Yorkshire Folk Singers* (EP), and in the Hudlestons' *Songs of the Ridings*
(2001), p. 183.
Roud 191; 45 entries.

Several nineteenth-century editors comment on how popular this song was across the country, particularly in the northern parts. Frank Kidson noted it from the singing of his mother, who heard it sung in Leeds around 1820. The version transcribed here was sung by three or four men, and the song seems to have been a popular one for unison singing, but it appears clear it was originally a duet song, for a male and female taking alternate verses but coming together on the chorus, and was presumably first written for the musical stage in the latter part of the eighteenth century.

The song was widely printed on broadsides, although the earliest that have survived date from only the 1790s. The colour of the cockade varies – white, blue or green – and although there is unlikely to be any real significance in that in traditional versions, it has been suggested that provincial broadside printers certainly tried to match the colour with particular local regiments.

A number of different tunes have been associated with this song, including 'The Banks of the Sweet Dundee' (No. 58). Mr Alderson's tune is the same as that collected by Kidson from his mother and elsewhere in Yorkshire. H. E. D. Hammond, Sabine Baring-Gould and Cecil Sharp also collected versions of this tune in the south-western counties of England. Mr Alderson and his singing companions perform this version in two parts, both of which have been transcribed here. Interestingly, the Copper family, who sing many of their songs in harmony, publish this one as a solo line, although their tune is much the same as that of Mr Alderson.

II
Down in Cupid's Garden …
Happy Relationships

21 Bold Fisherman

Sung by William Titchener, Stanton-in-the-Vale, Oxfordshire (c.1932);
collected by James Madison Carpenter (Carpenter MSS, pp. 00677–8). We
have added one verse from a similar version collected by Carpenter from
William Butler of Bampton, Oxfordshire (Carpenter MSS, p. 00646;
Cylinder 034 (sr252), Disc Side 067 (sr 034a)).
Roud 291, Laws O24; 58 entries.

This song was collected many times across the country, and its popularity was probably helped by its majestic tune and slightly mysterious words. It was also a favourite with broadside printers, and the earliest extant sheets date from about the 1820s. The words vary surprisingly little from version to version.

The early folk-song collectors sometimes took a leaf out of their folklorist cousins' book by indulging in flights of fancy about the age and origin of certain songs, and 'Bold Fisherman' has suffered from this unfortunate tendency. Lucy Broadwood decided that the 'three chains of gold', the river setting and the 'fisher-man' motif were indicative of a 'medieval allegorical origin' for the song, which incorporated features from Gnostic and early Christian symbolism (see *JFSS*, 5 (1915)). There is no evidence for this, and it seems to be wishful thinking, but the idea is often quoted by people commenting on the song. In fact, both the traditional and broadside versions make it pretty clear that it is a straight seduction narrative, of a maid by a higher-class man, but with a happy ending to prove his intentions were honourable and to make it romantic rather than sordid.

The difference between these two opposing perspectives is highlighted within the text itself. It is interesting to note that the traditional versions almost always include, in verse 4, the line 'He pulled off his morning gown and gently laid it down', but in the extant broadsides, which are all dated earlier, the same line is ren-dered, 'He pulled off *her* morning gown and gently laid *her* down'.

There is widespread consistency among the tunes to which this song has been sung. This is of note because it is one of a small class of tunes in the English folk-song repertoire sung with five beats to the bar, with an emphasis on the first and third beats. Five time is not commonly found in popular or art music, which makes its persistence in connection with this tune all the more intriguing.

22 Cupid the Pretty Ploughboy

'Kilpit the Ploughing Boy', sung by Mr W. Buckland, Lippenham, Buckinghamshire (18 September 1943); collected by Francis Collinson (Collinson MSS, COL/1/36).
Roud 986, Laws O7; 19 entries.

This song was collected a fair number of times in England, and occasionally in North America, but apparently not elsewhere. In Mr Buckland's version the ploughboy has acquired a rather prosaic name, but in virtually all the other renderings he is known as 'Cupid the Pretty Ploughboy'. Love across the class barrier is a regular theme in folk song, but does not always run so smoothly and end so happily as in this one. Indeed, the absence of any opposition or complication makes the storyline a little flat. But it was popular enough with singers, and appeared regularly on nineteenth-century broadsides. The song's origin, however, seems to lie in the third quarter of the eighteenth century, when it was included in chapbook garlands and songbooks, including the *Frisky Songster* (*c*.1785), which presented songs sung in the pleasure gardens of Vauxhall, Ranelagh, and so on. It was also one of the songs that American prisoner-of-war Timothy Connor, incarcerated in Forton Prison, Gosport, copied into his songbook in 1778 (see George G. Carey, *A Sailor's Songbag* (1976)).

23 Cupid's Garden

Sung by Mrs Nation, Bathpool, Somerset (c.1916); collected by Phyllis M. Marshall (Blunt MSS, JHB/10/1).
Roud 297; 20 entries.

Cuper's Gardens was a formal pleasure garden opened by Abraham Boydell Cuper about 1691, and until the 1750s was a well-known entertainment venue for Londoners, situated on the south side of the river, just east of the present Waterloo Bridge. Pleasure gardens like this offered eating, drinking, singing, dancing and flirting in tastefully arranged 'rural' walks and bowers, and Cuper's was particularly famous for its firework displays. At different times in its career it was the resort of the moneyed classes and of the general public, but there were always pickpockets and prostitutes around, and it constantly struggled against a bad reputation with the authorities. This may have been one of its attractions. It was probably inevitable that the gardens acquired the nickname 'Cupid's', and the phrase may have already existed. It is the name of a dance in Playford's *English Dancing Master* published in 1686.

We have several indications that 'Cupid's Garden' was an extremely popular song in the mid nineteenth century. William Chappell, for example, in his monumental *Popular Music of the Olden Time* (1859), wrote, 'This is one of the most generally known of traditional songs' (p. 727), and Sabine Baring-Gould noted in his manuscript notebook, about 1890, that it was 'Known to almost every old singer'.

The song bears all the hallmarks of an eighteenth-century pastoral, probably originating on stage or in one of the pleasure gardens, although we cannot be sure that it existed early enough to be sung at Cuper's itself. The earliest versions which have come to light are in printed chapbook garlands of the 1770s and 1780s, where it was usually entitled 'Lady Who Fell in Love with a 'Prentice Boy'. It was also very popular on broadsides from about 1800, the earlier ones being often called 'Lover's Meeting'.

Mrs Nation's tune exemplifies the widespread tune for the song which in turn is much the same as it appears in Chappell.

24 The Game of Cards

'The Game of All Fours', sung by Harry Westaway, Belstone, Devon (3 August 1950); recorded by Peter Kennedy. A few words in the first line of verse 4 are difficult to hear on the recording and may not be quite correct.
Roud 232; 32 entries.

A song found quite commonly in England, although nearly always in the southern half of the country, but almost never anywhere else.

All Fours was a widely popular card game in the past, and is still played in some quarters. It is one of the ancestors of whist, in that it is based on winning tricks by following suits, or by the use of trumps, and was already around in 1674 when its rules were first published. The descriptions of the game in collected versions of the song often seem a bit garbled, but this is partly because we no longer understand the rules. One recurrent phrase, for example, 'high-low- Jack', was an alternative name for the game.

The song is always regarded as mildly bawdy, with the game of cards as yet another euphemistic description of sex, which is certainly how many singers understood it. Nevertheless, a slightly different, and more subtle, interpretation is possible: the game of cards is part of the attempted seduction, with the girl's virtue as the stake; because the girl wins, she escapes unscathed, which gives the 'call again tomorrow' parting shot a different connotation. But this is probably just wishful thinking

'The Game of All Fours', or simply 'The Cards' was reasonably common on nineteenth-century broadsides, with a text which is almost exactly the same from printer to printer and very similar to most collected versions. The song is a little older than that, however, as is shown by a chapbook in the British Library entitled *The Chester All-Fours Garland,* published around 1750, probably in Newcastle.

Harry Westaway's melody is quite different from that usually found with this song, which is a triple-time tune.

25 *The Garden Gate*

Sung by Mr F. Scarlett Potter, Halford, Shipston-on-Stour, Warwickshire; published in Lucy Broadwood, *English County Songs* (1893), pp. 72–3.
Roud 418; 18 entries.

An inconsequential enough little piece, but immensely popular in the nineteenth century. Song collector James Henry Dixon commented in *Ancient Poems* (1846), 'This is one of the most pleasing of our rural ditties. The air is very beautiful. The editor lately heard it sung in Malhamdale, Yorkshire, by Willy Bolton, an old Dales'-minstrel, who accompanied himself on the union-pipes' (p. 226).

According to Sabine Baring-Gould in *English Minstrelsie* (1895), it was written by W. Upton and W. T. Parke and published in 1809, and it was popular enough to engender answer songs and sequels.

26 *Golden Glove*

Sung by Sally Withington, Edgmond, Shropshire (*c.*1883); collected by Charlotte Burne; published in Burne's *Shropshire Folk-Lore* (1883), pp. 552, 652. The lines in brackets were added by Burne from James Henry Dixon's *Ancient Poems* (1846). Sally learnt this song as a girl in farm service (1820–30), from the singing of her young mistress.
Roud 141, Laws N20; 49 entries.

A great favourite in England and Scotland, and also collected dozens of times in North America. This is just the sort of romantic narrative in which broadsides excelled, and the song was printed by nearly every known broadside printer of the nineteenth century. But it is older than that. We know, for example, that it was already around in 1777–9, because that was when American prisoner-of-war Timothy Connor, incarcerated in Forton Prison, Portsmouth, copied the text into his songbook (see George G. Carey, *A Sailor's Songbag* (1976), pp. 107–8). He called it 'A New Song', and his words are remarkably similar to Sally Withington's; it was popular enough to warrant at least one 'answer song'.

According to James Henry Dixon in *Ancient Poems* (1846), there was a tradition that the song was based on an incident which occurred in the reign of Elizabeth I, but that is almost certainly simply a legend.

27 Green Mossy Banks of the Lea

Sung by Mr Lockly (about eighty years old), sexton at High Ercall,
Shropshire (March 1908); collected by George Butterworth
(Butterworth MSS, GB/4/45).
Roud 987, Laws O15; 46 entries.

This song was widely collected in England, where Lucy Broadwood commented, 'the words are astonishingly popular amongst country singers' (*JFSS*, 2 (1906), 151), and was also well known on the other side of Atlantic. The story the song tells is most notable because the parents do not object and the course of true love runs uncharacteristically smooth.

The song was also widely printed on broadsides, at least from the 1820s onwards, in a text which is very similar to that collected from Mr Lockly (or Lockley – Butterworth used both spellings). Some writers have assumed an Irish origin, partly on the strength of the tune, but also because some broadsides give the fourth line as 'When I left Ireland my home', and the fifth line in the last verse as 'So now the poor Irish stranger'. American songster printers around the turn of the twentieth century also included the song in their compilations of 'Irish' songs. But the song was rarely collected in Ireland, in contrast to England, and the vast majority of the earlier broadsides place the stranger's home in Philadelphia; on present evidence it is most likely to be an English song with the American inserted into the story to give him a foreign, but not too foreign, backstory.

28 Hares on the Mountains

'Blackbirds and Thrushes', sung by Dicky Lashbrook, Kelly, Devon (27 May 1952); recorded by Peter Kennedy (BBC 17796).
Roud 329; 32 entries.

Regularly collected in England and Ireland, and quite widespread in North America, this song is often tangled up with 'Sally, My Dear' or 'Knife in the Window', which are usually sung to the same tune. It was already widespread when the Edwardian collectors were out in the field, but no broadside or chapbook printings have come to light, and without this evidence it is difficult to get to grips with the song's history. But we do know that it already existed in 1837, as it was included in Samuel Lover's novel *Rory O'More*, published in that year. Lover was an accomplished songwriter, so it is possible he wrote it from scratch, but a tune in George Petrie's *Complete Collection of Irish Music* (Part 2, no. 821), probably collected some years before Lover's book, is entitled 'If All the Young Maidens were Blackbirds and Trushes [sic]', which strengthens the idea that Lover was presenting an already existing song.

Bertrand Bronson included this song in his monumental *The Traditional Tunes of the Child Ballads*, under the heading of 'The Twa Magicians' (Child 44, Roud 1350) and several other editors have followed suit. 'Twa Magicians' is a relatively rare ballad in Britain, in which a female turns herself successively into a duck, a hare, an eel, and so on, to escape from a male pursuer, but he matches her every move and gets her in the end. To confuse the magical transformations in this ballad with the similes of our song, and to assume that one necessarily derives from the other, requires a giant leap of faith, backed by nothing more than the coincidence of hares, fish, and so on. Nevertheless, it is useful to have eleven tunes brought together in one volume.

In his *Erotic Muse* (1992), Edward Cray found more explicit versions of the song alive and well on college campuses in the USA (pp. 301–8), and it also survives in the British bawdy sing-song fraternity.

Although Bronson does not undertake an exhaustive study of the 'Hares on the Mountain' tunes, he comments that 'all the variants that I have seen are in triple time and seem at least distantly related' (*The Traditional Tunes of the Child Ballads*, I (1959), p. 350). Despite differences in their range, contour and tonality, there are certain resemblances among the tunes in terms of their distinctive rhythm, including the feminine endings at each line end, their phrase structure (AABC), the A-phrase cadence on the fifth degree of the scale and sometimes the melodic shape of the nonsense refrain. Petrie's tune stands out as somewhat different in that it is minor in tonality and its second half is reminiscent of 'Green Bushes' (see Cecil Sharp's *Folk Songs from Somerset*, II (1905), pp. 16–17), which, Sharp comments, 'in varying forms and set to different words, is constantly found in English folk-song' (p. 66).

Dicky Lashbrook's major plagal-range tune is closely paralleled by William Bailey's 'Hares on the Mountains' melody and also William Davis's tune for 'Sally, My Dear' (Bronson 3 and 11). The first half of these tunes is, in turn, very similar in contour and, to some extent, in rhythm, to 'London's Burning', a tune that dates back to at least 1580 (Lant MS, King's College Library, University of Cambridge, also known as KC1). The tune also bears a close resemblance to one of those used for 'Blackberry Fold' (No. 131).

29 The Indian Lass

Sung by William 'Jumbo' Brightwell, Leiston, Suffolk (1975); recorded by
Keith Summers; issued on *A Story to Tell*, Musical Traditions MTCD339-40
(2007). Jumbo's father, 'Velvet' Brightwell, can also be heard singing this
song on the CD *Good Order!* (Veteran VT140CD), recorded 1938/9.
Roud 2326; 27 entries.

Collected regularly across the country, and printed on numerous nineteenth-century
broadsides, back to at least the 1820s, this song is often claimed to have been a favourite with sailors. In a candid moment, leading folk-song expert Frank Kidson wrote
in *Traditional Tunes* (1891), 'Many of the old sailor songs are long dreary ballads, having
for their theme some naval engagement of the last century, or possibly some dismal
account of a shipwreck. Others, again, like the "Indian Lass", narrate in simple language the joys of a sailor's life ashore' (p. 110). His appreciation of the song did not
prevent him from leaving out the verse where they 'tossed and tumbled', believing
it to be too direct for his published book.

Folk songs are not always clear on the exact origin of 'foreigners' in their texts,
and Jumbo's song is ambiguous in this respect, but a verse which occurs in many
other versions, right back to the earliest broadside, indicates that the lass was a
Native American Indian:

> *This lovely young Indian on the place where she stood*
> *I viewed her sweet features and found they were good*
> *She was neat, tall and handsome, her age was sixteen*
> *She was born and brought up in a place near Orleans.*

'The Indian Lass' was also collected occasionally in North America, but on far fewer
occasions than a related song, 'The Little Mohee' (Roud 275, Laws H8), which was
very widely known there. G. Malcolm Laws sums up the latter in his *Native American Balladry* (1964), p. 233:

> The Indian girl invites the stranger to live in her cottage in the coconut grove. He
> replies that he must return to his true love in his own country. They part, and he last
> sees her waving to him from the shore as his ship sails. The girl at home proves untrue,
> and the sailor longs to return to the lass of Mohea.

It is usually assumed, probably correctly, that this is a more morally acceptable rewrite
of our 'Indian Lass', although the occasional American scholar argues that it is the
other way round.

30 Just as the Tide was a-Flowing

Sung by Harry Cox, Catfield, Norfolk (18 December 1945); recorded by

E. J. Moeran (BBC 17231); issued on *We've Received Orders to Sail*, Topic
TSCD662 (1998).
Roud 1105; 18 entries.

This song was collected a reasonable number of times in England, and a few times
in Canada, but not, apparently, elsewhere in Britain and Ireland or in the USA. It
was widely available on broadsides, from about 1830 onwards.

Roy Palmer has commented that it is not the innocent pastoral song which it
seems to be. After three verses of May mornings, birds singing and lambs skipping,
the couple end up rolling in the grass and the girl is sufficiently impressed to give
him money to spend on drink and other women. It is no wonder that it was, as
Frank Kidson noted in *Traditional Tunes* (1891), an 'old sailors' favourite' (p. 108).

Harry Cox sings a fine flowing version of the tune usually found with this song,
which Sharp characterized as 'a smooth sentimental melody'. Malcom Douglas and
Steve Gardham, the editors of Frank Purslow's *Marrow Bones* (2007), have located
it in Aird's *Selection of Scots, English, Irish and Foreign Airs* (1782) and several early
nineteenth-century Irish collections. Cecil Sharp also highlights its transformation
as 'The Blue-Eyed Stranger', a dance tune (*Folk Songs from Somerset*, II (1905), p. 68).

31 *The Knight and the Shepherd's Daughter*

'The Shepherd's Daughter', sung by Louise Holmes, Dinedor,
Herefordshire (14 October 1952); recorded by Peter Kennedy (BBC 18691).
Roud 67, Child 110; 23 entries.

This song was fairly widely collected in England but more common in Scotland, and
hardly noted at all in Ireland or North America; Francis J. Child prints twelve versions (all Scottish except one), and Bertrand Bronson only twenty-two tunes.

As it stands here, the song is a straightforward tale of a resourceful female who
refuses to go away quietly after a seduction or rape, and this is the core motif across
all the versions, but there are some important differences in detail and emphasis.
Sometimes it turns out that she is really a high-born lady and the knight is pleased
with his bargain, while in others, like Louise Holmes's, the last verses are rueful and
bode ill for the marriage. Another recurrent detail compounds the knight's ungal-
lant behaviour by having him try to trick her by giving a false name, or one in Latin.
Nearly all versions, however, have the delightful detail of the King answering his
own front door.

The earliest known version is on a black-letter broadside in the Roxburghe collection, entitled 'The Beautiful Shepherdesse of Arcadia', dating from the 1650s, and
under this name it was regularly printed in that century and the next. But, oddly
enough, few nineteenth-century printings have yet been discovered.

In Child's accompanying commentary, he draws attention to similarities with

Continental ballads which feature a high-born man being forced to marry a socially inferior, or in some cases hideous, bride to atone for his own misdeeds.

Various tunes are sung with this song, most of which feature a refrain of some kind (Bronson, *The Traditional Tunes of the Child Ballads*, II (1962), p. 535). Louise Holmes's tune has no refrain, however, being the tune often thought of as associated with 'The Banks of the Sweet Dundee' (No. 58). This catchy tune, with the form ABBA, flattened seventh and lack of the second degree, is frequently found with come-all-ye ballads (*compare* 'Captain Ward and the *Rainbow*', No. 3). In his *Folk Songs of the Catskills* (1982), Norman Cazden suspects it is Irish in origin (p. 193).

32 Little Gipsy Girl

Sung by Joseph Taylor of Saxby-All-Saints, Lincolnshire, on 78rpm record (Gramophone Co. matrix 8752e) (9 July 1908); recording organized by Percy Grainger; reissued on *Come Let Us Buy the Licence*, Topic TSCD651 (1998).
Roud 229, Laws O4; 21 entries.

Percy Grainger noted at least five different versions of this song, commenting that it was 'very generally sung in Lincolnshire', and many other collectors of his generation also came across it. It could be argued that this relatively inconsequential romantic song was probably as popular for its lively danceable tune as for its words, but Grainger's fellow folk-song experts were distinctly cool about the tune: 'The tune has been noted elsewhere, and to other words; I doubt it's being "country-made" or of any great age'; 'I have noted down this song once in Devonshire and twice in Somerset, and have always felt doubtful about its folk-origin' ; and 'it does not have the appearance of a genuine folk-air', wrote Lucy Broadwood, Cecil Sharp and Anne Gilchrist, respectively, in *JFSS*, 3 (1908), 221.

The relationship between Gipsies and non-Gipsies in England has not always been an easy one, and has often been founded more on stereotype than on fact. The theme of Gipsy women being adept at telling fortunes and other arcane arts has long been a social cliché on which both sides have traded, and the motif is taken for granted here. But there is a little more to the song than meets the eye. Nearly all the nineteenth-century broadside printers issued versions, and the later ones are textually very close to the traditional ones like Joseph Taylor's, above. But those printed in the 1820s and 1830s, such as the ones issued by James Catnach and John Pitts, give a different slant, by the insertion of two verses:

He took me to a house, it was a palace I'm sure
Where ladies were waiting to open the door
On a bed of soft feathers where I pleas'd him so well
In less than nine months after, his fortune I could tell.

My father he has got the babe, and he likes it so well

Here is twenty pounds a year for your fortune come tell
There was ladies of honour and every degree
But none to equal my pretty Betsy.

This appears to be trading on another stereotype, that Gipsy women have loose morals. Incidentally, these earlier broadsides explain that, in line 2 of the first verse, the girl's mother teaches her some 'cant' words, which makes more literal sense than 'camping'.

A new transcription of Grainger's cylinder recording is presented here, as Grainger's own notation is very complex and detailed. The tune is also associated with 'The Female Cabin Boy' (No. 6).

33 Lord Bateman

Sung by Mrs D. Gawthorpe, Padgate, Lancashire (22 December 1968); recorded by Fred Hamer; published in Hamer's *Green Groves* (1973), pp. 68–9.
Roud 40, Child 53; 89 entries.

A very large number of versions of this Child ballad have been collected in England and Scotland and quite a few in Ireland, but it was even more popular in North America, where hundreds have been noted. Francis J. Child printed 14 versions, and Bertrand Bronson 112, under the standard Scottish title 'Young Beichan'.

Mrs Gawthorpe's is a good long version, of which the collector, Fred Hamer, noted, 'Mrs Gawthorpe learnt this song when it was sung to her at the age of three by her sister who was 15 years older. As she is now 86, this would be prior to 1890.' But some versions are even longer, as singers seem to enjoy dwelling on the details of a romantic story which, in effect, is quite straightforward.

One significant element that is missing here is an account of Lord Bateman's trials and tribulations while in prison, which were heaped upon him primarily because he would not, as a faithful Christian, bend his knee to his heathen captors. This also makes the Turk's daughter even more courageous because she is willing to adopt Bateman's religion as well as to defy her father and travel halfway round the world. In some versions she does not even know that he owns half of Northumberland until she arrives there.

As Child points out, the story agrees in general outline with a well-known legend about Gilbert Becket, father of St Thomas, which was in circulation by at least 1300. This is not to argue that our song is that old, but it is likely that whoever wrote it already knew the Becket story and, probably quite consciously, adapted it for the broadside trade. In fact, we know little about its origin, as no early broadsides have survived and the first known versions are those noted by the late eighteenth-century Scottish ballad collectors. Pride of place goes to the version noted from the recitation of Mrs Anna Brown in 1783, but as she learnt most of her ballads in her youth we can speculate that it probably existed in the late 1750s. In contrast, numerous nineteenth-century printings have survived, as all the major broadside printers of the time issued versions.

Child notes that there are Norse, Spanish and Italian ballads with a similar story-line, and another, less well-known British song, often called 'The Turkish Lady' (Roud 8124, Laws O23) covers similar ground. Bronson notes that, despite the frequency with which this song appeared on broadsides, the tunes associated with it are remarkably similar to each other and have been so over a 200-year period (*The Traditional Tunes of the Child Ballads*, I (1959), p. 409). He takes this as evidence that the song was continually popular in oral tradition even though some singers might 'refresh' their memory of the words using the broadsides. Interestingly, the earliest tunes are in duple time and the later ones in triple, with some of the latter in five time. Mrs Gawthorpe's falls squarely into triple time, as transcribed.

Bronson subdivides the basic tune into groupings based on the degree of the scale on which the mid-point cadence falls. The two largest groups are the fifth and the second degree. Mrs Gawthorpe's falls on the third degree, aligning it with just seven of Bronson's 111 examples of the tune. Of these seven, Mrs Gawthorpe's tune also parallels the five from Kentucky in its phrase A and C cadences on the lower fifth.

A significant feature of Mrs Gawthorpe's tune is its third phrase, which repeats the music of the first phrase (giving it the form ABAC). This lends it a different feel from many of the other 'Lord Bateman' tunes, which have a varied form of phrase B at this point (ABB'A' or ABB'C).

34 Madam, Will You Walk?

'The Keys of Heaven', sung by William Fairbanks, Retford, Nottingham
(3 August 1906); collected by Percy Grainger (Grainger MSS, no. 254).
Grainger's music notation gives the words as 'five yards o' bibbin' in line 2.
Roud 573; 56 entries.

This was a well-known song in England, not so common in Scotland and Ireland, but very widely collected in North America. Several songs with a very similar format and storyline were formerly distinct, but have gradually become intertwined. The distinguishing feature is that they are dialogues, often sung as duets, between a potential lover and a female, in which he offers a range of gifts which she usually refuses, until the last, which she accepts. The gifts tend to escalate in value, verse by verse, often starting with a 'paper of pins' or a 'fine beaver hat', progressing through silk gowns and until we reach the keys to the man's treasure chest.

But the principal difference, which sets the moral tone for the song, is whether she accepts the material gifts or waits for him to change tack and offer the key of his heart, therefore showing that it is love which matters most to her. In some versions it is the other way round: he starts with an offer of love, which she refuses, but he then offers material gifts, and he scornfully rejects her at the end when she tries to accept them.

These songs go by a variety of titles, including 'A Paper of Pins', 'The Keys of Canterbury' and 'Madam, Will You Walk?' , and all show clear signs of originating on the stage, which is reflected in their later history. Several collectors in the late nineteenth and early twentieth centuries noted that their informants recalled these songs being regularly performed as dialogues between two singers – sometimes in all seriousness, but in other cases as a comic turn with the performers dressing up for their parts. There was also sometimes a dance sequence between some of the verses.

Oddly enough, these songs do not seem to have been printed on broadsides, so we must rely on other sources for dating. They do appear in the nursery tradition, however, and Iona and Peter Opie provide an informative historical entry in their *The Singing Game* (1985). The earliest versions so far found in England appeared in James Orchard Halliwell's *The Nursery Rhymes of England* (1844 and 1846 editions), but the Scottish tradition goes back further. A song called 'The Deil's Courtship', collected in the late 1820s, contains the usual offers, which the girl finally accepts, only to discover that she has been bargaining with the Devil (Emily Lyle, *Andrew Crawfurd's Collection of Ballads and* Songs, I (1975), pp. 104–5). It would not be too much of a surprise to find an eighteenth-century pleasure-garden or stage original for the English versions.

35 Queen of the May

'As I Walked Through the Meadows', sung by Shepherd Haden, Bampton, Oxfordshire (11 September 1909); collected by Cecil Sharp (Sharp MSS, FW 2159–60/FT 2390).
Roud 594; 28 entries.

A rather inconsequential little piece of pastoral romance, 'Queen of the May' was quite common in the country tradition in England, but not collected elsewhere, and it was also widely available on broadsides in the nineteenth century. Shepherd Haden's text follows the latter quite closely, although the printed versions usually start with verses explaining that the narrator is Johnny, a ploughboy 'as fresh as a rose'.

Frank Purslow, in *The Wanton Seed* (1968), called it 'an 18th century minor art-song', and while the song certainly has these characteristics, it has not yet been found before the early nineteenth century. To confuse the issue, a different song, also called 'Queen of the May' (Roud 23454), appears in David Herd's *Ancient and Modern Scottish Songs* (1776) and in late eighteenth-century garlands. This song has a similar pastoral setting and romantic theme, but is a dialogue between Jockey and Jenny.

Regarding the second note of bar 11, Sharp notes in the manuscript that 'this G was nearly always a clear [sharp], but sometimes a neutral G, never once [flat]'.

36 Searching for Lambs

'As Johnny Walked Out', sung by James Parsons, Lewdown, Devon
(November 1888); collected by Sabine Baring-Gould (Baring-Gould MSS,
SBG/1/1/65). Baring-Gould noted that 'he ran together verses 3 and 4 and
so lost the usual burden that concludes each stanza'. We have added the last
two lines of verse 3 from another version collected by him.
Roud 1437, Laws O9; 16 entries.

This eighteenth-century pastoral love song, with a similar storyline to 'The Spotted
Cow' (No. 38), has been found fairly regularly in England and a few times in Scotland
and Canada, but apparently not elsewhere.

In *Songs of the West* (1905), Baring-Gould identified a number of mid eighteenth-
century publications which contained this song, including *Six English Songs and
Dialogues as they are Performed in the Public Gardens* (*c.*1750), with music set by Mr
Dunn, but it does not seem to have been printed on nineteenth-century broadsides.

In our more knowing age, it is sometimes difficult to understand the attraction
of simple love songs such as this one, or to take them seriously. But when sung with
dignity and conviction (providing the tune is good), they can be most effective. See,
for example, the version of this song sung by George Spicer on *Up in the North and
Down in the South*, Musical Traditions MTCD 311-12 (2001) or Topic 12T 235.

37 Seventeen Come Sunday

'I'm Seventeen Come Sunday', sung by Alfred Atkinson, Redbourne,
Lincolnshire (31 July 1906); collected by Percy Grainger (Grainger MSS, no.
125).
Roud 27, Laws O17; 94 entries.

This was a very widely known song in England, and was also popular in Ireland and
Scotland. It is one of those which earlier editors, such as Sabine Baring-Gould and
Cecil Sharp, felt obliged to soften or rewrite for publication. It was also common on
broadsides throughout the nineteenth century, with the earliest being printed about
1810 and called 'Maid and the Soldier'. But the versions on the early broadsides have
a very different ending, with the soldier leaving the girl in the lurch and going off
without her, which changes the whole tenor of the song.

38 The Spotted Cow

Sung by Charles Lolley, Yorkshire (1880s); collected by Frank Kidson;
published in Kidson's *Traditional Tunes* (1891), pp. 70-71.
Roud 956; 34 entries.

This popular pastoral song, collected widely in England but rarely elsewhere, bears all the hallmarks of a stage song of the eighteenth century. It was certainly in print on broadsides and in songsters around 1800, sometimes called 'One Morning', and it continued to appear in the broadside printers' lists until at least the 1880s. The text varies remarkably little from version to version. The pastoral scenario of a girl looking for her animal charges, helped or hindered by a boy, is also found in the song 'Searching for Lambs' (No. 36), which dates from a similar period.

III
Let No Man Steal Your Thyme ...
Unhappy Love

39 Banks of Sweet Primroses

Sung by W. Buckland, Lippenham, Buckinghamshire (18 September 1943); collected by Francis Collinson (Collinson MSS, COL/1/30).
Roud 586, 54 entries.

An immensely popular song, which was so widely known in Edwardian times that the collectors did not attempt to note down every version they came across, and in *English Folk-Songs* (1891), William Alexander Barrett commented that the last two lines 'are often quoted as a crumb of comfort under adversity' (p. 80).

The song itself is something of a mystery, and it always seems as if we do not have the full story. What has the man done to deserve such an extreme and seemingly final rejection, especially as he states in the second verse that he does not know her (although in some versions the line is given as 'Not knowing me as she passed me by', thus implying simply that she did not recognize him). Although widely printed from at least the 1830s onwards, the broadsides do not help at all when it comes to explaining the story, as the collected and printed texts are extremely similar. It is quite feasible that it was written in this way, but it is also possible that there is an as yet undiscovered original which has verses to explain it all.

W. Buckland's tune is a prime example of the one that seems to have been used by nearly all singers for 'Banks of Sweet Primroses'. It also exemplifies a tune that seems to have been associated with only a few other texts (Broadwood mentions 'Young and Single Sailor', for which see 'Fair Maid Walking in Her Garden', No. 71). The relative stability of both the text and tune of 'Banks of Sweet Primroses' prompted Ralph Vaughan Williams and A. L. Lloyd to conclude that the song was 'unusually memorable and satisfactory' for singers and, in the absence of any other known stabilizing factor, such as an early commercial recording, it is hard to think of any other reason for this stability.

The collected versions suggest that some singers sang the three-syllable 'prim-e-roses' while others preferred 'primroses'. It is not unusual to find additional consonants like this cropping up in traditional singing where voiced consonants, such as *m* and *r*, might gain enough prominence to sound like an extra syllable, especially when allied to a separate note of the tune. W. Buckland seems to have a penchant for adding and modifying syllables, as he also sings 'to a-view' and 'love-lie' ('lovely') in this same rendition.

The time signature in bar 7 has been changed to 2/2 in place of 4/4, to keep the beat consistent.

40 Barbara Allen

Sung by Charlie Wills, Bridport, Dorset (19 October 1952); recorded by
Peter Kennedy (BBC 18692); issued on Topic 12T160/Rounder CD1775;
also recorded by Bill Leader (1971), issued on Leader LEA4041.
Roud 54, Child 84; 111 entries.

'Barbara Allen' is far away the most widely collected traditional song in the English language – equally popular in England, Scotland and Ireland, and with hundreds of versions collected over the years in North America. Francis J. Child, however, took little notice of the song, devoting only four pages to it, and printing only three early texts, but Bertrand Bronson makes up for this neglect with 198 tunes.

Many people have wondered why this particular song took such a hold on the public imagination, and it has come in for its share of criticism and even scorn. It is either deeply romantic or pointlessly sentimental, depending on your viewpoint, and even Bronson had a swipe at it: 'This little song of a spineless lover who gives up the ghost without a struggle, and of his spirited beloved who repents too late' (*The Traditional Tunes of the Child Ballads*, II (1962), p. 321. Indeed, the lover is so weak that he often does not even have a name.

In particular, singers and commentators alike have puzzled over the apparent lack of motive for Barbara's hard-heartedness, and she has been accused of being everything from a poisoner to a witch or a prostitute, but there is no indication that there is any hidden meaning or an ancient version which has been corrupted or suppressed. All the evidence agrees: she simply took offence at him and his buddies drinking healths to the other girls and leaving her out.

A closer examination of the song would still be useful, however. Bronson, for example, noticed a gradual softening in Barbara's character over the years, and another interesting feature is the mixture of voices – sometimes told in an impersonal third person, sometimes from one or other point of view, sometimes alternating as in a stage dialogue song.

We are fortunate to have evidence from when the song was, presumably, brand new, or at least in vogue, in the diary of Samuel Pepys. On 2 January 1666 he recorded fun and games at a New Year party: '... but above all, my dear Mrs Knipp, with whom I sang; and in perfect pleasure I was to hear her sing, and especially her little Scotch song of "Barbary Allen"'.

Pepys was an enthusiastic amateur musician, but Elizabeth Knip, or Knepp, was an actress, singer and dancer in the King's Company, and therefore a professional, and it is quite possible that the song was written originally for the stage. His calling it a 'Scotch song' does not necessarily mean that it was actually Scottish, but that it was probably 'in the style' of a Scottish ballad. We also have a black-letter broadside, dating from about the same time, in the Roxburghe Collection, entitled 'Barbara Allen's Cruelty or The Young Man's Tragedy; with Barbara Allen's Lamentation for her Unkindness to her Lover and Herself'.

Bronson divides the tunes for 'Barbara Allen' into four groups. Charlie Wills sings the verse part of his to a tune which falls clearly into Bronson's 'mainly English' Group A. Bronson also notes that many tunes in his Groups A and C (and, indeed, other groups too) are wholly or partially in five time and Charlie Wills's rendition is no exception. In fact, he perpetually varies the length of the bar, hence the changes of time signature in the transcription. These look complicated, but in practice give Wills's rendition an attractive lilt and movement. The 5/8 bars can easily be regularized to 3/4 by adding a dot to the crotchet, if desired.

A distinctive feature of Wills's 'Barbara Allen' is his inclusion of a refrain (with which, on this recording, others join in). Wills's refrain is made up of a number of features associated with many of Bronson's Group C tunes, namely, their mid-stanza feminine ending on the third to fifth degrees of the scale and the melodic shape of their final phrase, which descends to the lower dominant. Only a handful of other versions include a refrain, most of these collected in Dorset and Somerset. Unlike Wills's tune, the verse of these is sung to a melody which conforms to Bronson's Group C and which H. E. D. Hammond dubs 'the regular Dorsetshire tune' (Hammond MSS, D518).

Only the tune noted by Francis Collinson, probably c.1948, 'at the London Inn, near Bridport, Dorset' (Collinson MSS, COL/5/47B), not included in Bronson, shares the same form as Wills's tune. Indeed, it is almost identical to it except for its ending, which rises from the third below to the tonic, rather than repeating the tonic. It is probable that the London Inn notation is directly connected to Wills's version or even that it is from Wills himself.

The upbeat note for Wills's first stanza has here been altered down a tone to agree with the way it is sung in all the other stanzas. Similarly, the final note of bar 1 has been raised by a tone.

41 Bonny Light Horseman

Text from William Alexander Barrett's *English Folk-Songs* (1891) pp. 50–51;

tune sung by William Russell, Eynsham, Oxfordshire (26 April 1909);
collected by Cecil Sharp (Sharp MSS, FW 2039/FT 2185).
Roud 1185; 16 entries.

Although noted a fair number of times across the country, it is not easy to find a complete text and tune in the available collections, so we have combined a text from Barrett (who does not name his singer) with an unpublished tune from Sharp's collection.

It is possible that Barrett took his text from one of the many broadside printings; the earliest surviving example is in a garland printed by Robertson of Glasgow in 1802. Some of the collected texts start with a verse about Napoleon. The first 'light horse' regiment was formed in 1745.

Sharp comments that William Russell began his rendition with the chorus and, apart from the Cs in bars 21 and 22 of the first stanza, he consistently sang a flattened seventh, making the tune in the Mixolydian mode. Other collected versions tend to be straightforwardly major or lack the sixth degree. The majority are triple-time, authentic-range melodies with similarities to each other.

The slurring in Russell's tune has been adjusted here to fit the words from Barrett.

42 A Brisk Young Sailor

'A Brave Young Sailor Courted Me', sung by Alice Davies, Forest of Dean, Gloucestershire (11 August 1954); collected by Francis Collinson (Collinson MSS COL/4/51A).
Roud 60; Laws P25; 110 entries.

This widely collected song is an example of a group of popular traditional songs, loosely categorized under the title 'Died for Love', which have a similar theme and often share some verses. In *English Traditional Songs and Carols* (pp. 123–4), Lucy Broadwood commented on the popularity of the theme in 1908:

> The words of this song belong to a type of ballad which is extraordinarily popular amongst country singers both in England and Scotland. The subject (of a forsaken and broken-hearted girl, who directs how her grave shall be made), is the same in all versions, which however vary astonishingly in detail whilst having certain lines or stanzas always in common.

This song is a classic case of one of the problems of folk-song research: the so-called 'floating verses', which can turn up in any number of texts, but which sometimes coalesce into a recognizable song in their own right. It is only by a close comparison of a large number of versions, printed and collected, that a workable classification can be reached, but there remains the problem of where to place fragments and shorter versions. Steve Gardham has undertaken a study of the 'Died for Love' complex, which is so far unpublished. He maintains that there are relatively discrete, identifiably different songs within the mass, and that it is the combination of verses, and sometimes their order, that helps to differentiate different threads. Some of the main songs in this complex, with their numbers in *The Folk Song Index*, are as follows: 'Died for Love' (Roud 18828); 'The Butcher Boy' (Roud 18832); 'The Tavern in the Town', an American student song from about the 1880s (Roud 18834); 'The Rambling Boy' (Roud 18830); and 'Isle of Cloy' (Roud 23272); and in this volume, 'Early, Early All in the Spring' (No. 43), which contains several of these shared verses.

Our 'Brisk Young Sailor' was certainly around in the later eighteenth century. There is, for example, a broadside entitled 'A New Song Call'd the Distress'd Maid' in the Madden Collection (Slip Songs H-N no.1337) which is undated but looks late eighteenth or very early nineteenth century, and 'The Lady's Lamentation for the Loss of Her Sweetheart' in Manchester Central Library, which is older. Several seventeenth-century black-letter broadsides contain elements of the 'Died for Love' songs, but nothing concrete enough to be confidently called their ancestor.

A note on the manuscript states, 'Don't add known verses. Don't alter as given. Want to use it as it was sung in Forest of Dean.' Also 'Not 6/8' is written near the time signature at the start. 'Yes D' is written between the staves, presumably referring to the pitch of one or more of the cross-head notes that appear on the notation. These occur in bars 1, 2, 4 and 12 and have here been changed to low D each time.

43 Early, Early All in the Spring

Sung by Mrs Hollings, originally from Lincolnshire (*c.*1900?); collected by Frank Kidson; published in *JFSS*, 2 (1906), 293–4.
273 Laws, K12; 61 entries.

This is a very widely known song across Britain and Ireland, and was even more popular in North America, but its title, like its text, varies considerably. 'Sweet William', 'A Sailor's Life', 'The Sailor Boy' and 'Father, Father, Build me a Boat' are three of its common names, but there are many more. The core of the song usually remains the same – the girl's search for her lover and being told that he is dead – but it has a distinct tendency to attract verses from other songs. These are often simply general 'lamenting' verses, but in the case of Mrs Hollings's text, the last three verses are taken straight from a common version of the song 'Died for Love' or 'A Brisk Young Sailor' (No. 42).

The ending varies considerably but nearly always includes the heroine's death. In some versions she throws herself into the deep, in others she deliberately runs her boat on to a rock, and, as already noticed, in some she commits suicide at home. Occasionally, however, she declares that she will go to some 'silent shady grove', where she will mourn for ever, and this option gave the garland songwriters an opportunity for an 'Answer to the Sailor Boy', in which he has survived and happens to be in the same 'shady grove', so overhearing her lamentation. This latter song is in

a chapbook, *The Calleen Fuine*, printed in Limerick about 1800, so the original must
have been popular before that time.

Kidson comments on the 'curious rhythm' of Mrs Hollings's tune, which, as
Cecil Sharp points out, moves from 3/2 (3 minims in a bar) to 6/4 (two dotted minims in a bar) in bars 3 and 5. The same tune is found with 'The Isle of France' (No.
12) but without these implied changes of metre.

44 *The Foggy Dew*

Sung by Bob Hart, Snape, Suffolk (1969); recorded by Rod and Danny
Stradling; issued on *A Broadside*, Musical Traditions MTCD301-2 (1998).
Hart sang 'her eyes' rather than 'his eyes' in line 2 of the final verse,
presumably by mistake.
Roud 558, Laws O3; 48 entries.

This was a very widely collected song, across Britain and Ireland and North America, although the subject matter of premarital sex made the earlier collectors
uncomfortable. Sabine Baring-Gould called it 'a coarse song' (Baring-Gould MSS,
sbG/1/2/357), Frank Kidson printed only one verse (*Traditional Tunes* (1891), p. 167),
and for the first volume of Cecil Sharp's *Folk Songs from Somerset* (1904), the latter
completely rewrote the words. Later collectors were not so squeamish, so a large
number of versions have survived from the mid twentieth century, along with a
great many broadside printings from over a hundred years before.

'The Foggy Dew' has suffered more than most from the attentions of the secret-
meaning seekers of the folk-song world. The ambiguity of the phrase has led to a
number of fanciful claims, which need not be resurrected, although the one which is
on the increase – that the song is about 'the plague' – should be noted, and refuted.
It is no real surprise that this claim is on the increase: plague explanations are particularly popular at the moment, in a range of folkloric genres – especially legends,
ghost stories and explanations for odd geographical features. But there is no need
for fanciful speculation, as all is made perfectly clear by reference to earlier versions
of the song. In these, the girl is frightened into the man's bed by a ghost or monster,
which goes under various names such as 'bug-a-boo', 'Bogulmaroo' and 'bogle bo'.
It is worth noting that numerous dialect words for such creatures use the linguistic
root 'bug' or 'bog', which still survives as 'bogey' in modern usage.

The earliest known text is on a broadside in the Samuel Pepys collection (5.250),
entitled 'The Frightened York-Shire Damosel, or Fears Dispers'd by Pleasure', as
'printed and sold by J. Millet, next door to the Flower-de-Luce, in Little Brittain',
and conveniently dated 1689. It commences:

> *When first I began to court*
> *And pretty maids to wooe*

I could not win the Virgin Fort
But by the Bogulmaroo.

After getting what he wants, he marries her the next day. In that text it not quite clear how the 'Bogulmaroo' came about, but a version collected by John Bell in Newcastle in the 1810s or 1820s makes it clear that the man had set it all up: 'But I could ne'er her favour win till I hired the bogle bo' – he had paid a friend to dress up in a white sheet.

There is a lot more that could be done in respect of this song, now that the fanciful explanations can be set aside. It would be interesting to know how and when the song lost its rather obvious 'bugaboo' and gained its not-so-clear 'foggy dew', for example. The many extant broadsides printed from the 1820s onwards all involve the 'foggy dew', but we know from John Bell's Newcastle text that sometime in the first two decades of the nineteenth century the 'bogle bo' was still the main feature of at least one version. Is it simply that one broadside writer made the change – deliberately or not – and all the others followed, or is this a case of an 'oral' textual change being incorporated into the print tradition? The key will probably lie in the late eighteenth-century versions.

There is also much more to be done with a close comparison of orally collected texts. Sometimes the couple marry, for example, and sometimes she dies, and in the versions collected in the mid twentieth century there is great variation in the 'tone' of the song. In some it is quite tender, but in others it is characterized by a marked degree of offhand male bragging. These differences are sometimes brought out by performance style, but also by small differences in the words.

45 Green Bushes

Contributed in 1855 by Thomas Hepple of Kirkwhelpington to the Society of Antiquaries of Newcastle upon Tyne; published in Gwen Polwarth's *Folk Songs of Northumberland* (1966), pp. 26–7.
Roud 1040, Laws P2; 73 entries.

This was an immensely popular song, collected many times across England, although not so often elsewhere. It was also very popular with nineteenth-century broadside printers.

The song was given a tremendous boost by being included in a popular melo-drama, *The Green Bushes, or A Hundred Years Ago*, by J. B. Buckstone, which was first performed on 27 February 1845, at the Adelphi, London. In that play, which is set in Ireland and America, Nelly O'Neil, a simple but lively Irish 'peasant' girl, played by the 23-year-old Mrs (Ellen) Fitzwilliam, refers to the song several times, and although the published script only calls for her to sing a verse or two, the perform-ance was popular enough for the sheet music of the full song to be issued very soon afterwards. The play lasted in the repertoire of provincial and touring companies for a long time after its initial performance, and this must have helped to keep the song before the public eye. Incidentally, the same play introduced the celebrated 'Irish' song 'The Jug of Punch'.

The early collectors were all a little suspicious of the song because they sensed too much of the stage in both text and tunes. They were well aware of the influence of Buckstone's play, but they also identified possible eighteenth-century antecedents, including a 'Dialogue in Imitation of Mr H. Purcell – Between a Town Spark and a Country Lass' by Henry Carey, from about 1740, and also possible connections with other traditional songs such as the Scottish 'My Daddy is a Cankered Carle' and the English 'Whitsun Monday', in which one lover waits for the other 'Low down in the broom' rather than 'Among the green bushes'. Both of these date from the 1760s or 1770s, and they certainly have a similar storyline, but no real connection with our song beyond the 'outdoor waiting' motif.

The real early history of our 'Green Bushes' song has yet to be properly ascertained. It was certainly in existence in the 1820s or 1830s, because it appears on broadsides printed by Catnach and Pitts, as well as others of the time. But one broadside printed by the latter (Bodleian Library Broadside Ballads, Harding B 11(52)) introduces another confusion. On this sheet, the song called 'Among the Green Bushes' is a different song, although closely related to ours. It has the same scenario, but an almost opposite meaning, in which a young man walking through the meadows in May sees a maid. He offers her diamonds, gowns and silk petticoats, and his hand in marriage. She tells him to ask her father, who is a shepherd. Father gives consent and 'To church they went without delay'. But to underline the connection, the last line in four of the six verses is 'Among the green bushes my Jenny meets me'. However, on the same sheet is another song, 'The False Lover', which turns out to be our 'Green Bushes'. Whether one of these was a parody or rewrite of the other remains to be seen, as does the question of whether they were deliberate rewrites of the earlier 'broom' songs.

Lucy Broadwood (JFSS, 5 (1915), 178) divides the tunes associated with this song into two broad categories. The first comprises variants of a major tune, such as that sung by Frederick Fennimore (George B. Gardiner collection), which is closely related to 'Whistle and I'll Come to Ye' (James Johnson, The Scots Musical Museum, II, no. 106). Broadwood states that it is this form of the tune which is sung by Mrs Fitzwilliam in Buckstone's play but, despite being attributed to her in the published sheet music, the tune was widespread in Britain and Ireland well before the mid nineteenth century.

The second category comprises variants of the tune made famous by Ralph Vaughan Williams in his English Folk Song Suite and also by Percy Grainger in his Passacaglia for orchestra. These crop up in both major and minor tonalities, and frequently employ one of the modes, as in Thomas Hepple's example (which is Aeolian, although sharpening the lower seventh at one point). This is again a very widespread tune. It is found with a number of other songs in Ireland and England and is the form of the tune found in Carey's 'Dialogue'. As Anne Gilchrist describes (*JFSS*, 5 (1915), 179):

> It ... consisted of nine verses, eight sung alternately by the Town Spark and the Country Lass, and the last by both. The Town Spark sang his four verses all to the same tune, but the Country Lass had a different melody for each ... The tune or tunes are so much of the same character as some of the traditional 'Green Bushes' airs (the one in *Traditional Tunes* especially) ... which must surely have been known to the writer of 'Green Bushes' – or, conversely, elaborated from the ballad.

The tune collected by Hepple differs in form from most other 'Green Bushes' tunes in this group, being structured ABB'A rather than AA'BA. It also lacks the feminine ending cadence (from the lower seventh to the tonic) at the end of the B phrase found in other variants.

46 Green Grow the Laurels

Sung by John Gregson, Burley, Lancashire (1977); collected by Gordon Cox; published in *Lore & Language*, 3:7 (1982), 61.
Roud 279; 26 entries.

Very popular across Britain and Ireland, and in North America as well, this song has often puzzled commentators because it seems somehow incomplete, although this does not seem to have bothered the singers. The problem is that nowadays we expect there to be neat and tidy systems of, for example, colour and plant symbolism, but real folklore does not work that way and is always far messier. Indeed, it is a crude but useful rule of thumb that the more organized and comprehensive a system is, the more likely it is to be a recent invention, like the Victorian 'language of flowers' or rhymes such as 'Monday's Child'.

Although some plants have relatively well-known attributes – weeping willows for sadness, rue for regret, for example – others are more fluid and may even be present in a text more for the rhyme than for the symbolism. And then singers bring their own meanings. Many versions of this song have the line 'Change the green laurel for the orange and blue', which leads some writers to assume an Irish political origin. But in the same place, others have 'violet so blue', or even 'bonnets so blue'. This is the undoing of Tristram P. Coffin's brave but ultimately unsuccessful study of this song published in the *Journal of American Folklore*, 65 (1952), 341–51, because every new variation has to be fitted into a scheme which was probably bogus to start with.

The song appears, in various forms, on a few nineteenth-century broadsides, and some from the last quarter of the eighteenth century, but these do not help a great deal as they, too, seem unsatisfyingly incomplete or inconclusive. The earliest is entitled 'Can't You Love Whom You Please', and starts, 'When first in this country a stranger I came'. It includes sentiments that occur in other songs, such as 'I often have wondered how men can love maids' and 'Can't you love little and can't you love long'. The 'Green grows the laurel' theme comes only in the fourth verse of five.

There is a real need for someone to undertake an in-depth analysis of the song, but only if they can avoid worrying about what the colours *mean*.

The tune is 'Villikins and His Dinah' (see note to 'All Jolly Fellows Who Follow the Plough', No. 91). The final note of bars 4 and 8 has been changed from a crotchet to a dotted crotchet, and the tied semiquaver has been added in bar 9 in order to make these bars rhythmically complete.

47 If I Were a Blackbird

Sung by Amy Ford, Low Ham, Somerset (14 March 1974); recorded by Bob and Jacqueline Patten; published in the Pattens's *Somerset Scrapbook* (1987), p. 72 and accompanying cassette.
Roud 387; 37 entries.

Frank Purslow commented in *The Wanton Seed* (1968), p. 131:

> Still one of the most widely known songs in the English countryside. At one time many versions of the tune could have been noted but since a popular radio artist made it his signature tune some years ago, everyone now tends to sing the same form of the tune. Very few people can now remember more than the first verse.

Most of the recent collected versions have remarkably similar words, and as Purslow noted, this is mainly due to recordings and media appearances by popular singers in the post-war period, including Michael O'Duffy (1949), Josef Locke (1950) and Ronnie Ronalde, billed as 'The Yodelling Whistler' (1950). The song rapidly became a staple of the 'Irish ballad' repertoire, and the recording that started it all off was the one made by the widely popular Irish singer Delia Murphy, in 1939. All subsequent records and published sheet music credit her as the song's author, although it was clearly around long before her time. It is tempting to assume, but without proof, that she learnt it from Colm O'Lochlainn's *Irish Street Ballads*, published in the same year, which has exactly the same text as Murphy's first recording. O'Lochlainn, in turn, noted his source as 'Dublin street singers about 1920; and afterwards from J. M. Kerrigan', who was a popular Irish character actor (1884–1964). It is still regarded as an Irish song, and appears regularly on 'Celtic' CD compilations and in popular folk circles, but at present there is no evidence that it was originally Irish – apart from the mention of Donnybrook Fair in the lyrics of some versions. Indeed, the earliest known texts were collected in the English countryside before the First World War, by George B. Gardiner, Cecil Sharp and Ralph Vaughan Williams. But without further evidence, it is not clear how the song got there.

A careful comparison of the tune records for this song, which come from both before and after Delia Murphy's 1939 recording, enables a more nuanced view of the situation outlined by Purslow. It suggests that the homogenizing influence of the Murphy recording and its commercial successors is not quite as great as Purslow feared.

The pre-1939 oral recordings confirm that there is more than one tune associated with the song during this period, such as those sung by William Tucker (collected by Sharp), Mrs Krause (Carey) and J. W. Wright (Vaughan Williams), Wright's tune being one often associated with 'Three Maids to Milking Did Go' (No. 87). Nevertheless, the majority of tunes from this time are clearly much the same as the one popularized by Delia Murphy. The situation is similar for the post-1939 recordings. Most use the same basic tune as Murphy but among them is still another distinct tune for the song. According to Fred Hamer, May Bradley, the singer of this version (1959), 'likes to explain that she has heard "a modern song" like this, but she sings it "in the old way"' (Garners Gay (1967), p. 52). This illustrates an important principle in the historical study of oral literature, namely that the date at which a version is collected is unlikely to be an accurate guide to the period from which the version itself comes.

If we look at the detail of the tune most commonly found with 'If I Were a Blackbird', we find that the English versions collected before 1939 have, as a group, several features which make them distinct from Delia Murphy's version. They share the same phrase structure as the Murphy tune – ABAB' (where B' begins the same as B but modifies the end of the phrase slightly) – with the first B phrase cadencing on the second degree of the scale and the final one on the tonal centre. The A phrases of the traditional versions, however, cadence on the fifth degree of the scale while Murphy's A phrases cadence on the second degree, the notes immediately leading up to them having a slightly different contour as a result.

Secondly, the ascending melodic figuration in Murphy's penultimate bar is not found in any pre-1939 traditional versions. None of the English ones contain any chromaticism either, a feature of the Murphy tune (in bars 1, 5, 9 and 13). This gives us something of a baseline against which to assess the post-1939 traditional tunes. Some of these have features associated with the early versions while others, such as that of Caroline Hughes, collected by Ewan MacColl and Peggy Seeger in 1962, follow the Murphy tune in these details. Amy Ford's tune shows a mixture of these older and newer traits. The first half of her tune follows the pattern of the early English versions and the second half follows the Murphy tune in its details. This results in a phrase structure of ABA'C.

Wider comparison of the tune as manifested elsewhere in Britain and Ireland, as well as beyond, is needed to provide a complete picture, but the song makes an interesting case study of the ways in which material is appropriated within traditional and commercial song contexts. As to the origin of Delia Murphy's version, the tune given in O'Lochlainn contains chromaticism in the B phrase but otherwise follows the pattern noted with the early English versions. Interestingly, there is some precedent in one of the earlier English notations (collected from Florence Lockett by Sharp) and one of the earlier Irish notations (collected by Sam Henry), for Delia Murphy's distinctive A-phrase ending.

The tune for the chorus is the same as for the verse. Amy Ford sings with rhythmic freedom, which adds to her lyrical performance. The tune is the same tune as that used for the verse, but not the chorus, of 'The Wild Rover' (No. 88).

48 Lord Thomas and Fair Eleanor

Sung by F. Wheeler, Weobley, Herefordshire; collected by Ella M. Leather and A. M. Webb; published in Leather's *The Folk-Lore of Herefordshire* (1912), pp. 200–202. Leather inserted verses 2–6 from a version collected by H. E. D. Hammond, which we have decided to keep.

Roud 4, Child 73; 42 entries.

Very popular in Britain, though less so in Ireland, the huge number of versions collected in North America bring Lord Thomas into the 'top five' Child ballads, in terms of widespread popularity in the anglophone world. Francis J. Child printed 8 versions, and Bertrand Bronson amassed 147 tunes.

The earliest versions are black-letter broadsides entitled 'A Tragical Ballad of the Unfortunate Love of Lord Thomas and Fair Eleanor' in the Pepys and Roxburghe collections, published in the 1680s, and a number of eighteenth-century prints have also survived, which cover the period between these and the plethora of nineteenth-century broadside printings. Indeed, we have an unusually full printed record for this song, which shows that the song has gradually got shorter but has preserved the core story intact over the centuries.

Child also detailed a number of Scandinavian ballads based on similar love-triangle scenarios, in which there are various permutations as to who kills who first, and there is an alternative telling in an English broadside, 'The Unfortunate Forester, or Fair Elener's Tragedy', which may well pre-date the 'Tragical Ballad'. It tells basically the same story, but stresses Thomas's mother's role in preventing his marrying for love, and ends with Elener committing suicide, and Thomas following suit.

The story of Lord Thomas was obviously a popular one, and is an example of the lack of sympathy for innocent bystanders in ballads. We should perhaps spare a thought for the 'brown girl' who is taunted by her new husband's ex on her wedding day and, like the boyfriend in 'Barbara Allen' (No. 40), is not even given a name. Who can blame her for lashing out as she does?

As Bronson points out, the principal tunes associated with 'Lord Thomas and Fair Eleanor', 'Lord Lovel' (No. 122) and 'The Outlandish Knight' (No. 127) in English tradition form a well-defined family (*The Traditional Tunes of the Child Ballads*, II (1962), p. 189). The renditions we have selected here are particularly close. Yet, on closer inspection, each has its distinctive features. 'Lord Lovel' is a five-phrase tune and lacks the seventh degree of the scale (C) in the upper octave, while 'The Out-landish Knight' tune has a flattened seventh and so is Mixolydian. 'Lord Thomas' has a range of an octave while the other two have a range of a ninth. Each has its own melodic twists and turns. They sound similar because of the closeness of their rhythm, metre and stressed pitches, their common sequence of cadence points, and their overall melodic contour. Together they form a neat example of the way in which what presumably started out as one tune can be subject to a myriad varia-tions and yet retain its identity as it has been passed on, performed and adapted to different sets of words.

49 Mowing the Barley

Sung by Charles Chivers of Basingstoke, Hampshire (1906); collected by
George B. Gardiner (Gardiner MSS, GG/1/9/494).
Roud 922; 28 entries.

This song seems only to have been collected in England, and no further north than Warwickshire and Shropshire, but was clearly popular in the southern counties. Cecil Sharp, in the first volume of his *Folk Songs from Somerset* (1904), called it a 'dainty little ballad' (p. 60), and included a short version in his influential *English Folk-Songs for Schools*, which he compiled in collaboration with Sabine Baring-Gould in 1906.

But the song has a noticeable split-personality problem. The basic premise is the same in all versions – a lawyer meets a pretty girl and tries to win her with promises of riches and a high position in society – but the outcome is very different from ver-sion to version. In most, as in Charles Chivers's song, she refuses his advances, scorns his offers and vows to marry a poor man. In others she initially refuses, but when he persists she relents and they marry.

No nineteenth-century broadsides seem to have survived, but we have three printings from the eighteenth century to guide us, and the earliest, entitled 'The Lawyer and the Farmer's Daughter', was printed by John Garnet, of Sheffield, in 1745. This is presumably the original song and it solves our dichotomy by having it both ways. The lawyer is even more persistent and explicit in his advances than in the collected texts, but it turns out he was only testing her, and once convinced of her virtue goes to her parents and asks for her hand, like a proper honourable gentle-man. This is something of a surprise, as usually in folk song (and in popular culture in general), lawyers have a very bad reputation for duplicity and are rarely goodies.

50 An Old Man Once Courted Me

'Maids, When You're Young, Never Wed an Old Man', sung by Sam Larner,
Winterton, Norfolk (1959); recorded by Ewan MacColl and Peggy Seeger;
issued on *Now is the Time for Fishing*, Folkways FG3507/Topic TSCD511

(2000); published in McColl and Seeger's *The Singing Island* (1960), p. 34.
Roud 210; 26 entries.

Quite commonly collected in England and Scotland, but less often elsewhere. The theme of the marriage or courtship of an old man and a young woman features in a number of songs, and often the girl is under pressure to accept him, although here there is no hint of compulsion. Sam Larner's chorus is unusual, and in most versions the song has instead a 'Hey down derry down' refrain.

It has proved difficult to trace the song's history because of gaps in the documentary record. Our song is clearly related to one from the late eighteenth century, entitled 'Scant of Love, Want of Love', a phrase that recurs as the second line in each verse. It is found in David Herd's manuscript of the 1770s (published as *Ancient and Modern Scottish Songs*) and was also published in a number of collections of the period, with titles such as *The Nightingale or Vocal Songster* (1780), *The British Songster* (1788), *The Chearful Companion* (1783) and *The Skylark or the Lady's and Gentleman's Harmonious Companion* (1785) – in each case written 'By a Lady'.

But no more is seen of the song until a text very similar to the traditional versions and called 'Never Maids Wed an Old Man' appeared on a broadside printed by John Harkness of Preston, probably in the 1840s. Five copies of this broadside have survived, but no other printings have come to light, which is highly unusual.

Tune records for 'An Old Man Once Courted Me' start appearing from the 1880s when they began to be noted from oral tradition. From this time onwards, the same basic melody has been found with this song in England, Ireland, Scotland and Canada, although it is not the only tune to which it has been sung.

Among the earliest tunes to be written down are two from North Yorkshire, one noted by T. C. Smith in Rillington in 1888 (*JFSS*, 2.4 (1906), 273) and the other printed by Frank Kidson in 1891. Despite differences in a number of details, both Kidson's tune and the second strain of Smith's show clear parallels with the melody sung here by Sam Larner. They illustrate some of the many permutations of the tune, which, nowadays, has become best-known in the variants sung by Sam Larner and Jeannie Robertson.

As so often with humorous songs, the tune is in 6/8. In performances of which there are sound recordings, it is clear that many singers feel at liberty to play with the speed and rhythm, as in Sam Larner's rendition here, in order to put the song's innuendo and humour across.

51 *Rosemary Lane*

Sung by Lucy Woodall, Old Hill, Worcestershire (*c.*1976); recorded by Mike Yates; issued on *It Was on a Market Day 2*, Veteran VTC7CD (2006).
Roud 269, Laws K43; 60 entries.

An extremely widespread song, in Britain and America. Its potential for bawdry means that it was popular in male-centred contexts such as rugby clubs, army barracks, and particularly in the navy, where it can still be heard, but traditional versions were often collected from women as well as men. The Victorian and Edwardian collectors encountered the song regularly, but were not keen to publish it in full – Sabine Baring-Gould, for example, commented that 'the words are objectionable' and used the tune for one of his own compositions.

The most interesting thing about the song, however, is its versatility in terms of core meaning and emotional tone. Not only was it sung by both men and women, but it is also couched in both first- and third-person language, and sometimes the narrator is the girl, sometimes the sailor. The bawdier versions go into more detail, of course, but in many versions the girl takes the initiative, and even when she does not she is usually a willing participant.

Sung by a man, to a relatively rollicking tune, it is a devil-may-care song about a sailor with a girl in every port, who shows his heart of gold when he throws money into the girl's apron with a debonair gesture. At the other extreme, it is a rueful lament of a girl regretting her impulsive behaviour, or a bitter complaint on the perfidy of men – although in some versions she declares in the last verse that she will 'dry up her tears' (or, as the broadsides say, 'dry up her milk' after the baby is born), and 'pass for a maid in a new country'.

The locale of the song varies from version to version, but is most often Rosemary Lane, and this seems to have been in the original. Rosemary Lane, otherwise known as Rag Fair, was a notorious part of London, not far from the docks. It was renowned for its second-hand clothing stalls and other low-class establishments, and had a most unsavoury reputation. It was renamed Royal Mint Street in 1850.

Somehow or other, by late Victorian times, 'Rosemary Lane' had gathered to itself the chorus from an otherwise unrelated song variously called 'The North Country Maid', 'Northern Lasses Lamentation' or 'The Oak and the Ash', and it became 'Home, Dearie, Home' or 'Bell-Bottom Trousers'.

A number of broadsides featured it, although not as many as one would expect, given the song's later popularity, the earliest being from the London printers Jennings and Pitts in the first quarter of the nineteenth century. They called it 'The Servant of Rosemary Lane'.

The singing is very slow and deliberate in the rendition in this volume, rhythmically quite free with frequent pauses at the ends of the clauses.

52 The Seeds of Love

Sung by Mrs Baker, Hammer, Sussex (Oct 1912); collected by Clive Carey
(Carey MSS, Sx265/265a).
Round 3; 117 entries.

'It is no exaggeration to say that this song is known to the peasant folk all over England,' said Cecil Sharp in the first volume of *Folk Songs from Somerset* (1904), p. 57, and
it holds a special place in the hearts of folk-song enthusiasts because it was the first
song which he collected, in Hambridge, in 1903. Sharp was visiting his friend, the
Revd Charles Marson, and heard the gardener, John England, singing it. We also have
the authoritative word of the musical antiquarian William Chappell on the popularity of the song half a century before Sharp's time. Writing in his *Popular Music of the
Olden Time* (1859), he commented:

> If I were required to name three of the most popular songs among the servant maids of
> the present generation, I should say, from my own experience, that they are 'Cupid's
> Garden', 'I Sowed the Seeds of Love', and 'Early one Morning'.

Dozens of versions have been collected, and reading them gives at first an
impression of great textual variety, but closer examination shows that this is only
superficial, and many are in fact very similar to each other and to the numerous
nineteenth-century broadside texts, which seem to have acted as a stabilizing force.

But beyond the consensus over popularity, folk-song scholars have long disa-
greed about this song and its history, to the extent that a modern researcher might
be reluctant to enter into such treacherous waters and offer an opinion. Even a syn-
opsis of the argument is complex, and readers may wish to skip straight to the end.

The first problem is its relationship to 'The Sprig of Thyme' (No. 53) and whether
or not we are dealing with two songs or one. It is quite possible to see two songs
here – to oversimplify, 'The Seeds of Love' is couched almost entirely in the symbolism of flowers while 'The Sprig of Thyme' uses similar language but focuses on
thyme, rue, an oak tree, and so on. There are some versions which are thus starkly
differentiated, but the majority combine elements of the two – and the tunes are
apparently fully interchangeable. James Reeves, in *The Everlasting Circle* (1960), sits
on the fence, and declares the 'impossibility of deciding whether we have one song
which has developed in several directions or several songs which have coalesced in
the popular tradition' (p. 238). Frank Kidson wrote, 'The air and words of "I Sowed
the Seeds of Love" are so entangled with those of "The Sprig of Thyme" that the
two ballads are often regarded as identical' (*JFSS*, 1 (1902), 211), but two years later,
in the notes to the first volume of Cecil Sharp's *Folk Songs from Somerset* (pp. 57–8),
he stated categorically, '"The Sprig of Thyme" and "I Sowed the Seeds of Love" are
certainly one and the same ballad.'

In *Marrow Bones* (1965), Frank Purslow was equally insistent that the songs were
originally separate and claimed that 'The Sprig of Thyme' was a woman's song,
while 'The Seeds of Love' was clearly a man's. His argument seems to stem mainly
from the idea that sowing seeds was an active occupation, whereas women's songs
are more passive. But he then ventures further on to thin ice by claiming that 'The
Seeds of Love' is more usually sung to 'masculine' tunes ('bold and strident'), while
'Sprig of Thyme' tunes are of more feminine character (p. 110).

Roy Palmer, in his *Folk Songs Collected by Ralph Vaughan Williams* (1983), also differentiates the two songs on gender lines, but on the safer ground that the first person 'narrator' in 'Seeds' is male, while in 'Sprig' she is female. He also discusses the plant symbolism, and states that 'thyme' stands for the womb, and by extension, virginity (p. 133).

Perhaps the earliest versions will help – or perhaps not. What we have is a broadside in the Pepys collection (5.246), published by Alexander Milbourne in 1696, headed 'An Excellent New Song Called the Young-Man's Answer to the Maids Garden of Tyme', but unfortunately we do not have the song to which this a reply. This song includes the verse:

You say a young man went
Into your garden fine
And there unto your discontent
He pluckt up all your time.

So its forerunner could well be our 'Sprig of Thyme' song, but even if it is we do not know whether or not it included the flowers of 'Seeds'. The 'Answer' is also fairly unsubtle in its sexual euphemisms, with talk of fountains and bushes, but again this is no evidence that the original had the same tone.

We are on surer ground a few decades later. Two chapbook texts, 'The Maid's Lament for the Loss of her Maiden-head' of 1766 and 'The Encouraging Gardener' (*c.*1760–80), both start with verses based on the theme of 'thyme' being stolen and then progress to the gardener standing by, who offers flowers or herbs. Interestingly, however, these two chapbook texts, while recognizably the same song, vary a good deal more than one would expect of two songs printed so close in time.

And then there is the claim that the original song was written about 1689, by a Mrs Fleetwood Habergham (d. 1703), of Whalley, in Lancashire, in sorrow over her husband's extravagance and vice, according to *An History of the Original Parish of Whalley* (1800), by Thomas Dunham Whitaker. It is very difficult to disprove local claims, for which no evidence beyond assertion is given, but it is unlikely that the song is based on a real event or personal circumstance.

Just for the record, another song, 'The Gardener' (Roud 339, Child 219), is sometimes thrown into the equation, in which a gardener attempts to woo a lady by offering to dress her in flowers, but is rejected. This has no real connection with our other song(s) but is occasionally confused with them in people's minds.

Another complicating factor to its history is that 'The Seeds of Love' is also one of those songs which have existed in very different contexts and at different levels in the social scale, apparently at the same time. Like 'Barbara Allen' (No. 40) and 'The Lincolnshire Poacher' (No. 138), it has often had something of a split personality in this respect. As 'The Encouraging Gardener', mentioned above, it appears in a collection called *The British Harmony* (Part 2), which comprises songs sung 'this and the last seasons at both the theatres, Vauxhall, Ranelagh, Sadler's Wells, etc.', so there is more than a hint of the professional stage in the song's development in the eighteenth century. Chappell mentioned a burlesque version performed at the Manchester Theatre, a little before 1839, and it was also sung, with great success, by the popular singer Mrs Honey in the dramatic entertainment of *The Loan of a Lover,* by J. R. Planché, at the Olympic Theatre in 1834. Lucy Broadwood commented that following the song's appearance in Chappell's *Old English Ditties* (1868) with piano accompaniment by Sir George Macfarren, 'it became a favourite in Victorian drawing-rooms'. It was parodied on the music-hall stage, and in 1906 it was included in Baring-Gould and Sharp's *English Folk-Songs for Schools,* and was subsequently warbled by several generations of schoolchildren in classrooms up and down the land. And in the post-war Revival it took on a new lease of life as 'Let No Man Steal Your Thyme'. There is no doubting its enduring popularity.

53 *The Sprig of Thyme*

Sung by Charles Lolley, East Riding, Yorkshire; collected by Frank Kidson; published in Kidson's *Traditional Tunes* (1891), p. 69. In his book, Kidson puts a row of dots between verses 4 and 5, probably indicating omitted words. The broadside texts are so similar to Kidson's that it seems permissible to insert the missing verse here (from a sheet printed by Forth of Hull).

In Charles Lolley's rendition, the tune is quite distinct from Mrs Baker's 'Seeds of Love' tune.

See the note to 'The Seeds of Love', above.

54 *Susan, the Pride of Kildare*

Sung by George 'Pop' Maynard, Copthorne, Sussex (1959); recorded by Brian Matthews; issued on *Down at the Cherry Tree*, Musical Traditions MTCD400 (2000).
Roud 962, Laws P6; 24 entries.

This was one of Pop Maynard's favourite songs and, when singing it, he often repeated the last two lines of some verses. 'Pretty Susan' was surprisingly popular in England, and collected fairly regularly in North America, but not much elsewhere. It was also widely printed on broadsides from the 1820s and possibly a little earlier.

In the catalogue of songs which are laments for faithless lovers, the female voice predominates, but there is a handful of well-known songs like this (for example 'A Week Before Easter', No. 56) in which it is the man who is left in sorrow.

Pop Maynard's tune is a fine example of the tune found almost universally with this song. Lucy Broadwood notes that the melody is 'met with in so many forms,

Irish and Scottish' and that it was used by the poet Thomas Moore for his song 'The Meeting of the Waters' in *Irish Melodies*, I (1808) (*JFSS*, 6 (1918), 11–12).

55 The Trees They Do Grow High

Sung by Mrs Joiner, Chiswell Green, Hertfordshire (7 September 1914); collected by Lucy Broadwood (Broadwood MSS, LEB/2/46); published in *JFSS*, 5 (1915), 190–91.
Roud 31, Laws O35; 77 entries.

Judging by the number of versions gathered in the major manuscript collections and later sound recordings, this song has been a firm favourite with singers in Britain, Ireland and North America for a long time. The wording varies surprisingly little across the English versions and the story is always the same, and these probably derive from nineteenth-century broadside printings, of which there were many.

The early history of the song, however, as so far known, refers to Scottish versions and is not straightforward. The earliest sighting is a two-verse fragment in the manuscript collection of David Herd, dating from the 1770s (published by Hans Hecht in 1904). Robert Burns used this fragment as a basis for his poem 'Lady Mary Ann', which he contributed to the *Scots Musical Museum* in 1792, and which also entered the tradition. Ballad editor James Maidment published a version which he called 'The Young Laird of Craigstoun' (*North Countrie Garland*, 1824) and he claimed that the song was based on the true story of thirteen-year-old John Urquhart of Craigston who in the early 1630s was married to his older cousin by her manipulative father. Over the years this explanation has been discounted as circumstantial by various editors, but in one of the latest scholarly ballad books, *The Glenbuchat Ballads* (2007), David Buchan and James Moreira give full credence to the story, so we must at least accept its possibility.

In a bid to claim the ballad back for England, Sabine Baring-Gould, in his *Songs of the West* (1905), pp. 2–3, quoted a verse from a song in Fletcher and Beaumont's play *Two Noble Kinsmen* (1634) that he claimed was similar to some words in a version of 'The Trees They Do Grow High' he had collected in Devon. Unfortunately for his argument, the similarity is far-fetched, and the words quoted not typical of our song, so, on balance, the Scots still claim the ballad.

Broadwood marks the verse of this Dorian tune as 'very slow and expressive'. Her dynamic markings have been omitted here. Tune variations (a) and (c) are labelled as 'variants used very occasionally'. Of variation (d), which is stanza 6, Broadwood states that the G sharps are 'decidedly more *sharp* than *natural*, though a little difficult to determine'. The first crotchet of bar 15 has been made into a dotted crotchet here to make the bar complete.

56 A Week Before Easter

Sung by Harry Burgess, Glynde, Sussex (19 June 1956); recorded by Mervyn
Plunkett; also issued on *As Me and My Love Sat Courting*, Topic TSCD665
(1998). Harry started two verses with 'The first time'
which is why there is no 'third time'.
Roud 154; 41 entries.

This was clearly a popular song with traditional singers, with versions appearing in
most of the major collections in England and Scotland, and it was one of the songs
the Northampton poet John Clare noted from his mother and father's singing in the
1820s. The traditional texts vary more than usual and appear under a number of titles,
including 'The False Bride', 'The Forlorn Lover' and 'The Despairing Lover'.

It is surprising that, given how widely collected the song was, few nineteenth-
century broadside printings have survived. But this lack is more than remedied by
the survival of several eighteenth-century copies and even some dating from the
late seventeenth century, housed in the Roxburghe, Douce and Euing collections.
A printed ballad entitled 'The Forlorne Lover' was entered in the Company of Stationers' Register on 1 March 1675. These earlier versions are far wordier than the
traditional sets of the later centuries, taking sixteen verses to tell the story, and, as
is usually the case, the shorter texts are far more satisfying as songs, with a much
tighter emotional core.

In this recording, Harry Burgess sings the word 'didn't' to the final semiquaver
of bar 12. The rhythm of this bar has been slightly amended here so that 'didn't' falls
on the final two notes of the bar.

IV

Since Love Can Enter an Iron Door ...
Lovers' Tricks, Disguises and Obstacles Overcome

57 The Baffled Knight

'Blow the Windy Morning', sung by Emily Bishop, Bromsberrow Heath,
Herefordshire (13 October 1952); recorded by Peter Kennedy (BBC 18679);
issued on Topic 12T161/Rounder 11661-1776-2.
Roud 11, Child 112; 45 entries.

This was an immensely popular song in the English tradition and was also known in
other parts of the English-speaking world. Francis J. Child prints five early versions,

and discusses its history and connections with similar songs from Spain, Portugal, France, Italy, Denmark and Germany, while Bertrand Bronson amasses thirty-nine tunes.

As it stands, Bishop's is the central core of a much longer song which has been around since at least the early seventeenth century. Her version is perfectly viable as a short song, but does miss out a rather crucial part of the story. After her verse two, the shepherd propositions the girl and she says they would be much more comfortable at her house, or at an inn, which gives her the opportunity to fox him by locking him out.

The earliest known text is in Thomas Ravenscroft's *Deuteromelia* (1609), as 'Yonder Comes a Courteous Knight', and numerous versions were issued on broadsides and in songbooks over the following 300 years. While the general tendency is for the oral tradition to shorten stories, print gives the opportunity for extension. In the later seventeenth century, new versions were issued which repeated the joke by describing how she baffled him again and again with different ruses, although these do not seem to have lasted in traditional singers' minds as they have preferred to keep it simple. It is also noticeable that in earlier versions the protagonist is a knight rather than a shepherd, and the difference in social class between him and the girl adds to the humour.

Bishop's tune, with its 'blow the windy morning' chorus, is an example of the 'jolly plagal tune' most commonly found with this song in the twentieth century (Bronson, *The Traditional Tunes of the Child Ballads*, I (1959), p. 547). It has a distinctive opening phrase, however, ending with an ascending figuration reminiscent of that in 'The Shepherd's Son', a nineteenth-century Scottish tune for the ballad, reproduced by Bronson (II (1962), no. 5, p. 550). In other details it is closer to Cecil Sharp's version from Mrs Richards, Little Sodbury, Gloucestershire, rather than the tunes collected from West Country singers.

58 The Banks of the Sweet Dundee

Sung by Mrs Burge, Bathpool, Somerset (1916/1917); collected by Janet
Blunt (Blunt MSS, JHB/10/16).
Roud 148, Laws M25; 56 entries.

In *Traditional Tunes* (1891), Frank Kidson wrote, 'This has been popular in nearly every district in England, and in a number of places in Scotland as well. Though sublime doggerel, the song is even now a great favourite with the old folk who still remember it. Perhaps this is on account of the good air to which the song is set' (p. 53). But a song needs more than a good tune to be as widely known and to last as long as this one has. It is, in fact, a good example of the strengths and weaknesses of 'broadside ballads': a strong melodramatic plot, told sequentially and simply, with good triumphing over evil, and love more important than money. It was often called

'Undaunted Mary', which also emphasizes the 'strong heroine' aspect of the story.

The song was collected widely and was equally popular on broadsides, with almost all the well-known nineteenth-century printers offering versions, although the earliest so far found date from only about the 1820s. Texts vary surprisingly little.

Nearly all the traditional versions, like Mrs Burge's, as well as the broadsides, leave Mary happy in her wealth, but make no mention of William's fate. Occasionally, however, an additional verse is found, as in the following, from W. H. Long's *The Dialect of the Isle of Wight* (1886), pp. 134–5:

> *About a twelvemonth after, or perhaps a little more*
> *The fleet returned to England, and William came ashore*
> *He hastened to his Mary and who so glad as she?*
> *They soon were wed, and happy lived, on the banks of sweet Dundee.*

But the story was far too good to be left with this weak ending, and the broadside presses soon provided an 'Answer to Undaunted Mary' (Roud 5649) in which William takes part in a great sea battle, is wounded, but arrives home with his prize money. He hastens to Mary but first puts her through the traditional test of telling her that her William has died before revealing his identity, and they get married. This sequel does not seem to have grabbed the attention of singers in England, but some versions were collected in Scotland. Another sequel was entitled 'The Banks of Inverness' (Roud 3813).

Cecil Sharp dubs 'The Banks of the Sweet Dundee' tune 'the stock-in-trade of every English folk-singer', suggesting that singers often resort to it when 'at a loss for a tune' (*English Folk-Song: Some Conclusions* (1907), pp. 93–4). Norman Cazden points out that there are a number of tunes sung for 'The Banks of the Sweet Dundee' and cautions against 'any reference to *the* tune of *The Banks of Sweet Dundee* as though that were a specific and identifiable entity' (*Folk Songs of the Catskills* (1982), p. 183). As far as the melodies collected in England are concerned, one tune tends to predominate in association with this song but it can be divided into several subgroups, as follows.

Group I is exemplified by Mrs Burge's tune. It is either major or Mixolydian (major with a flattened seventh) in tonality and has an A phrase beginning with a descending jump from the fifth to the first degrees, followed by a rising scale back up to the fifth degree again. Group II begins as the Group I tunes. The first B phrase in this group, however, introduces a sharpened fourth which implies a change of key (modulation) to the dominant. The Group I melodies cadence on the same degree of the scale but do not inflect the fourth. Another feature of the Group I and II tunes is the descending 4-3-1 figuration in the penultimate bar of the A phrase. In Group III this pattern is given increased prominence by appearing in the first full bar of the A phrase as well. This seems to be associated with a B phrase in which the upper tonic is approached by means of a scale or arpeggio figure, rather than a direct jump. Group III tunes are allied with Group I in that they do not modulate. They also share their characteristics with certain tune variants found in association with 'Van

Diemen's Land' (No. 145), such as that sung by Harry Cox (MacColl and Seeger, *The Singing Island*, 1960), although Cox's tune mostly implies a minor tonality.

Cecil Sharp also uses 'The Banks of the Sweet Dundee' tune to exemplify the common phrase structure ABBA. As he describes, 'the second B is often a free rendering of the first, rather than an exact reproduction of it' and this is sometimes true of the A phrase too (Sharp, *English Folk-Song: Some Conclusions*, pp. 93–4). Interestingly, Benjamin Holgate's tune, printed by Kidson, opens with the Group III form of the A phrase and varies its reappearance with the Groups I and II form of the phrase. In all cases, the 'free rendering' of the repeated phrases does not affect the cadence pattern usually associated with the ABBA structure, which is on the first (A phrase) and fifth (B phrase) degrees of the scale.

For more about the ABBA form, see Introduction to the Music (p. xlvii). There is no text underlay in Janet Blunt's tune manuscript for Mrs Burge's rendition, so that given here is conjectural. All slurring is editorial. The final note has been changed from a dotted crotchet to a dotted minim in order to complete the bar.

59 Basket of Eggs

'Eggs in Her Basket', sung by Fred List, Suffolk (*c*.1975); recorded by Keith Summers; issued on *Good Hearted Fellows*, Veteran VT154CD (2006).
Roud 377; 26 entries.

This song on the theme of girl tricks boy to get her own back was quite common in England and Scotland, but rare in Ireland and North America. Collected versions often end happily, with the sailor owning up to his previous misdeeds and the couple getting married, but earlier broadside versions end with his bad temper at being outwitted. It was probably this revenge aspect which attracted singers in earlier times, and broadside versions were often called, or subtitled, 'The Biter Bit'.

Surprisingly few nineteenth-century broadside printings have survived, but we have several eighteenth-century examples to sketch in its early history. These include 'Luck in a Basket, or The Biter Bit', printed for Sam Cook in Southwark, probably about 1750; and 'The Jovial Sailor, or The Biter Bit' in *The Royal Wedding Garland* of the 1760s. The song was also called 'Eggs and Bacon'.

There are a number of distinct tunes associated with this song, some having a major tonality, others in the 'minor' Dorian and Aeolian modes, and still others shifting between major and minor through the singer's inflecting of the third degree of the scale. Fred List's is major and has a particularly wide compass, being a major twelfth.

His tune also illustrates features common to a number of those found with this song, despite their melodic diversity. One of these is that his tune ends on the fifth degree of the major scale rather than the more usual first degree. Cecil Sharp's version from Mrs Laurence does likewise, and several other collected versions finish on the sixth degree. These can strike the modern listener as making the tune sound unfinished or open-ended because of their relative distance from the expected tonal centre.

Perhaps even more striking is the rhythmic flexibility of Fred List's rendition, which in many bars is in five time (*compare* 'Bold Fisherman' (No. 21), with which it has some occasional melodic similarities). A number of the other tune transcriptions and recordings of this song also dip in and out of five time, including several collected by George B. Gardiner, and by Cecil Sharp, Ralph Vaughan Williams and Ewan MacColl. The emphasis always falls on the first and third beats, giving the tune a lilt all of its own.

Fred List's 'Basket of Eggs' tune is much the same as tunes collected by Sharp, Percy Grainger and Vaughan Williams for 'Lord Bateman' (No. 33), some of which are also in five time.

60 The Blind Beggar's Daughter of Bethnal Green

'The Blind Beggar of Bethlem Green', sung by Mr Rugman and Mr Lough,
farm labourers, Dunsfold, Surrey (1898); collected by Lucy Broadwood;
published in *JFSS*, 1:4 (1902), 202–3.
Roud 132, Laws N27; 15 entries.

This song tells a well-known story, although it has not very often been collected from English singers. The earliest manifestations of the ballad are found on a black-letter broadside of about 1680 and in the manuscript that Thomas Percy used for his *Reliques of Ancient English Poetry* (1765), which is usually dated to about 1650. But the story also appeared in prose form, and it is known that a play on the subject was performed as early as 1600, so it is often assumed that the ballad itself dates from the time of Elizabeth I. The early broadsides were much longer (over 250 lines long), and the versions collected from traditional singers all stem from a severely curtailed broadside text which first appeared in the early nineteenth century.

One detail may seem puzzling: the 'dropping' of the money in verses 8 and 9. In most other versions the money is *thrown* down, a much more dramatic gesture, and redolent of the competitive display of riches which proved that the beggar had far more money than his detractors.

Lucy Broadwood published two versions of this song from Dunsfold, each with a different melody (*JFSS*, 1 (1902), 202–3). These exemplify the two principal tunes to which 'The Blind Beggar's Daughter' has been sung in England. Both are in triple time and feature predominantly crotchet movement. That from Mr Lough is major and has brief echoes of 'Villikins and His Dinah' and 'Flash Company' (see No. 80). That from Mr Rugman is minor in tonality (the Dorian mode) and recalls the tune of 'The Cunning Cobbler' (see No. 78).

Comparison of the major and modal tune traditions shows that they are not totally distinct. They share the same phrase structure (ABCD) and melodic contour and sometimes the same cadence points (in the first, second and fourth phrases) as well as some specific pitch progressions.

William Chappell prints two tunes for the song (*Popular Music of the Olden Time* (1859), I, pp. 158–60). These are similar to each other but distinct from the more recently collected melodies in their meter, being in common time, although they have some points of resemblance in their contour, range and minor tonality. Chappell cites Edward Rimbault's claim that one of the tunes, under the name of 'The Cripple', was written by Rogers, 'a celebrated lutenist of the reign of Charles II'. Chappell also finds a number of songs from the mid seventeenth century sung to the melody known as 'Pretty Bessy'. The second tune he prints exemplifies how the song is 'sung about the country'.

61 The Bonny Blue Handkerchief

Sung by F. Kitching, Guildford, Surrey (5 February 1952); collected by
Francis Collinson (Collinson MSS, COL/2/27A).
Roud 378; 19 entries.

Not so well known as other 'returned lover in disguise' songs, 'The Bonny Blue Handkerchief' was nevertheless collected quite widely in England, as well as a few times in Scotland, Ireland and North America, and it appeared regularly on broadsides from at least the 1820s onwards.

Not only is blue the sign of loyalty ('true blue'), but some versions also make it clear that the maiden's lover was a sailor and gave her the handkerchief to match his traditional blue jacket. The connection is taken one step further on a broadside printed by James Catnach of London, dating from the 1820s, where it is paired with another song, 'The Bonny Blue Jacket'. The latter is either an 'answer to' or a parody of 'The Bonny Blue Handkerchief' and reverses the scenario of the latter: it is the girl who meets, and tempts, the sailor boy, who is looking for his sweetheart, and the refrain line is 'The bonny blue jacket this lad was dressed in'.

There appears to be no generally accepted tune for this song. Most are major-key, triple-time melodies, some containing echoes of other well-known tunes. The A phrase of Mrs Kitching's tune, for example, is that of the major-key 'Green Bushes' tune (see No. 45) and her B phrase recalls one of the tunes associated with 'All Jolly Fellows Who Follow the Plough' (see No. 91).

62 Bonny Labouring Boy

Sung by Ernest Glew, North Bersted, Sussex (*c.* 1958); recorded
by Mervyn Plunkett.
Roud 1162, Laws M14; 21 entries.

Very widely sung in England, with a fair few versions collected in Ireland and North America, but not, apparently, in Scotland, 'Bonny Labouring Boy' is another treatment on the common theme of parental disapproval of young people's choices in love. In this case it is the girl who is of the higher status as she is a farmer's daughter falling for one of her father's labourers, but like all true ballad heroines she stands firm against their opposition.

Ernest Glew's version is pared down to the bone, but even the longer collected versions seem curiously truncated and do not appear to tell the full story. A seven-verse treatment, sung by Harry Cox of Norfolk, can be found in Peter Kennedy's *Folksongs of Britain and Ireland* (1975), p. 346, and on Topic CD TSCD 512D. Two key verses, taken from a broadside printed by W. R. Walker of Newcastle in the 1840s (Bodleian Library Broadside Ballads, Firth c.12 (442)), fill out the text but do not advance the story a great deal:

> *His cheeks are like the roses red, his eyes as black as sloes*
> *He's mild in his behaviour wherever that he goes*
> *He's merry, neat and handsome, his skin as white as snow*
> *And in spite of my parents' malice with my labouring boy I'll go.*

> *This couple they got married and joined in unity*
> *In peace and comfort to live, in love and loyalty*
> *Her parents' riches she disdains for her love and only joy*
> *May prosperity attend her with her bonny labouring boy.*

The description of his skin as 'white as snow' shows the poetic rather than the realistic nature of such songs: it is unlikely that many nineteenth-century farm labourers could have boasted such a complexion. The song was also very popular with broadside printers, dating probably from about 1830.

The widespread tune for this song is akin to the melodies used for 'Erin's Lovely Home' (No. 70) and a number of other folk songs. Ernest Glew sings a different tune, a 6/8 variant of the first strain of 'The Wearing of the Green'. His tune is distinct in having a fairly restricted melodic range of a sixth. The beginning of his B phrase thus diverges from that of 'The Wearing of the Green', which jumps to the octave at this point before descending with its characteristic 6-5-3-1 figure (*compare* 'Brennan on the Moor', No. 132). Anne Gilchrist traces the origin of 'The Wearing of the Green' to a Scottish march entitled 'The Tulip' (*Southern Folklore Quarterly*, 9 (1945), 119–26). It was composed by James Oswald as one of his *Airs for the Seasons* (*c*.1747). Norman Cazden in his *Folk Songs of the Catskills* (1982), pp. 317–19, provides a useful overview of the scholarship on the song's text and tune history.

63 Broomfield Hill

'Bonny Green Woods', sung by Miss Anne Hiles, Kirton in Lindsey, Lincolnshire (March 1904); collected by Mabel Peacock and Edgar C. Robinson; published in *JFSS*, 4 (1910), 110–16
Roud 34, Child 43; 42 entries.

This was very well known across England and Scotland, but rare in the USA; Francis J. Child printed six versions, and Bertrand Bronson presented twenty-four tunes. Texts and tunes of this song vary considerably but the basic story remains pretty constant. In Anne Hiles's version, an unusual, perhaps unique, feature is that the girl drugs the young man, but commentators most often assume that the sleep which overcomes him is induced by the girl's magical powers. Occasionally she visits a witch, who tells her what to do, and in some versions she strews certain herbs and flowers at his feet and head – but in the latter case he must already be asleep when she arrives, so the magic here must be merely to keep him sedated. Many versions, however, including the earliest broadside, do not bother to explain why his sleep was so deep, nor is it ever explained why, in most renderings, the knight proclaims that he was planning to kill the girl.

The earliest text so far located is probably the broadside printed by Thomas Norris in London in the Douce collection, which dates from between 1679 and 1732, or another in the same collection, by John White of Newcastle, which dates from about 1720. Attempts to link the song with earlier ones that mention 'broom' and 'hills' are unconvincing. But Child comments that very similar stories occur in Swedish, Danish and Icelandic ballads which are a little older than our English ones, and all may well derive from a tale published in the *Gesta Romanorum,* the collection of anecdotes and tales compiled about 1300.

Anne Hiles called her version 'Bonny Green Woods', and 'hare and hounds' in verse 4 is more usually 'hawk and hounds'. Traditional versions most often start with the words 'A wager, a wager'.

Although it is 'full of charm and interest', Bronson notes much diversity among the tunes for this song (*The Traditional Tunes of the Child Ballads*, I (1959), p. 336). Accordingly, Anne Hiles's tune is melodically closer to that noted by Lucy Broadwood in Sussex and Surrey for 'The Bailiff's Daughter of Islington' (Roud 483) and 'The Seeds of Love' (No. 52) than it is to other 'Broomfield Hill' tunes (see Broadwood, *JFSS*, 1.4 (1902), 209). Broadwood highlights further parallels with several other English and Scottish songs, but these lack the bouncy rhythm that characterizes Miss Hiles's tune. Bronson also notes similarities with 'The Mermaid' (No. 13), many of whose tunes, although authentic in range rather than plagal like that of Miss Hiles's, have the dotted rhythm and a similar feel.

64 Butter and Cheese and All

'The Cook's Choice', sung by Leslie Johnson, Fittleworth, Sussex (8 November 1954); recorded by Bob Copper (BBC 22762); also published in Copper's *Songs and Southern Breezes* (1973), pp. 236–7.
Roud 510; 15 entries.

Reasonably well known across England, but not so common elsewhere, this song also appeared regularly on broadsides from about 1830, under titles such as 'Cookey's Court-ship' or 'Cupboard Love'.

One of the main reasons why so many employers insisted that their servants had 'no followers' was to safeguard their morals, but there was also a well-grounded fear that visitors below stairs would be entertained at the family's expense or, even worse, would be strangers casing the joint for a future burglary. The young man who was sweet on the cook simply for the food he could get was thus a recognizable scenario.

Nearly all the tunes sung for this comic song are major-key tunes in a rollicking 6/8 metre. Several bear a close resemblance to Leslie Johnson's tune, such as that sung by Walter Weller in Stubbs, *The Life of a Man* (1970), pp. 38–9.

65 Caroline and Her Young Sailor Bold

'Caroline and her Young Sailor Boy', sung by Mrs Fanny Pronger, East Grinstead, Sussex (1960); collected by Ken Stubbs; published in Stubbs's *The Life of a Man* (1970), pp. 22–3.
Roud 553, Laws N17; 22 entries.

Although this song has elements of 'family opposition to lovers' and 'girl dresses as sailor to accompany her lover', these plotlines do not have the punch they usually do in traditional songs, and even the sailor lad is here decent enough to warn the young woman not to get involved with sailors. Nevertheless, the song was popular with traditional singers and was collected often in England and a fair number of times in Scotland and Ireland as well.

It was even more popular on broadsides and was issued by most of the nineteenth-century printers, and it is on one of the surviving sheets that we get a clue of the song's origin. As mentioned elsewhere, we know very little about the people who wrote songs for the broadside trade, but the one exception is John Morgan. Thanks to the earlier writings of Charles Hindley, and the recent researches of James Hep-burn, we know something of Morgan's life and some of the songs he wrote. On one sheet, printed by Taylor of Waterloo Road, London, the song 'Young Sailor Bold' is actually signed by 'J. Morgan', and as Taylor was at that address for only a short time we can date it to about 1836. But there is another clue on this sheet, as it states that our song is an answer to 'The Gallant Hussar' (Roud 1146), and is probably written to that tune. This song features a 'damsel of great beauty' who falls in love with a soldier, and it is similar in many respects to 'Caroline …', but despite being equally well known on broadsides was collected much more rarely.

The melodic tradition for this song is very stable and consistent. Fanny Pronger's rendition exemplifies the tune that is associated with most collected versions and in much the same form. The same tune is found with 'The Gallant Hussar', as was common with songs which claimed to be an 'answer' to an existing song. It is also commonly associated with 'The Rakish Young Fellow' (Roud 829).

66 Claudy Banks

'Cloddy Banks', sung by Archer 'Daddy' Lane, Winchcombe Workhouse,
Gloucestershire (5 April 1908); recorded by Percy Grainger; transcribed
from Grainger's cylinder by Gwilym Davies, *FMJ*, 6:3 (1992), 148–9.
Inaudible lines supplied by Davies in his *Grainger in Gloucestershire* (1994)
booklet.
Roud 266, Laws N40; 16 entries.

On the surface, 'Claudy Banks' appears to be one of the 'returned lover in disguise'
songs such as 'Fair Maid Walking in Her Garden' (No.71). It was popular with singers in England and also regularly collected in Scotland and Ireland, and is well known
in the post-war Revival from the singing of the Copper Family and others such as
George 'Pop' Maynard. But perhaps it has been misunderstood. Evidence from the
earliest broadsides, and a close reading of some traditional performances, demonstrate
that this was not originally a 'broken token' song, in which the faithful lover returns
in disguise after years abroad. In fact, Johnny has been a faithless lover (and is described
so), and the girl is looking for him precisely because he has left her. This explains the
'six long weeks' line in many versions, including Archer Lane's given here, which
some commentators presume is a mistake for 'six years'. She is actually being told,
'Well, you've just missed him, he's gone to sea and been shipwrecked.' Johnny of
course has a change of heart, and the story ends happily.

The song was also very popular on broadsides and most of the major nineteenth-
century printers published versions, with the earliest being about 1818. It is usually
assumed that the 'Claudy' in the song (although spelling and pronunciation varies
widely) is the village in County Londonderry, and that the song is therefore Irish in
origin, but there is no real evidence for this either way.

In most cases nineteenth-century broadsides did not give any indication of the
tune to which the song they contained should be sung, so tunes from other songs
were fitted to the words by the broadside seller or the singers who purchased the
sheet. This seems to have been the case for 'Claudy Banks', which has been sung to
a number of different tunes. 'Daddy' Lane's rendition is distinct from those sung
by the Copper family and Pop Maynard, for example, but resembles that collected
from Joanna Slade by Cecil Sharp in Somerset. This same tune was also sung by Mrs
Lock, another of Sharp's Somerset contributors, for 'High Germany' (Roud 904).
It is a good example of a modal tune – in this case the Dorian mode – so prized by
the Edwardian folk-song collectors. Indeed, the tune (deriving from Mrs Lock) was
incorporated by Ralph Vaughan Williams into his *English Folksong Suite* (1923).

67 Dabbling in the Dew

'Rolling in the Dew', sung by Leslie Johnson, Rustington, Sussex (8

November 1954); recorded by Bob Copper (BBC 22762); published in
Copper's *Songs and Southern Breezes* (1973), pp. 238–9.
Roud 298; 50 entries.

This is a very widely collected song – Cecil Sharp alone noted fourteen versions – and very effective when sung as a male–female duet, which is how it was originally designed. No doubt it was the maid's sassy answers which appealed in the past, as now. The refrain line in different collected versions varies from 'rolling' or 'roving' to 'dabbling' in the dew, and this presumably refers to the widespread notion that morning dew – especially on May Day – is good for the complexion.

The song was popular on broadsides, and was printed by most of the well-known printers in the nineteenth century. It also entered the juvenile tradition, being included in books such as James Orchard Halliwell's *Nursery Rhymes and Nursery Tales of England* (1870 edn), suitably cleaned up, of course. But its roots are much older. What is presumably the original black-letter broadside can be seen in the Wood collection in the Bodleian Library, entitled 'A Merry New Dialogue between a Courteous Young Knight and a Gallant Milk Maid', printed in London for W. Thackeray, about 1688. See also the Opies' *Oxford Dictionary of Nursery Rhymes* (1951), pp. 281–3 for further historical information.

The broadside is directed to be sung to the tune called 'Adams fall, or Jocky and Jenny', or 'Where art thou going my pritty maid'.

Many of the tunes associated with this song in oral tradition exhibit melodic parallels which give the impression of resemblance despite differences in tonality (in terms of specific modes and overall major or minor tonality), metre (4/4 and 6/8) and specific melodic figurations. The tune sung by Leslie Johnson illustrates these common characteristics in its authentic range, the overall melodic contour and range of each phrase, and the mid-cadence on the fifth degree of the scale and first-phrase cadence on the tonic. In its specifics, it has a very close counterpart in the tune sung by the Somerset singer Samuel Weekes (Maud Karpeles, *Cecil Sharp's Collection of English Folk Songs*, I (1974), p. 439).

68 Dark-Eyed Sailor

'Fair Phoebe and Her Dark-Eyed Sailor', sung by Mrs Hill (old family nurse, native of Lincolnshire) (November 1893); collected by Lucy Broadwood; published in *JFSS*, 4 (1910), 129–30.
Roud 265, Laws N35; 71 entries.

Often called 'Fair Phoebe and Her Dark-Eyed Sailor', this was probably the most popular of the 'broken token' songs in England, and was not only noted regularly by all the Edwardian collectors, but also still being widely sung when the post-war fieldworkers turned up with their tape recorders. It is usually assumed to be of eighteenth-century origin, but so far no printed texts have been found earlier than those issued by the London printers Pitts and Catnach, which were produced some-time in the first three decades of the nineteenth century.

Many collectors comment on the persistence of the same basic tune with this song. Lucy Broadwood also points to the tune's association with 'The Female Smuggler' (Roud 1200) and its similarity to the four-time melody of 'All on Spurn Point' (Roud 599) (*JFSS*, 4 (1910), 131).

69 The Daughter in the Dungeon

Sung by Jack Barnard of Bridgwater, Somerset (17 April 1906); collected
by Cecil Sharp (Sharp MSS, FW 940–42/FT 871). Jack's version lacked four
important lines in the last verse, and we have supplied these from a text
collected by Lucy Broadwood from Walter Searle, Amberley, Sussex (1901),
published in her *English Traditional Songs and Carols* (1908), pp. 38–9.
Roud 539, Laws M15; 31 entries.

Under a number of evocative titles – 'The Daughter in the Dungeon', 'The Iron Door', 'The Cruel Father and Affectionate Lovers' – this song was particularly popular in England and Canada, but less so in Scotland, Ireland and the USA. In its somewhat pedantic, step-by-step narrative it is typical of songs written for the broadside trade, which, it must be admitted, are far better heard than read. The words are remarkably faithful to the printed versions, the earliest of which dates from about the 1820s.

70 Erin's Lovely Home

Sung by John Edbrook, Bishop's Nympton, Devon (11 January 1905);
collected by Cecil Sharp (Sharp MSS, FW 167–9/FT 107).
Roud 1427, Laws M6; 38 entries.

This was a very popular song in Britain and Ireland, and regularly encountered in North America, although apparently better known in Canada than the USA. It is another treatment of the 'family opposition' theme, narrated by the young man who is waiting to be transported for seven years. It is never made clear what crime he has been charged with, as such details are not always thought necessary in folk-song texts. On the evidence of other songs on the same theme, he would have been framed by the father, but it is good to know that his sweetheart plans to wait the seven years for him, as sweethearts should.

'Erin's Lovely Home' was also popular with nineteenth-century broadside print-ers, and on the evidence of surviving sheets probably dates from the 1840s.

John Edbrook's common-time tune exemplifies the basic melody to which

English versions of this song are generally sung. It is characterized by minor tonality (the Dorian or Aeolian mode), authentic range, and the common phrase structure ABBA with its associated cadences on the tonic and the fifth degrees of the scale. Versions of the song have also been collected in which the phrases of this tune are sung in a slightly different arrangement (such as that by Mrs Munday, collected by George B. Gardiner, GG/1/17/1064), or combined with further melodic material (such as Henry Hills, *JFSS*, 1 (1901), 117). There is at least one example of the same basic tune sung in a major tonality and with an extended overall range of an eleventh (Mrs Curling, Gardiner MSS, GG/1/8/430).

Cecil Sharp claims that 'a large number of English Folk-tunes are modelled on the same pattern' (*JFSS*, 2 (1906), 168), including 'Young Henry the Poacher' (Roud 221), 'The Sheffield Apprentice' (No. 141), 'On Board a Ninety-Eight' (Roud 1461), and 'Napoleon's Farewell' (Roud 1626). He also suggests a possible connection with the tune of 'Lazarus' (Roud 477), but the resemblance is loose at best, given the distinctive cadences and differing form of the latter.

Outside England, 'Erin's Lovely Home' is frequently sung to a major tune in 6/8 time.

71 Fair Maid Walking in Her Garden

'Young and Single Sailor', sung by Mrs Vaisey, Hampshire (September 1892); collected by Lucy Broadwood; published in *JFSS*, 4 (1910), 127–8.
Roud 264, Laws N42; 49 entries.

Probably the second most popular of the 'broken token' songs ('Dark-Eyed Sailor' is number one, see No. 68), this song was widely collected in England and Scotland, and even more often in North America. It also appeared on numerous nineteenth-century broadsides, with similar texts, but under a variety of titles, including 'Sailor's Return', 'Loyal Sailor' and 'Young and Single Sailor', although the earliest probably date from the late eighteenth century.

It is a mark of the astonishing conservatism of the Anglo-American tradition that certain textual details, which are not obviously crucial to the story, seem to be hard-wired into the song. In this case, of the 332 entries in *The Folk Song Index* for which we know the first line, 287 specifically set the scene in a 'garden'.

Mrs Vaisey's tune is a good example of that commonly associated with this song. Nearly all versions, though they differ in melodic detail, contain the distinctive feature of a large ascending leap of a seventh, here found in bars 5 and 7. Cecil Sharp commented on 'the bold sweep and vigour of this melody', versions of which he had often found to be in an irregular rhythm (*Folk Songs from Somerset*, II (1905), p. 72).

72 Polly Oliver's Rambles

Sung by George Dunn, Quarry Bank, Staffordshire (5 June 1972); collected
by Roy Palmer; published in *FMJ*, 2:4 (1973), 286–7, and on *Chainmaker*,
Musical Traditions MTCD 317-18 (2002). On the day that he was recorded,
George had forgotten some of the lines of the song, so we have taken the
liberty of repairing the text with lines from a broadside printed by J. Russell
of Birmingham (Madden collection, Cambridge University Library),
designated by square brackets, as suggested by Roy Palmer.
Roud 367, Laws N14; 25 entries.

'Polly Oliver's Rambles' was regularly found in England and North America, but
was much rarer elsewhere in Britain and Ireland. 'Girl dresses as soldier to follow her
lover' is a well-known theme in folk song, with plenty of examples in this book, but
'Polly Oliver's Rambles' is a little different from the normal case. Instead of an open-
ended commitment to soldiering, Polly has a specific practical joke in mind. The joke
is tame enough, but the song caused blushes on the part of earlier editors. Both Sabine
Baring-Gould and William Chappell supplied completely new words in their publications, and even Frank Kidson omitted the verses where they share a bed. The
modern excuse of 'nothing happened' obviously cut no ice with them.

Baring-Gould noted in 1895 that it was 'A still popular song among the English peasantry', but Frank Purslow points out in *The Foggy Dew* (1974), p. 116 that
its continued popularity was probably due to its regular performance on the early
music-hall stage, where it was regarded as a somewhat saucy song.

The song was also widely printed on broadsides in the nineteenth century, and
was included in a number of song garlands in the second half of the eighteenth,
often entitled 'The Maid's Resolution to Follow Her Love'. Nevertheless, it may
well be older, as a song called 'The Pretender's Army', published in a forty-six-page
collection of songs, *Mughouse Diversion, or a Collection of Loyal Prologues and Songs* in
1717, commences:

As Perkin one morning lay musing in bed
The thought of three kingdoms ran much in his head,

which is presumably based on 'Polly Oliver's Rambles' (rather than the other way
round).

The rather strange image of Polly riding a 'green dragon' in verse 2 of George
Dunn's song has been brought about by a mishearing somewhere down the line.
The broadsides usually have 'On her father's black gelding like a dragoon did ride',
or something similar.

73 The Pretty Ploughboy

Sung by Mrs Nation, Bathpool, Somerset (c.1916); collected by Phyllis M.
Marshall (Janet Blunt MSS, JHB/10/7).
Roud 186, Laws M24; 52 entries.

'The Pretty Ploughboy' – sometimes he was 'Jolly' or 'Simple', but mostly he was
'Pretty' – was a particularly popular song in England, and was also often found in
Scotland and Ireland, and fairly frequently in North America. The text varies little
between versions. In traditional song, one of the standard responses of parents faced
with unsuitable suitors for their daughters is to threaten to bribe the press gang to
take him away. It is indeed well documented that the press gang was open to bribery
in this way, although it is impossible to know how often this really happened. And
then we must admire her spirit in going after him.

The song was also very widely available on broadsides, with nearly all the main
nineteenth-century printers offering versions for sale. Some of these may be as early
as about 1800, but no definite eighteenth-century version has yet been found.

The many variants of Mrs Nation's tune associated with this song tend to be
modal, often Mixolydian, or, as with hers, Dorian. This same basic melody has also
been collected in both compound time, as here, and simple time.

74 William and Mary

Sung by Mr Hale, West Kirby, Cheshire; collected by Dorothy Dearnley;
published in Dearnley's *Seven Cheshire Folk-Songs* (1967).
Roud 348, Laws N28; 15 entries.

One of the many simple 'returned lover in disguise' storylines, although here he is
at least disguised as a beggar, which explains why she does not recognize him after
only three years. It was only moderately popular in England, and nowhere near
as widespread as others in the genre, such as 'Claudy Banks' (No. 66) and 'Fair
Maid Walking in Her Garden' (No. 71), but it was collected much more often in
North America.

Nearly all the main nineteenth-century broadside printers issued versions,
including Catnach and Pitts in London, and Kendrew of York, but the earliest so far
found seems to be by Evans, in 1794. The text varies little from version to version.

75 William Taylor

'Billy Taylor', sung by Clara Gillam, Adderbury, Oxfordshire (1913);
collected by Janet Blunt (Blunt MSS, JHB/1A/13B).
Roud 158, Laws N11; 59 entries.

An immensely popular song in England – both Lucy Broadwood and Cecil Sharp called it a 'favourite song' among country singers – 'William Taylor' was also collected many times in North America, but less frequently in Scotland and Ireland. It was also very common on broadsides and was often included in more substantial songsters and songbooks.

The song features on one of the earliest recordings we have of an English traditional singer. Percy Grainger arranged for the Gramophone Company to record his star Lincolnshire singer, Joseph Taylor, in 1908, and that recording can be heard on the Topic CD *Tonight I'll Make You My Bride* (TSCD 656). Earlier texts vary considerably, but versions collected from Victorian times onwards are more stable. In some versions William is press-ganged just before his wedding with Sally, rather than enlisting voluntarily, so it was not all his fault. The song is popular with many people nowadays because of its strong female lead, although modern sensibilities might be a little bruised by the fact that she shoots both William and his bride, which seems a little hard on the latter.

In part because there are so many extant versions, the history of the song is not quite as clear as we would like. Most traditional singers seem to have sung the song in all seriousness, but for much of the nineteenth century is was regarded in a very different light and was published and widely performed as a comic number, often under the title of 'Billy Taylor'. At this distance it is not always easy to tell from the text alone whether the intention was comic, as the comedy seems to have relied much on the style of performance rather than on the actual words.

The comic version was already in print around 1804, and possibly before, but the earliest dated example of the song, where there is no hint of comedy, seems to be a chapbook in the British Library called *Four New Songs*, printed in Alnwick in 1792. The song is there called 'Billy Taylor', but another early broadside title is 'The Female Lieutenant, or The Faithless Lover Rewarded', which certainly sounds more serious.

A close reading of the many available texts, both oral and printed, might reveal more of the history of the song, but what looks likely at the moment is that a late eighteenth-century 'serious' song was quickly picked up and performed as a burlesque, which remained a staple of the comic-song repertoire well into the third quarter of the nineteenth century. Traditional singers then learnt the burlesque words and started to sing them 'straight', and in their performances it became a serious song again.

V

My Parents Reared Me Tenderly ...
Lust, Infidelity and Bad Living

76 The Ball of Yarn

Sung by Ray Hartland, Eldersfield, Gloucestershire (1980); recorded by
Mike Yates; issued on *It Was on a Market Day 2*, Veteran VTC7CD (2006).
Roud 1404; 23 entries.

An extremely widely known song, but for obvious reasons it appeared only rarely
in folk-song collections until recent years, and we need to look to the few collectors
who specialized in 'bawdy' material to piece together its history. The earliest references come from America, where the song is also very well known. Three of the
singers who sang the song to Vance Randolph in the Ozarks in the 1940s claimed to
have first heard the song in the 1880s or 1890s, one of them specifically at sea, and the
Texan collector John Lomax mentions a cowboy version of the same vintage. The
song has clearly remained a favourite of what could be called the 'minor' bawdy
canon, that is the songs with obvious sexual meaning but innocent enough to be
generally performed, by both men and women. Some versions are more explicit than
others, of course, and as always it is the skill of the singer and the appropriateness of
the occasion which makes or breaks any performance.

It is easy to get carried away when discussing bawdy songs and to presume either
that there is a deep psychological significance to everything mentioned, or to con-
centrate on the physical attributes of the objects or actions mentioned and to seek
sexual similarities. But both approaches often lead to some pretty silly conclusions.
Perhaps the only principle to understand is that almost any human activity can be
given a sexual twist, in the context and performance of a song, and it is the inven-
tiveness of the imagery, or lack of it, which makes the song clever and interesting
or just plain crude and silly. But the original imagery itself may have no intrinsic
sexual reference.

Folk-song scholars have noticed some similarity between 'The Ball of Yarn' and
an older song known to Robert Burns called 'The Yellow Yellow Yorling'. Some of
the lines are similar but the imagery in the old song is concerned with birds, rather
than yarn, as 'yorling' is a Scots name for the yellowhammer. Bird imagery is common in songs about sex, but no one has explained how this was translated into the
'ball of yarn'. Two of the standard commentaries on the latter are that it must refer
to sailors winding up a rope (because it was sung as a shanty), or because of the
context of the action it must refer to female pubic hair, because they cannot find

anything else 'stringy' enough to be relevant. But to understand the origin of the song it is necessary to delve deeper into the art of knitting rather than fornication.

'Winding Up Her Little Ball of Yarn' was a pop song, with words by Earl Marble and music by Miss Polly Holmes, published in 1884, and the sheet music can be seen online in the Lester S. Levy Collection of Sheet Music in Johns Hopkins University Library. It concerns a young man courting a young lady, and its chorus, 'Ball of yarn, ball of yarn ...', is clearly the origin of that in the bawdy version. Previous generations would have immediately understood the cultural references in the song, but most modern readers need some explanation. It refers to the days, up to the 1950s, when knitting wool (called 'yarn' in America) came in loose hanks and had to be wound into balls by the knitter before use. A regular task which men were usually reluctant to undertake was to sit with the wool around their outstretched hands while their mother, sister or wife wound it into a ball. Not surprisingly, the only time men did this willingly was when courting, and it was a mildly flirtatious thing to do. The picture on the front of the original sheet music shows this quite clearly.

What has happened is pretty evident. The marked sentimentality of Marble and Holmes's song quickly attracted a bawdy parody, and whoever constructed it was probably familiar with 'The Yellow Yellow Yorling' or a derivative. As with all parodies, the original point would be its deliberate debunking of the innocence of the original, and would rely on the hearer's recognition of this cultural reference. But, as sometimes happens in this kind of situation, the new 'Ball of Yarn' song took on a life of its own, and has long outlived its original referent.

There is one potential problem in this explanation of the origins of the song. In his book on American pop music, *Lost Chords* (1942), Douglas Gilbert, used the bawdy 'Ball of Yarn' as an example of the type of song sung in taverns in the 1870s, and if this were true it would suggest that the copyrighted song published by Marble and Holmes was a cleaned-up version of an already existing song. It is unfortunately typical of Gilbert's imprecise style of writing that this impression is given because he does not actually say that the song existed in the 1870s, nor does he offer any evidence to support the idea. But it has been quoted as fact by many later writers.

Ray Hartland's tune exemplifies well the melody to which this song is commonly sung in England. It corresponds fairly closely to the sheet music and, where it deviates from it, shows remarkable consistency with other versions from England and the US. Interestingly, Ray Hartland's tune, in common with many other oral versions, has a greater melodic compass (of a minor tenth) than the sheet music (major seventh).

77 Bold Grenadier

'Water Rattle', sung by Arthur Howard, Hazlehead, Yorkshire (1981); recorded by Ian Russell; issued on *Merry Mountain Child*, Hill and Dale HD006 (1981).
Roud 140, Laws P14; 35 entries.

This was a widely known song in England and even more popular in North America, but not apparently collected in Scotland or Ireland. The sexual symbolism of the fiddle and string are fairly transparent, although it is quite possible that the song as sung by Arthur Howard could have been a perfectly innocent romantic ballad. Other versions continue with the girl asking him to marry her, and he usually says that he is already married but ends hopefully with the idea that if he comes this way again perhaps they could hear the nightingales again.

The history of the song is strangely unclear. A ballad entitled 'The Souldier and His Knapsack' was registered with the Stationers' Company on 4 November 1639, which might be our song, although soldiers and knapsacks are a rather commonplace pairing. But half a century later, the ancestor of our song was definitely in existence, as shown by surviving broadside editions of 'The Nightingale's Song or the Souldier's Rare Musick and Maid's Recreation' dating from the 1680s and 1690s, which can be found in the Roxburghe, Pepys and Douce collections.

Many of our folk songs which go back to the seventeenth or eighteenth centuries show evidence of being rewritten and severely reduced in length about 1800, probably by the broadside printers of the day. But it is not clear if this is the case with our 'Souldier' or 'Grenadier'. The problem is that after the late seventeenth-century printings, we can find no evidence of the song's existence until about 1840, despite the online availability of so much eighteenth-century material nowadays. In addition, far fewer nineteenth-century printings have survived (only four or five) than we would expect from such a popular traditional song. So we simply do not know whether the song persisted in the oral tradition for over 140 years or was reintroduced in the nineteenth century by a broadside author and/or printer.

This song has mostly been sung to triple-time tunes with an ABBA phrase structure. Among these there is some variety in terms of range (plagal or authentic), tonality (some are straightforwardly major; others have a flattened third, giving them a minor feel) and contour. Arthur Howard's triple-time, major-key tune stands out, having an ABCD structure and a contour quite unlike other collected versions except in its D phrase, which echoes the A phrase of one of the more widespread tunes (compare that sung by Raymond and John Cantwell in Peter Kennedy's *Folksongs of Britain and Ireland* (1975), pp. 414–15).

78 The Cunning Cobbler

'The Little Cobbler', sung by John Johnson, Reigate, Surrey (*c.*1954); collected by Bob Copper; published in Copper's *Songs and Southern Breezes* (1973), pp. 224–5.
Roud 174; 21 entries.

Versions of 'The Cunning Cobbler' were noted down by several of the Edwardian collectors, including Cecil Sharp, H. E. D. Hammond, Percy Grainger and Ralph

Vaughan Williams, but for obvious reasons if they published it at all it was only the tune or the first verse. Vaughan Williams commented, 'The rest of the words are not suitable for publication and have little interest except, perhaps, in giving a modern example of the kind of rough fun which we find in Chaucer ... The words are evidently modern, or modernized, since a policeman is one of the characters introduced' (*JFSS*, 2 (1906), 156–7). This is one of several humorous songs in which the husband comes home to catch his wife with her lover; see, for example, 'The Bold Trooper' (Roud 311) and 'The Boatswain's Chest' (Roud 570).

Many of the nineteenth-century broadside printers issued the song, and the text varies remarkably little between them and the traditional versions. The earliest so far located is 'The Cunning Cobler [*sic*] Done Over', printed by James Catnach in London, probably in the early 1830s, and his text, interestingly enough, already includes the policeman. As the Metropolitan Police were founded in 1829, this may well be the original of the song, but it is possible, though perhaps not likely, that the song existed before that without the policeman character.

Bob Copper collected John Johnson's tune for 'The Cunning Cobbler' from his elder son, also called John, as Johnson had died eleven years previously. It exemplifies the most commonly found tune for this song. Among the collected examples, some have an even subdivision of the beat, as in John Johnson's example, while others are sung with a bouncy, uneven subdivision. Johnson's tune initially alternates between 6/8 and 4/4 , reflecting these slightly different rhythmic manifestations of the basic melodic pattern. This latter is often minor in tonality, with flattened third and seventh degrees (the Dorian mode), though it is sometimes found in the major, with a flattened seventh (the Mixolydian mode).

The same basic tune is found with other songs, such as 'Irish Bull' (Roud 918), as collected by Sharp in Somerset, 'My Father Was a Good Old Man' (Roud 1631), as collected by Gardiner in Hampshire, and 'O Rare Turpin, Hero' (Roud 621). See also 'The Blind Beggar's Daughter of Bethnal Green' (No. 90 in this volume).

Some performers sing the song very fast (for example Henry Stansbridge, William Short and George Smith), while Frank Purslow (*Marrow Bones* (1972), pp. 119–20) comments on the way George Spicer 'commences his performance in a normal speaking voice ... gradually changing to a singing voice in the course of the second line. The result is excellent, especially as Mr Spicer retains an emphasis on story-telling right through the piece, rather than on singing a song'.

79 The Devil and the Farmer's Wife

'The Farmer's Curst Wife', sung by Leslie Lawson, Southrepps, Norfolk (7 February 1955); recorded by Peter Kennedy (BBC 21903). Leslie sang the first verse differently from the others, without the refrain and repeat; we have regularized it to simplify the notation.

Roud 160, Child 278; 24 entries.

This song was collected many times in England, Ireland and Scotland, and hundreds of times in the USA, although its early history remains something of a mystery. Francis J. Child prints only two versions, with nothing earlier than Henry Dixon's 1846 text (see below), but he comments, 'A curst wife who was a terror to demons is a feature in a widely spread and highly humorous tale, Oriental and European' (*The English and Scottish Popular Ballads*, V, p. 107). There seems to have been a Scottish song, which Robert Burns rewrote as 'Kellyburnbraes' (1792), but that earlier song has not been found, and Burns's text bears little similarity to the English versions, although the story is the same.

There are surprisingly few surviving broadsides, but one was printed by John Pitts in London about 1810–20, where it is called 'The Sussex Farmer', and sometime in the first half of the nineteenth century it acquired a whistling chorus and was often later called 'The Sussex Whistling Song'. Henry Dixon printed a version in his *Ancient Poems* (1846), pp. 210–11, and claimed that it was 'a great favourite'. He described the way it was generally performed at that time:

> This is a countryman's whistling-song, and the only one of the kind which the editor remembers to have heard ... The tune is 'Lilli Burlero' and the song is sung as follows: the first line of each verse is given as a solo; then the tune is continued by a chorus of whistlers, who whistle that portion of the air which in 'Lilli Burlero' would be sung to the words, 'Lilli burlero bullen a la'. The songster then proceeds with the tune and sings the whole of the verse through, after which, the strain is concluded by the whistlers. The effect of the song, when accompanied by the strong whistles of a tribe of hardy countrymen, is very striking, and cannot be described by the pen.

In *Folk-Songs of the Upper Thames* (1923), Alfred Williams also calls it the 'Sussex Whistling Song', and comments that it was 'very popular in the Thames Valley eighty years ago' (that is, about 1840). The song often ends with the lines,

> *This shows that the women are worse than the men*
> *They get taken to hell and brought back again.*

A different song, 'The Devil in Search of a Wife', which was also popular on nineteenth-century broadsides, shares the same sentiments and occasional lines with 'The Devil and the Farmer's Wife'.

Bronson notes that about a quarter of the seventy-one tunes he located for this song have a whistling refrain while the others have a refrain of nonsense words. These nonsense refrains are often on lines 2 and 4 of the stanza but in some cases are extended into a fifth line. Still others have the refrain on lines 2, 5 and 6, as in Leslie Lawson's rendition. Despite this, the tunes to which the song has been sung are very similar and Leslie Lawson's is no exception. It is major and in 6/8 time, like many humorous songs, with a range of a tenth. It bears a particularly close resemblance to the tune sung by the Northumberland shepherd Jimmy White, collected by Peter Kennedy (see Bertrand Bronson, *The Traditional Tunes of the Child Ballads*, IV (1972), no. 6) and the tune from a Belfast singer noted by O'Lochlainn (see Bronson, IV, no. 7), both of which also have the nonsense refrain and the six-phrase form.

Leslie Lawson sings the final stanza more deliberately and brings the song to a rousing finish by raising the final three notes of the penultimate bar.

80 Flash Company

Sung by Cyril Poacher, Blaxhall, Suffolk (1972); recorded by Keith Summers; issued on *A Story to Tell*, Musical Traditions MTCD339-0 (2007).
Roud 954; 22 entries.

'Flash Company' was quite commonly found in England, but not much sung in Scotland or Ireland, and only one or two versions have been reported in North America. It is something of a schizophrenic song, which explains why some commentators have found it puzzling or incomplete. This is not simply a question of 'floating verses', which flit from song to song and seem to have no real home, but more a demonstration of how very different meanings in a song can be constructed by reordering a set of common verses linked with a couple of different ones; at bottom, two separate songs have become entwined – 'Flash Company' and 'The Wandering Girl'.

The two main branches within the song's history are distinguished by the sex of the narrator, because this is one of those songs which can be told from the male or female perspective. Probably the earliest from the female perspective is 'The Wandering Girl or Bud of the Rose' in which the girl is simply lamenting that she has been left holding the baby by a false young man, but in another strand the girl is in sorrow because her sweetheart/husband is being transported for some unspecified crime, hence the 'remembrance' motif. A third set of versions often starts, 'First I loved Thomas and then I loved John', and implies that the girl's fickleness and love of a good time has brought her to ruin. In the second main category, as sung by Cyril Poacher and most singers in recent times, it is the man whose fast living has brought him to poverty.

In its different guises, the song was popular on nineteenth-century broadsides from about 1820 onwards. The striking 'yellow handkerchief' motif does not appear in all versions, but was certainly present in some of the earliest, and is, surprisingly, a factual detail within the fiction of the song. Yellow handkerchiefs, or more what we would call neckerchiefs, were indeed popular in flash circles – particularly those in the prize-fighting and boxing fraternities in the early nineteenth century.

There is some research to be done on the tune of this song. It seems that many of the earlier collected versions comprise the first half of 'Green Bushes' (see note to No. 45, especially Lucy Broadwood's second category of tunes), while the second two phrases are much as in Cyril Poacher's version, with the distinctive rise to the upper tonic. One wonders if the first half of Poacher's tune, also commonly found with this song, is a more recent development. When a version was published in the *JFSS*, Cecil Sharp commented that it was 'a curious medley of "Green Bushes", "Turtle Dove", and "Amble Town" ("The Oak and the Ash", etc.) tunes' (*JFSS*, 5 (1915), 175). The tune is found with other songs, such as 'The Lakes of Cold Finn' (No. 120).

81 The Gipsy Laddie

'Gipsies-O', sung by Harry Cox, Catfield, Norfolk (1946); collected by Francis Collinson (Collinson MSS, COL/5/75); published in *JEFDSS*, 5 (1946), 14–15; different recordings from the same singer issued on Topic TSCD512D; BBC 22914/Topic 12T161/Rounder CD1776. In verse 5, it is not clear whether Harry sang 'black-guarded' (pronounced 'blaggarded') or 'black-hearted' (pronounced 'blackarted').
Roud 1, Child 200; 72 entries.

Definitely in the top five Child ballads in terms of widespread popularity, and possibly second only to 'Barbara Allen', the Gipsies stealing the lady, or, to put it the other way round, the lady running off willingly with the sexy Gipsies, has caught singers' attention all over the anglophone world for more than 200 years. For obvious reasons the song has long been a favourite with members of the travelling community.

Francis J. Child printed eleven versions, and Bertrand Bronson reprinted 128 tunes, and most of the nineteenth-century broadside printers issued versions, so there is a great deal of material available for the comparative researcher to work on. The song goes under a wide variety of titles, including 'The Dark-Eyed Gipsy', 'The Draggletail Gipsies', 'Seven Little Gipsies', 'Johnnie Faa' and 'Black Jack Davy (or David)'.

The basic story is nearly always the same, but the details at key points in the plot vary considerably, and these have a major effect on the moral tone of the piece. Sometimes, for example, the Gipsies cast a spell on the lady, but sometimes she just falls for them of her own volition; when her husband finds her she defiantly rejects him, or resignedly says she must stick to the choice she has made; some versions end there, but in many the last verse matter-of-factly informs us that all the Gipsies were hanged. We are rarely told what happened to her.

Despite the plethora of material, the early history of the song is still unclear and is not really helped by attempts by many commentators to link the song with events between 1541 and 1624 concerning recurrent attempts by the Scottish authorities to expel all Gipsies, and occasions when some were executed for staying. These events took place at least a hundred years before our song was known to have been in existence, and there is no reason to connect them apart from the fact they are both about Gipsies. There was also a strong local tradition that the original song referred to an incident in the life of John, sixth Earl of Cassilis and his wife, Lady Jean Hamilton (who died in 1642). The story goes that the 'Gipsies' were really the supporters of a rival suitor in disguise. The main supporting evidence is that many of the older Scottish versions name the Lord as 'Cassilis', but this is most likely an example of post-facto tinkering. Rather than being corroborative evidence for a legend's truth, details like this are changed in the song to support the existing, or emerging, legend. Others argue more simply that 'Cassilis' was a mishearing or misreading of the word 'castle', and the legend was created to explain it. Either way, the connection with Cassilis is shown to be mythical, although we will return to this thread in a moment.

Hard facts in the history of the song are hard to come by. What is possibly the earliest version of the song is on a broadside in the Roxburghe collection, entitled 'The Gypsy Loddie'. Commentators usually date this to about 1720, but it bears no imprint and there is unfortunately nothing to support or refute this dating. The next sighting is 'Johny Faa, the Gypsie Laddie' in the 1740 edition of Allan Ramsay's collection of Scottish ballads, *Tea-Table Miscellany*, and after that there are several other late eighteenth- and early nineteenth-century printings, often simply reprinting Ramsay's text.

Looking more closely at the two earliest printings provides some useful questions about the song's early development, but no definitive answers. The Ramsay text, for example, goes straight from the Lord saddling his steeds to the execution, and therefore lacks the dialogue between him and his wife which is present in 'The Gypsy Loddie' and virtually all other early versions. Similarly, 'The Gypsy Loddie' includes the decidedly peculiar lines, in verse 2:

As soon as her fair face they saw
They called their grandmother over.

But this is easily explained as a mishearing or misunderstanding of the Scottish 'They cast their glamour (glaumry, etc.) o'er her', meaning they cast their spell or enchantment over her. In Allan Ramsay's version the line is 'They coost the glamer o'er her'.

It is also highly suggestive that the first two known published versions are textually quite different. A close comparison of such details strongly suggests that neither of these is the 'original' text, but that there was an earlier version – or more probably versions – from which they both derive, but what or when is unknown.

Which brings us back to the putative Cassilis connection. Bertrand Bronson noticed that a tune in the Skene Manuscript, in the National Library of Scotland, dating from before 1630, is closely related to one of the tunes commonly used later for versions of 'The Gipsy Laddie', and is entitled 'Lady Cassilles Lilt'. Bronson maintains that this is evidence that the song existed at that time and that the tradition linking it with the Cassilis family was already in place, although the evidence is again circumstantial. The tune may well have become associated with the song precisely because the Cassilis legend had become attached to it.

Bronson divides the many tune records for this song into three main groupings. The first of these is well documented in oral tradition over a period of more than 300 years, the earliest record being 'Lady Cassilles Lilt'. Harry Cox's tune is from Bronson's second group, whose tunes open with a repeated descending melodic figure. Some of these are in a minor tonality while others, like that of Harry Cox, are major. Overall, this group is the tune most commonly found with this song in

English tradition although, as Bronson notes, it is not confined to England. Harry Cox gives his own 'twist' to the tune by lengthening the final note of several phrases and the initial note of lines 4 and 7. Bars 6–7 (which coincide with the first of these) have here been changed from 4/4 and 2/4 respectively to one 3/2 bar in order to be consistent with bar 13 (the second occurrence).

82 Marrowbones

'There Was an Old Woman in Yorkshire', sung by Harry Cox, Catfield, Norfolk (1953–6); recorded by Peter Kennedy; issued on *English Love Songs*, DTS LFX4 (1965), and *Seventeen Come Sunday*, Folktracks FSA032 (1975).
Roud 183, Laws Q2; 20 entries.

In folk song the battle of the sexes is usually treated humorously and direct action is often preferred to more subtle means. Wife-murder is perhaps not morally acceptable, but at least the husband can say, 'She started it.'

The song was widely collected in England, and was just as well known in Ireland and in Scotland, under titles such as 'The Wife of Kelso' or 'The Wily Auld Carl'. The main difference in the Scottish versions is that the wife is advised to give her husband ground-up marble rather than marrowbones.

'Marrowbones' was already in the oral tradition by about 1840, as is shown by a version in the Robert Bell manuscripts in Newcastle University Library, but for such a popular song surprisingly few printed sources have been found. Only one broadside is known, by John Pitts of London, probably from the 1820s, and another printing, called 'There Was an Old Woman in Our Town', in a chapbook of 1818 (in the Robert White collection in Newcastle University Library).

A similar song, 'Johnny Sands' (Roud 184), was written by John Sinclair about 1840 and also became popular with local singers. The plot is similar, except that the husband says he is tired of life and wants to drown himself, but in case his courage fails at the last minute she should tie his hands together and push him in. As in 'Marrowbones', he makes sure that she is the one to fall in, and he then declares he cannot help because his hands are tied.

83 The Molecatcher

Sung by Frank Cole, North Waltham, Hampshire (c.1952); collected by Bob Copper; published in Copper's *Songs and Southern Breezes* (1973), pp. 268–9.
Roud 1052; 17 entries.

One of those songs whose popularity is difficult to gauge because it offended some of the people who usually provide us with evidence. The early collectors obviously came across it, but it was not to their taste and they usually noted the tune and first verse only. Sabine Baring-Gould commented, 'rest very gross, not taken down' and referred to a version in an 'old garland' in the British Museum where the page had been torn out, 'probably for the same reason why I did not take down the ballad' (Baring-Gould MSS, SBG/1/2/304). Three Norfolk versions of the tune were published in the *JFSS*, 4 (1910), with the terse comment by Vaughan Williams, 'the words are unsuitable for this journal'. H. E. D. Hammond and George B. Gardiner, however, noted full texts, in Dorset and Hampshire respectively, although they did not publish them.

Apart from the general subject of adultery, which is, after all, dealt with in quite a few songs in a humorous way, it seems that the problem lies with the fact that the song's imagery is too direct, and its text too explicit. But even here the evidence is lacking. To modern eyes it is pretty tame stuff. The euphemism 'ploughing my ground' in verse 5 is common, but it is verse 4 that causes more problems in this respect. The rhyme of sport/coat, given here, is sometimes lap/trap, but can also be frolics/bollocks or frolic/jacket. Recent singers have been known to change the line in accordance with the audience and context of performance, and there is no reason to believe that our predecessors were not capable of similar subterfuge.

No nineteenth-century broadside printings have come to light as yet, although they probably did exist. The garland with the missing pages, mentioned by Baring-Gould, is a copy of *Daniel Cooper's Garland* in the British Library, published by Viner and Nailer in Bristol, and therefore dating from about 1765. According to the garland's cover, the song was called 'The Farmer and the Mole-Catcher', and it also appears under that name in *The Frisky Songster*, a deliberately risqué collection in the Bodleian Library, dated 1776, although this is a 'new edition', so the original was probably published a few years earlier. This version is somewhat more explicit than any of the collected versions or indeed those commonly sung in rugby-club-type circles today.

There are several tunes associated with this song, some in simple time, others in a bouncing compound time, as here.

84 The Nutting Girl

'A-Nutting We Will Go', sung by William Hands, Chipping Camden, Gloucestershire (c.1932); recorded by James Madison Carpenter (Carpenter MSS, pp.00561–2; Cylinder 130 (sr350)).
Roud 509; 35 entries.

A very widely known song in England, but not so often collected elsewhere in Britain or in North America, this was another that was encountered by many of the earlier collectors but never published by them in its full form. As Sabine Baring-Gould commented in *Songs of the West* (1905), p. 24, 'The broadside ballad consists of fourteen verses, and is very gross. I have had to considerably tone down the words.'

The song is a fairly straightforward account of sex in the open air between willing partners, and can be seen as a bit of good clean bawdy fun or an exercise in male wishful thinking, depending on your viewpoint. Twentieth-century singers tended to call it 'The Nutting Girl', while a hundred years before it was usually 'The Nut Girl' for broadside printers. But the earliest versions were called 'The Jolly Plough Boy' or 'The New Ploughboy'.

Two symbolic references underpin the story which would have been readily understood by rural singers and listeners in England from at least the mid seventeenth century onwards. The first is the notion of the ploughboy as the epitome of manhood – strong, handsome, direct, and irresistible to women – which occurs in many songs. The other is that 'going nutting' was a well-known metaphor for al fresco sexual, or at least amorous, encounters, and parents and moralists constantly warned girls against the practice. It was a widely quoted proverb that 'a good year for nuts is a good year for babies'. So, for example, lascivious Squire Philidor, in James Howard's play *All Mistaken, or The Mad Couple* (1667), when confronted by three nurses carrying his illegitimate children exclaims, 'A very hopeful generation! Sure this was a great nut year.'

As is to be expected, the words vary somewhat, but William Hands's version is very similar to the standard text printed and reprinted by the main nineteenth-century broadside houses, back to that of John Pitts in the 1820s. But the song was also included in song garlands of the later eighteenth century and the texts varied a little more. In one chapbook version, before the generalized moral warning to young females, the girl says to her ploughboy that if she proves with child he must marry her, but:

> When twenty weeks were over, she thicken'd in the waist
> She wrote to John a letter, but he had left his place ...

and she is, predictably, left alone with her baby.

Frank Purslow notes that this melody cropped up with various texts during the nineteenth century and that some of these described various pastimes, of which the best known seems to have been 'A-Hunting We Will Go' (Roud 509) (*The Constant Lovers* (1972), p. 115).

85 Our Goodman

'As I Came Home So Late Last Night', sung by Harry Scott, Eaton Bray,
Bedfordshire (18 February 1958); recorded by Peter Kennedy (BBC 26071);
also collected by Fred Hamer and published in his *Garners Gay* (1967), p. 24.
Roud 114, Child 274; 58 entries.

This was an immensely widespread song, probably known all over the English-speaking world, with the wording varying considerably but the structure and basic story remaining the same. Francis J. Child printed only two versions, almost at the end of his seminal collection, but Bertrand Bronson mustered fifty-eight versions with tunes.

The song first appears in the second half of the eighteenth century, but it is not clear whether the original was Scottish or English. A version does appear in the David Herd manuscripts of the 1770s, published as *Ancient and Modern Scottish Songs, Heroic Songs, etc.* (1869) and the same text, with tune, in the *Scots Musical Museum*, 5 (1796), but these are probably pipped at the post by a London broadside, 'printed and sold at the Printing-Office in Bow Churchyard', entitled 'The Merry Cuckold and Kind Wife', which dates from about 1760. The latter is noteworthy for the fact that the man sees *three* horses, swords, boots, breeches, hats and heads, and that he is named, Old Witchet, rather than being simply an anonymous fool. It could be argued that these Scottish and English versions are so dissimilar that the song had probably been in circulation for some time before these printings, but this is at present pure speculation.

Child, as was his wont, listed a number of analogous ballads and tales from across Europe, with varying degrees of similarity to our song, but none seem to pre-date the British examples. Indeed, one of his descriptions serves as a caution not to jump to conclusions in cross-national comparisons. He gives details of a very similar German ballad, very popular on broadsides, which spread into Scandinavia and Hungary from 1790 onwards. But this ballad started as a direct translation, by Friedrich Wilhelm Meyer, of the Bow Churchyard broadside listed above.

Considering its widespread popularity with singers, it is odd that few nineteenth-century broadsides seem to have survived. If this is a true picture of the situation, and not simply an accident of survival, it demonstrates that although printed forms are considered to be crucial to the life of traditional song in general, it does not *necessarily* follow that all songs needed print to live and multiply.

As in many humorous songs, Harry Scott's tune for 'Our Goodman' is very straightforward in both pitches and rhythm, presumably in the service of putting across the comedy of the narrative. Quite a few of the pitches are repeated up to four times in a row (for example bar 5) and melodic movement tends to be stepwise or in thirds. The rhythm often follows the rhythm of the words as they might be declaimed. Almost all the tune is restricted to the first six degrees of the scale. The chorus becomes a more rounded melody, incorporating more variety of melodic and rhythmic movement, and a greater melodic compass.

The earliest extant tune dates from 1796 (James Johnson, *The Scots Musical Museum*). Bronson comments on the similar feel of most of tunes sung for this song, despite their many superficial differences. They are almost all major in tonality and in two- or four-time, as is Harry Scott's melody.

86 Spencer the Rover

Sung by Arthur Wood, Middlesbrough, Yorkshire, on *Yorkshire Folk Singers* E.P. (private pressing) recorded by Mary and Nigel Hudleston; also in the Hudlestons' *Songs of the Ridings* (2001).
Roud 1115; 30 entries.

Lucy Broadwood noted this as 'a great favourite amongst country singers', and Alfred Williams called it 'A simple yet pleasing song, with genuine human feeling expressed within its lines'. He thought it must have been composed in Yorkshire, but Anne Gilchrist, on the other hand, thought it was originally Irish.

It is surprising to learn that some of the early collectors thought the song really was composed by the man named in the first line. So, for example, Frank Kidson wrote, after saying how popular it was with singers in Yorkshire, 'The words are on Yorkshire ballad sheets, and no doubt they are the production of the aforesaid Spencer, some wandering ballad singer, who has not been endowed with much poetical genius' (*Traditional Tunes* (1891), p. 154). It must be said that the song is better heard than read.

The earliest collected version, from 'a Derbyshire peasant', appears in M. H. Mason's *Nursery Rhymes and Country Songs* (1878), but there are many broadside printings, from all over the country, back to sheets printed in London in the 1820s or 1830s.

Arthur Wood's tune appears to be widespread but no other versions, as documented, contain the extensive melodic variation that he introduces into his rendition.

87 Three Maidens to Milking Did Go

Sung by Fred Hewett, Mapledurwell, Hampshire (26 July 1955); recorded by Bob Copper (BBC 21860); also published in Copper's *Songs and Southern Breezes* (1973), pp. 280–81, and issued on Topic 12T317 and *Who's That at My Bedroom Window?* TSCD660 (1998).
Roud 290; 32 entries.

In full versions the symbolism of birds and bushes is not particularly subtle, and although this song was noted by many of the earlier collectors, including Cecil Sharp, Sabine Baring-Gould, George B. Gardiner, H. E. D. Hammond, Frank Kidson and Ralph Vaughan Williams, it was presumably the tunes which attracted them as they were not impressed with the words and either did not publish them or edited them heavily. Indeed, Kidson writes, 'This air my friend, Mr Holgate, remembers being sung in and about Leeds. If not very old, it is good, and it could be wished that the succeeding verses to the first (the only one which I have printed), were equally meritorious and more suitable to this work' (*Traditional Tunes* (1891), pp. 72–3) .

Nevertheless, Sharp collected ten different versions, so it must have been well known. Alfred Williams published an innocuous version in his *Folk-Songs of the Upper Thames* (1923), p. 229, which shows signs of deliberate bowdlerization, but as his manuscript text reads the same as that in the book, it may have been the singer (Eli Dawes of Southrop), or someone before him, who amended it, rather than the collector.

The song's early history is unclear, and the broadside printings are something of a mystery. A handful of sheets have survived, from various nineteenth-century provincial presses, including Kendrew (York); Ross, Walker and Williamson (Newcastle); Birmingham (Dublin); and Jackson (Birmingham); but remarkable by their absence are all the prolific London producers – Catnach, Pitts, Disley, Fortey, Such, and so on. Of the surviving examples, the earliest is probably that of Kendrew, who was in business in York from 1803 to 1838. Nevertheless, the song appears in Thomas Lyle's *Ancient Ballads and Songs* (1827), with the comment, 'From recollection – air plaintive and pastoral'. Lyle was born in Paisley in 1792, and notes to other songs in his book imply that he was remembering material from about 1810 to 1815.

The tune used for this song is is very stable. There are many slight variations in detail and occasional versions in 3/4, though often mixed with bars of two- or four-time, but the basic tune is always recognizable. Fred Hewett omits the second phrase of the tune in stanzas 2 and 3, and the first and second phrases of the tune in stanza 4.

88 The Wild Rover

Sung by Sam Larner, Winterton, Norfolk (1958–1960); recorded by Ewan MacColl and Peggy Seeger; issued on *Now Is the Time for Fishing* (Folkways FG3507/Topic TSCD511).
Roud 1173; 20 entries.

A reasonably common song in the traditional corpus, which was probably more widely known than is indicated by the number of collected versions. Its somewhat slight storyline combines the sentiments of 'Spencer the Rover' (No. 86) with 'The Green Bed' (No. 10). 'The Wild Rover' is one of the songs which the post-war Revival groups made extremely famous, and it is often assumed to be Irish as a result, but it is not. Indeed, it was possibly Sam Larner's version which was the source on which the Revival standard was based.

'The Wild Rover' was very widely printed by broadside houses throughout the nineteenth century, in texts which do not vary much, but it is not clear whether it was in circulation in this form before 1800. The earliest evidence so far discovered is in a twelve-page songster in the British Library called *A Collection of Choice Songs*, published by J. Clarke of Stockport and therefore dating from between 1778 and 1809, and the next is a broadside by J. Jennings of London from about 1815.

But the roots of the song go back much further. In the Roxburghe collection (2.200-201) of black-letter broadsides is a song written by Thomas Lanfiere entitled 'The Good Fellow's Resolution, or The Bad Husband's Return from His Folly', which was printed about 1678–80. It tells the same story as 'The Wild Rover', but at much greater length, and has a number of verbal similarities, such as the first two lines:

I have been a bad husband this full fifteen year
And have spent many pounds in good ale and strong beer

and the chorus:

> *For now I will lay up my money in store*
> *And I never will play the bad husband no more*

while the incident with the landlady is told in almost the same words as in later versions. The term 'Wild Rover' does not appear, but it is one of a number of 'bad husband' songs printed about that time. Nevertheless, we do not know how and when the 'Bad Husband' was turned into the 'Wild Rover'.

It makes little difference to the song itself, but our modern view of the main character is to a certain extent coloured by the last verse, which varies considerably. In Sam Larner's song the man determines to return to his parents, so we see him as a wayward young fellow coming to his senses. But in some he resolves to return to his wife, who has presumably been waiting patiently for his change of heart. In others he will return to his father and get himself a wife, as part of the settling-down process.

The tune used for the verse of Sam Larner's 'Wild Rover' is the same as that of 'If I Were a Blackbird' (No. 47). Other melodies have also been collected, including one whose chorus is the same tune as 'The Saucy Sailor Boy' (No. 17).

89 Young Ramble Away

Sung by James Parsons, Lew Down, Devon (25 May 1891); collected by
Sabine Baring-Gould (Baring-Gould MSS, SBG/1/2/442).
Roud 171; 20 entries.

'I remember the time when I liked a red-coat myself very well – and indeed so I do still at my heart.' So said Mrs Bennet in Jane Austen's *Pride and Prejudice* (1813), and she was not the only one. Indeed, the fatal attractions of the soldier's red coat for eighteenth- and nineteenth-century girls was proverbial, and young Ramble Away clearly knew it.

The name of the fair in verse 2 varies considerably from version to version, appearing as Brimbledon, Brocklesby, Burlington, Derry Down, Nottingham and others, and is often given as the title of the song, but in the broadside texts it is almost always Birmingham Street or Fair. Although the earlier collectors encountered it a fair number of times, it was not often published in full by them, unless in a cleaned-up version like Cecil Sharp's in his *Folk Songs from Somerset*, III (1906).

The song was found regularly only in England, but was printed by most of the broadside houses from about the 1810s onwards, and there was even a follow-up song, 'Answer to Young Ramble Away', which shows that the original must have been popularly known. In this, Ramble Away learns the error of his ways and returns to marry his Nancy and claim his son.

The first note of bar 5 is unclear in the manuscript. It looks like an E and this is what is reproduced in the published version. Magnification of the page in the manuscript indicates that the notehead is on the line (D), as reproduced here.

90 Young Sailor Cut Down

'The Sailor Cut Down in His Prime', sung by Herbert Prince, Warminster, Wiltshire (6 October 1954); recorded by Peter Kennedy (BBC 21497).
Roud 2, Laws Q26; 65 entries.

Very widely known across England, Ireland and North America but less so in Scotland, this is without doubt one of the most versatile songs in the Anglo-American tradition, as it seems able to adapt itself to any group or situation. It always concerns someone who is dying (or recently dead), but this can be a 'young soldier' or 'young sailor', 'airman', 'cowboy' or 'lumberman', or sometimes simply a 'young man' or 'young girl'. But whoever the unfortunate hero is, the military-style funeral with drums, pipes and rifles seems perfectly appropriate.

Herbert Prince's version makes it clear that the sailor is dying of venereal disease, and while some versions include other explicit clues such as 'Lock Hospital', treatment with mercury, and euphemisms such as being 'disordered' by the girls, many versions manage to avoid or disguise this element and leave the reason for the illness unspecified. But if some singers were not aware of the song's background, collectors were embarrassed by it. When the tune was first printed in the *JFSS* (1 (1904), 254) only one verse of the text was included, with the comment, '"The Unfortunate Lad" is a ballad that will scarcely bear reprinting in its entirety.' But a few years later they were bold enough to print a whole text, and Lucy Broadwood commented, 'a version of this was sung to me, inappropriately enough, by a little girl of seven, in a Sussex field' (*JFSS*, 4 (1913), 326).

Despite the number and variety of collected versions, the early history of the song is still unclear, and surprisingly few nineteenth-century broadside copies have survived. This may be because the subject of the song put printers off, although they happily printed other, more explicit items, or it may simply be that the broadside collectors did not like to have copies in their collections. An undated broadside in the Madden collection, entitled 'The Buck's Elegy', which concerns the death of a young man about town is clearly the earliest and appears to date from between 1790 and 1810. There is also a single verse and tune, collected in Cork in December 1848, in P. W. Joyce's *Old Irish Folk Music and Songs* (1909), p.249, collected from a man who heard it sung there about 1790. The song is probably at least half a century older than this, but at present we have no evidence to support such a theory.

VI
I Can Guide a Plough ...
Rural Life and Occupations

91 *All Jolly Fellows Who Follow the Plough*

Sung by John Hodson of Aldbrough, Yorkshire (1972); collected by Steve
Gardham; published in Gardham's *An East Riding Songster* (1982), p.15.
Roud 346; 74 entries.

One of the most widespread songs of rural life in England, perhaps only second to
'The Farmer's Boy' for popularity (see No. 94), but rarely collected elsewhere in
Britain or North America. Cecil Sharp wrote, 'I find that almost every singer knows
it, the bad singers know but little else. Perhaps it is for this reason that the tune is
very corrupt, the words are almost always the same' (quoted in Sabine Baring-Gould,
Songs of the West (1905), notes, pp.18–19).

To some it smacks too much of rural contentment to ring true, but others recognize the pride of the farm labourer in his work, and the spark of independence
shown in verses 6 and 7 greatly increases its verisimilitude. Texts vary remarkably
little from version to version, and it was widely printed on broadsides in the nineteenth century. But the earliest found so far is in the British Library, printed by
Evans of London in 1794.

As George B. Gardiner noted in 1909, and others have commented since, this
song is commonly sung to the tune of 'Villikins and His Dinah' and John Hodson's melody is no exception. This tune has been used for many English folk songs,
including 'Lord Randal' (Child 12, Roud 10), 'Green Grow the Laurels' (No. 46)
and 'The Cruel Ship's Carpenter' (No. 117). The earliest records date from the early
1850s, when the song 'Villikins and His Dinah', a parody of 'William and Dinah', as
sung by Frederick Robson (and soon after Sam Cowell), wowed theatre audiences
in London, Cork, Dublin and Edinburgh (Norman Cazden, *Folk Songs of the Catskills*
(1982), pp. 156–7). The tune began to be named on broadsides from around the same
period.

The first records of the tune as sung in oral tradition for 'All Jolly Fellows' date
from the late nineteenth century. They are rather more varied than one might imag-
ine for a tune that is often described as 'ubiquitous'. Most are in triple time and have
similarities with the standard 'Villikins' tune (as printed in sheet music and exemplified by John Hodson's tune). Several, however, have become modal (either flattening
the seventh to become Mixolydian, or the third as well, making them Dorian and
minor-sounding). Others adopt a different melodic contour in places and the notes
on which the musical phrases cadence are not always the same as those in the 'Vil-

likins'. There are even a few versions of 'All Jolly Fellows' sung to tunes distinct from the 'Villikins' tune family, such as the two- and four-time examples among the Gardiner and Hammond manuscripts.

92 The Barley Mow

Sung by George Spicer, Copthorne, Sussex (4 February 1956); recorded by
Peter Kennedy (BBC 23093).
Roud 944; 40 entries.

One of the most well known of the many cumulative folk songs, this was particularly popular, for obvious reasons, in pub sessions. In the hands of an accomplished singer like George Spicer 'The Barley Mow' was quite a tour de force, and it was quite astonishing how the speed and rhythm of the ever-lengthening chorus could be maintained. In the middle or end of a pub singing session, of course, it could also be seen as a test of sobriety. Some singers even elongated it and sang health to the army, the navy, the royal family, and so on, but the last verse was nearly always 'the company'. In some versions, the wording is 'We'll drink out of ...' instead of 'Jolly good luck to ...', and in this case the list often continues after the barrel with the pipe, the well, the river, the River Thames and the ocean.

Only a few nineteenth-century broadside printings have survived, which gives some support to a theory mentioned elsewhere in these notes that cumulative and highly structured repetitive texts did not need print to survive, whereas lyrical and narrative songs have needed its aid far more.

We have an unusually early text, in Thomas Ravenscroft's *Deuteromelia* (1609). This is definitely our song, which goes through the sizes of drinking vessels and storage, although the actual words are quite different from modern versions. But it is the second line in each verse – 'Sing gentle butler balla moy' – which introduces another line of enquiry. It has been suggested that in the 'balla moy' phrase we have the origin of 'barley mow'. Furthermore, a sixteenth-century drinking song, usually called 'How, Butler How!' after its first line, had the line 'Gentle butler, bell amy', which the editors gloss as 'good friend'. The phrase 'barley mow' seems to fit into the song text so well that it hardly needs an ancestor, but it appears to have one all the same. See Richard Leighton Greene's *The Early English Carols* (1936), p. 285, and R. T. Davies' *Medieval English Lyrics* (1963), p. 276, for the sixteenth-century song.

Peter Kennedy calls this song 'a tongue-twisting cumulative catalogue of drinking companions' in his *Folksongs of Britain and Ireland* (1975). The expandable section, which carries the accumulating words (bars 9–10 of the version given here), is generally sung to a repeated note or a simple melodic figure that is repeated over and over, the singer varying the rhythm as needed to accommodate the words, before leading into the final phrase. Many tunes found with this song, including that printed by William Chappell in 1859, are in compound time, which lends itself to a rollicking performance style. George Spicer's fine rendition has the added feature of a rapid, and seamless, shift from compound metre (6/8 in the transcription) to simple time (3/4) in the cumulative section and back again.

93 Buttercup Joe

Sung by Bob Mills, Alresford, Hampshire (1977); recorded by Paul Marsh; published on *Let This Room Be Cheerful*, Forest Tracks Cassette FTC 6025 (1991).
Roud 1635; 41 entries.

Immensely popular in England, but hardly noticed elsewhere, 'Buttercup Joe' is one of a host of 'country yokel' songs which, despite poking fun at country people, was readily adopted and sung by them. Most of the early collectors did not note it, although there is one version each in the manuscripts of Cecil Sharp (1904), George B. Gardiner (1905) and Alfred Williams (1918), and we do not know if the others deliberately ignored it or it was simply not popular enough for them to come across it. Post-war collectors have reported that it was one of the most commonly known songs in England, but much of this popularity stems from a Zonophone 78 rpm record, sung by Albert Richardson, issued in 1928.

The song is clearly a late nineteenth-century music-hall-type song, but considering how recent the song is, it has proved surprisingly difficult to pinpoint its origin. The earliest known versions are printed in the *New Prize Medal Song Book*, no. 9 (June 1872) and on a Pearson (Manchester) broadside, almost certainly about 1870, and both of these mention, 'as sung by Harry Garratt', but its author remains unknown.

Richardson's recording seems to have led to, or at least encouraged, the standardization of the tune for this song. The two versions (collected by Sharp and Gardiner) noted before 1928 were sung to melodies which are distinct from each other and from the Richardson tune, although they are in the same metre and have much the same rhythm. Extant versions collected after 1928 are sung to more or less the same tune as Richardson's. This is certainly true of Bob Mills's tune, which, although rhythmically freer, has several melodic details in common with the recording, including the varied final bar of verse 2.

Bob Mills sings with a certain amount of freedom, pausing here, speeding up there, for dramatic effect. This has to some extent been regularized in the transcription for the sake of clarity.

94 The Farmer's Boy

Sung by Mark Wyatt, Enborne, Berkshire; published in Lucy Broadwood, *English County Songs* (1893), pp. 120–21.
Roud 408, Laws Q30; 76 entries.

Extremely widely known in Britain and also in North America, 'The Farmer's Boy' is for some the archetypal English folk song and was often used as a semi-official rural anthem at union meetings and harvest suppers. Most of the early collectors noted versions and they commented on how common it was. Sabine Baring-Gould, for example, wrote, 'One of the most popular and widely known folk-songs in England. It would be hard to find an old labourer who has not heard it' (*English Minstrelsie*, I (1895), p. xxx). Some later writers, however, have baulked at the rosy view of farm work and the picture of worker-farmer relations which it portrays. See Michael Pickering, 'The Farmworker and The Farmer's Boy' in *Lore and Language* (1983) for more on this aspect of the song.

Despite attempts by several of our best researchers to pin down its early history, the origin of the song still eludes us. The earliest concrete date we can find is that the song was in existence in 1832, which is when it was included, as 'The Lucky Farmer's Boy', in James Catnach's catalogue of broadside ballads, and his rival John Pitts also printed it, at an address which he occupied from 1819 onwards. Another broadside, printed by J. Kendrew of York, is possibly earlier, as he was in business from 1808 to 1838, but it could be later, and several other printings can be confidently dated to the 1830s.

There are several red herrings, however. Robert Bloomfield (1766–1823), Suffolk farm labourer turned shoemaker turned poet, made his name with his best-selling poem 'The Farmer's Boy', published in 1800. But this poem bears no relationship to our song. Then there is another, totally different song, called 'The Farmer's Boy', which was printed on broadsides and in songsters at the same time as the folk song and indeed was included in the same 1832 catalogue of James Catnach. It commences:

Indeed my simple tale is true
A farm my father had

and goes on to explain that the father died, and the mother lost the farm and died, leaving the 'farmer's boy' an orphan and seeking employment, the boy saying, 'O I can drive the team at plough…' The subject matter and sentiment are the same as our folk song, but the words are completely different. And then there is the claim from Little Leigh in Cheshire (on the C. C. Publishing website, www.cc-publishing.co.uk):

The composer was Charles Whitehead who was born [in Cheshire] in 1792, and the song concerned his brother-in-law Charles Smith who, at the age of fifteen, unsuccessfully sought employment at various local farms … A century later the story was confirmed by Whitehead's grand-daughter who related that her aunt, Naomi, had actually been present at the time the song was written.

In the *Cheshire Life* magazine (February 1968), the same story is told but it is Thomas Smith who is immortalized in the song. Sources such as these, which do not provide any clue about where they got their information, must always be treated with caution. They may be true, but are more likely to be another example of the post-facto claim of authorship which often attaches itself to well-known songs. Further research into 'The Lucky Farmer's Boy' is clearly necessary.

95 Fathom the Bowl

Sung by Robert Hard, South Brent, Devon (October 1888); collected by Sabine Baring-Gould (Baring-Gould MSS, SBG/1/1/82). Robert Hard's text had two lines missing, which have been supplied from other versions. At the end of the verses in Hard's text, Baring-Gould does not give the format of the chorus, but simply writes 'etc.'. The format given here is that published by him in the first edition of his *Songs and Ballads of the West,* but even then it is not clear whether one should repeat the words he labels as the 'chorus' each time or change them in accordance with the words of the relevant verse.
Roud 880; 18 entries.

Apparently not noted outside England, and even there collected only in the southern half of the country, 'Fathom the Bowl' is one of several traditional paeans to male-bonding over alcohol, complete with the seemingly obligatory snipe at wives' disapproval (another one is 'O Good Ale', Roud 203).

Frank Purslow regarded it as an 'arty' nineteenth-century drinking song (*The Wanton Seed*, 1968), and it has to be said the song has a slightly fake feel, as if it were written for a middle-class glee-club clientele, but no early sheet music has turned up and it was widely available on broadsides, where it is more commonly called 'The Punch Ladle'. John Pitts and James Catnach both printed it, and as it is listed in the latter's 1832 catalogue of songs it already existed by that time, but no earlier versions have yet emerged. In his *English Folk-Songs* (1891), however, William Alexander Barrett states that it dates from about 1770, but on what grounds is not clear.

The odd detail in verse 4 about the brothers being dead in the sea is, in nearly all other versions (including the broadsides), 'My father is dead ...', although it makes little difference to the meaning. It has recently been suggested that this line, and the fact that the song mentions brandy and rum, indicates that the song was originally about smuggling, but it is always unwise to extrapolate thus from internal details without corroborating evidence. It probably means little more than 'nothing in the world matters except drink and good company'.

Alfred Williams, in his *Folk-Songs of the Upper Thames* (1923), p. 88, offered the following toast to follow the song:

Here's to the large bee that flies so high
The small bee gathers the honey
The poor man he does all the work
And the rich man pockets the money.

In the music notation, the last note of bar 16 is given here as in Baring-Gould's manuscript but is written a tone higher in his printed version.

96 Green Brooms

'The Broomdasher', sung by George Tompsett, Cuckfield, Sussex (1959); recorded by Mervyn Plunkett.
Roud 379; 44 entries.

This song was collected many times across England, with very similar texts, and was also well known on nineteenth-century broadsides. The earliest available text is in Thomas D'Urfey's *Wit and Mirth; or, Pills to Purge the Melancholy* (1720 edition), where it is called 'The Jolly Broom-Man, or the Unhappy Boy Turn'd Thrifty', and was also printed in a chapbook as *The Jolly Broomsman's Garland*. This has the feeling of a stage song, probably sung by a broom seller – a well-known character in dramas and a staple of the 'Street Cries of London' type of publication, popular from the mid sixteenth to the nineteenth century. The 1720 song is longer, but similar in storyline to that of the later traditional versions, although it has a very different ending: instead of the boy marrying the lady, it ends with verses praising his broom-selling trade.

97 John Barleycorn

Sung by Harry Wiltshire, Bampton, Oxfordshire (*c.*1930); collected by James Madison Carpenter (Carpenter MSS, pp. 00538–9; Cylinder 104 (sr323), Disc Sides 229 (sr117a), 230 (sr117b), 311 (sr158a)).
Roud 164; 75 entries.

This was a very widespread traditional song indeed, which Alfred Williams said was 'everywhere popular' (*Folk-Songs of the Upper Thames* (1923), pp. 246–7) and Lucy Broadwood dubbed 'a constant favourite', across Britain and Ireland but more particularly in England (*JFSS*, 6 (1918), 27–8). It was perhaps inevitable that this song would attract the ritual-origins theorists, who claimed that it was all to do with corn spirits and resurrection, but it is now generally agreed that such notions were romantic wishful thinking and there is no evidence either for the theories themselves or for this song to be anything but a clever allegory.

If we stick to what we do know, a ballad called 'Sir John Barleycorne' was entered into the register of the Stationers' Company on 14 December 1624. Several printings of a black-letter broadside entitled 'A Pleasant New Ballad to Sing Eve'ning and Morn, of the Bloody Murder of Sir John Barley-Corn', from later in the seventeenth century, have survived in the major collections, such as Douce, Euing, Pepys and Roxburghe, and it is likely that this is the song which was registered. This is recognizably the ancestor of our song, but is much longer. By the mid eighteenth century, however, somebody had taken the 'Pleasant New Ballad' and rewritten it in much shorter order as 'Sir John Barleycorn', and this was repeatedly printed in chapbook garlands and subsequently on a wide variety of broadsides in the nineteenth century.

However, these were not the only items that relied on a personification of John Barleycorn, and he was clearly a well-known character. A number of prose chapbooks, for example, were issued during the eighteenth century with titles such as *The Dying Groans of Sir John Barleycorn: being his Grievous Complaints Against the Brewers of Bad Ale* (1790), and *The Arraigning and Indicting of Sir John Barleycorn, Knt., newly composed by a Well-Wisher to Sir John and all that love him* (1770?). There is also another, much less well known, traditional song called 'John Barleycorn Is a Hero Bold' (Roud 2141), written by Joe Geoghegan about 1870, which appears half a dozen times in the folk-song collections.

But if our 'modern' 'John Barleycorn' song is a rewrite of the early seventeenth-century 'Pleasant New Ballad' broadside, it is also possible that that in its turn was a rewrite of an earlier Scottish song called 'Allan-a-Maut', which certainly existed before 1568 and which covers something of the same ground. Anyone interested in a more detailed examination of the history of the song is recommended to read Peter Wood's article in *FMJ*, 8:4 (2004).

98 The Jolly Waggoner

Sung by John Taylor, Sheffield, Yorkshire (27 March 1970); recorded by Ian Russell; printed in *FMJ*, 5:3 (1987), 348–9.
Roud 1088; 25 entries.

In a very real sense, carters, waggoners and carriers were the life's blood of the rural community before the coming of the railways and for a long time afterwards, carrying equipment, materials, produce, animals and people around the farm, the village, and to and from the towns. Several songs featured waggoners, but 'The Jolly Waggoner' (sometimes 'The Warbling Waggoner') was one of the most popular. Alfred Williams commented in 1918, for example, 'Formerly a great favourite throughout the Thames valley. I have met with it in many places' (*Folk-Songs of the Upper Thames* (1923), p. 157). It was also widely available on broadsides, and the earliest surviving copy is dated 1794.

John Taylor's version has three of the usual four verses, but the other verse adds little to the song, which is somewhat inconsequential. Sabine Baring-Gould noted that it was sung about 1835 by the singer and comedian Paul Bedford (1792–1871), in costume, and that he had added topical verses about the coming of steam threatening to ruin the waggoning trade (*A Garland of Country Song* (1895), pp. 34–5). But these verses were already present in the earliest known broadsides. It was also a hit for other professional singers, including Sam Cowell (1820–64).

99 *The Lark in the Morning*

'The Ploughboy', sung by Lily Cook, North Chailey, Sussex (September
1955); recorded by Bob Copper (BBC 22736).
Roud 151; 28 entries.

According to the documentary record, this song was quite common in the English
tradition, but it was probably even more popular than the collected versions indicate.
'This song is a favourite throughout England,' wrote Sabine Baring-Gould, but he
also noted that it had 'two or three objectionable stanzas' (*A Garland of Country Song*
(1895), pp. 58–9). There is something schizophrenic about 'The Lark in the Morning',
as it exists in three rather different forms, which we can separate sufficiently for
discussion, although in the real world the picture is less clear-cut.

What we have here from Lily Cook is perhaps the core of the song: the pastoral
image of the lark ascending and the conventional praise of the ploughboy. But in
the earlier broadsides the tone of the rest of the song is quite different. When the
ploughboy and his 'sweet lass' return from the country fair:

> *Where the meadows is mowed and the grass is cut down*
> *If they chance for to tumble among the green hay*
> *It's 'Kiss me now or never' the damsel will say.*

And later on:

> *Come Molly and Dolly let's away to the wake*
> *There the plow boys will treat us with beer, ale and cake*
> *And if in coming home they should gain their ends*
> *Never fear but they'll marry and make it amends.*

It is to be hoped that their faith in their ploughboys was not misguided. But the story
in the nineteenth-century broadsides progressed differently:

> *And as they return from the wake to the town*
> *The meadows being mown and the grass cut down*
> *We chanc'd to tumble all on the new hay*
> *It's 'Kiss me now or never' the maiden did say.*

> *When twenty weeks were over and past*
> *Her mamma ask'd her the reason why she so thicken'd in the waist*
> *'It was the pretty ploughboy,' the damsel did say*
> *'That caus'd me to tumble on the new-mown hay.'*

No mention of marriage here.

Traditional versions collected from singers either miss out the sex altogether,
or tend towards the nineteenth-century broadside texts, but they occasionally

show the influence of the earlier broadsides. But our picture is incomplete because the early collectors were not keen on the sexual encounters and noted down, or published, only the safe pastoral verses.

The oldest known versions date from the last quarter of the eighteenth century and tend to be called 'The Plowman's Glory'. The earliest is in *Four Excellent New Songs*, a garland printed in Edinburgh in 1778.

100 The Miller's Three Sons

'The Miller and His Sons', from J. Collingwood Bruce and John Stokoe,
Northumbrian Minstrelsy (1882), pp. 94–5.
Roud 138, Laws Q21; 19 entries.

Reasonably widespread in England, but hugely popular in North America, this song relies on the traditional distrust of millers, which was endemic in British popular culture for centuries. In feudal times, the lord of the manor owned the mill and locals had no choice but to use its services and pay the stipulated toll. In later periods the miller was independent, but still took his payment in kind as a proportion of the flour he produced for each individual customer, and this system was wide open to abuse. The song is also interesting for the motif of three sons, each addressed individually, which is a common feature of many traditional folk tales.

Although not published till 1882, this version was probably collected in the 1850s, when the Newcastle Society of Antiquaries launched their project to note local songs and tunes. The history of this song is a bit of a mystery. At least two different printings have survived from the mid eighteenth century, and it was included in the catalogue of 'old ballads' issued by William and Cluer Dicey of London, in 1754, under the title of 'The Miller's Advice to his Three Sons in taking of Toll'. But no other broadside prints have survived. It is, of course, possible that the song survived in oral tradition without the aid of print, and its simple repetitive nature would have helped, but it is unlikely that this is the true case, and nineteenth-century printings will probably turn up one day.

101 The Painful Plough

Sung by Robert Metcalf, Ilkley, Yorkshire (5 December 1909); collected by
T. S. Carter and F. Ferguson (Lucy Broadwood MSS, LEB/5/114).
Roud 355; 23 entries.

The importance of farming to the health and stability of the nation is a regular theme of songs of previous centuries, and 'The Painful Plough' was a well-known example. James Henry Dixon, in his early collection *Ancient Poems* (1846), noted its popularity:

This is one of our oldest agricultural ditties, and maintains its popularity to the present hour. It is called for at merry-makings and feasts in every party of the country. The tune is in the minor key, and of a pleasing character.

It is probably not quite as ancient as he seemed to think, as it cannot be shown to be older than the later eighteenth century. The earliest known version is in an eight-page chapbook entitled *The Ploughman's Garland*, printed at Darlington in 1774 (Bodleian Library, Harding A36/11), where it is described as 'an Excellent New Song', which takes twenty-two 8-line verses to tell the story. It was presumably cut down to a manageable length by a broadside printer in the early nineteenth century, and most of the later printers issued the shorter text at one time or another. The collected traditional versions follow the broadsides quite closely. It should be explained that 'painful' in this context signifies painstaking, diligent, or hard-working.

In the music notation, a dot has been added to the final minim to complete the bar. The melodic variation is indicated in the manuscript by means of a note 'Sometimes sung E' beneath the final note of bar 6, and a notated E above the D on the first beat of the next bar. It is possible that the written indication refers to the same thing as the music notation, but I have interpreted them here as referring to separate notes.

102 Twankydillo

Sung by Gabriel Figg, West Chiltington, Sussex (4 July 1965); recorded by
Joy Hyman (BBC 29821).
Roud 2409; 17 entries.

This song has been a puzzle to song enthusiasts ever since it was first collected in the Victorian and Edwardian period. Who was old Cole and young Cole (or Coal?), for example, and what is meant by 'Twankydillo'? Where evidence is tangled and inconclusive it is usually replaced by speculation, which invariably starts the investigation off in the wrong direction. It is often assumed, for example, that this song is indelibly linked to the blacksmith's trade, and that it is a remnant of some ancient ritual to do with the craft. But this is a prime example of the tendency in folklore writing to assume that things which are connected at one point in time have always been so, and that everything goes back a very long way. In this case it seems that neither is correct. An example here is Lucy Broadwood's assertion that the reference to bagpipes should be read as 'blowpipes', as this is more relevant to the smithy setting of the song (*English County Songs* (1893), pp. 138–9), but in fact the bagpipe reference is one of the few constants in the song's tangled history.

An article by Frederick Sawyer, 'Sussex Songs and Music', in the *Journal of the British Archaeological Association* 42 (1886), 306–27, firmly places the song in the 'Old Clem' celebrations of local blacksmiths which took place on St Clement's Day (23

November) every year, and other singers over the next couple of decades confirm the connection with the trade, beyond the simple mention in the text. But in piecing together the history of the song, the connection with Old Clem may well be a red herring anyway. The song actually makes no reference to Clem at all, and the connection between blacksmiths and St Clement in Britain seems to date only from the early nineteenth century. So perhaps it had been adopted (and adapted) by the blacksmiths at a relatively late date.

Three extant broadsides (Jennings, Catnach and Pitts) dating from around 1810–30 have texts similar to ours but are called 'The Bold Farriers' and make no mention of blacksmiths as such. And in these, the word 'Twanky Dillow' appears just once at the end of the chorus rather than being repeated. Another sheet printed by Hurd (Shaftesbury) around 1830 has the 'blacksmith' words, but the chorus is given as 'Twang dillo …', a small but significant difference, to which we will return.

An undated broadside in the Madden collection, probably from the turn of the nineteenth century, entitled 'The Envied Shepherd', makes no mention of blacksmiths at all but is about shepherds and is clearly related to our song, including the lines:

> Green willow, green willow, green willow, willow, willow
> And he plays upon his bagpipe made of the green willow.

This 'shepherd' version of the song lasted into the twentieth century, as it was collected by H. E. D. Hammond from John Hallett in Dorset in June 1906 (Hammond MSS, HAM/4/21/11) and appears in his collection as 'Twankydillo'.

Before the turn of the nineteenth century we can find no mention of the song, but there are numerous references in the eighteenth century to the words 'twangdillo' and 'tangdillo', meaning the twanging of a stringed musical instrument, often in a derogatory sense (see *OED*). In addition, these words appear in choruses to several songs, including a nursery rhyme, 'The Goose and the Gander', and 'Twangdillo', a rather risqué song in D'Urfey's *Wit and Mirth* (1719), and in each case the word is repeated in the same way as the 'twankydillo' in our song.

To sum up: the connection with blacksmiths gets weaker and disappears as we move further back in time. The 'twankydillo' is usually a semi-onomatopoeic reference to music and was used as a generic chorus line in a number of songs. There is no evidence for any ritual origin for the song.

VII
The Sons of Harmony …
Animals and Nonsense

103 Bryan O'Lynn

'Brian O'Flynn', sung by Mrs Todd, Chesterfield, Derbyshire (1960s);
recorded by Fred Hamer; published in Sam Richards and Tish Stubbs, *The
English Folksinger* (1979), p. 61.
Roud 294; 23 entries.

Alfred Williams, who prints a similar text, commented that 'Bryan O'Lynn' was a
favourite along the Thames side, from Malmesbury to Faringdon and in the neigh-
bouring villages as far as Aldsworth (*Folk-Songs of the Upper Thames* (1923), p. 181),
and versions were collected all over Britain, Ireland and North America. It is often
the case that the songs which make little sense turn out to be some of the oldest, and
this one goes back at least 500 years. It seems to have been a popular song in the mid
sixteenth century, with three separate printed references: 'Thom of Lyn' is mentioned
in the *Complaynt of Scotland* (1549) and a 'Ballett of Thomalyn' was entered in
the register of the Stationers' Company in 1557/8. What seems to confirm these
as our song is the verse about the bridge, and the character Tom a Lin, which occur
in a play by W. Wager, *The Longer Thou Livest the More Fool Thou Art* (*c.*1560). The
song was printed regularly in chapbooks and garlands throughout the nineteenth
century, and it also entered the children's song repertoire, as shown in James Orchard
Halliwell's important collection *The Nursery Rhymes in England*, in 1843.

It is sometimes assumed that this is an anti-Irish song, and it probably was in
some singers' minds, but it was widely sung in Ireland, and the first verse often
started 'Tommy Linn was a Scotchman born', or '… a Dutchman born', and so on.
On balance, it seems more often to have been thought to concern a 'village idiot'
rather than an ethnic one.

This is a simply constructed tune based on a stepwise ascending motif, each time
with a different twist at the end. This results in an AA'A" structure. The majority
of tunes associated with this song revolve around 1-3-2-1 figurations, or sequences
based on this pattern. In terms of range, Mrs Todd's tune and most other versions
are confined to the first five degrees of the scale, plus the lower fifth, which is usually
employed as an upbeat. The simplicity of the tune and its pretty much ubiquitous
compound metre allow the song to be performed at a gallop, as in Mrs Todd's performance. A number of singers, including Mrs Todd, momentarily hold up the gallop
with a sustained note or deliberate gap at strategic points in the text, such as the ends of
the first or final phrases, or immediately before the chorus, adding to the comic effect.

'Bryan O'Lynn' was printed in *The Dublin Comic Songster*, where it is reported as 'sung by Mr Purcell the celebratd [*sic*] Irish Vocalist, with unbounded applause' (Dublin: James Duffy, 1845, p. 17).

104 The Crabfish

Sung by Charlotte Renals, Cornwall (1978); recorded by Pete Coe; issued on
Catch Me If You Can, Veteran VT 119CD (2003).
Roud 149; 20 entries.

A very widely known song across the English-speaking world, and much more popular than the number of entries implies, because the 'coarse' nature of its humour kept it out of most earlier collections and publications, although Cecil Sharp did publish a cleaned-up version for the sake of its tune. It is still widely sung and is found under a variety of titles, including 'The Lobster', 'The Sea Crab' and 'The Codfish', and it nearly always has a lively, nonsense-sounding chorus.

The earliest reference in the English tradition is in the manuscript on which Thomas Percy based his *Reliques of Ancient English Poetry*, which dates from about 1650, but the basic story is much older and can be said to be almost worldwide in its reach. Roger deV. Renwick's excellent book *Recentering Anglo/American Folksong* (2001) identifies numerous versions from around the world, as a prose tale, a song, poem or jest, with the earliest documented example being an Italian literary retelling by Franco Sacchetti (1330–1400).

In English versions the humour is sometimes extended by the crab grabbing the husband's nose with its other claw, or by the couple chasing it around the room armed with shovel and broom. Sometimes the song ends with a baby being born, which has confused some commentators, but this is easily explained by reference to earlier versions where the wife is pregnant at the start, and the reason why the husband is so keen to buy a crab or lobster is that it is one of her 'cravings'. It was formerly very widely believed that an expectant mother's cravings must be satisfied for the sake of the baby's well-being. Another element here is that it was (and still is) also widely believed that any fright or sudden shock to the mother would result in a birthmark or other 'defect' on the baby, so in this case the child would expect to have, at the very least, the shape of a crab or lobster on its private parts.

As one would expect in a comic song, the rhythm is quite punchy, particularly the simple time versions, such as the one in Charlotte Renals's rendition.

105 Creeping Jane

Sung by Joseph Taylor, Saxby, Lincolnshire (9 July 1908); collected by Percy
Grainger; issued on Gramophone 2-2974 (matrix 8751e).
Roud 1012, Laws Q23; 25 entries.

Quite widely recorded in England, but rarely elsewhere, 'Creeping Jane' was also printed on numerous broadsides from the 1830s onwards or perhaps a little earlier, but little more is known of its history. Song researchers have spent some time trying to find out if there is any factual basis to the song, but most have reluctantly concluded that it is purely fictional. One problem is that 'Creeping Jane' was quite common as a racehorse name, and there were many so called throughout the eighteenth and nineteenth centuries. Something of a red herring is thrown up by a song headed 'The Ballad of Jenny the Mare' that appears in Edward Fitzgerald's novel *Euphranor* (1851), which reproduces much of the 'Creeping Jane' text but credits it to the horse 'Yorkshire Jenny'. This novel certainly post-dates the earliest broadsides, but the author implies that the song is old.

Of Joseph Taylor's performance on this recording, Patrick O'Shaughnessy writes, 'The flexibility of his seventy-five-year-old voice and the rhythmic vitality of his singing are remarkable' (*21 Lincolnshire Folk Songs* (1968), p. 28). The tune is close to many of the others associated with this song, which are either transcribed in 6/8 time or a ('lazy') dotted rhythm, as here. Joseph Taylor's verse moves immediately into the chorus without a sustained note and also finishes with this little melodic twist, in common with versions collected by Frank Kidson and Cecil Sharp. The tune is reminiscent of 'All for the Grog' (Roud 475), especially as sung by Sharp's contributor, Louie Hooper.

106 The Derby Ram

'The Old Tup', sung by Mr L. Colbeck and Mr E. J. Houghton, Braithwell,
Yorkshire (8 November 1945); collected by Ivor Gatty; published in
JEFDSS, 5:1 (1946), 24–6. See the same article for other versions from the
Sheffield area.
Roud 126; 53 entries.

'The Derby Ram', or 'The Old Tup', was widely sung all over England and North America, but collected only a few times in Scotland and Ireland. The earliest known version is entitled 'The Old Ram of Derby' and was included in *A Garland of New Songs*, printed by Angus of Newcastle about 1790, and the text given there is very similar to later collected versions. Local writer Llewellyn Jewitt, in his *Ballads and Songs of Derbyshire* (1867), p. 115, claimed that the ram (if not the song) had been famous before that time: 'Derby people have, I know by allusions to it, been fond of their Ram for more than a century'. But the earliest known 'collected' version is, in fact, Scottish: 'The Ram of Diram', published in George Ritchie Kinloch's *Ballad Book* of 1827.

It is difficult to know what to make of songs like this and 'The Herring's Head' (No. 109) and 'The Cutty Wren' (Roud 236), which involve hyperbolic descriptions of animals. Over the last few generations it became commonplace to assert that they had an ancient ritual basis, despite the complete lack of evidence to support such a notion. But many people still want to believe that such a song must have a more interesting origin than the fact that somebody just wrote a nonsense song.

The 'Derby Ram' song is sung all over the country, but in certain areas – particularly around Sheffield – it was also known as an annual custom, usually called the 'Old Tup'. Sometime over the Christmas period, lads of the village would dress one of themselves as the ram and go round pubs and houses singing the song and enacting its main story. They would then collect money or food and move on. This puts it squarely into the category of seasonal customs, which have also been assumed to be ancient and pagan, but again there is no evidence for the ram or tup custom before the mid nineteenth century. It is likely that the custom evolved from the song and not the other way round, and it is interesting that Jewitt makes no mention of the custom.

Certainly, the ram is popular in Derby. It features heavily as the emblem of the city and the county football club, and appears often in local public art; a real ram was adopted as the official mascot of the 95th Derbyshire Regiment in 1858. But it is not even clear whether the emblem was suggested by the widespread song, or the song was written about an already existing local icon. Much more research is needed.

107 The Foolish Boy

'My Father Died and I Cannot Tell How', sung by Mrs L. H. Haworth, Huddersfield, Yorkshire (1940s); sent to Francis Collinson (Collinson MSS, COL/4/26A).
Roud 469; 28 entries.

This was a widely collected ditty, even more common in North America, and was often called 'The Swapping Song'; many people remembered it from their childhood but continued to sing it in adulthood. The verses vary little between versions, although in some a few more animals or items are added to the list, but the choruses vary widely in terms of words, if not in sounds. In the classic children's rhyme book *Gammer Gurton's Garland* (1810), which contains the earliest printed version of the song, it is recorded as:

With my wing wang waddle oh
Jack sing saddle oh
Blowsey boys bubble oh
Under the broom.

That the song was already in circulation at that time is confirmed by the Cumberland poet John Woodcock Graves, who wrote the original 'John Peel' song; he remembered 'The Foolish Boy' from his childhood and he was born in 1795.

The song seems to have survived without the aid of broadside versions, although printed nursery-rhyme collections will have served a similar purpose. Mrs Haworth's text is uncannily close to an Isle of Man version published in the 1843 edition of James Orchard Halliwell's 1843 edition of *The Nursery Rhymes of England*, and one suspects that she, or the person who taught her, learnt it from print, although as that book did not have music, somebody must have added the tune on the way. The motif of the series of foolish bargains is not uncommon in traditional tales.

Mrs Haworth notes in the manuscript, with reference to note 4 of bar 4, 'I am uncertain whether the last note goes up or down. It might be down.' The dotted rhythms she gives in bars 5, 6 and 8 feel too slow for the character of the tune (and in bar 5 lead to a five-beat bar) so have here been changed to a dotted quaver-semiquaver pattern in each case. The penultimate note of bar 4 is unclear on the manuscript, so may be an E rather than the D given here.

108 The Frog and the Mouse

'The Frog's Wooing', sung in the Mitford Family, Mitford, Northumberland; published in M. H. Mason, *Nursery Rhymes and Country Songs* (1878).
Round 16; 37 entries.

Very widely known across Britain and Ireland, and even more so in North America, this is a good example of a song which was found even more commonly in the nursery tradition than in adult circles and was therefore much more widely known than the number of collected instances would suggest. It is probably true to say that in the nineteenth century, at least, everybody in the country would have known it, and most people still do in some form or other.

In addition to appearing regularly in nursery literature, the song was kept in the public eye by becoming a popular comic song in the stage routines of performers such as Grimaldi and John Liston, as a dance tune ('Lord Frog') on numerous popular prints and broadsides, and in other forms of popular culture. Influential publications such as Sabine Baring-Gould and Cecil Sharp's *English Folk-Songs for Schools* (1906) and Revival recordings by Burl Ives (1954) and others ensured that each succeeding generation could learn the song anew.

A song called 'The Frog cam to the mil dur [mill door]' was mentioned in *The Complaynt of Scotland* (1549), and 'A Most Strange Weddinge of the ffrogge and the mowse' was registered with the Stationers' Company on 21 November 1580, but the earliest extant text was published in Thomas Ravenscroft's *Melismata* (1611). The early history is thus well documented, but the song's later development would certainly repay close scrutiny, precisely because it was so well known, and would be an ideal candidate for a study of long-term continuity and change. Until about fifty years ago, for example, versions for children as well as adults nearly always ended up with the frog, mouse and rat being chased and eaten by local cats and ducks, but nowadays it is less acceptable to interest children in cute little animals and then kill them off. It is also intriguing to see how different words have been used over the years to tell the same story. But the most obvious marker for different strands within the song's development is the range of refrain and chorus lines, such as 'Roley Poley gammon and spinach', 'Kitty alone' and 'Uh huh', which help to reveal the genealogy of each particular manifestation of the song.

109 The Herring's Head

Sung by Jack Elliott, Birtley, County Durham (1960s); published in Gwen and Mary Polwarth, *North Country Songs* (1969); issued on *Jack Elliott of Birtley*, Leader LEA4001 (1969).
Roud 128; 43 entries.

Jack spoke and sang with a broad Durham accent, which does not translate well to the written page, and anyone thinking of singing the song should do so in their own accent anyway. We have decided to give the text in 'standard' English. The first verse of the Polwarths' rendering of Jack's accent is as follows:

> *What'll I do wi' me harrin's heid*
> *Oh what'll I do wi' me harrin's heid?*
> *We'll mak' 'em into loaves of breid*
> *Harrin's heid, loaves o' bried*
> *An' aal manner o' things*
> *Of aal the fish that live in the sea*
> *The harrin is the one for me*
> *How are ye the day, how are ye the day*
> *How are ye the day, me hinny O?*

It was an extremely widespread cumulative nonsense song that varies widely from version to version but is always based on making unusual things from bits of the herring – things that are seemingly chosen to serve the rhythm and rhyme, rather than from any intrinsic meaning. Enthusiasts of the 'secret meanings' school like to think that songs which detail animal parts, such as this one, 'The Derby Ram' (No. 106) and 'The Cutty Wren' (Roud 236), must have ancient ritual origins, but there is not the slightest evidence that this is the case, or that the songs are based on anything more than a love of hyperbole and nonsense.

Frank Purslow, interestingly enough, suggests that this might have previously been a 'forfeit song', the leader or chairman addressing his questions to different members of the company, who must improvise a verse or pay a penalty – probably a round of drinks (*The Wanton Seed* (1968), p. 130). James Madison Carpenter noted that one of the versions he collected about 1932 in Oxfordshire was 'a drinking song, learned in a pub'. There is evidence that other cumulative songs – for example 'The Twelve Days of Christmas' – started life as memory-game songs.

That said, it is difficult to gauge the age of a song like this, simply because it does not seem to have appeared on broadsides, so we have no datable printed sources to guide us. It was clearly in circulation in late Victorian times: Sabine Baring-Gould noted a Devon version in 1891, and another was printed in Sarah Hewett's *The Peasant Speech of Devon* in 1892, but oral testimony takes us back even further. James Olver, one of Sabine Baring-Gould's singers, claimed that he had 'learned it in 1810 from Jan and Tom Hive, two old men in Liskeard' (Baring-Gould MSS, SBG/1/2/338), and there is a version in the manuscripts of Scottish collector Peter Buchan from about 1840.

The singing becomes slower in bars 9–14, possibly due to the fact that in this recording the audience join in with the chorus.

110 *The Hungry Fox*

'The Fox', sung by Bob and Ron Copper, Rottingdean, Sussex (1963); recorded by Peter Kennedy.

Roud 131; 53 entries.

A very widely known song across Britain and Ireland, and also in North America, it was previously thought highly appropriate for children and included in numerous nursery-rhyme books, as well as in the adult folk-song collections. Collector Fred Hamer commented, 'My mother used to sing me to sleep with her Irish version of this song and wherever I go I seem to pick up another version' (*Garners Gay* (1967), p. 75).

The story remains the same from version to version, although there is a fair amount of variation in the actual text, and in performance the Coppers' version is unusually complex in the rhythm of its words and tune. The earliest reference is a single verse ('Old Mother Widdle Waddle jumpt out of bed …') in *Gammer Gurton's Garland*, a small book devoted to nursery rhymes, published in 1810. It does not seem to have been popular with broadside printers, and only one, issued by Disley of London in the 1860s or 1870s, has so far turned up.

Both parts of the Coppers' two-part rendition have been transcribed here.

111 *The Keeper*

Sung by Sam Bennett, Ilmington, Warwickshire; collected by Cecil Sharp (12 January 1909) (Sharp MSS, FW 1919–20/FT 2052), and James Madison Carpenter (*c.*1930) (Carpenter MSS, pp. 00563–00564). This version is a combination of the two sources.

Roud 1519; 17 entries.

This song has been collected a fair number of times from traditional singers in England and occasionally in the USA, but it achieved a much wider circulation after the 1920s by being included in the campfire and community-song repertoire of certain youth organizations and other societies. Cecil Sharp, Ralph Vaughan Williams, George Butterworth, Henry Hammond and Sabine Baring-Gould collected the song, but the latter published a severely bowdlerized text. He described the text as 'gross' or 'coarse' and declined to note down all the verses, even in his manuscript notebooks.

To be frank, even the broadsides and the one or two collected texts in the manuscripts which have not been 'edited' are hardly 'gross', although they do obviously refer, somewhat clumsily, to men chasing women. Examples from the 'Frolicksome Keeper' broadside are:

> The seventh doe she prov'd with fawn
> And to the Keeper she made great moan
> Wishing he had but let her alone
> Among the leaves so green O.

> The one [doe] cryed out to the other
> I am serv'd as my father serv'd my mother

And at least two of the traditional singers from whom the song was collected were women.

Cecil Sharp noted that 'This is one of the few two-men folk-songs' (*English Folk Songs*, II (1920), p. xvii). Evidence is coming to light, however, that quite a few traditional songs were designed to be sung by more than one person. Alfred Williams, for example, includes a number of duets in his *Folk-Songs of the Upper Thames* (1923), although these were usually sung by a male and a female (or a man pretending to be a female), but perhaps it was the 'call and response' of the chorus which interested Sharp.

No nineteenth-century broadside of 'The Keeper' seems to have survived, but we have some evidence of the song's earlier history. The earliest known texts are on black-letter broadsides from the 1680s, in the Pepys, Douce and Roxburghe collections. These are entitled 'The Huntsman's Delight, or The Forester's Pleasure' and were by J.M. (presumably Joseph Martin), and there is no reason to doubt that one of these was the original. A shorter version, called 'The Frolicksome Keeper: A New Song', which is much closer to the traditional texts, appeared on a late eighteenth-century sheet. The originals can be seen on the Bodleian Library Broadside Ballads and the English Broadside Ballad Archive websites.

In Sharp's manuscript the call-and-response section is transcribed in 2/4 but here the 4/4 time signature has been retained throughout.

112 *Old King Cole*

Sung by Charles Lay, Bampton, Oxfordshire (*c.*1931); recorded by James Madison Carpenter (Carpenter MSS, pp. 00647–8; Cylinder 033 (sr253), Disc Side 071 (sr036a)).
Roud 1164; 20 entries.

This falls into one of the categories of song in which the number of entries in *The Folk Song Index* is relatively meaningless because it has long been in the general nursery-rhyme tradition and nearly everybody in the nation knows at least a bit of 'Old King Cole'. The investigations of Iona and Peter Opie (*The Oxford Dictionary of Nursery Rhymes* (1951), pp.154–5) turned up a reference in William King's *Useful Transactions in Philosophy* (1708–9) where the author quotes a few lines and speculates on the original identity of 'Old King Cole', so it was clearly already well known by that time. The song was printed regularly throughout the eighteenth century, particularly in Scottish songbooks.

Although texts vary considerably, they seem to fall into a handful of categories. The most common, which appears to be the original pattern, is to enumerate musicians and the noises their instruments make, but other versions introduce a different trade in each verse, followed by characteristic sounds, actions or words. There are also versions specific to a particular community, in particular army ones, which are often extremely bawdy, and there have been many parodies. As with all such cumulative songs, it can be sung solo, in unison or in a group with different people taking parts.

There are also different endings to each chorus. Charles Lay, above, offers one common set invoking the 'sons of harmony', but the earliest version has:

For 'twas my lady's birth-day
Therefore we keep holy-day
And come to be merry.

And Scottish versions often have:

There no lass in a' Scotland
Compared to our sweet Marjorie.

A great deal of ingenuity has been devoted to pinning down the original Old King Cole, although none have any evidential backing. The fact that he can be called Coul, Coal, Coil, and so on, provides plenty of scope for invention, but the real problem is with the original assumption that he must have been a real or at least a well-known fictional person before the song was composed. This in itself is at best speculative.

Carpenter's recording contains the first and last stanzas only. As sung on this occasion, the end of line 1 is omitted and conflated with the beginning of line 2 so we have mended this here by incorporating the first two bars from the final-stanza tune.

113 *Three Sons of Rogues*

Version 1: 'King Arthur's Servants', traditional in the Mitford family
of Northumberland; published in M. H. Mason, *Nursery Rhymes and
Country Songs* (1878).

Version 2: 'When Good King Arthur Ruled this Land', from James Orchard

Halliwell, *The Nursery Rhymes of England* (1842), p.1.
Roud 130; 30 entries.

This was a widely known song in North America as well as in Britain. It often features King Arthur, but the king's name is not significant: different versions have Henry, Edward and George, while in America it usually starts 'In good old colony times'. Whatever the historical period, the characters are often 'three sons of rogues'. It appears, however, that this may be a euphemism for 'three sons of whores', as we shall see.

For such a small innocuous ditty, its history is something of a tangle. The first version given above, from the Mitford family in the 1870s, is perhaps the stand-ard version and the one which appears in most collections, although with some variations. It rarely appeared on broadsides, but there are plenty of other nine-teenth-century sightings: John Bell collected a version in Newcastle, probably in the 1820s; it is printed in the hardback songster *The Quaver* (1844), and James Orchard Halliwell's *The Nursery Rhymes of England* (1842); while Thomas Hardy included a verse in Part 4, Chapter 2 of his novel *Under the Greenwood Tree* (1872).

However, the earliest version so far found is in the Bodleian Library on a broad-side dated 12 December 1804 and published by Laurie and Whittle of London, who specialized in sheets with large illustrations and short songs. The picture shows a fearsome devil carrying off a tailor (with a roll of cloth under his arm), and the title is 'Miller, Weaver and Little Tailor: A Much admired Song sung by Mr Chas John-ston, & proper to be sung at all Musical Clubs'. If this is the original, which is likely, it strongly suggests that the song started its life as a comic stage song.

The second text, which can be sung to the same tune, is clearly related to the first but was much less widely known. It was already in circulation in the early 1840s when Halliwell compiled his *Nursery Rhymes of England* and Flora Thompson mentions it being sung heartily by villagers in her childhood on the Northampton-shire–Oxfordshire border in the 1880s. She describes it as a rousing chorus song, and also adds her child's-eye view of the matter: 'Every time Laura heard this song she saw the queen, a gold crown on her head, her train over her arm, and her sleeves rolled up holding the frying-pan over the fire. Of course, a queen would have fried pudding for breakfast: ordinary common people seldom had any left over to fry (*Lark Rise* (1939), Chapter 4).

But then there is a third text, also published in hardback songbooks in the early nineteenth century – for example *The Vocal Library* (1820) – which starts with 'When Arthur first in court began' and features three thieves: an Irishman, a Scotsman and a Welshman. This was composed by prize-winning glee writer John Wall Callcott (1766–1821). Callcott's heyday was in the 1790s, so it is possible that this song pre-dates the Laurie and Whittle song, which may turn out to be a parody after all.

It seems that the song has existed in different forms in different contexts almost from the beginning – stage song, children's ditty, pub song, and in glee clubs and urban sing-song societies.

And the whores? Well, the Laurie and Whittle broadside refers to them as 'Three sons of whores', while the other published texts speak of rogues. But Thomas Hardy, in a letter dated 1889, makes it clear that he regarded 'whores' as the proper reading. So perhaps it is an example of a song which changes with the company it keeps.

The minims in the original notation have been changed to dotted crotchets tied to a quaver to conform to the time signature.

114 The Tree in the Wood

Sung by John Thornber, Burney, Lancashire (20 November 1914); collected by Cecil J. Sharp (Sharp MSS, FT 3068).
Roud 129; 38 entries.

This was a very popular cumulative song which was equally well known in North America and is still widely sung. Versions have also been collected in Ireland and Scotland, where it is sometimes called 'The Bog Down in the Valley'. Although the actual words vary somewhat, the structure is always the same – in order of diminishing size – hill, tree, branch, twig, nest, bird, egg, and so on – which is much easier to remember than many other cumulative sequences.

Many writers comment on how close our song is to other European songs – in Breton, Welsh, Danish, Swiss, French, Dutch, for example – but until someone carries out a thorough international investigation it is not clear which came first. The history of the song in Britain is certainly unclear. Only a couple of nineteenth-century broadsides have so far been found, with one of the earliest, called 'The Tree in the Wood', printed by John Pitts in London sometime around 1820. But an earlier version, 'The Tree on the Hill', was included in *Two Excellent New Songs,* a chapbook printed in London, probably in the 1790s. Then there is silence in the printed record. Perhaps it is simply that straightforward cumulative songs do not need the help of print to last in singers' repertoires.

Nor is the song found in the Victorian or Edwardian nursery literature or child-lore collections in England, where it would be expected, apart from John Hornby's *Joyous Book of Singing Games* (1913), p.110, where it is given as a cumulative song without actions. William Wells Newell included it in his *Games and Songs of American Children* (1903 edition), but he implied that it was not widely known and that the song had been adapted from a French game. These two publications came out at exactly the same time as our major collectors were finding numerous versions being sung in the English countryside.

As is often the case, it is interesting to compare the modern versions with the earliest ones. The similarities are more common than the differences, but in the chapbook text dating from the 1790s, the repeated lines at the end of the cumulation are intriguing:

And the tree on the hill
And the hill stand still
And evermore will
By the side of a gill
While my name's John Hill!

And the song goes further than the chick in the egg, which puts a very different complexion on the matter:

And in that feather there was a bed [sic], etc.
And in that bed there was a lass, etc.
And in that lass there was a lad, etc.

The song is nowadays often described as being concerned with the natural life cycle and that subject so beloved of those looking for hidden symbolic meaning: fertility. This theory is based almost entirely on a rare, possibly unique, version entitled 'The Everlasting Circle' in Sabine Baring-Gould's manuscripts (see VWML website, Baring-Gould MSS, SBG/1/1/491), and reprinted by James Reeves in the book of the same name, in 1960. In this version, the maid and the man verses are followed by a baby, who grows up and plants an acorn. Neat, of course, but unconvincing, and doubly so because the last verses have such a different textual feel that it is quite likely the collector added them himself.

VIII
Cruel Death Has Put an End ...
Songs of Death and Destruction

115 *The Constant Farmer's Son*

Sung by Mrs Fred Nation, Taunton, Somerset (*c.*1916); collected by Janet Blunt (Blunt MSS, JHB/9/8). The second line of verse 5 is missing in Mrs Nation's version, so we have supplied it from a Hampshire version in the George Gardiner MSS (GG/1/17/1104).
Roud 675, Laws M33; 27 entries.

Regularly collected in England and North America, but more rarely in Scotland, 'The Constant Farmer's Son' was also widely available on broadsides, with similar texts, from about the 1820s onwards. It tells more or less the same story as another traditional song, 'Bruton Town' (Roud 18, Laws M32), but the latter was much less frequently found. The storyline of 'Bruton Town', or 'The Bramble Briar', follows quite closely part of a tale included by Boccaccio in his *Decameron* (*c.*1358), 4th Day, 5th Story, which was in turn used as a basis for four different works by the German poet Hans Sachs (1494–1576) and again in Britain by Keats, *Isabella or The Pot of Basil* (1820). The basic theme of brothers plotting to get rid of their sister's sweetheart is also treated in 'The Bristol Garland', a song which appeared on a number of broadsides and chapbooks in the second half of the eighteenth century. These three songs – 'The Constant Farmer's Son', 'Bruton Town' and 'The Bristol Garland' – often include textual echoes of each other, as well as sharing general plot similarities, but it still remains unclear which takes precedence and in which direction any potential influences operated.

Frank Purslow comments that 'the tunes to which ['The Constant Farmer's Son'] is sung are usually of the "street ballad" variety' (in Gardiner MSS, GG/1/15/955). Among these various melodies is a group of tunes which not only resemble each other quite closely in their melodic outline but share certain distinctive characteristics. Mrs Nation's tune illustrates these characteristics well. Whereas most folk-song tunes are eight or sixteen bars in length, depending on whether they comprise two or four 4-bar phrases, Mrs Nation's tune and the others of its kind are eighteen bars long, the final phrase consisting of six bars. This phrase is essentially a repetition of the first phrase of the tune but with two bars added to the middle of it. Another distinctive feature, found in Mrs Nation's tune and most of the others in the group, is the three-note slurred figuration which occurs on the final word of line 3 in each verse (bar 12).

Mrs Nation's tune is in simple time but others in the group, such as that collected by Gardiner from James Channon, are in compound time, and one (collected by Cecil Sharp from Mrs Edbrook) mixes the two. Purslow suggests that Channon's tune has 'something of "The Verdant Braes of Skeen" about it' (Gardiner MSS, GG/1/15/955) and there is certainly a strong resemblance in the opening phrase of each.

This rendition finishes on the third degree rather than the expected first degree. The pause indicated on the penultimate beat of phrases 1 and 2 is also unusual.

116 *The Cruel Mother*

Sung by Cecilia Costello, Birmingham (1951); recorded by Marie Slocombe and P. Shuldham-Shaw; published in Roy Palmer, *Songs of the Midlands* (1972), p. 67; issued on Leader LEE4054.
Roud 9, Child 20; 27 entries

Widely collected across Britain and Ireland, and in North America, 'The Cruel Mother' has clearly struck a chord with singers over a number of generations. We will never quite know why, of course, but in performance the combination of the matter-of-fact handling of a difficult subject and the repeated rhythmic refrain often creates a stark and hypnotic tale, which is extremely effective. Many versions omit even the first verse(s) which explain that the woman is not only expecting illegitimate children, but that the father is of a lower status and the shame thereby doubled. Nevertheless, there have also been parodies and even children's versions over the years. One of the latter, called 'Old Mother Lee', which was still widely sung over the last fifty years, progresses at a rapid pace through the story, in successive verses: 'There was a woman called Old Mother Lee', 'She had a penknife long and sharp', 'She stuck it in the baby's heart', 'The forty police came running up', 'The Magistrate said you must die', 'That was the end of Old Mother Lee', and so on.

Francis J. Child printed thirteen versions, mainly from Scotland, and Bertrand Bronson published fifty-six tunes. The earliest evidence of the song being in traditional circulation is in David Herd's manuscripts of the 1760s, and this is one of the relatively rare songs which seem to have been popular without the aid of the broadside presses, as no printed copies from the eighteenth and nineteenth centuries have yet turned up. But the song was printed at least once, in London about 1690, and this broadside might well be its original form. Entitled 'The Duke's Daughter's Cruelty, or the Wonderful Apparition of Two Infants whom she Murther'd and Buried in a Forrest, for to hide her Shame', the broadside already has many of the structural and verbal features of later collected versions, including the second- and fourth-line burden in each verse.

Although the subject matter of infanticide might seem unusual or even unpleasant to modern sensibilities, our song was only one of several treatments of the theme in the seventeenth century. A prose chapbook entitled 'The Cruel Mother', for example, with the subtitle 'being a true relation of the bloody murther committed by M. Cook, upon her dearly beloved child ...', was printed by W.R. in London in 1670, and another broadside, 'No Natural Mother, but a Monster', which was written by Martin Parker, was licensed in 1634 (reprinted by Hyder E. Rollins, *A Pepysian Garland* (1922)). Other Child ballads, such as 'The Maid and the Palmer' (Child 21, Roud 2335) and 'Mary Hamilton' (Child 173, Roud 79), also include the theme.

In the real world of the seventeenth century, the authorities were increasingly aware of the problem of the killing of babies, and infanticide was distinguished from other forms of murder in 1624. It was also illegal to 'conceal a birth' because it was usually impossible at a later date to distinguish a stillbirth from the victim of a murder. For more on this song, and on infanticide in general, see David Atkinson, 'History, Symbol, and Meaning in The Cruel Mother', *FMJ*, 6:3 (1992) and Vic Gammon, 'Folk Song Collecting in Sussex and Surrey', *History Workshop Journal*, 10 (2008).

Cecilia Costello's haunting tune, with its first-half minor tonality and second-half suggestion of the major, seems well suited to the 'Cruel Mother' story. It is not particularly close to any of the examples in Bronson's *Traditional Tunes of the Child Ballads*, which themselves are wide-ranging (although see Bronson addenda, p. 456). As Bronson discusses (I (1959), p. 276), what gives these tunes a certain unity is the rhythm of the refrain lines (2 and 4), which is essentially the same in nearly all versions. This is certainly true of Costello's tune, although the rising melodic contour with which hers ends is very much a feature of her version. She learnt the song from her father, of Ballinasloe, County Roscommon. According to Marie Slocombe, Costello had vivid recollections of her father singing it: '"He sang it", she told us, "with his eyes closed, hands clasped, bending over, with great emphasis and drama, very slow – he used to frighten us children with it"' (*JEFDSS*, 7:2 (1953), 96).

117 *The Cruel Ship's Carpenter*

'Polly's Love', sung by Henry Burstow, Horsham, Sussex (1893); collected
by Lucy Broadwood; published in *JFSS*, 1:4 (1902), 172–73.
Roud 15, Laws P36A/B; 39 entries.

This song was very widely collected in Britain and Ireland, with a huge number of versions found in North America, where it is one of several songs regularly called 'Pretty Polly'.

In some murdered sweetheart ballads, the crime is seemingly carried out on the spur of the moment and is described in an almost matter-of-fact way. But in others, like 'The Cruel Ship's Carpenter' here, the symbol of premeditation is the open grave 'with the spade lying by'.

Our song derives directly from a mid eighteenth-century garland entitled 'The Gosport Tragedy, or The Perjured Ship's Carpenter', which includes a very much longer text that someone (presumably a broadside printer) cut down to manageable size around the year 1800. The shorter version, usually called 'Polly's Love, or the Cruel Ship Carpenter', is a much tighter text and a better song, and was in turn widely printed in the nineteenth century. The text produced by John Pitts about 1820 and Henry Such about 1870 are very close to each other and are also very similar to collected versions such as the one given here from Henry Burstow. The song was sufficiently popular to attract a burlesque, ' Molly the Betrayed or The Fog-Bound Vessel'.

Tunes for 'The Cruel Ship's Carpenter' are almost always in triple time. Those in the major key sometimes incorporate echoes of the widespread 'Villikins and His Dinah' tune or 'All Jolly Fellows Who Follow the Plough' (No. 91) while retaining their own identity. Henry Burstow's tune, on the other hand, comprises the 'Villikins and His Dinah' tune in its entirety. A handful of other versions use the Dorian-mode tune associated with 'The Blind Beggar's Daughter of Bethnal Green' (No. 60). Its minor tonality seems more in keeping with the tragic narrative and it may be for this reason that Frank Purslow commented, 'I think this is the best tune I have heard to the "Cruel Ship's Carpenter"' (in Hammond MSS, HAM/5/34/26).

118 *Edwin in the Lowlands Low*

'Young Edmund', sung by Harry Cox, Catfield, Norfolk, recorded by Peter
Kennedy (9 July 1956); also recording in Ewan MacColl collection (National
Sound Archive), issued on *It Fell on a Day, a Bonny Summer Day*,
Topic TSCD667 (1998).
Roud 182, Laws M34; 21 entries.

Harry Cox was recorded singing this song a number of times, and it would be an interesting project for someone to compare his different renditions. Certainly, there are a number of verbal differences, and he did not even always sing all the verses. An example of the difference is the second line of the first verse, which he sang as either

Concerning gold as we are told that leads so many wrong

or

Whilst I unfold concerning gold that leads so many wrong.

It is even extraordinarily difficult to distinguish 'lowlands low' from 'lowland low'; he definitely sings both, but it was not uncommon for his Norfolk accent to miss out the 's' in plurals. The text given here is an amalgamation of four performances.

This was an extremely widespread song in England, Scotland, Ireland, and even more so in North America, where dozens of versions have been collected. Collected texts are often full, and it was clearly a story which kept singers' attention. The song was also printed by everybody who was anybody in the broadside trade, but, on present evidence, only from the 1820s onwards. The plot would seem a natural for the melodrama stage or the cheap nineteenth-century 'shocker' novel, and a number of somewhat similar stories had appeared on the Continent and in Britain, which usually told of a man (often a soldier) coming home in disguise, or simply unrecognized, after many years and his parents unwittingly murdering him. Versions of this tale appeared in Britain in chapbooks such as *News from Perin, Cornwall* (1618) and *The Liverpool Tragedy* (*c.*1760s), and in a play by George Lillo called *Fatal Curiosity* (1736), but no direct parallels to our song have yet come to light. It is possible it was deliberately adapted from the older tales by a nineteenth-century broadside writer, but this at present is conjecture.

119 Hugh of Lincoln

'Sir Hugh', sung by James Pike, Portsmouth, Hampshire (August 1907);
collected by George B. Gardiner (Gardiner MSS, GG/1/14/842).
Roud 73, Child 155; 33 entries.

This song was widely collected in England and Scotland and was even more common in North America, but less well known in Ireland. It was one of the songs included in Francis J. Child's classic ballad collection, and he printed eighteen versions of the text, while Bronson presented sixty-six tunes from the Anglo-American tradition.

The subject matter, however, is disturbing, and reminds us that folklore is not always nice and cosy. Indeed, racists, xenophobes, political zealots and religious fundamentalists have always used legends, rumours, songs, jokes and other lore to support and spread their beliefs and to indoctrinate their young, and in particular to denigrate and stereotype outsiders and the victims of their bigotry.

Probably the longest-running and most pernicious of all racial or religious prejudice is the virulent anti-Semitism which lurks just below the surface in the Christian
West. The direct roots of our song lie in a report of an incident which supposedly
took place in Lincoln in 1255, although that in its turn was simply the latest manifestation of a legend which was already centuries old. Based on the idea that Jews
kidnap Christian children and crucify them in contempt of Christ, and/or use the
child's blood in their own rituals, the report declared that a young boy called Hugh,
who lived in Lincoln, had been murdered in this way by Jews, and to really bring
the moral home, it was made clear that this was not an isolated incident but a regular practice, and that delegates had gathered from Jewish communities all over the
country to take part. Like all good legends the story had corroborating detail, such
as that when the Jews tried to dispose of the body the river refused to accept it, as
did the earth, and when the boy's mother was seeking him his body (or his ghost)
called out to her. Bells rang, heavenly light flooded the scene, a blind woman who
touched the body had her sight restored instantly, and so on. The Jews were all
rounded up and executed.

The story had the multiple propaganda purpose of giving believers a common
enemy to scapegoat, of showing how despicable our religious enemies are, and how
wonderful our own religion is. Lincoln Cathedral did very well out of the hordes of
pilgrims who flocked there because of stories of Hugh's miracles, and the establishment therefore had another vested interest in keeping the legend going. The story
has never gone away, and surfaces regularly. Child, for example, cited numerous
similar legends across Europe, from medieval times onwards, together with perse-
cutions and murders of local Jews as a result of people believing such stories, right
into the 1880s. In Britain we are constantly reminded of the story because it forms
the basis of the Prioress's Tale in Chaucer's *Canterbury Tales*.

It is not known quite how this traditional song came into being. It suddenly
seems to spring into life in the 1760s, in Scottish sources, and although it appears
in various ballad manuscripts and literary collections, it is decidedly odd that no
eighteenth-century garlands or nineteenth-century broadside printings of the song
seem to have survived.

James Pike's tune exemplifies the central tune tradition of this ballad, which
Bertrand Bronson finds to be concentrated in the Appalachians as well as in Pennsyl-
vania, Indiana, New York, Ohio, and in one example from Somerset (*The Traditional
Tunes of the Child Ballads*, III (1966), p. 73). The tune is characterized by major tonality, authentic range and 6/8 time, with a mid-cadence on the fifth degree. Unlike
most of the other 'Sir Hugh' tunes in this group, Pike's melody does not repeat the
final line to make a refrain. All these tunes clearly comprise the same basic tune as
that associated with 'Lord Lovel' (No. 122) and 'The Outlandish Knight' (No. 127)
and Pike's is particularly reminiscent of Fred Jordan's rendition of the latter (for
example, as recorded on *A Shropshire Lad*, Veteran VT148CD (2003)).

120 *The Lakes of Cold Finn*

Sung by Arthur Nightingale, Didbrook, Gloucestershire (*c*.1932); recorded
by James Madison Carpenter (Carpenter MSS, p.00638; Disc Side 307
(sr156a)). Carpenter wrote, 'Learned from Grandmother, Mrs Davis, 50
years ago.'
Roud 189, Laws Q33; 28 entries.

Widely known in England, but also collected regularly in Ireland, Scotland and
North America, 'Willie Leonard' or 'The Lakes of Coolfin' is particularly interesting
for the matter-of-fact way in which the story of a relatively minor domestic tragedy
is related. It has fascinated song commentators, who find it tantalizing because it
does not seem to be the sort of song a broadside songwriter would invent out of the
blue, and one cannot help wondering what prompted it.

It does not seem to be very old, and it is noticeable that the surviving English
broadsides are not from the early printers but from what could be called the third
generation of nineteenth-century printers such as Fortey, Disley and Pearson, who
were active around the middle of the century. Nevertheless, one sheet printed by
Haly of Cork, and lodged in the Bodleian Library (Harding B 26(681)), could possibly be as early as the late 1820s. The song is there entitled 'A New Song Called Willie
Leonard', and the lake is 'Colfin', and this seems to support the general assumption
that the song was originally Irish. But apart from the place name in the song, which
varies widely, there is no real evidence to tell us where the song originated, and
efforts by Irish song-researcher John Moulden to pin down the place or to find a real
event behind the story have so far proved negative.

Some American researchers of a previous generation were fond of the idea that
Willie was not drowned but carried away by some sort of water-fairy. This is simple
wishful thinking typical of the 'secret meanings' school, but one cannot help thinking there is more to be discovered about the song, somewhere.

The tune is a variant of 'Flash Company' (No. 80).

121 *Lambkin*

'The Ballad of Cruel Lambkin', sung by Mrs Lines, Adderbury, Oxfordshire
(April 1916); collected by Janet Blunt (Blunt MSS, JHB/3/5). Blunt wrote,
'Mrs Lines would sing through the ballad fairly fast and cheerfully, with a
great relish for verses 5 and 6, 15 and 19.'
Roud 6, Child 93; 22 entries.

'Lambkin' is not one of the major-league Child ballads in terms of popularity, but
it was widely known in England and Scotland, and even more so in North America.
Francis J. Child printed twenty-two versions and Bertrand Bronson presented thirty

tunes. The central character's name varies considerably, including, in just the English versions, 'Lamkin', 'Lankin', 'Lincoln' and 'Limkin', and he is variously referred to as 'Long', 'Bold', 'Cruel' and 'False'.

There is plenty of violence in Child's *English and Scottish Popular Ballads*, but this is the song which really grabs attention in this respect, and this is especially true of the versions like Mrs Lines's which offer no clue about the reason for Lambkin's animosity to the Lord's family. The oldest versions, and those collected in Scotland, have a more coherent narrative, and the first verse usually declares Lambkin to be a mason who has built a castle for the Lord (whose name also varies), but has been cheated out of his payment, or otherwise slighted. In her study of the ballad ('Lambkin: A Study in Evolution', *JEFDSS*, 1 (1932), 1–17), Anne Gilchrist identified two threads to the song's history – one Scottish and the other Northumbrian. In the latter tradition, she argued, the early loss of the 'mason' verse forced successive singers to introduce other elements to fill in Lambkin's back-story. Hence, there are versions where he is a rival lord, a border ruffian, or even the slighted suitor of the Lady's daughter. Most versions collected in England stem from this Northumbrian ancestor.

Gilchrist also identified a confusion of characters in the centre of the action, especially in the supporting female roles. In many, as here, the Lady somewhat unheroically offers Lambkin her daughter, but in other versions the daughter, or a faithful servant, offers their life to save the Lady, and it is sometimes a daughter and sometimes a maid who greets the Lord with the bad news at the end.

Unusually for Child's chosen ballads, there are no known European analogues to 'Lambkin', and this is often taken as an indication that the ballad is based on a real event. Quite naturally, both Scotland and Northumberland claim the story, and have locations such as Ovingham and Balwearie Castle where local tradition insists that the events took place. Unfortunately there is no evidence to even suggest that the story was ever real, let alone where it happened.

The earliest known versions, reprinted by Child, date from about 1775, but unusually for a widely known song only one nineteenth-century broadside copy of it has so far turned up, printed by John Pitts of Seven Dials in London in the 1820s or 1830s. Various wild theories about fairies (Lambkin was a supernatural being employed to build the castle), lepers (because of the blood in a silver basin), and other flights of fancy, can be dismissed as just that – flights of fancy.

The tune tradition for 'Lambkin' is quite diverse and Bronson makes nine groupings from the thirty tunes he locates for the song. Apart from its triple time and metrical pattern – similar, as Bronson notes, to that of 'The Cherry-Tree Carol' and 'A Virgin Unspotted' (see Nos. 147 and 151 in this volume respectively) – Mrs Lines's tune is quite distinct. It is minor in tonality and may be heard as plagal, with its tonal centre on A; or authentic, with its tonal centre on E. The F natural preceding bar 1 reflects what is noted in the manuscript, but may be sung as an F sharp if preferred.

122 *Lord Lovel*

Sung by Emily Bishop, Bromsberrow Heath, Herefordshire (13 October
1952); recorded by Peter Kennedy (BBC 18678).
Roud 48, Child 75; 34 entries.

Immensely popular in England and Scotland and even more widely collected in
North America, 'Lord Lovel' has obviously taken singers' fancy for over 200 years.
Francis J. Child cited nine versions from England and Scotland, while Bertrand
Bronson presented seventy-one tunes, drawn from both sides of the Atlantic. The
earliest versions to come to light so far are those given by Child, and date from about
1770, and the song was also widely available on nineteenth-century broadsides.

Many of the great ballad scholars have had trouble with 'Lord Lovel', which they
felt gets perilously close to the line between simplicity and silliness, and it has been
mercilessly parodied down the years. This uneasiness caused Child to defend simple
songs (*The English and Scottish Popular Ballads*, II, p. 204):

> It can scarcely be too often repeated that such ballads as this were meant only to be
> sung, not at all to be recited. As has been well remarked of a corresponding Norwe-
> gian ballad, 'Lord Lovel' is especially one of those which, for their due effect, require
> the support of a melody, and almost equally the comment of a burden. No burden
> is preserved in the case of 'Lord Lovel' but we are not to infer that there never was
> once. The burden, which is at least as important as the instrumental accompaniment
> of modern songs, sometimes, in these little tragedies, foreshadows calamity from the
> outset, sometimes, as in the Norwegian ballad referred to, is a cheerful sounding for-
> mula, which in the upshot enhances by contrast the gloom of the conclusion.

Bronson called it a 'too too insipid ballad', and also commented on the music as its
saving grace: 'its great popularity for at least a hundred years is powerful testimony
to the life-giving energy of a memorable tune' (*The Traditional Tunes of the Child
Ballads*, II (1962), p. 189); and Frank Kidson also had reservations: 'This song was
very popular in the forties and fifties of the nineteenth century from its use by such
comic singers as Sam Cowell ... I have always looked upon the ballad as a mock-
pathetic travesty or burlesque of some serious original (*JFSS*, 6 (1918), 32). Steve
Gardham, one of the best of our current crop of song researchers, writes, 'To me,
"Lord Lovel" is a burlesque of a lost ballad or just a skit on the whole genre' (private
communication).

Nevertheless, there is no evidence that the dozens of singers whose versions were
annotated and recorded in the twentieth century regarded it as a comic song. It is
interesting to note that the versions which were published as 'comic' are almost
word-for-word the same as the 'straight' versions collected from traditional singers,
except for one interpolated verse, and it was clearly the way it was sung which provided most of the comedy. Davidson's *Universal Melodist* (1848), for example, directs

the song to be sung in a 'Mock pathetic' style', and the give-away extra verse is:

Then he flung his self down by the side of the corpse
With a shivering gulp and a guggle
Gave two hops, three kicks, heav'd a sigh, blew his nose
Sung a song, and then died in the struggle.

Bishop's version is even simpler than most, as it leaves out the final verses which are included in most other texts. In these verses, Lovel meets the funeral, asks who is dead, asks for the coffin or grave to be opened, and, as in 'Barbara Allen' (No. 40), dies; the lovers are then buried together. It could be argued that this formulaic ending, which occurs in so many other ballads, adds to the stereotypical nature of 'Lord Lovel', and that Bishop's song gains by their omission.

Child also provides references to a number of Scandinavian and Germanic ballads which are closely analogous to our 'Lovel'. Some are as simple as the British song, but others have a little more incident and a harder edge in that the girl is pregnant and the man's departure more reprehensible, and in some cases she even dies in childbirth.

The fascination of this song's melody is its remarkable consistency across the many oral versions collected in England, Scotland, Ireland and the USA (Bronson, *The Traditional Tunes of the Child Ballads*, II (1962), p. 189). Emily Bishop's tune is no exception though she gives it her own twist by holding the final word of lines 3 and 4. This adds an extra beat to bars 6 and 8 and momentarily confounds the listener's expectation of a regular metre throughout. The tune is also associated with 'Lord Thomas and Fair Eleanor' (No. 48) and 'The Outlandish Knight' (No. 127).

123 Maria Marten

Sung by Robert Feast, Ely, Cambridgeshire (11 September 1911); collected by Cecil Sharp (Sharp MSS, FT 2659/FW 2211).
Roud 215; 22 entries.

Whenever a high-profile murder took place the broadside printers and sellers had a field day. They issued a succession of sheets that, typically, covered the discovery of the crime, the hunt for the perpetrators, the arrest, the trial, and so on. And before 1868, when public executions were abandoned, broadsides were printed that contained the 'last dying speech' of the criminal (written of course by the broadside hacks), which were sold at the foot of the gallows to the crowds who had gathered to watch the spectacle.

These 'last dying speeches' often included a song, which typically gave details of the crime, the murderer's remorse and a warning to others not to follow the paths of crime. These songs were mostly too topical and ephemeral to survive long in singers' repertoires, but 'Maria Marten' was the exception, as it was still being sung 150 years after the event.

In May 1827, in Polstead, Suffolk, William Corder was courting Maria Marten, the daughter of a local molecatcher. Not long before, she had given birth to William's baby (her third, by different fathers), but the baby had died. On the pretence of taking her away to get married, Corder met Maria at a local barn (soon to be dubbed 'the red barn' by the media), murdered her and buried her under the floor. He gave out that she had gone away and, after a while, he also left the village. Eleven months later, Maria's father discovered her body, and rumour had it that he was guided to the spot by a recurring dream reported by his wife. Corder was found, in Ealing, married to a schoolmistress, and he was eventually tried, convicted and executed. See Judith Flanders, *The Invention of Murder* (2011) for more details of the crime and the way it was handled in the media of the time.

124 *Mary Across the Wild Moor*

Sung by Mr Holgate, Yorkshire; collected by Frank Kidson; published in Kidson's *Traditional Tunes* (1891), pp. 77–8.
Roud 155, Laws P21 ; 17 entries.

'Mary Across the Wild Moor' was probably much more popular than the number of index entries would imply, because many of the early collectors would probably have passed it by as too redolent of Victorian popular culture. Both Frank Kidson and Alfred Williams, who published versions, commented on its relatively recent origin, but in his *English Folk-Songs* (1891) William Alexander Barrett remarked that it was 'Popular throughout the country'. The picture is very different in North America, where versions appear in nearly all the major folk-song collections.

The young woman with baby at the mercy of the elements is a common enough motif in nineteenth-century song and drama, but in Mary's case we are not told whether she has been shunned by her family because her child was illegitimate or because she had married against her parents' wishes and had been abandoned by her husband.

Judging by the numerous broadside printings, the song probably originated in the 1820s. Kidson comments, 'I have found that the song is known in the North and East Ridings to the same tune. Both air and song appear to be not much earlier than the beginning of the present century' (*Traditional Tunes* (1891), p. 77).

125 *Mary in the Silvery Tide*

Sung by Jane Gulliford, Combe Florey, Somerset (8 September 1908); collected by Cecil Sharp (Sharp MSS, FW 1704-1705/FT 1858).
Roud 561, Laws O37; 17 entries.

In the standard 'murdered sweetheart' ballad scenario, it is the girl's young man who turns nasty and murders her, but in this case, while she is, as usual, innocent, the perpetrator is very different. The story is suitably melodramatic: Mary is goodness personified, the Captain is likewise bad, and it is Henry's lot to find the body, with the help of a dream. But traditional singers apparently took it perfectly seriously, and it would not be surprising to learn that some thought it a true story. Nevertheless, the real moral for the modern reader seems to be that when trussing up your victim, never use a monogrammed handkerchief.

Most of the main nineteenth-century broadside printers issued the title, and as is often the case, the sheets printed by Catnach and Pitts, dating probably from the 1820s, provide the earliest evidence so far recorded of the song's existence.

126 The Mistletoe Bough

Sung by Freda Palmer, Bampton, Oxfordshire (26 February 1978); recorded
by Steve Roud.
Roud 2336; 14 entries.

This was another immensely popular song, which the Victorian and Edwardian collectors largely ignored because of its recent origin. The song was written by Thomas Haynes Bayly, probably early 1830s, with music by Sir Henry Bishop.

Bayly (1797–1839) was one of the most prolific popular songwriters of his day and he also wrote drama and poetry, but he did not invent the story itself. He based his song on 'Ginevra', a poem by Samuel Rogers, published in his book *Italy* in 1823. This tells of seeing a portrait of Ginevra in Modena, and an old chest placed beneath it. She was the fifteen-year-old bride of her childhood sweetheart, Francesco Doria, and she had playfully hidden in the chest during her wedding feast, with tragic results. But it was Rogers himself who had introduced the Italian setting; as he wrote: 'This story is, I believe, founded on fact, although the time and place are uncertain. Many old houses in England lay claim to it.' So it was already known over here, although earlier versions have not yet come to light.

It was a stroke of genius of Bayly to introduce the Christmas setting, if it was he who did so, because it ensured its revival at concerts, theatres and home entertainments every year at that season, and there could have been few Victorians who did not know it well. There is no doubt that many singers of 'The Mistletoe Bough' believed it to be a true story, and even now many houses in England claim to be the spot where the tragedy took place. Some possess the very chest in which she hid herself, while others base their claim on the fact that the name Lovel occurs locally. Contenders include Minster Lovell (Oxfordshire); Bramshill House, Marwell Old Hall and Malsanger (all in Hampshire); Brockdish Hall (Norfolk); and Bawdrip and Shapwick (Somerset); see Jennifer Westwood and Jacqueline Simpson, *The Lore of the Land* (2005), pp. 302–3.

The broadside printers were not slow in picking up the song, and it was available in this form from the 1830s onwards. Broadsides rarely give information about sources, but an early sheet by Catnach reprints the explanatory commentary from Rogers's Italian book.

The singer begins a little shakily in this performance so the first bar of stanza 2 has been substituted in the transcription.

127 The Outlandish Knight

Sung by Mrs Sarah Phelps, Avening, Gloucestershire (c.1930); collected by James Madison Carpenter (Carpenter MSS, pp. 06997–8; Cylinder 131 (sr 351), Disc Side 310 (sr 157b)).
Roud 21, Child 4; 116 entries.

In the timescale covered by this book, about half a dozen of the ballads chosen by Francis J. Child have proved in a class of their own as regards widespread popularity, and 'The Outlandish Knight' is up there with 'Barbara Allen' and 'The Gipsy Laddie' (see Nos. 40 and 81) in being collected time and again all over the English-speaking world. Bertrand Bronson called it 'one of the most impressive of all ballads for the geographical sweep of its popularity and vital tenacity' (*The Traditional Tunes of the Child Ballads*, I (1959), p. 39).

The song goes by many names, including 'False Sir John' and 'May Colven' in Scotland, but 'The Outlandish Knight' is the nearest we get to a standard title in the English tradition. Influenced by foreign ballads, Child, rather confusingly, called it 'Lady Isabel and the Elf Knight'.

Child himself only printed six versions, but provided a wealth of background material, and Bronson amassed 141 tunes. Much of Child's discussion is concerned with the many Continental analogues, and he shows that similar ballads exist in the traditions of Holland, Denmark, Sweden, Norway, Germany, Serbia, France, Spain, Portugal and others. The British ballad is particularly close to the Dutch ballad 'Heer Halewijn', and it seems pretty clear that the British ballad was not an indigenous growth but was originally imported from the Continent, and probably not that long ago.

Despite its archaic feel and close foreign relatives, the song does not seem to be very old, at least in Britain. An undated broadside in the Roxburghe collection, entitled 'The False Knight Outwitted', is almost certainly from the second half of the eighteenth century, and 'May Colvin' is published in David Herd's *Ancient and Modern Scottish Songs, Heroic Ballads, etc.* (1776), but no earlier versions have yet been located.

The song was also very common on later broadsides, and many of the collected texts, including Sarah Phelps's, are remarkably similar to those printed in the nineteenth century, from Catnach and Pitts in about 1820 to Henry Such sometime after the 1860s, even down to the puzzling line in verse 13, 'Although it is made of a tree'. Indeed, these texts are also very similar to the eighteenth-century example already mentioned, except for one key element in the plot. In most versions the girl tells the knight to turn his back while she takes off her dress, but in some, including the Roxburghe broadside, she demands that he cut down the nettles which are growing on the brim, and while engaged with his sickle he is thrown in. On present evidence the song seems to have been more than usually influenced by printed texts in its history.

It is a great disappointment to many that the song as found in Britain, in contrast to many of its Continental cousins, has no obvious supernatural element (apart from the talking parrot, of course), and it is usually assumed that these motifs have been lost, rather than they were never there. It has been suggested, for example, that because the False Knight drowns his victims he must originally have been some form of water-monster, but why such a being can be killed by throwing him in the water is never explained.

Carpenter's cylinder recording contains four verses of the song whose melody is the same as that of 'Lord Thomas and Fair Eleanor' and Lord Lovel' (see notes to Nos. 48 and 122 respectively).

128 Oxford City

Sung by Freda Palmer, Witney, Oxfordshire (1973); recorded by Mike Yates; issued on *Up in the North and Down in the South*, Musical Traditions MTCD311-2 (2001).
Roud 218, Laws P30; 51 entries.

A straightforward tale of tragic love. Under various titles, such as 'Jealousy' and 'Poison in a Glass of Wine', this song was widely collected across Britain and Ireland and in North America. It also widely printed on broadsides, with the earliest sheets so far identified being from the Pitts and Catnach era, around the 1820s, and texts vary little from version to version.

The upbeat notes to stanza 1 have been changed to D from E as E only occurs in stanza 1. The notated rhythm is somewhat approximate as the singing is fairly free in places.

129 The Oxford Girl

'Ekefield Town', sung by Harry Cox, Catfield, Norfolk (12 June 1960); recorded by Mervyn Plunkett.
Roud 263, Laws P35; 25 entries.

Widely sung in England, not quite so common in Scotland and Ireland, but with numerous North American versions, this song was one of the most popular 'murdered sweetheart' accounts in the tradition. It goes under many names, often based on the place concerned – 'The Oxford Girl', 'The Wexford Girl' and, in the USA, 'Expert Town', 'Lexington Murder', 'Knoxville Girl' – or focusing on the perpetrator as 'The Cruel Miller', 'The Bloody Miller', and so on.

It was widely available on broadsides in the nineteenth century, and collected versions are usually quite close to these printed texts, but these later broadsides were in turn based on a widely printed eighteenth-century account entitled 'The Berkshire Tragedy, or The Wittam Miller'. This was a much longer and wordier treatment of the story, and, as happened with many other songs of the period, was deliberately cut down to suit the fashion for shorter songs sometime soon after 1800.

The song may have the hallmarks of a 'generic' murder ballad, but there is some evidence that it may have started as a report of a real crime, although we have two potential ancestors. The first, a black-letter broadside in the Pepys collection, entitled 'The Bloody Miller', dating from 1684, claims to record how Francis Cooper, a miller's servant of Hocstow, near Shrewsbury, murdered his pregnant sweetheart, Anne Nicols. But beyond the general similarity, the details of the crime and the text of the song itself bear little relation to our song, although there is a curious coincidence in the mention of a nosebleed, which occurs when Cooper hears his sentence passed by the judge.

The second candidate is much closer. We have seen that the 'Berkshire Tragedy' broadsides show clear textual similarities to the collected versions of the song, and the two earliest printings to come to light so far are chapbooks, published in York and Edinburgh respectively, which claim that the song reports a real and recent crime. They both end with 'The Last Dying Words and Confession' of the murderer, John Mauge, a miller, who was executed at Reading for killing his sweetheart, Anne Knite. 'Wittam', which appears in the titles of both versions, is presumably Wytham, near Oxford, and they are dated 1744. It is possible that they are telling the truth, but street literature such as this is notoriously untrustworthy, and as it has proved impossible to find any independent corroboration of the facts of the case so far, it may well be fiction after all.

130 *The Unquiet Grave*

'Cold Blows the Wind', sung by Jane Jeffrey, Dunterton, Devon (1893);
collected by Sabine Baring-Gould (Baring-Gould MSS, SBG 3/1/42).
Lucy Broadwood also collected a version from the same singer in 1893 and
published it in her *English Traditional Songs and Carols* (1908), p. 119.
Roud 51, Child 78; 89 entries.

An immensely popular song in England, but much rarer in Scotland and North America. Cecil Sharp called it 'a great favourite' with his Somerset singers, and Sabine Baring-Gould commented that 'there are few old singers who do not know it'. Francis J. Child gives five versions, including one from Scotland, while Bertrand Bronson musters forty-three tunes. Folklorists tend to follow Child in referring to the song as 'The Unquiet Grave', but most singers seem to have simply called it 'Cold Blows the Wind', after its common first line.

For such a simple song, 'The Unquiet Grave' has attracted a fair amount of commentary; partly because it was included by Child in his seminal ballad collection, but also because it has a marked supernatural element, which is surprisingly rare in English songs. The identification of the song as an old *ballad* has in itself coloured the way it is handled. Child started it all off with the comment, 'this may suggest a suspicion that this brief little piece is an aggregation of scraps. But these repetitions would not strike so much if the ballad were longer, and we must suppose that we have it only in an imperfect form.

Later writers have taken as read the idea that what we have is incomplete and have hoped to find a more satisfyingly complex predecessor, but to achieve this they have had to look abroad. There is no doubt that the central motif – that immoderate or too-lengthy mourning by the living disturbs the rest of the dead – existed across Britain and Ireland independently of the song and was a widespread motif in folklore across Europe, particularly in Scandinavia and Germany, where ballads on the subject can also be found. But as often happens in ballad study, it requires a substantial leap of faith to square this particular circle. Ruth Harvey, for example, in an otherwise useful study of the song published in the *JEFDSS*, automatically assumes it to be 'a song which certainly goes back to pre-Christian traditions' (4 (1941), 49–66), despite the fact that there is no evidence of its existence before the nineteenth century. Put simply, the problem with 'ancient' motifs which have remained current in society, as this one had, is that they are available for incorporation into a song at any given time in their history, not just at the beginning of it, and their presence is therefore no proof of antiquity.

To complicate matters, however, some versions include another well-known 'ballad' motif, the setting of impossible or difficult tasks, but it is not clear whether these formed part of the 'original' 'Unquiet Grave' song or were grafted on later. For an investigation of this aspect, see David Atkinson, 'The Wit Combat Episode in The Unquiet Grave', *Lore & Language*, 12 (1994).

There is one small straw at which those who hope to find an ancient history for the song can grasp in Richard Leighton Greene's *The Early English Carols* (1935), pp. 127–8. He published the text of a carol, written down about the end of the fifteenth century, which starts with the two lines:

There blows a cold wynd todaye, todaye
The wynd blows cold todaye

And although the carol has no other similarity to 'The Unquiet Grave', Bertrand Bronson thought these lines close enough to the latter to suggest its existence in that period.

But what we do know of the song's history is more prosaic, and inconclusive. In *Songs of the West* (1905), Sabine Baring-Gould seems to say that he first came across the song from someone who had learnt it from an old nurse about 1830, so it was already in 'oral' circulation at that time.

However, surprisingly few broadside printings of the song have survived. Of the six known sheets which have printers' names, four of them were produced in Birmingham, while the others are from Portsea and Liverpool. Two of these printers were in business from 1820, the others much later. Nevertheless, two slip songs in the Madden collection, which unfortunately have no imprints, look to be from about 1800, or just before, but efforts to find a definite eighteenth-century printing have so far been in vain. The most noticeable thing, however, is that as yet there is no evidence of the song being printed by any of the most prolific London businesses, or others from Manchester, Preston, and so on. This may simply be an accident of history, but it is decidedly strange that such a widely known traditional song has left such a limited paper trail.

Lucy Broadwood commented, 'Mrs Jeffreys' great age and ill-health made it impossible to note more than the tune and the two beautiful concluding verses here printed. The other verses were so much the same as in the Shropshire version ... that the latter has been re-printed here, up to the point where Mrs Jeffreys' materially differed.'

The music transcriptions by Broadwood and Frederick Bussell, Baring-Gould's collaborator, are almost identical. Bussell's first-bar notation is ambiguous, the stem direction of the second note appearing to imply an alternative pitch but without supplying a corresponding note to which it would form the alternative. Broadwood's transcription gives a B at this point so this has here been taken as the missing note which completes the bar while Bussell's alternative notations are presented below.

Jane Jeffrey's tune is unusual among those for 'The Unquiet Grave' in being triple time, but its melodic contour is akin to the tunes with authentic range in Bronson's principal melodic grouping, that is, his group Ab (see *The Traditional Tunes of the Child Ballads*, II (1962), p. 234). The Baring-Gould manuscript notes 'compare with Chevy Chase' beside the tune notation, and it certainly appears that Jeffrey's tune is a close analogue of the 'O Ponder Well' tune tradition associated with 'Chevy Chase' (Child 162, 'The Hunting of the Cheviot'; Roud 223), particularly in Northumberland (J. Collingwood Bruce and John Stokoe, *Northumbrian Minstrelsy* (1882), p. 2). The same tune appears in *The Beggars' Opera* (1728) and is associated with the song 'Children in the Wood' (Roud 288). According to William Chappell, the tune goes back to Elizabethan times (*Popular Music of the Olden Time* (1859), I, p. 200).

Bar 1 of the manuscript is ambiguously notated in that the second quaver stem appears to suggest a melodic alternative. It is here given as part of the main tune, however, as two quavers at the start of the bar is characteristic of the tune elsewhere.

IX

Me and Five More ...
Poachers, Highwaymen and Other Criminals

131 Blackberry Fold

Sung by Eve Champion, Slough, Buckinghamshire (1 November 1950);
collected by Francis Collinson (Collinson MSS, COL/2/46B). Last two
verses from Harry Cox, Catfield, Norfolk, recorded by Peter Kennedy (19
July 1956) (BBC 22914).
Roud 559, Laws O10; 25 entries.

This was a popular enough song in its own right, but nowhere near as widespread
as 'The Banks of the Sweet Dundee', which has a similar storyline (see No. 58). Eve
Champion's version stops short of what is the usual denouement, so we have taken the
liberty of adding the two last verses from the singing of Harry Cox of Norfolk. Nevertheless, it must be said that only in the fantasy world of song would it be deemed a
happy ending that Betsy marries the man who had tried to rape her at sword point.

There are other aspects, below the surface, which to the modern eye change the
tenor of the narrative. In the common broadside text, for example, it is Betsy who
draws 'her own dagger knife', rather than using his sword, and the last line was often
'He's made her his lady instead of his whore', which is certainly more direct and
realistic about the squire's motives, but mars the romantic 'happy ending' a little.

Broadside texts have survived from various times in the Victorian era and the
earliest date from the first two decades of the nineteenth century, the printers often
calling the song 'The Squire and the Milkmaid' or 'Young Squire'. But the song
was not quite brand new at that time. It is a deliberate rewrite of an older broadside
ballad, 'The Virtuous Milk-Maid's Garland', dating from sometime between 1765
and 1780, which takes over 130 lines to tell the same story. A number of other songs
that entered the tradition in the early nineteenth century were the result of a similar
cutting-down treatment, and in every case, including this one, a much better song
was created in the process.

The tunes associated with 'Blackberry Fold' are always, it seems, in triple time
and for the most part are major. A range of distinct melodies is evident in the tune
tradition, a handful of which contain an echo of the 'Villikins and His Dinah' tune
in one or another feature, such as the thrice-repeated note which ends the first,
second and fourth phrases (see Jacob Baker's tune, collected by H. E. D. Hammond,
Hammond MSS, HAM/5/34/26). A few other tunes are a version of the full 'Villikins' tune (for example Florrie Coomber's, collected by Anne Gilchrist, and Miss
E. Bull's, by Lucy Broadwood). None of this is enough evidence to support Frank

Purslow's claim that 'most collected versions of the tune have apparently been affected by contact with the ubiquitous "Villikins"' (*The Foggy Dew* (1974), p. 104).

Eve Champion's tune is one of a group of related tunes for the song characterized by the phrase structure AABC. Some of these have a compass as wide as an eleventh, but the bulk of the tune in each case tends to emphasize the first five degrees of the scale. Interestingly, the Dorian tune collected by E. J. Moeran from George Hill in Suffolk is similarly formed in terms of its phrase structure and compass so one must disagree with Gilchrist that this tune is 'quite different' from the major ones of this group (*JFSS*, 8 (1931), 269). Likewise, Purslow's view that this is 'a decidedly strange tune which is not at all representative of English folk song' seems misplaced (*The Foggy Dew*, p. 104). Gilchrist also points to a resemblance between the major tunes in this group and the tune commonly associated with 'Spencer the Rover' (*JFSS*, 6 (1918), 36; see No. 86) but although there is a general similarity, the latter does not emphasize the first five degrees of the scale in the way so characteristic of the 'Blackberry Fold' tune. The first note of bar 9 in Collinson's notation of Champion's tune has here been changed from a dotted crotchet to a minim to make a complete bar.

132 Brennan on the Moor

Sung by Charlie Wills, Bridport, Dorset (19 October 1952); recorded by
Peter Kennedy (BBC 18693); also in Kennedy's *Folk Songs of Britain and
Ireland* (1975), pp. 697–8.
Roud 476, Laws L7; 22 entries.

This song was very widely sung in Victorian times, as shown by Frank Kidson's comment in *Traditional Tunes* (1891) that it 'is, or was, sung all over England'. William Brennan really did exist, and was one of the most famous Irish criminals of the period. It is not easy to get authoritative information about him, mainly because legend quickly obscured fact, and even his date of death is not known for sure; 1804 is most regularly cited, but there are other references to 1809 and even 1812, and while most sources claim that he was taken by the authorities and formally executed, there is also a tradition that he was killed by one of his potential victims in a highway robbery which went wrong.

The song is typical of outlaw ballads in that it portrays the miscreant as some sort of hero. 'Robbing from the rich' is, of course, one of the most common motifs in songs of this kind, and the mention of Dick Turpin brings in another romantic hero. Even being outsmarted by the pedlar is probably drawn from a similar episode in the Robin Hood cycle.

The song was widely available on British and Irish broadsides, which are typically undated, but on present evidence the earliest of these date from the 1830s, so the song was probably written several decades after the real Willie Brennan's exploits were over, and it is mentioned in an article in *Chambers's Journal* in 1863 as typical of the street ballads of the time. The traditional texts, like Charlie Wills's given here, follow the broadsides quite closely.

There are a number of tunes associated with this song, including 'Villikins and His Dinah', 'The Banks of the Sweet Dundee' (No. 58) and 'The Wearing of the Green'. Although different, they contain rhythmic similarities, especially the use of the 'Scotch snap' pattern (as on the first beat of bar 7 in Charlie Wills's rendition). The rhythmic resemblance is particularly noticeable in the chorus on the words 'Brennan's on the moor', which in just about all versions is realized by the same rhythm, if not the same pitches. Even when the tune for the verse is in 6/8 time, it changes to simple duple time to make the characteristic rhythm of the chorus (see the tune sung by J. Halls in Roy Palmer's *Folk Songs Collected by Ralph Vaughan Williams* (1983), for example).

Charlie Wills's tune is particularly close to that collected by Francis Collinson from an unnamed singer (Collinson MSS, COL/4/33) and it is very likely that the Collinson notation is another transcription of Wills himself. Like several other 'Brennan' tunes, the final phrase of Wills's verse and chorus is the same as the B phrase of 'The Wearing of the Green'. Except in stanzas 8 and 9 on this recording, Charlie Wills habitually prolongs the second beat of the penultimate bar of the verse (bar 7 in the transcription) to make a 5/4 bar at this point, whereas at the corresponding place in the chorus he keeps to the regular 4/4 metre.

For more on 'The Wearing of the Green' melody, see 'Bonny Labouring Boy' (No. 62).

133 Dick Turpin

Sung by David Belton, Ulceby, Lincolnshire (26 July 1906); collected by
Percy Grainger (Grainger MSS, no. 181).
Roud 621, Laws L10; 31 entries.

By far the most popular of several traditional songs about the famous highwayman's exploits (see also Roud 620 and 856), this was collected widely in England under titles such as 'Turpin Hero' and 'O Rare Turpin', but rarely elsewhere.

The real Turpin was born in Hempstead, Essex, about 1705, and died on 7 April 1739. He started as a butcher's apprentice, but soon progressed to a life of crime, which included receiving, deer poaching, horse stealing and burglary as well as the highway robbery for which he later became famous. Turpin's fictional fame began to take shape in chapbooks published around the end of the eighteenth century, but was given a huge boost by the best-selling novel *Rookwood* by William Harrison Ainsworth (1834), which presented a romanticized notion of highwaymen as 'gentlemen of the road'. In the course of this process of literary romanticizing, legends which had been told of previous criminals became attached to Turpin. The death-defying ride to York to provide himself with an alibi, for example, had previously been told of William (John) Nevison (d. 1684) and others.

It is interesting to note that on top of the fiction underlying the story as sung by David Belton, the last verse includes a historical reference to the suitably ignominious end to Turpin's sordid criminal career. Too well known to operate around London, he moved to Yorkshire, where he lived under the name of Samuel Palmer. Instead of lying low, he created a scene by shooting his neighbour's cockerel and threatening to shoot the man as well. He was arrested for disturbing the peace, and while in custody was linked to some local horse theft, then recognized, tried and executed at York.

Jack Catch in the last line refers to Jack Ketch, who was the public executioner in the late seventeenth century. He became so well known in his time – partly through ballads and other printed sources – that his name lived on long after his death as the generic name for any executioner or hangman.

The earliest example of the present song is as part of a much longer text, detailing several of Turpin's fictional exploits, which appeared in a late eighteenth-century chapbook entitled *The Dunghill Cock, or Turpin's Valiant Exploits*, but it was later printed as a separate song by many of the nineteenth-century broadside firms.

134 *The Female Highwayman*

'Cecilia', sung by Mabs Hall, Horsham, Sussex (1980s); recorded by Mike Yates; issued on *As I Went Down to Horsham*, Veteran VT115CD. The last three verses are added from the singing of Hall's son Gordon on *Good Things Enough*, Country Branch CBCD095 (2001).
Roud 7, Laws N21; 42 entries.

Hall's version is perfectly good the way it stands, but we could not resist adding the last three verses from Gordon's singing, just to round things off nicely. It was a very widely collected song, also popular on broadsides, from at least 1800 onwards and probably a little earlier. Despite widespread transmission, texts of the song do not vary a great deal, and Hall's words are uncannily close to a broadside printed by John Pitts about 1820. But the girl's name varies considerably, most commonly as Sylvia or Sylvie, but sometimes Sovie, and so on. The broadsides often had the more formal title of 'Sylvia's Request and William's Denial'.

There is more than a handful of 'strong women' in the English folk-song tradition, but with one or two exceptions they are permitted to step outside their female roles only to a certain degree. As with the female tar songs, their motives are still circumscribed by gender conventions, and Cecilia cannot become a highwayman just for the hell of it. She can only do it to test her sweetheart's love. A further last verse, where she says that she would have shot him if he had given up the ring, so popular with Revival singers, does not seem to appear in traditional or broadside versions. What usually happens, as in verse 7 above, is that he worries about what would have happened if he had fought back and shot her, or she had accidentally shot him.

The first half of the tune seems to become stable in this rendition only in stanza 3, so that stanza has been used in the transcription given here. The performer sings the rhythm fairly freely, and there has been some attempt to show this in the transcription, hence the several time signatures.

135 The Gallant Poachers

'The Gallant Poacher', sung by Henry Adams, Sturminster Newton, Dorset (August 1905); collected by H. E. D. Hammond (Hammond MSS, HAM/2/6/7).
Roud 793, Laws L14; 17 entries.

Collected regularly across England, but rarely elsewhere, 'The Gallant Poachers' is one of the liveliest of our many poaching songs, but with a tragic storyline. Henry Adams's text is remarkably similar to the earliest known broadside, by James Catnach of London, dating from the 1820s, but it is more likely to have been derived from sheets printed later in the century (for example by Henry Such) which used the same words.

A. L. Lloyd (in *Folk Song in England* (1967), p. 243), and Roy Palmer (in *Everyman's Book of English Country* Songs (1979), pp. 98–100) have both noticed that a Luddite song, 'The Croppers' Song' of about 1812, is clearly based on 'The Gallant Poachers'. It starts:

Come cropper lads of high renown
Who love to drink strong ale that's brown
And strike each haughty tyrant down
With hatchet, pike and gun.

136 Geordie

'Spare Me the Life of Georgie', sung by Mary Hayes, Hartlebury, Worcestershire (30 November 1908); collected by W. K. Clay; published in his *Four Folk Songs from Hartlebury, Worcestershire* (1908?). Clay writes that Hayes 'had learnt it from a dairy maid in Upton Warren parish fifty-seven years before'.
Roud 90, Child 209; 48 entries.

Extremely well known in England, Scotland and North America, but apparently rarer in Ireland, 'Geordie' is one of those Child ballads which has distinct English and Scottish traditions, almost to the extent of being two different songs. Francis J. Child printed fourteen traditional Scottish versions, plus two English broadsides from the seventeenth century, while Bertrand Bronson presented fifty-eight tunes from the Anglo-American traditions. It is noticeable that the American versions are much closer to the English, rather than Scottish texts.

Ballad aficionados strongly favour the Scottish ballad. As Child himself commented in *The English and Scottish Popular Ballads*, IV (1972), p. 126, 'The Scottish ballads have a proper story, with a beginning, middle and ... a good end, and they are most certainly original and substantially independent of the English.' In these, Geordie is a nobleman and his lady's pleading is successful, while in the English he is a confessed criminal (albeit a noble one), of one sort or another, and his lady is too late to save him so he dies. Scottish versions are most often called some variant of 'Geordie', but other titles include 'Gight's Lady' and 'The Laird o' Geight', and it is often claimed – on slim evidence – that the story is based on a real-life character, identified by some as George Gordon, Earl of Huntly in the 1550s.

There are sufficient similarities between the two national traditions to suggest either a common ancestor or a major influence one way or another, and if the latter, on present evidence the English must take precedence. Scottish versions were first recorded in the later eighteenth century, at least a hundred years after the earliest evidence south of the border.

The earliest version of the English 'Geordie' to come to light so far is a black-letter broadside in the Pepys collection, 'The Life and Death of George of Oxford', printed in London between 1672 and 1696. It has all the key elements of the later song – London Bridge, Lady Gray, conversation with judge, hanging on a silken string – although the actual wording has changed over the years. But there is an even earlier broadside, preserved in the Roxburghe collection and dating from between 1601 and 1640, with the long title typical of the period, 'A Lamentable New Ditty Made Upon the Death of a Worthy Gentleman, named George Stoole, dwelling sometime on Gate-Side Moore and sometime at Newcastle in Northumberland, with his Penitent End'. This has a rhythm and rhyming scheme which connects it to 'Geordie', and includes some key verbal similarities, such as the lines:

> *I never stole no oxe nor cow*
> *Nor never murdered any.*

This ballad has a chorus in which 'heigh-ho' is repeated several times, and a ballad registered with the Stationers' Company on 1 June 1629, entitled 'Hey Hoe George', may well be the same.

It is likely that the 'George of Oxford' ballad in the Pepys collection was either based on or influenced by 'George Stoole', and it is usually assumed that this is the case. It is further assumed that the events described in 'George Stoole' are true, and it is confidently stated that they took place in 1610 (which seems to derive from the 'estimate' put forward by Joseph Ritson, an eighteenth-century ballad scholar). But there is no independent evidence to confirm or deny the existence of Stoole, or his trial and execution, so we must reserve judgement on whether the song is 'truth' or 'fiction'.

But to return to the song as it was collected from late nineteenth- and twentieth-century singers. Most of the leading nineteenth-century broadside producers issued the song, and despite being widely dispersed in time and place, the collected versions are textually very similar, and have probably been stabilized by these printed editions.

The most common tune for this ballad among English singers is minor in tonality. It is also employed for many other songs as well (see Bronson, *The Traditional Tunes of the Child Ballads*, III (1966), p. 268). The 'Geordie' versions sung to this tune have textual connections with the 'George of Oxford' broadside. Whether this is the same tune as that named on the broadside as 'a pleasant New Tune, called, Poor Georgy', however, is debatable because the broadside has a fairly extensive chorus or 'burden' which is not preserved in the extant oral texts or tunes of this group. The 'George Stoole' broadside is directed to be sung 'To a delicate Scottish Tune'.

Mary Hayes's tune is major in tonality and, in its first phrase and rising fourth in the final bar, sounds very like the widespread minor tune transformed into the major (compare Bronson's note to 'Geordie' as sung by Mrs Glover, Huish Episcopi, no. 43). All slurs in the melody are editorial.

137 Highwayman Outwitted

'The Yorkshire Boy', sung by Sam Fone, Mary Tavy, Devon (4 October 1892); collected by Sabine Baring-Gould (Baring-Gould MSS, SBG/1/2/633).
Roud 2637, Laws L1; 29 entries.

This will have to stand as representative of three very similar songs, each concerning a highwayman being tricked by someone carrying money on their way home from market. In 'The Farmer in Cheshire' or 'The Highwayman Outwitted' (Roud 2638, Laws L2) the protagonist is a girl, and while the robbery is taking place, the highwayman foolishly demands that she hold his horse. She leaps on the horse and rides off home. In the least well-known of the three, 'The Crafty Farmer' or 'Saddle to Rags' (Roud 2640, Child 283) it is the farmer himself who is stopped on the highway. He throws his saddlebags over the hedge, and while the robber goes to retrieve them, rides off with his horse.

All three first appear on broadsides and chapbooks in the second half of the eighteenth century, and were perpetuated by many broadside printers in the nineteenth. Our one is often called 'The Yorkshire Bite' and more often than not concerns a boy from Yorkshire, relying on listeners understanding that people from that county are famous for their shrewdness.

The music manuscript includes the symbol for a turn in bar 4 and a mordent in bar 10. Suggested interpretations have been added to the notation here. The text underlay of the refrain as given in the source does not fit the notation in any obvious way so this wording has been slightly reworked here and several notes subdivided so that the text scans well.

138 The Lincolnshire Poacher

'Gloucestershire Poacher', sung (probably) by Mrs Williams, Sonning-on-Thames, Berkshire; collected by Clive Carey (Carey MSS, Gl.227). Two short pieces of text missing from Mrs Williams's version, have been supplied from a Gloucestershire version printed in Alfred Williams,
Folk-Songs of the Upper Thames (1923).
Roud 299; 23 entries.

This song was very widely known in traditional forms but was also extremely popular in other milieux such as the stage and the concert hall as an accredited 'old English song'. Clearly, when sung by a village labourer or other worker it would have meant something different than to a concert professional or a middle-class parlour singer, but the latter presumably sang about poaching in the same way as they did about being Gipsies or shepherdesses. The repeated line 'For it's my delight on a shiny night in the season of the year' was particularly well known, and became almost proverbial.

William Chappell commented, 'This song is rather *too* well known among the peasantry. A friend informed me, twenty years ago, that he had heard it sung by several hundred voices together, at Windsor, on the occasion of one of the harvest-homes of King George IV' (*Popular Music of the Olden Time* (1859), p. 732). But Alfred Williams implied that by 1918 it was more 'known' than sung at village level: 'This was once very popular. It is to be met with in most collections of folk-songs. I had known part of it from childhood, and heard it spoken of in many places, but I was a long time in finding one who really included it in his list of "live" songs' (*Folk-Songs of the Upper Thames* (1923), p. 175). Versions are often localized in the first verse – Lincolnshire is the most common, but Gloucestershire, Yorkshire, Somersetshire and others are also found.

For such a well-known song, its origin is strangely obscure. Sabine Baring-Gould (*English Minstrelsie*, III (1895), p. ii) states that it was William Thomas Moncrieff who introduced the song to public notice. He quotes from that author's *Original Collection of Songs* (1850): 'The writer first heard the old part of this song sung at a small road-side public-house in the little village of Lillishal, Warwickshire and was so pleased with the humour of it, that he was induced to add half-a-dozen new verses to it.' He presumably meant Lillishall, in Shropshire. Moncrieff (1794–1857) was a major force in the London theatrical world for many years. He wrote over 200 dramatic pieces, and his speciality was adapting current novels for the stage, but many of his dramas were too ephemeral to have been published. He also produced poems, guidebooks and countless other written works, and was a theatre manager and general theatrical fixer. He was certainly in just the right position to introduce a new hit song.

The song was extremely widely disseminated on broadsides and in more substantial songsters during the nineteenth century. These publications are rarely dated, but the song collection called *The Evergreen*, printed by James Catnach, was already in print when he issued his catalogue in 1832, and the song there is described as 'sung by Mr Richards'. In the *London Vocalist* (*c.*1840) it is described as 'A Celebrated comic song, sung by Mr Howell, at the Surrey Rotunda'.

Given these scraps of information, if Moncrieff's claim is correct, he probably launched his 'new' song in the late 1820s, and it must have been clear to everyone of his generation that it was a 'playhouse' song – which makes it particularly puzzling that William Chappell, the most knowledgeable of the song antiquarians of his generation, should include the song in his section entitled 'Traditional songs of uncertain date', as if he were unaware of its provenance. Added to this, in *Ballads and Songs of the Peasantry of England* (1857), Robert Bell's revision of James Dixon's work, the editor clearly states that the oldest copy he had seen was printed at York and dated from about 1776.

Perhaps this was the original on which Moncrieff worked his magic, or perhaps he was claiming credit that was not his due. Either way, there is clearly much more to be learnt about 'The Lincolnshire Poacher'.

A final repeat mark is given in the Clive Carey manuscript, along with a note that reads, 'This does not indicate which portion of the tune is to be repeated; probably the final 4 bars.' This is how the repeat has been interpreted here.

139 *The Lost Lady Found*

Sung by Mrs Hill of Stamford, Lincolnshire (1893); published in Lucy
Broadwood, *English Traditional Songs and Carols* (1908), pp. 86–91. Lucy
Broadwood noted, 'Mrs Hill, an old family nurse, and a native of Stamford,
learned her delightful song when a child, from an old cook who danced as
she sang it, beating time on the old kitchen-floor with her iron pattens.'
Roud 901, Laws Q31; 43 entries.

The song's story does not quite ring true. The woman who is abducted by the Gipsies is not a child but an adult, and seems to have made no effort to free herself, find her way home, or tell anyone in Dublin of her plight. But this does not appear to have worried the singers, and its popularity is indicated by the number of times it was collected. Many broadside printers, from about the 1820s onwards, included it in their stock, with very similar texts, and Lucy Broadwood has clearly completed Mrs Hill's text from a sheet printed by Such, of London.

Several different tunes are sung to this song and even similar tunes show variety in their length, structure, mode, tonality and range, although all seem to be in triple time. Mrs Hill's melody has an AA'BA phrase structure, authentic range and is Dorian. Lucy Broadwood notes that 'the tune should be compared with that of "The Lament of the Duchess of Gloucester" (words modern), in Gill's *Manx National Songs* (Boosey & Co.), and with certain Dorian versions of "Green Bushes"' (*English Traditional Songs and Carols* (1908), p. 123).

140 *The Poor Smuggler's Boy*

'The Orphan Boy', sung by Jack Barnard, Bridgwater, Somerset (16 April 1906); collected by Cecil Sharp (Sharp MSS, FW 963–4, FT 93). We have taken the liberty of tidying up the tenses of some of the verbs in Mr Barnard's rendering to make a little more literal sense of the story.
Roud 618; 18 entries.

The song was quite widely known in England, but not, apparently, elsewhere. The theme of a poor boy or girl (usually an orphan) begging in the street and being taken in by a kind lady or gentleman was clearly a popular one in nineteenth-century England, and several songs were devoted to the subject, including 'The Farmer's Boy' (No. 94) and 'The Poor Fisherman's Boy' (Roud 912). In 'The Poor Smuggler's Boy' the father's calling seems to be no obstacle to our pity, presumably because smuggling, like poaching, was widely thought of as no crime at all.

The song was also popular on broadsides from about 1830 onwards, and often had a chorus:

'Oh pity I crave, or give me employ
For alone I must wander,' cried the poor smuggler's boy.

Jack Barnard's tune contains echoes of 'Flash Company' (No. 80). The final note of bar 11 is unclear in the manuscript and may be an E rather than a D as given here.

141 *The Sheffield Apprentice*

'Died for Love of You', sung by Charles Pottipher, Ingrave, Essex (4 December 1903); collected by Ralph Vaughan Williams (VW MSS, British Library 54188, 4 to 1 MS bk, p. 8).
Roud 399, Laws O39; 31 entries.

This was clearly a popular song, with numerous versions appearing in the major English collections, although it was not so often published by the collectors; it was also well known in Scotland and in North America.

In the world of traditional song, love across class lines is relatively common, and although it rarely runs smooth it usually has a happy ending. But where the love (or lust) is unreciprocated, it is almost always the higher-class character who turns out to be bad – such as the squire in 'The Banks of the Sweet Dundee' (No. 58) – and the 'lady' in 'The Sheffield Apprentice' runs true to form.

The song was widely printed on broadsides, with the earliest dating from the 1790s, and traditional texts follow the broadsides closely.

142 Thorneymoor Woods

Sung by Sam Bennett, Ilmington, Warwickshire (23 August 1909); collected by Cecil Sharp (Sharp MSS, FW 2114–18/ FT 2320); also collected from the same singer by James Madison Carpenter (early 1930s) (Carpenter MSS, pp. 00569–70, 00573).
Roud 222; 28 entries.

One of the most widespread of poaching songs. The spelling of the locality in which the song is set naturally varies considerably from version to version, but there are two main contenders in the real world. One is Thorney Wood Chase, near Nottingham, and the other Thornehagh Moor Woods, near Newark. Roy Palmer, who knows more about such things than most, plumps for the latter (*Everyman's Book of English Country Songs* (1979), pp. 96–7).

It is not usual for poachers in songs to be let off by the magistrates, and it is perhaps this incident which led to the unlikely notion, reported by James Henry Dixon in his *Ancient Poems* (1846): 'There is a prevalent idea that the song is not the production of an ordinary ballad-writer but was written by a gentleman of rank and education, who, detesting the English game-laws, adopted a too successful mode of inspiring the peasantry with a love of poaching.'

The song is sometimes assumed to be of late eighteenth-century origin, but the earliest broadsides so far found date only from around 1800. Most of the later printers also issued versions, but it was already in oral circulation by the early 1840s, being collected by John Broadwood's *Old English Songs* in 1843 as well included in Dixon's *Ancient Poems*.

143 Three Butchers

'Two Jolly Butchers', sung by Walter Pardon, Knapton, Norfolk (1975); recorded by Mike Yates; issued on *A World Without Horses*, Topic TSCD514 (2000).
Roud 17, Laws L4; 43 entries.

'Three Butchers' was a very widely known and popular song in England, Scotland and North America, and most of the major collections include versions. Details vary: there may be two or three butchers, sometimes they are 'merry', sometimes 'jolly', and occasionally they are 'sportsmen' or 'huntsmen' rather than butchers. Their names also vary somewhat, Ips and Gips, for example, or Wilson and Gibson, but the hero is almost always called Johnson.

The song has lasted well for at least 300 years. Several black-letter broadsides from the late seventeenth century have survived, dating from as early as 1672, and one of them is signed by its author, Paul Burges. But although the different printings tell basically the same story, there are significant differences and they are clearly not simply copied from each other. In one, for example, after attacking Johnson from behind, the treacherous woman cold-bloodedly murders his two companions (who had been tied up by the robbers) and then all the surviving villains avoid justice by taking ship and going abroad.

Most of the nineteenth-century broadside printers also offered this song for sale, but, as is usually the case, these versions are much shorter and textually tighter. There is no real trace of the seventeenth century in the wording of the collected traditional renditions, which are clearly derived from the later sheets.

Walter Pardon sings the final phrase more slowly than the other phrases, sometimes close to half speed. In general, his tempo and metre are quite elastic so the rhythm as transcribed is somewhat approximate.

144 *The Undaunted Female*

Sung by Mrs Philip Castle, West Adderbury, Oxfordshire, (1915); collected
by Janet Blunt (Blunt MSS, JHB/1/8). First verse taken from version sung
by Henry Potter, Standlake, Oxfordshire (*c.*1918); collected by Alfred
Williams; published in Williams's *Folk-Songs of the Upper Thames* (1923), pp.
280–81.
Roud 289, Laws L3; 53 entries.

Mrs Castle's song is perfectly good as it is, but it does lack the introductory verse which most versions start with. We have inserted the first verse from another Oxfordshire version, but it is not strictly necessary. Alfred Williams commented about this song: 'Formerly a very special favourite in the Vale [of the White Horse] I have been offered it at least twelve times.'

Often called 'The Box on Her Head', this is one of several songs which started life as a long broadside ballad in the mid eighteenth century – in this case called 'The Staffordshire Maid', 'The Staffordshire Maid's Garland' or, in *The Swimming Lady's Garland*, 'The Jolly Young Stratford Maid' – which were cut down to manageable size, for the broadside trade, sometime around the turn of the nineteenth century. There are several copies of the eighteenth-century original in the Bodleian and Madden broadside collections, along with many sheets with the shorter text, with words very similar to Mrs Castle's.

Mrs Castle's tune is that found with 'The Banks of the Sweet Dundee' (No. 58).

145 *Van Diemen's Land*

'The Gallant Poachers', sung by Henry Burstow, Horsham, Sussex (1893);
collected by Lucy Broadwood (Broadwood MSS, LEB/2/11); published in
JFSS, 1:4 (1902), pp. 142–3.
Roud 519, Laws L18; 21 entries.

There are many songs about poaching in the English tradition, but of the songs that
focus on the punishment, this is the most widespread. Transportation to the colonies
had been regularly used as a legal punishment since the seventeenth century, but the
American Revolution forced the British authorities to find another destination. The
First Fleet departed for Australia in 1787, and from then until 1868 about 162,000
convicts were shipped there. The scene where this song is set is the notorious Van
Diemen's Land (Tasmania) colony, which was founded in 1803.

In the *Folk Music Journal*, 3:2 (1976), Roy Palmer argues persuasively that this song
was probably written and first printed in or soon after 1828, when the already tough
Game Laws were further tightened and it was decreed that if three men were found in
a wood, and one of them carried a gun or bludgeon, all were liable to be transported
for fourteen years. Two high-profile trials of poachers, which bear some resemblance
to the circumstances reported in the song, took place in Warwickshire in 1829, and
it is feasible that the author consciously drew on these. But the author was clearly
not writing from experience, unless the 'tigers' in verse 3 is simply poetic licence.

The song was widely disseminated on broadsides and was certainly in print by
1832, as it was listed in the catalogue of songs available from the London printer
James Catnach in that year.

Many of the tunes to which 'Van Diemen's Land' is sung resemble each other.
Like Henry Burstow's melody, they tend to be in a minor tonality with natural
third and seventh degrees (Dorian mode). An exception to this is Mr Broomfield's
melody, as noted by Ralph Vaughan Williams, which is a major form of the tune.

A feature of Burstow's melody is the distinctive cadence on the seventh degree
of the scale in the penultimate phrase. This results in the form ABB'A, cadencing
on the first, fifth, seventh and first degrees. Mr Broomfield's major version does
likewise. The third-phrase cadence is also found in Marina Russell's tune, collected
by H. E. D. Hammond (Hammond MSS, HMA/5/33/45), which is in many ways
parallel to Burstow's but with the first two phrases in reverse order. Harry Cox sings
another tune which resembles that of Burstow but with a straight ABBA structure,
thus cadencing 1, 5, 5, 1 (Ewan MacColl and Peggy Seeger, *The Singing Island* (1960);
compare Collinson (Collinson MSS, COL/6/86); see also the commentary on 'The
Banks of the Sweet Dundee', No. 58). Benjamin Arnold's tune flattens the sixth
(Aeolian mode) and demonstrates yet another shaping of this same melodic material. It comprises the structure BBBA in terms of Burstow's melody, prompting

George B. Gardiner to comment 'the tunes are similar towards the end' (Gardiner MSS, GG/1/11/637). George Petrie refers to a 6/8 ABBA variant of this tune as 'a Donegal melody' which he acquired from William Allingham (*The Complete Collection of Irish Music* (1902–5), no. 808).

146 Wild and Wicked Youth

'The High-Way Man', sung by James Townsend, Holne, Devon (May 1890); collected by Sabine Baring-Gould (Baring Gould MSS, SBG 1/2/153).
Roud 490, Laws L12; 36 entries.

A widely known song in England and North America, but much rarer in Scotland and Ireland, this song goes under a variety of titles, including 'Adieu Adieu', 'The Flash Lad', 'The Highwayman's Fate' and 'The Robber'. Although the verbal details of the song vary considerably, the core story of the young man's descent into criminality and his final regretful fate remains the same from version to version, and is typical of a type of song which is often termed a 'goodnight ballad'. These ballads are closely related to the 'Last Dying Speeches' of the broadside presses, which purported to be the actual confessions of particular convicted criminals, and have prompted some writers to assume that there are real-life criminals behind these songs, but there is no evidence of that.

James Townsend's version lacks the first verse found in most of them, which usually goes something like this:

> *In Newry Town I was bred and born*
> *In Stephen's Green I died with scorn*
> *I served my time to the saddling trade*
> *And always was a roving blade.*

Although the place in the first line varies considerably, including Dublin, Norwich, Kerry, Newbury and London.

Commentary on this song has been skewed by claims that it refers to an Irish highwayman called Charles Reilly, but this stems largely from a misreading of earlier writings which were concerned with tunes, and extrapolating these on to the texts. John Moulden, the leading expert on Irish traditional songs and their broadside manifestations, can find no Charles Reilly and, indeed, believes that the evidence points to the song being of English origin (private communication).

Confusion is further compounded by the appearance of Irish place names in many versions of the song, but these are usually followed by London landmarks, such as Grosvenor Square and Covent Garden, and again it is clear that although the young man is portrayed as an Irishman, the song takes place on this side of the Irish Sea. Nevertheless, the two earliest known printed texts were both produced in

Ireland and date from the 1780s and 1790s, and it was subsequently issued by all the major English printers in the nineteenth century.

X
What Is the Life of a Man ...
Traditional Religious Songs

147 *The Cherry-Tree Carol*

First verse and tune sung by Mary Anne Clayton, Chipping Campden, Gloucestershire (13 January 1909); collected by Cecil Sharp (Sharp MSS, FT 2069). The rest of the text taken from version sung by Anne Roberts, Winchcombe, Gloucestershire; collected by Sharp (Sharp MSS, FW 2018/FT 2151). Published in this composite form in Sharp's *English Folk Carols* (1911).
Roud 453, Child 54; 21 entries.

'The Cherry-Tree Carol', often called 'When Joseph Was an Old Man', was extremely well known in England and also very popular in North America, but not collected often in Ireland or Scotland. Francis J. Child printed four texts, and Bertrand Bronson gives thirty-two versions with tunes.

The incident of Mary and the fig tree was first recorded in the Gospel of Pseudo-Matthew, one of the New Testament Apocrypha texts written to fill out the details of Christ's early life, which was probably compiled about AD 600. The story was already in circulation in England in the late fourteenth century as it is featured in the Mystery play from Coventry, with the tree being localized as a cherry. On present evidence, however, our song dates only from the later eighteenth century, when it started to appear on broadsides and in printed garlands. Child also gives references to the story as it appeared in songs and tales on the Continent.

Tunes for this carol have been collected in oral tradition since the early nineteenth century and are broadly similar, with a few exceptions. Mary Anne Clayton's tune is an example of what Bronson regarded as the core melodic tradition. It is in triple time and has the distinctive first-half rhythm, found in many of the 'Cherry-Tree Carol' tunes, which echoes that of another popular and long-lived song, 'Love Will Find Out the Way' (see William Chappell, *Popular Music of the Olden Time* (1859), I, pp. 305–6). Unlike the latter, the carol tune is plagal in range, often cadencing on the second or fifth degree midway through. Mary Anne Clayton's tune is unusual in cadencing on the fourth, and also in having a refrain created by repeating the second two lines of text and, with a slight change, tune.

148 The Joys of Mary

'The Nine Joys of Mary', sung by James Thomas, Camborne, Cornwall
(August 1915); collected by T. Miners and H. E. Piggott; published in *JFSS*,
5 (1916), 319–320.
Roud 278; 25 entries.

One of the most popular religious folk songs in England, it was also collected in
Ireland, but not, it seems, in Scotland. It was also widely known in North America.

'The five joys of Mary' were popular in medieval Roman Catholic devotional
art and literature, and symbolized the 'joyous' events in Christ's life: Annuncia-
tion, Nativity, Adoration, Resurrection and Ascension. They were later extended
to seven, nine or even twelve, and there were also the 'seven sorrows of Mary' for
more sombre occasions.

The popularity of the theme in medieval and early modern England is attested by
a number of literary references, including the famous fourteenth-century poem *Sir
Gawain and the Green Knight*. In this, the pentangle on Gawain's shield is explained in
terms of his five senses, five fingers, the five wounds of Christ, and 'when he fought
his courage came from the five joys the high Queen of Heaven had of her child' (Part
2, sections 27–8). In a selection of Christmas carols in the manuscript known as *Richard
Hill's Commonplace Book*, compiled in the first quarter of the sixteenth century but
probably copied from an earlier written source, another song on the theme appears,
which starts 'Mary, for the love of thee' and continues through the five joys:

> *The fyrst joy was sent to thee*
> *Whan Gabryell gretyed thee*
> *And sayd 'Hayle, Marye, in chastite!*
> *Officiaris gravida.'*

But although the underlying theme and structure is medieval, this is not to argue
that our current song is quite that old. It is most likely to have been written much
more recently, based on the earlier traditions or drawn from contemporary Catholic
belief elsewhere. Our first record of the song is in 1764, as 'The First Good Joy Our
Mary Had', which was one of the Christmas carols included in the catalogue of the
printers Dicey and Marshall, of Aldermary Churchyard, London, issued in that year.
'The Joys of Mary' continued to be popular on nineteenth-century broadsides, both
as an ordinary sheet and also on the special extra-illustrated large format collections
of carols printed each year for the season.

149 The Life of a Man

Sung by George Townshend, Lewes, Sussex (7 February 1960); recorded by

Brian Matthews; issued on *Come Hand to Me the Glass*, Musical Traditions
MTCD304 (2000).
Roud 848; 27 entries.

Regularly collected in England, and mostly in the southern half of the country, this
song does not seem to have been popular anywhere else, apart from Canada, where
a couple of versions have been reported.

It may not be the thing nowadays to go around reminding people of their inevitable end, but our Victorian ancestors did not shrink from dwelling on death, and all
brands of religion of the time included plenty of reminders. As many commentators
have pointed out, the comparison of human life to flowers or trees is at least as old
as Homer and the Bible, and is homely enough to appeal particularly to rural folk.

The song appeared on plenty of broadsides, usually under the title of 'The Fall of
the Leaf', and surviving prints date perhaps from about 1810 onwards. The broadside
texts tend to be longer and more stiffly formal, and the versions collected from singers have definitely been improved by having the corners knocked off over the years.

The upbeat to stanza 1 is sung as an E in this rendition but has here been changed
to a D in line with the later verses. The singing style is very deliberate and slow in
this performance, with additional slowing down on the final line of the chorus.

150 *The Moon Shines Bright*

Sung by Emily Bishop, Bromsberrow Heath, Herefordshire (13 October
1952); recorded by Peter Kennedy (BBC 18685).
Roud 702; 32 entries.

One of the most popular of 'folk carols', 'The Moon Shines Bright' was a particular
favourite with parties of both Christmas and May Day carollers, and even when it
entered the mainstream official carol literature it still retained this link with institu-
tional singing. In William Henry Husk's *Songs of the Nativity* (1868), for example, it
is entitled 'The Bellman's Song', which the author explains: 'The functionary known
in bygone times as the Bellman was a kind of nightwatchman, who, in addition to
his staff and lantern, carried a bell, and at a certain period of the year was wont to
arouse the slumbering inhabitants of the town to listen to some such effusion as [this]'
(p. 62). In Henry Ramsden Bramley and John Stainer's *Christmas Carols New and Old*
(1871) it is 'The Waits Song'. The Waits had previously been musicians on the munic-
ipal payroll of particular towns, but by the nineteenth century were more usually
semi-official carollers active at Christmas.

The song appeared regularly on broadsides issued each year specifically for the
Christmas market, from the late eighteenth century onwards.

151 *A Virgin Unspotted*

Sung by Emily Bishop, Bromsberrow Heath, Herefordshire (13 October 1952); recorded by Peter Kennedy (BBC 18684).
Roud 1378; 26 entries.

Frank Kidson commented that 'This carol appears to have been popular, at one time, in almost every English county. Gentility has in some cases altered the term "unspotted" to "most pure", but otherwise the words have generally adhered to an accepted version pretty closely' (*JFSS*, 5 (1916), 324).

It was printed at various times in the eighteenth and nineteenth centuries on broadsides, chapbooks and collections of carols, but the earliest version of the words appears to be in *New Carolls for this Merry time of Christmas* (London, 1661) in the Bodleian Library.

Bibliography

Abrahams, Roger D., and George Foss, *Anglo-American Folksong Style* (Englewood Cliffs, NJ: Prentice-Hall, 1968).

Adkins, Roy and Lesley, *Jack Tar: The Extraordinary Lives of Ordinary Seamen in Nelson's Navy* (London: Little, Brown, 2008).

Andersen, Flemming G., *Commonplace and Creativity: The Role of Formulaic Diction in Anglo-Scottish Traditional Balladry* (Odense: Odense University Press, 1985).

Anderson, Hugh, *Farewell to Judges and Juries: The Broadside Ballad and Convict Transportation to Australia 1788–1868* (Victoria: Red Rooster, 2000).

Ashton, John, *A Century of Ballads* (London: Elliot Stock, 1887).

———, *Modern Street Ballads* (London: Chatto & Windus, 1888).

———, *Real Sailor-Songs* (London: Leadenhall Press, 1891).

Atkinson, David, 'History, Symbol, and Meaning in The Cruel Mother', *Folk Music Journal*, 6:3 (1992), 359–80.

———, 'The Wit Combat Episode in The Unquiet Grave', *Lore & Language*, 12 (1994), 11–30.

———, *The English Traditional Ballad: Theory, Method and Practice* (Aldershot: Ashgate, 2002).

An Authentick Narration of all the Occurrences in a Voyage to Greenland in the Year 1722 (Durham: G. Sowler, c.1772).

Banfield, Stephen and Russell, Ian, 'England (i)', 23 November 2011, Grove Music Online/ Oxford Music Online, http://www.oxfordmusiconline.com/subscriber/article/grove/music/40044.

Baring-Gould, Sabine, *A Garland of Country Song* (London: Methuen, 1895).

———, *English Minstrelsie*, 10 vols. (Edinburgh: Jack, 1895–6).

———, *Songs of the West*, revised edn (London: Methuen, 1905).

Baring-Gould, Sabine, and Cecil J. Sharp, *English Folk-Songs for Schools* (London: Curwen, 1906).

Barrett, William Alexander, *English Folk-Songs* (London: Novello, 1891).

Bearman, C. J., 'Who Were the Folk? The Demography of Cecil Sharp's Somerset Folk Singers', *Historical Journal*, 43:3 (2000), 751–75.

———, 'Cecil Sharp in Somerset: Some Reflections on the Work of David Harker', *Folklore*, 113 (2002), 11–34.

———, 'Percy Grainger, the Phonograph, and the Folk Song Society', *Music & Letters*, 84:3 (2003), 434–55.

Bell, John, *Rhymes of the Northern Bards* (Newcastle: J. Bell, 1812).

Bell, Robert, *Early Ballads Illustrative of History, Traditions and Customs* (London: Parker, 1856).

Bohlman, Philip V., *The Study of Folk Music in the Modern World* (Bloomington, IN: Indiana University Press, 1988).

Boyes, Georgina, *The Imagined Village: Culture, Ideology and the English Folk Revival*, revised edn (Leeds: No Masters Co-operative, 2010).

Bramley, Henry Ramsden, and John Stainer, *Christmas Carols New and Old* (London: Novello, 1871).

Bratton, J. S., *The Victorian Popular Ballad* (London: Macmillan, 1975).

British Film Institute, *Here's a Health to the Barley Mow*, 3 DVD set (London: BFI, 2011)

Broadwood, John, *Old English Songs* (London: Balls & Co., 1847).

Broadwood, Lucy, *English County Songs as now Sung by the Peasantry of the Weald of Surrey and Sussex* (London: Cramer, 1893).

——, *English Traditional Songs and Carols* (London: Boosey, 1908).

Bronson, Bertrand Harris, *The Traditional Tunes of the Child Ballads*, 4 vols. (Princeton, NJ: Princeton University Press, 1959–1972).

——, *The Ballad as Song* (Berkeley, CA: University of California Press, 1969).

Brown, Mary Ellen, *Child's Unfinished Masterpiece: The English and Scottish Popular Ballads* (Urbana, IL: University of Illinois Press, 2011).

Brown, Roly, 'Glimpses into the 19th Century Broadside Trade', ongoing series of articles on Musical Traditions website, www.mustrad.org.uk.

Bruce, J. Collingwood, and John Stokoe, *Northumbrian Minstrelsy* (Newcastle: Society of Antiquaries, 1882).

Buchan, David, and James Moreira, *The Glenbuchat Ballads* (Jackson, MS: University Press of Mississippi, 2007).

Burne, Charlotte, *Shropshire Folk-Lore* (London: Trubner, 1883).

Burstow, Henry, *Reminiscences of Horsham* (Horsham: Free Christian Church Book Society, 1911).

Butterworth, George, *Folk Songs from Sussex* (London: Augener, 1913).

Carey, Clive, *Ten English Folk-Songs* (London: Curwen, 1915).

Carey, George G., *A Sailor's Songbag: An American Rebel in an English Prison 1777–1779* (Amherst, MA: University of Massachusetts Press, 1976).

Cazden, Norman, Herbert Haufrecht and Norman Studer, *Folk Songs of the Catskills* (Albany, NY: State University of New York Press, 1982).

Chappell, William, *The Ballad Literature and Popular Music of the Olden Time* (London: Chappell, 1859).

Child, Francis J. *The English and Scottish Popular Ballads*, 5 vols. (Boston: Houghton Mifflin, 1882–1898).

Clay, W. K., *Four Folk Songs from Hartlebury, Worcestershire* (no publisher, 1908?).

Coke, David, and Alan Borg, *Vauxhall Gardens: A History* (New Haven, CT: Yale University Press, 2011).

Collinson, Francis, and Dillon, Francis, *Songs from the Countryside* (London: Paxton, 1946).

——, *Folk Songs from Country Magazine* (London: Paxton, 1952).

Collinson, Robert, *The Story of Street Literature: Forerunner of the Popular Press* (London: Dent, 1973).

Colls, Robert, *The Collier's Rant: Song and Culture in the Industrial Village* (London: Croom Helm, 1977).

Copper, Bob, *A Song for Every Season: A Hundred Years of a Sussex Farming Family* (London: Heinemann, 1971).

——, *Songs and Southern Breezes* (London: Heinemann, 1973).

——, *Early to Rise: A Sussex Childhood* (London: Heinemann, 1976).

Cowdell, Paul, 'Cannibal Ballads: Not Just a Question of Taste', *Folk Music Journal* 9:5 (2010), 723–47.

Cowdery, James R., 'A Fresh Look at the Concept of Tune Family', *Ethnomusicology*, 28:3 (1984), 495–504.

Cray, Ed, *The Erotic Muse: American Bawdy Songs*, 2nd edn (Urbana, IL: University of Illinois Press, 1992).

Cubbin, Sue, *That Precious Legacy: Ralph Vaughan Williams and Essex Folksong* (Chelmsford: Essex Record Office, 2006).

Davidson's Universal Melodist (London: G. H. Davidson, 1848).

Davies, Gwilym, *Grainger in Gloucestershire* (Cheltenham: The Author, 1994).

Davies, R. T., *Medieval English Lyrics: A Critical Anthology* (London: Faber and Faber, 1963).

de Val, Dorothy, *In Search of Song: The Life and Times of Lucy Broadwood* (Aldershot: Ashgate, 2011).

Dawney, Michael, *Doon the Wagon Way: Mining Songs from the North of England* (London: Galliard, 1973).

——, *The Iron Man: English Occupational Songs* (London: Galliard, 1974).

——, *The Ploughboy's Glory: A Selection of Hitherto Unpublished Folk Songs Collected by George Butterworth* (London: English Folk Dance and Song Society, 1977).

Deacon, George, *John Clare and the Folk Tradition* (London: Sinclair Browne, 1983).

Dearmer, Percy, Ralph Vaughan Williams and Martin Shaw, *The Oxford Book of Carols* (Oxford: Oxford University Press, 1928).

Dearnley, Dorothy, *Seven Cheshire Folk-Songs* (London: Oxford University Press, 1967).

Dhu McLucas, Anne, *The Musical Ear: Oral Tradition in the USA* (Farnham: Ashgate, 2009).

Dillon, Francis (ed.), *Country Magazine: The Book of the BBC Programme* (London: Odhams, 1949).

Dixon, James Henry, *Ancient Poems* (London: Percy Society, 1846).

Dixon, James Henry, and Robert Bell, *Ballads and Songs of the Peasantry of England* (London: Parker, 1857).

Downing, Sarah Jane, *The English Pleasure Garden* (Oxford: Shire, 2009).

Dugaw, Dianne, *Warrior Women and Popular Balladry 1650–1850* (Cambridge: Cambridge University Press, 1989).

Dunn, Ginette, *The Fellowship of Song: Popular Singing Traditions in East Suffolk* (London: Croom Helm, 1980).

Dunstan, Ralph, *The Cornish Song Book* (London: Ascherberg, Hopwood & Crew, 1929).

——, *Cornish Dialect and Folk Songs* (London: Ascherberg, Hopwood & Crew, 1932).

D'Urfey, Thomas, *Wit and Mirth; or, Pills to Purge Melancholy* (London: F. Tonson, 1719–20).

Flanders, Judith, *The Invention of Murder: How the Victorians Revelled in Death and Detection and Created Modern Crime* (London: Harper Press, 2011).

Folk Music Journal (FMJ) (1965 to date) (English Folk Dance and Song Society).

Friedman, Albert B., *The Ballad Revival: Studies in the Influence of Popular on Sophisticated Poetry* (Chicago: University of Chicago Press, 1961).

Gammer Gurton's Garland, or The Nursery Parnassus (London: R. Triphook, 1810).

Gammon, Vic, 'Folk Song Collecting in Sussex and Surrey, 1843–1914', *History Workshop Journal* 10 (1980), 61–89.

——, 'Babylonian Performances: The Rise and Suppression of Popular Church Music, 1660–1870', in *Popular Culture and Class Conflict, 1590–1914*, ed. Eileen and Stephen Yeo (Brighton: Harvester, 1981).

——, 'Not Appreciated in Worthing? Class Expression and Popular Song Texts in Mid-19th Century Britain', *Popular Music*, 4 (1984), 5–24.

——, 'Singing and Popular Funeral Practices in the Eighteenth and Nineteenth Centuries', *Folk Music Journal*, 5:4 (1988), 412–47.

——, 'Grand Conversation: Napoleon and British Popular Balladry', *RSA Journal*, 137 (1989), 665–73.

——, *Desire, Drink and Death in English Folk and Vernacular Song 1600–1900* (Aldershot: Ashgate, 2008).

Gardham, Steve, *An East Riding Songster* (Lincoln: Lincolnshire and Humberside Arts, 1982).

Gardiner, George B., *Folk Songs from Hampshire* (London: Novello, 1909).

Gerould, Gordon Hall, *The Ballad of Tradition* (Oxford: Clarendon Press, 1932).

Gilbert, Davies, *Some Ancient Christmas Carols*, 2nd edn (London: Nichols, 1823).

Gilbert, Douglas, *Lost Chords: The Diverting Story of American Popular Songs* (New York: Doubleday, 1942).

Gilchrist, Anne, 'Lambkin: A Study in Evolution', *JEFDSS*, 1 (1932), 1–17.

Gillington, Alice E., *Eight Hampshire Folk Songs* (London: Curwen, 1907).

——, *Old Christmas Carols of the Southern Counties* (London: Curwen, 1910).

——, *Songs of the Open Road* (London: Joseph Williams, 1911).

Gomme, Alice Bertha, *The Traditional Games of England, Scotland, and Ireland*, 2 vols. (London: David Nutt, 1894/1898).

Grainger, Percy, 'Collecting with the Phonograph', *Journal of the Folk-Song Society*, 3 (1908), 147–69.

Greene, Richard Leighton, *The Early English Carols* (Oxford: Clarendon Press, 1935).

Gregory, E. David, *Victorian Songhunters: The Recovery and Editing of English Vernacular Ballads and Folk Lyrics 1820–1883* (Lanham, MD: Scarecrow Press, 2006).

——, 'Fakesong in an Imagined Village? A Critique of the Harker-Boyes Thesis', *Canadian Folk Music*, 43:3 (Fall 2009), 18–26.

——, *The Late Victorian Folksong Revival: The Persistence of English Melody 1878–1903* (Lanham, MD: Scarecrow Press, 2010).

Gregson, Keith, *Cumbrian Songs and Ballads* (Clapham: Dalesman, 1980).

Haggard, Lilias Rider (ed.), *I Walked by Night: Being the Life and History of the King of the Norfolk Poachers* (London: Nicholson & Watson, 1935).

Halliwell, James Orchard, *The Nursery Rhymes of England* (London: Percy Society, 1842; and later editions).

——, *Popular Rhymes and Nursery Tales of England* (London: John Russell Smith, 1849; and later editions).

Hamer, Fred, *Garners Gay: English Folk Songs* (London: EFDS Publications, 1967).

——, *Green Groves: More English Folk Songs* (London: EFDS Publications, 1973).

Hammond, H. E. D., *Folk Songs from Dorset* (London: Novello, 1908).

Harker, Dave, *Fakesong: The Manufacture of British 'Folksong' 1700 to the Present Day* (Milton Keynes: Open University Press, 1985).

Harker, D. I., *Songs from the Manuscript Collection of John Bell* (Gateshead: Surtees Society, 1999), vol. 196.

——, *Songs and Verse of the North-East Pitmen c.1780–1844* (Gateshead: Surtees Society, 1999), vol. 204.

Harland, John, *Ballads and Songs of Lancashire* (London: Whittaker, 1865).

Harman, H., *Sketches of the Bucks Countryside* (London, Blandford, 1934).

Hecht, Hans, *Songs from David Herd's Manuscript* (Edinburgh: William J. Hay, 1904).

Hepburn, James, *A Book of Scattered Leaves: Poetry and Poverty in Broadside Ballads of 19th Century England* (Lewisburg, PA: Bucknell University Press, 2000).

Herd, David, *Ancient and Modern Scottish Songs, Heroic Ballads, etc.* (Edinburgh: Wotherspoon, 1776; new edn, Glasgow: Kerr & Richardson, 1869; Edinburgh: Scottish Academic Press, 1973).

Herzog, George, 'Song: Folk Song and the Music of Folk Song', in Maria Leach, *Funk and Wagnalls Standard Dictionary of Folklore, Mythology and Legend*, one-volume edn (New York, Harper & Row, 1984) pp. 1032–50.

Hewett, Sarah, *The Peasant Speech of Devon*, 2nd edn (London: Eliot Stock, 1892).

Hill, Geoffrey, *Wiltshire Folk Songs and Carols* (Bournemouth: W. Mate, 1904).

Hodgart, M. J. C., *The Ballads* (London: Hutchinson, 1950).

Hopkins, Harry, *The Long Affray: The Poaching Wars 1760–1914* (London: Secker & Warburg, 1985).

Horn, Pamela, *The Rise and Fall of the Victorian Servant* (London: Gill & Macmillan, 1975).

Hornby, John, *The Joyous Book of Singing Games* (London: E. J. Arnold, 1913).

Horsfall Turner, J., *A Yorkshire Anthology: Ballads and Songs, Ancient and Modern* (Bingley: The Author, 1901).

Howson, John, *Songs Sung in Suffolk* (Stowmarket: Veteran Tapes, 1992).

Howson, Kate, *Blyth Voices: Folk Songs Collected in Southwold by Ralph Vaughan Williams* (Stowmarket: East Anglian Traditional Music Trust, 2003).

Hudleston, Mary and Nigel Hudleston, *Songs of the Ridings: The Yorkshire Musical Museum* (Scarborough: G. A. Pindar, 2001).

Hugill, Stan, *Shanties from the Seven Seas* (London: Routledge & Kegan Paul, 1961).

Huntington, Gale, *Songs the Whalemen Sang* (Barre: Barre Publishers, 1964).

Husk, William Henry, *Songs of the Nativity* (London: John Camden Hotten, 1868).

Jewitt, Llewellyn, *The Ballads and Songs of Derbyshire* (London: Bemrose, 1867).

Johnson, James, *The Scots Musical Museum* (1787–1803; facsimile reprint, Aldershot: Scolar Press, 1991).

Joyce, P. W., *Old Irish Folk Music and Songs* (London: Longmans, Green, 1909).

Journal of the English Folk Dance and Song Society (JEFDSS) (1932–64).

Journal of the Folk-Song Society (JFSS) (1899–1932).

Journal of the Irish Folk Song Society (JIFSS) (1904–32).

Karpeles, Maud, *Cecil Sharp: His Life and Work* (London: Routledge & Kegan Paul, 1967).

——, *Cecil Sharp's Collection of English Folk Songs* (London: Oxford University Press, 1974).

Kennedy, Peter, *Folksongs of Britain and Ireland* (London: Cassell, 1975).

Kidson, Frank, *Traditional Tunes: A Collection of Ballad Airs* (Oxford: Chas. Taphouse, 1891).

——, *A Garland of English Folk-Songs* (London: Ascherberg, Hopwood & Crew, 1926).

Kidson, Frank, and Alfred Moffat, *English Peasant Songs* (London: Ascherberg, Hopwood & Crew, 1929).

Kidson, Frank, and Mary Neal, *English Folk-Song and Dance* (Cambridge: Cambridge University Press, 1915).

Kinloch, George Ritchie, *The Ballad Book* (Edinburgh: (no publisher), 1827).

Laffin, John, *Jack Tar: The Story of the British Sailor* (London: Cassell, 1969).

Lanham, Neil, *There's a Story that My Mother Told …* (Helions Bumpstead: Traditions of Suffolk, 2007).

Laws, G. Malcolm, *American Balladry from British Broadsides: A Guide for Students and Collectors of Traditional Song* (Philadelphia: American Folklore Society, 1957).

——, *Native American Balladry: A Descriptive Study and a Bibliographic Syllabus*, revised edn (Philadelphia: American Folklore Society, 1964).

Leach, MacEdward, and Tristram P. Coffin, *The Critics and the Ballad* (Carbondale: Southern Illinois University Press, 1961).

Leather, Ella M., *The Folk-Lore of Herefordshire* (Hereford: Jakeman & Carver, 1912).

Leather, Ella M., and Ralph Vaughan Williams, *Twelve Traditional Carols from Herefordshire* (London: Stainer & Bell, 1920).

Lloyd, A. L., *Folk Song in England* (London: Lawrence & Wishart, 1967).

——, *Come All Ye Bold Miners: Ballads and Songs of the Coalfields*, 2nd edn (London: Lawrence & Wishart, 1978).

Lloyd, Christopher, *English Corsairs on the Barbary Coast* (London: Collins, 1981).

Long, W. H., *The Dialect of the Isle of Wight* (London: Reeves & Turner, 1886).

Lyle, Emily, *Andrew Crawfurd's Collection of Ballads and Songs*, 2 vols. (Edinburgh: Scottish Text Society, 1975 and 1996).

Lyle, Thomas, *Ancient Ballads and Songs, Chiefly from Tradition, Manuscripts, and Scarce Works* (London: L. Relfe, 1827).

MacColl, Ewan, and Peggy Seeger, *The Singing Island* (London: Mills Music, 1960).

——, *Travellers' Songs from England and Scotland* (London: Routledge, 1977).

Maidment, James, *A North Countrie Garland* (Edinburgh, The Author, 1824).

Mason, M. H., *Nursery Rhymes and Country Songs* (1878; 2nd edn, London: Mezzler, 1908).

Mayhew, Henry, *London Labour and the London Poor* 4 vols. (London: Griffin, Bohn, 1861).

Merrick, W. P., *Folk Songs from Sussex* (London: Novello, 1912).

Moeran, E. J., *Six Folk Songs from Suffolk* (London: Augener, 1924).

——, *Six Suffolk Folk-Songs* (London: Curwen, 1932).

Moore, Thomas, *A Selection of Irish Melodies*, 10 vols. (Dublin: Power's Music and Instrument Warehouse, 1808–34; and countless later editions, usually entitled *Moore's Irish Melodies*).

Morrish, John, *The Folk Handbook: Working with Songs from the English Tradition* (New York: Backbeat, 2007).

Newell, William Wells, *Games and Songs of American Children*, 2nd edn (New York: Harper, 1903).

Northall, G. F., *English Folk-Ryhmes* (London: Kegan Paul, 1892).

O'Lochlainn, Colm, *Irish Street Ballads* (Dublin: Three Candles, 1939).

Opie, Iona, and Peter Opie, *The Oxford Dictionary of Nursery Rhymes* (Oxford: Oxford University Press, 1951).

——, *The Singing Game* (Oxford: Oxford University Press, 1985).

O'Shaughnessy, Patrick, *Seven Lincolnshire Folk Songs* (London: Oxford University Press, 1966).

——, *21 Lincolnshire Folk Songs* (London: Oxford University Press, 1968).

——, *More Folk Songs from Lincolnshire* (London: Oxford University Press, 1971).

——, *Yellowbelly Ballads*, 2 parts (Lincoln: Lincolnshire and Humberside Arts, 1975).

——, *Late Leaves from Lincolnshire* (Lincoln: Lincolnshire and Humberside Arts, 1980).

Palmer, Roy, *Songs of the Midlands* (East Ardsley: EP, 1972)

——, *A Touch on the Times: Songs of Social Change, 1770–1914* (Harmondsworth: Penguin, 1974).

——, *The Rambling Soldier: Life in the Lower Ranks, 1750–1900* (Harmondsworth: Penguin, 1977).

——, *Everyman's Book of English Country Songs* (London: Dent, 1979).

——, *Everyman's Book of British Ballads* (London: Dent, 1980).

——, *Folk Songs Collected by Ralph Vaughan Williams* (London: Dent, 1983).

——, *The Oxford Book of Sea Songs* (Oxford: Oxford University Press, 1986).

——, *The Sound of History: Songs and Social Comment* (Oxford: Oxford University Press, 1988).

——, *What a Lovely War: British Soldiers' Songs from the Boer War to the Present Day* (London: Michael Joseph, 1990).

——, *Boxing the Compass: Sea Songs and Shanties* (Todmorden: Herron, 2001); new edn of *The Oxford Book of Sea Songs*.

——, *Working Songs: Industrial Ballads and Poems from Britain and Ireland 1780s–1980s* (Todmorden: Herron, 2010).

Paton, Charlotte, *The King of the Norfolk Poachers: His Life and Times* (Ipswich: Old Pond, 2009).

Patten, Bob and Jacqueline, *Somerset Scrapbook* (Ina Books, 1987).

Petrie, George, *The Complete Collection of Irish Music*, ed. Charles Villiers Stanford (London: Boosey, 1902–5).

Pickering, Michael, *Village Song and Culture: A Study based on the Blunt Collection of Song from Adderbury, North Oxfordshire* (London: Croom Helm, 1982).

——, 'The Farmworker and The Farmer's Boy', *Lore and Language*, 3:9 (1983), 44–64.

——, *Blackface Minstrelsy in Britain* (Aldershot: Ashgate, 2008).

Pickering, Michael, and Tony Green, *Everyday Culture* (Milton Keynes: Open University Press, 1987).

Polwarth, Gwen, *Folk Songs of Northumberland* (Newcastle: Oriel Press, 1966).

Polwarth, Gwen, and Mary Polwarth, *North Country Songs* (Newcastle: Frank Graham, 1969).

——, *Folk Songs from the North* (Newcastle: Frank Graham, 1970).

Porter, James, *The Traditional Music of Britain and Ireland: A Research and Information Guide* (New York: Garland, 1989).

Purslow, Frank, *Marrow Bones: English Folk Songs from the Hammond and Gardiner Manuscripts* (London: EFDS Publications, 1965; revised edn edited by Malcolm Douglas and Steve Gardham, London: English Folk Dance and Song Society, 2007).

——, *The Wanton Seed: More English Folk Songs from the Hammond and Gardiner Manuscripts* (London: EFDS Publications, 1968).

——, *The Constant Lovers: More English Folk Songs from the Hammond and Gardiner Manuscripts* (London: EFDS Publications, 1972).

——, *The Foggy Dew: More English Folk Songs from the Hammond and Gardiner Manuscripts* (London: EFDS Publications, 1974).

Ramsay, Allan, *The Tea-Table Miscellany: A Collection of Scots Songs*, 4 vols. (Edinburgh, The Author, 1723–37).

Ravenscroft, Thomas, *Pammelia: Music's Miscellanie, or Mixed Varietie of Pleasant Roun-*

delayes and Delightfull Catches ... (London, 1609; reprinted, American Folklore Society, 1961).

——, *Deuteromelia, or the Second Part Musick's Melodie or Melodious Musicke of Pleasant Roundelaies* ... (London, 1609; reprinted, American Folklore Society, 1961).

——, *Melismata: Musical Phantasies Fitting the Court, Citie, and Countrey Humours* (London, 1611; reprinted, American Folklore Society, 1961).

Reeves, James, *Idiom of the People: English Traditional Verse from the MSS of Cecil Sharp* (London: Heinemann, 1958).

——, *The Everlasting Circle: English Traditional Verse* (London: Heinemann, 1960).

Renwick, Roger DeV., *English Folk Poetry: Structure and Meaning* (London: Batsford, 1980).

——, *Recentering Anglo/American Folksong: Sea Crabs and Wicked Youths* (Jackson, MS: University Press of Mississippi, 2001).

Reynardson, H. F. Birch, *Sussex Songs: Popular Songs of Sussex* (London: Stanley Lucas, Weber & Co. [1889]).

Richmond, W. Edson, *Ballad Scholarship: An Annotated Bibliography* (New York: Garland, 1989).

Richards, Sam, and Stubbs, Tish, *The English Folksinger* (London: Collins, 1979).

Rogers, Nicholas, *The Press Gang: Naval Impressment and Its Opponents in Georgian Britain* (London: Continuum, 2007).

Rollins, Hyder E., *A Pepysian Garland: Black-Letter Broadside Ballads of the Years 1595– 1639* (Cambridge, MA: Harvard University Press, 1922).

Roud, Steve, and Paul Smith, *Catalogue of Songs and Song Books Printed and Published by James Catnach, 1832* (West Stockwith: January Books, 1985).

Roud, Steve, Eddie Upton and Malcolm Taylor, *Still Growing: English Traditional Songs and Singers from the Cecil Sharp Collection* (London: English Folk Dance and Song Society, 2003).

Russell, Ian, *Singer, Song and Scholar* (Sheffield: Sheffield Academic Press, 1986).

——, 'Stability and Change in a Sheffield Singing Tradition', *Folk Music Journal*, 5:5 (1987), 317–58.

Sainsbury, A. B., *The Royal Navy Day by Day*, 2nd edn (Shepperton: Ian Allen, 1992).

Sandys, William, *Christmas Carols: Ancient and Modern* (London: Richard Beckley, 1833).

Seeger, Charles, 'Prescriptive and Descriptive Music-Writing', *Musical Quarterly*, 44 (1958), 184–95.

Seeger, Peggy, and Ewan MacColl, *The Singing Island: A Collection of English and Scots Folksongs* (London: Mills Music, n.d.).

Senelick, Lawrence, *Tavern Singing in Early Victorian London* (London: Society for Theatre Research, 1997).

Sharp, Cecil J., *Folk Songs from Somerset*, 5 vols. (London: Simpkin Marshall, 1904–9).

——, *English Folk-Song: Some Conclusions* (London: Simpkin, 1907).

——, *English Folk Carols* (London: Novello, 1911).

——, *One Hundred English Folk Songs* (Boston: Oliver Ditson, 1916).

——, *English Folk Songs* (London: Novello, 1920).

——, *English County Folk Songs* (London: Novello, 1961).

Shepard, Leslie, *The Broadside Ballad: A Study in Origins and Meaning* (London: Herbert Jenkins, 1962).

——, *John Pitts, Ballad Printer of Seven Dials, London* (London: Private Libraries Association, 1969).

Simpson, Claude M., *The British Broadside Ballad and Its Music* (New Brunswick: Rutgers University Press, 1966).

Smith, Audrey, *A Little Book of Northamptonshire Song* (Stroud: No. 9 Publications, 2006).

Stark, Suzanne J., *Female Tars: Women Aboard Ship in the Age of Sail* (London: Constable, 1996).

Stokoe, John, and Samuel Reay, *Songs and Ballads of Northern England* (Newcastle: Walter Scott, 1899?).

Stubbs, Ken, *The Life of a Man: English Folk Songs from the Home Counties* (London: EFDS Publications, 1970).

Sumner, Heywood, *The Besom Maker and Other Country Folk Songs* (London: Longmans Green, 1888).

Thompson, Flora, *Lark Rise to Candleford* (originally published as three books; Oxford: Oxford Univ. Press, 1939–43).

Vaughan Williams, Ralph, *Folk-Songs from the Eastern Counties* (London: Novello, 1908).

——, *Eight Traditional English Carols* (London: Stainer & Bell, 1919).

——, *National Music and Other Essays*, 2nd edn (Oxford: Oxford University Press, 1987).

Vaughan Williams, Ralph, and A. L. Lloyd, *The Penguin Book of English Folk Songs* (London: Penguin, 1959).

——, *Classic English Folk Songs*, edited by Malcolm Douglas (London: English Folk Dance and Song Society, 2003); new edn of *The Penguin Book of English Folk Songs*.

Venning, Annabel, *Following the Drum: The Lives of Army Wives and Daughters, Past and Present* (London: Headline, 2005).

Vicinus, Martha, *Broadsides of the Industrial North* (Newcastle: Frank Graham, 1975).

Westwood, Jennifer, and Jacqueline Simpson, *The Lore of the Land* (London: Penguin, 2005).

Whittaker, W. G., *North Countrie Ballads, Songs and Pipe Tunes* (London: Corwen, 1921).

Wilgus, D. K., *Anglo-American Folksong Scholarship since 1898* (New Brunswick: Rutgers University Press, 1959).

Williams, Alfred, *Folk-Songs of the Upper Thames* (London: Duckworth, 1923).

Wood, Pete, 'John Barleycorn: The Evolution of a Song Family', *Folk Music Journal*, 8:4 (2004), 438–55.

——, *The Elliotts of Birtley* (Todmorden: Herron, 2008).

Yates, Mike, 'Percy Grainger and the Impact of the Phonograph', *Folk Music Journal*, 4:3 (1982), 265–75.

——, *Traveller's Joy: Songs of English and Scottish Travellers and Gypsies 1965–2005* (London: English Folk Dance and Song Society, 2006).

Manuscript and Audio Collections

VWML: Vaughan Williams Memorial Library, 2 Regent's Park Road, London NW1 7AY (www.efdss.org)
Take 6 website: http://library.efdss.org/archives/

At the time of writing, a major digitization project is in preparation, which it is hoped will add nearly all the remaining major English manuscript collections to the VWML's Take 6 website, from 2013 onwards. The new project is entitled 'Full English' and is planned to include those collections marked ** below.

Albino, H. H. **
VWML

Baring-Gould, Sabine
Mostly Devon County Record Office, Exeter; available online on Take 6 website

Bell, John
Newcastle University Library.

Blunt, Janet
VWML; available online on Take 6 website

Broadwood, Lucy**
VWML.

Butterworth, George
VWML; available online on Take 6 website

Carey, Clive**
VWML.

Carpenter, James Madison
Library of Congress, Washington DC; digital copy and microfilm available at VWML. Catalogue available online at http://www.hrionline.ac.uk/carpenter/
Collinson, Francis
VWML; available online on Take 6 website

Gardiner, George B.
VWML; available online on Take 6 website

Gilchrist, Anne G.
VWML; available online on Take 6 website

Grainger, Percy**
Grainger Museum, University of Melbourne; copies at VWML

Hamer, Fred **
VWML.

Hammond, H. E. D.
VWML; available online on Take 6 website

Kidson, Frank**
Mitchell Library, Glasgow

Plunkett, Mervyn
In private hands, but some items available on the British Library's National Sound Archive website: http>//www.bl.uk/nsa

Sharp, Cecil J.**
Clare College, Cambridge University; copies at VWML

Vaughan Williams, Ralph**
British Library; microfilm copy at VWML

Williams, Alfred**
Wiltshire and Swindon History Centre, Chippenham; microfilm copy at VWML; transcripts on Wiltshire Council website: http://history.wiltshire.gov.uk/community/folksongsintro.php

Major Collections of Early Broadsides

Bagford
British Library

Douce
Bodleian Library; available online on Bodlerian Broadside Ballad website: http://www.bodley.ox.ac.uk/ballads/ballads.htm

Euing
Glasgow University Library; available online on English Broadside Ballad Archive: http://ebba.english.ucsb.edu/

Madden
Cambridge University Library; microfilm copy available at VWML

Pepys
Cambridge University Library; available online on English Broadside Ballad Archive: http://ebba.english.ucsb.edu/

Roxburghe
British Library; available online on English Broadside Ballad Archive: http://ebba.english.ucsb.edu/

Major Websites

Bodleian Library Broadside Ballads: http://www.bodley.ox.ac.uk/ballads/ballads.htm

English Broadside Ballad Archive: http://ebba.english.ucsb.edu/

English Folk Dance and Song Society (EFDSS): www.efdss.org

Musical Traditions Internet magazine: http://www.mustrad.org.uk/

National Sound Archive: http://www.bl.uk/nsa

Vaughan Williams Memorial Library (VWML): http://library.efdss.org/cgi-bin/home.cgi

Yorkshire Garland: http://www.yorkshirefolksong.net/default.aspx

Discography

The current state of availability of recordings of English traditional singing is complicated and in flux. Numerous recordings that have been made available over the years, usually issued by small labels and dedicated enthusiasts, were on LP records and cassettes, and have not made the transition to CD or digital download. Many are now very hard to find. It is not feasible to list all those deleted releases here, although most can be found in *The Folk Song Index* and a copy is usually preserved in the Vaughan Williams Memorial Library.

The following discography focuses solely on CD issues and digital downloads that are currently available from established organizations.

EFDSS

2 Regent's Park Road, London NW1 7AY; www.efdss.org

Various, *A Century of Song: A Celebration of Traditional Singers Since 1898*, CD002 (1998)

Musical Traditions

1 Castle Street, Stroud, Gloustershire GL5 2HP; www.mustrad.org.uk

Bob Hart, *A Broadside*, MTCD301-2 (1998)
Cyril Poacher, *Plenty of Thyme*, MTCD303 (1999)
George Townshend, *Come Hand to Me the Glass*, MTCD304 (2000)
Walter Pardon, *Put a Bit of Powder on It, Father*, MTCD305-6 (2000)
Wiggy Smith, *Band of Gold*, MTCD307 (2000)
Pop Maynard, *Down at the Cherry Tree*, MTCD400 (2000)
Various, *Just Another Saturday Night: Sussex 1960*, MTCD309-10 (2001)
Various, *Up in the North and Down in the South*, MTCD311-12 (2001)
George Dunn, *Chainmaker*, MTCD317-18 (2002)
Various, *Here's Luck to a Man: Gypsy Songs and Music from South-East England*, MTCD320 (2003)
Various, *The Birds Upon the Tree and Other Traditional Songs and Tunes*, MTCD333 (2004)
Various, *A Story to Tell: Keith Summers in Suffolk 1972–79*, MTCD339-40 (2007)
Brazil Family, *Down by the Old Riverside*, MTCD345-7 (2007)
Bill Smith, *Country Life: Songs and Stories of a Shropshire Man*, MTCD351 (2011)

National Sound Archive

British Library, 86 Euston Road, London NW1 2DB: http://sounds.bl.uk

The 'Traditional Music in England' project has gathered many privately made post-war sound collections to preserve them for posterity. Over 20,000 recordings are available for free access on the archive's website.

Rounder

www.Rounder.com

Various, *Classic Ballads of Britain and Ireland 1*, CD 1775 (2000)
Various, *Classic Ballads of Britain and Ireland 2*, CD 1776 (2000)
Various, *Songs of Seduction*, CD 1778 (2000)
Harry Cox, *What Will Become of England?*, CD 1839 (2000)

Saydisc

The Barton, Inglestone Common, Badminton, Gloucestershire GL9 1BX;
www.saydisc.com
Most of the Saydisc catalogue is available as download albums and tracks.

Various, *Sea Songs and Shanties: Traditional English Sea Songs and Shanties from the Last Days of Sail*, CD-SDL405 (1994)
Various, *Songs of the Travelling People*, CD-SDL407 (1994)
Various, *English Customs and Traditions*, CD-SDL425 (1998)

Topic

Fernie Business Park, Station Road, Uppingham, Rutland LE15 9TX;
www.topicrecords.co.uk

For many years, Topic was the main source of LPs of traditional English songs, and dozens of important records were issued. These LPs are no longer available and are not listed here, although some of the material has subsequently been reissued on CD, and Topic has a policy of providing all their past catalogue as downloadable tracks.

The most important CD release for many years was the *Voice of the People* series, a twenty-volume anthology edited by Reg Hall, issued in 1998 (CDs also available individually):

1 *Come Let Us Buy the Licence: Songs of Courtship and Marriage*, TSCD651

2 *My Ship Shall Sail the Ocean: Songs of Tempest and Sea Battles, Sailor Lads and Fishermen*, TSCD652

3 *O'er His Grave the Grass Grew Green: Tragic Ballads*, TSCD653

4 *Farewell My Own Dear Native Land: Songs of Exile and Emigration*, TSCD654

5 *Come All My Lads That Follow the Plough: The Life of Rural Working Men and Women*, TSCD655

6 *Tonight I'll Make You My Bride: Ballads of True and False Lovers*, TSCD656

7 *First I'm Going to Sing You a Ditty: Rural Fun and Frolics*, TSCD657

8 *A Story I'm Just About to Tell: Local Events and National Issues*, TSCD658

9 *Rig-a-Jig: Dance Music of the South of England*, TSCD659

10 *Who's That at My Bedroom Window? Songs of Love and Amorous Encounters*, TSCD660

11 *My Father's the King of the Gypsies: Music of English and Welsh Travellers and Gypsies*, TSCD661

12 *We've Received Orders to Sail: Jackie Tar at Sea and on Shore*, TSCD662

13 *They Ordered Their Pints of Beer and Bottles of Sherry: The Joys and Curse of Drink*, TSCD663

14 *Troubles They Are But Few: Dance Tunes and Ditties*, TSCD664

15 *As Me and My Love Sat Courting: Songs of Love, Courtship and Marriage*, TSCD665

16 *You Lazy Lot of Bone-Shakers: Songs and Dance Tunes of Seasonal Events*, TESCD666

17 *It Fell on a Day, a Bonny Summer Day: Ballads*, TSCD667

18 *To Catch a Fat Buck Was My Delight: Songs of Hunting and Poaching*, TSCD668

19 *Ranting and Reeling: Dance Music of the North of England*, TSCD669

20 *There Is a Man Upon the Farm: Working Men and Women in Song*, TSCD670

Various, *Hidden English: A Celebration of English Traditional Music*, TSCD 600 (1994)

Various, *English Originals*, TSCD706 (1999)

Sam Larner, *Now Is the Time for Fishing*, TSCD511 (2000)

Harry Cox, *The Bonny Labouring Boy*, TSCD512D (2000)

Walter Pardon, *A World Without Horses*, TSCD514 (2000)

Copper Family, *Come Write Me Down*, TSCD534 (2001)

Various, *You Never Heard So Sweet: Songs by Southern English Traditional Singers*, TSCD671 (2012)

Various, *I'm a Romany Rai: Songs by Southern English Gypsy Traditional Singers*, TSCD672D (2012)

Various, *Good People Take Warning: Ballads Sung by British and Irish Traditional Singers*, TSCD673T (2012)

Veteran

PO Box 193, Stowmarket, Suffolk IP14 3WZ; www.Veteran.co.uk

Various, *Stepping It Out: Traditional Folk Music, Songs and Dances from England*, VTC1CD (1993)

Various, *When the May Was All in Bloom: Traditional Singing from the South East of England*, VT131CD (1995)

Phoebe Smith, *The Yellow Handkerchief*, VT136CD (1998)

Various, *Songs Sung in Suffolk*, VTC2CD (2000)

Various, *Comic Songs Sung in Suffolk*, VTC3CD (2000)

Various, *Good Order! Ladies and Gentlemen Please: Traditional Singing and Music from The Eel's Foot, Eastbridge, Suffolk*, VT140CD (2000)

Various, *Down in the Fields: An Anthology of Traditional Folk Music from Rural England*, VTC4CD (2001)

Various, *When the Wind Blows: An Anthology of Traditional Folk Music from Coastal England*, VTC5CD (2001)

Various, *Pass the Jug Round: Traditional Songs and Music from Cumberland*, VT142CD (2001)

Charlotte and Betsy Renals, Sophie Legg, *Catch Me If You Can: Songs from Cornish Travellers*, VT119CD (2003)

Fred Jordan, *A Shropshire Lad*, VT148CD (2003)

Various, *Uncle Tom Cobleigh and All: Folk Songs Sung in the West Country*, VTC9CD (2004)

Various, *It Was on a Market Day 1: English Traditional Folk Singers*, VTC6CD (2005)

Various, *Heel and Toe: Traditional Folk Songs, Music Hall Songs and Tunes from Norfolk, Cambridgeshire and Essex*, VT150CD (2005)

Tom, Jean and Ashley Orchard, *Holsworthy Fair: Songs, Tunes and Stepdances from a Devon Gypsy Family*, VT151CD (2005)

Various, *It Was on a Market Day 2: English Traditional Folk Singers*, VTC7CD (2006)

Viv Legg, *Romany Roots*, VT153CD (2006)

Various, *Good Hearted Fellows: Traditional Folk Songs, Music Hall Songs and Tunes from Suffolk*, VT154CD (2006)

Ray Hubbard, *Norfolk Bred*, VT155CD (2007)

Mabs and Gordon Hall, *As I Went Down to Horsham*, VT115CD (2008)

Various, *Many a Good Horseman: Traditional Music-Making from Mid-Suffolk*, VTC8CD (2009)

Harry Green (and others), *The Fox and the Hare: Folk Songs, Music Hall Songs and Recitations*, VT135CD (2010)

Acknowledgements

One of the genuine pleasures of compiling this book has been the generous support we have received from others working in the field. Everyone who was approached for permission to include material gave their immediate consent, and many others helped with information, access to material, advice and technical assistance. We must also express our gratitude to all the singers and collectors down the years who between them have provided us with such a wealth of archived and recorded songs. Modern life would be much the poorer if they had not made the effort to pass on this important part of our cultural heritage.

For permission to reprint material and for other assistance, our thanks to Merriol Almond of the Baring-Gould Corporation; David Atkinson; Elaine Bradtke; Clare College, Cambridge; Pete Coe; the Copper Family; Gordon Cox; Tony Engle of Topic Records; Martin and Shan Graebe; Reg Hall; Hugh Hamer; Dave Hillery; John Howson of Veteran; the Library of Congress (Carpenter Collection); Paul Marsh; Brian Matthews; Bob and Jackie Patten; Ian Russell; Derek Schofield; Rod and Danny Stradling of Musical Traditions; Bob Walser; and Mike Yates; and to our two professional colleagues Julian Elloway and Caroline Pretty, for the immense amount of care they have taken in (respectively) producing the music notations and copy-editing the text.

A special thank you, as always, to Malcolm Taylor, Peta Webb, Rebecca Hughes and Laura Smyth of the Vaughan Williams Memorial Library for continued professional support, information, gossip, tea and sympathy.

And three colleagues who deserve special mention for their unstinting help way beyond the call of duty: Steve Gardham, John Moulden and Roy Palmer.

Index of Titles and First Lines

First lines in italic; numbers refer to song numbers, not page numbers

Index of Collectors' and Singers' Names

Collectors' names in italic; numbers refer to song numbers, not page numbers